Women
in the 20th Century

MAUREEN HILL

Women
in the 20th Century

MAUREEN HILL

CHAPMANS
1991

Chapmans Publishers Ltd
141-143 Drury Lane
London WC2B 5TB

A CIP catalogue record for this book is available
from the British Library.

ISBN 1-85592-711-X

First published by Chapmans 1991

Photoset by Monoset Typesetters, London

Printed and bound in Great Britain by
Butler & Tanner Ltd, Frome and London

Acknowledgements

Christine Couch
Jocelyn Creighton
Bob Dignum
John Emery
Tony Fordham
Don Foxwell
Muriel Good
Mary Goodwin
Elaine Hoile
Yvonne Holland
Christine Hoy
Vivien James
George Johnson
Roger Lightfoot
Richard McHale
Paul Rossiter
Dave Shepherd
Dave Stanley
Steve Torrington
Pam Webb
Clayton Westcott

Also by Maureen Hill

Growing up at War
The London Blitz

For Frances, Duncan,
Alice, Corinne and Greg

Contents

Introduction

The inspiration for this book came from the 'women's pages' of the *Daily Mail*. Since the beginning of the century, the newspaper has published, initially monthly and then with increasing frequency, a page to attract the interest of women readers. The pages did not deal solely, as I had imagined, with fashion, beauty and jam making, but included articles on women and politics, women in employment and business, sports for women, and debates about the relative joys of being a woman or a man. However, news reports, sometimes in the very same editions, testified to the restrictions imposed on women. So that while in March 1910 the *Daily Mail* magazine section, which carried a weekly page for women readers, published an interesting and thoughtful article on 'Women and the County Councils', Lady Constance Lytton had only recently been released from prison, having been force fed after she had gone on hunger strike as part of the campaign to gain women a vote in parliamentary elections.

The finished book is structured to reproduce a facsimile 'women's page' for most of the years of the century, except for during the First World War where the contents of the facsimile pages are outweighed by a wealth of interesting and fascinating photographs. During the Second World War and into the early 1950s, paper shortages meant that the newspaper sometimes contained only two pages, and while women's interest articles were included they amounted to a very few column inches. The 'women's pages' have been selected to reflect a wide range of topics including cooking, fashion, mothercraft, work, travel and sport. They are complemented by pictures from the *Daily Mail* picture archive, which relate to the year in question and illustrate the variety of the lives of ordinary women as well as the more extraordinary or famous women of the century.

The accompanying text tells the story of how life was, and charts the changes in the role and status of ordinary women this century. Here, too, is a celebration of the achievements of women who fought to change the system, or who worked hard to reach the top in all-male professions, or who became famous for their skills as entertainers, sportswomen or politicians, and references and brief sketches of the lives of some of them are included.

Information for the text was gleaned from a number of sources. The *Daily Mail* archive with its articles, photographs and captions was the initial source, but obviously there were many issues, especially early in the century, which were never written about in newspapers. I found a number of books invaluable including *Hidden from History* by Sheila Rowbottom, *Out of the Doll's House* by Angela Holdsworth, *Lady into Woman* by Vera Brittain, *Bombers and Mash* by Raynes Minns, *Longman's Chronicle of the Twentieth Century* edited by Derrik Mercer, *Guinness Guide to Twentieth-Century Fashion* by David Bond, *Elizabeth's Britain* by Philip Ziegler, and *Collins Illustrated Encyclopedia of Famous People* by Keith and Valerie McLeish. Another rich source of information, which has served to underwrite and highlight many of the facts discovered in my research was conversations with women friends and relatives of all ages about their experiences, thoughts and feelings on a whole range of issues.

Maureen Hill
June 1991

DAILY MAGAZINE.

HOW WOMEN CAN HELP OUR SOLDIERS

CHAS. J. FOLKARD.

THEIR URGENT NEED.

Plenty of Opportunity for Willing Workers.

HUNDREDS of welcome parcels pour into Room 44 of the "Daily Mail" office every morning. All are sent out as fast as they come, and the cry is still for more. Forward anything that strikes you as likely to be useful to Tommy wounded and returning home, Tommy out at the front, who is particularly cold at night, and Tommy's women-folk and children who are coming to cold England from various hot parts, including South Africa and India, in a great hurry, and with nothing in the least bit adequately warm for such a winter as this of fog, rain, and frost.

Send in shirts, tam-o'-shanters, Balaclava helmets, socks, cushions, women's skirts, little children's gloves, scarves, shawls, and stockings. Other comforts this page suggests, and direct your parcels to Room 44, the "Daily Mail," Tallis-street, London, E.C.

CHANGE OF CLIMATE.

Flannel Shirts by the Thousand are Required.

When our men come back from the battlefield they possess in the majority of cases no clothes except those in which they stand up. And this means much less than the ordinary man in England would understand by the expression. Save their khaki uniforms, thin are worn as they are—for these men have been in the brunt of battle, and their clothes are mere reminiscences of what they were when they went out so taut and trim—they have scarcely anything else to call their own.

It is difficult, therefore, to put into sufficiently illuminating words the crying need there is now for shirts, which garments should be made of flannel and be as simple of construction as they can be compatibly with comfort. They should be of a good medium size, rather too large for the average slim man than a fit. This rule it would be well to recollect when making all the comforts that are being so widely constructed. Knitted things should be loosely knitted, and tight knitters should cast on more stitches than those given in the recipes for average knitters.

It is a good fault to have all garments comfortably large, and the socks sent should not be an exception to the rule.

Every wife has her husband's favourite flannel shirt pattern by her to act as a guide. Men are very much alike in their preferences and dislikes, and what will suit the tennis player or angler in this way will also suit Tommy admirably. Some men there are who like a shirt with a chest protector front. This is a very specially splendid pattern, for there are certain to be colds easily caught by the wounded in a low state of health on their return to England.

A diagram is shown below illustrating how a 27in. flannel may be best cut. A shirt is taken that will serve either for daytime or night wear.

For the day shirt 27in. width flannel would

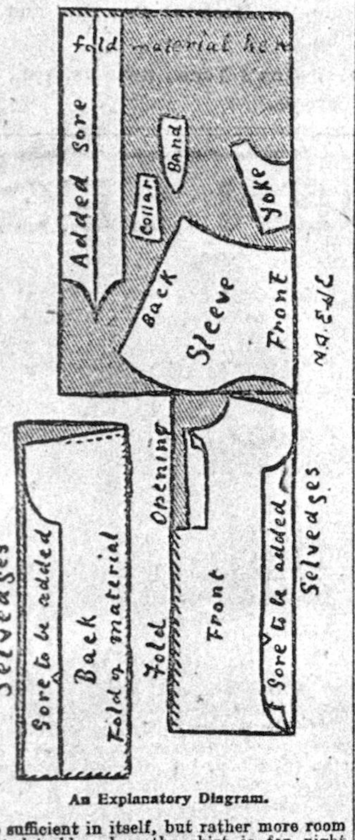

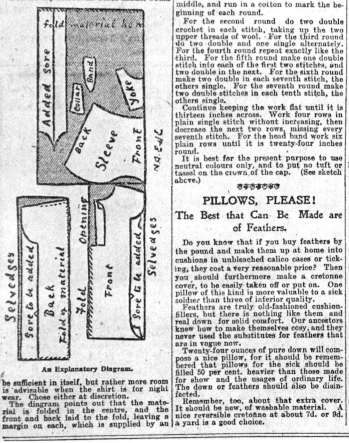

An Explanatory Diagram.

be sufficient in itself, but rather more room is advisable when the shirt is for night wear. Chose either at discretion.

The diagram points out that the material is folded in the centre, and the front and back laid to the fold, leaving a margin on each, which is supplied by an added gore obtained from another piece of stuff; this latter giving also the collar, yoke, and cuffs. Such an addition makes the shirt roomy, fit for night or day.

It must be remembered that the gore at both sides is joined to the back as well as to the front, and therefore it takes its length from the former, and after being slit up the centre it is easy to shorten the front half to the required length. A three-cornered gusset is inserted where the flaps begin to prevent the material tearing.

The yoke joins straight on to the shoulder

The Approved Pattern Tam o'Shanter.

in front, but at the back the material is gathered and sandwiched between the two folds.

The front opening is demonstrated in the diagram, cut down the centre and across the base, then fold back to be hemmed; this is the right side. The left is turned under rather wider, and instead of being hemmed is stitched into a tuck of the material to give the box-pleat, which is then folded over the right side, and the superfluous material at the base is laid in neat folds on the inside and firmly stitched across with a neatening strip of tape over the turnings. Double material must be used for the neckband; but it is optional whether the collar is single or double. A plain neckband is just as serviceable as a turn-over pattern.

It is the sloped side of the sleeve that is set to the back, the seam coming on a line with the centre of the gore. Allow five yards of flannel for this shirt, and remember that Tommy is said to prefer a flannel he can "feel" rather than one of the finely-dressed kinds women would naturally choose.

FOR THOSE WHO CROCHET.

A Useful Tam-o'-Shanter for Tommy.

One of the recipes Mrs. Postlethwaite approves of is a tam-o'-shanter cap created after the following method: Procure three ounces of single Berlin wool and a medium-sized crochet needle. Make three chain, join and work six double crochet into the middle, and run in a cotton to mark the beginning of each round.

For the second round do two double crochet in each stitch, taking up the two upper threads of wool. For the third round do two double and one single alternately. For the fourth round repeat exactly like the third. For the fifth round make one double stitch into each of the first two stitches, and two double in the next. For the sixth round make two double in each seventh stitch, the others single. For the seventh round make two double stitches in each tenth stitch, the others single.

Continue keeping the work flat until it is thirteen inches across. Work four rows in plain single stitch without increasing, then decrease the next two rows, missing every seventh stitch. For the head band work six plain rows until it is twenty-four inches round.

It is best for the present purpose to use neutral colours only, and to put no tuft or tassel on the crown of the cap. (See sketch above.)

PILLOWS, PLEASE!

The Best that Can Be Made are of Feathers.

Do you know that if you buy feathers by the pound and make them up at home into cushions in unbleached calico cases or ticking, they cost a very reasonable price? Then you should furthermore make a cretonne cover, to be easily taken off or put on. One pillow of this kind is more valuable to a sick soldier than three of inferior quality.

Feathers are truly old-fashioned cushion-fillers, but there is nothing like them and real down for solid comfort. Our ancestors knew how to make themselves cosy, and they never used the substitutes for feathers that are in vogue now.

Twenty-four ounces of pure down will compose a nice pillow, for it should be remembered that pillows for the sick should be filled 50 per cent. heavier than those made for show and the usages of ordinary life. The down or feathers should also be disinfected.

Remember, too, about that extra cover. It should be new, of washable material. A nice reversible cretonne at about 7d. or 9d. a yard is a good choice.

A PINCUSHION FAIR.

The Stallwomen Dress as Red Cross Nurses.

It is not possible for many women to do what one wealthy lady is accomplishing. She is giving up her house to make a private hospital for wounded officers whose own homes cannot receive them.

A girl of sweet seventeen has evolved the notion of a pincushion fair, at which all the ladies who sell are to be dressed as Red Cross nurses. A pretty costume is shown in the sketch below, which can easily and quite inexpensively be carried out.

The notion of selling pincushions, and pincushions only, is a good one. Though a great deal of ingenuity may be lavished on the different shapes of the pincushions, the brain is not racked for ideas as it is at a bazaar comprising miscellaneous goods.

THE TRIPLE SKETCH.

Various Ways of Making These Models.

There are numbers of garments that could more easily be made in flannel or cloth than by knitting or crotchet. Such is the man's Cardigan jacket, a sleeveless comfort admirably made in double khaki-coloured flannel or in blue or scarlet serge. It is worn over the shirt and beneath the coat. Bound with stout binding, and made to fasten down the centre with buttons and buttonholes, it is a garment with a great deal of service in it.

The child's skirt (see the large sketch opposite) is illustrated as a reminder. Any number of petticoats of all sizes for women and children are needed to meet the pressing demands of the cry, "We are so cold."

Knitters will be glad of a good "Weldon" recipe for a child's petticoat. It is suitable for girls from four to six years of age. It is knitted in three breadths, allowing two breadths for the back of the petticoat and a wider breadth for the front, and these are joined together and set into a linen waistband. Procure 4oz. or 5oz. of grey single Berlin wool and a pair of No. 11 long bone knitting needles. Begin for the front breadth by casting on 150 stitches. Work

We Cannot all be Nurses.

for the flounce, for the first row, knit 3 and purl 3 alternately to the end. For the second row repeat this. Continue till 12 rows of this ribbing are accomplished, or more rows may be done if you prefer the flounce to be deeper.

For the next row, knit 2 together all along, and now there will be 75 stitches on the needle for the top of the skirt. Work 80 rows of all plain knitting. In the next row, to reduce for the waist, knit 3, knit 2 together, knit 6, and repeat to the end. Now do 12 rows of ribbing, 1 stitch plain and 1 stitch purl alternately, and cast off rather tightly. Work the two back breadths in the same manner, casting on 114 stitches for the beginning of each. Sew up the breadths, but leave a few inches open at the back for a placket hole. Cut a band of grey linen the right size for the waist, and sew the knitting thereto; make a buttonhole on one side of the waistband, and put a button on the other side.

A petticoat for an older child can be made with the same number of stitches, but using Alloa wool or three-thread fleecy, and No. 9 knitting needles.

For the women, how useful a nice shawl in crochet will be to throw over the shoulders! To make a nice-sized shawl, use a long tricot needle and 1lb. of five-ply fingering. Make a chain of rather more than one yard long. For the first row, draw up a loop in every stitch of the chain, leaving each stitch on the needle, wool over, and draw through the last loop. Then put the wool over, and draw through the next two loops, and so on, until all the stitches are worked off, and only one stitch remains on the needle.

For the second row, work a loop through the perpendicular loop of the last row, and bring the wool to the front of the work, and pick up a stitch through the next loop. Then put the wool over, and draw through the stitch just lifted up. Put the wool to the back of the work, and repeat from the

Comforts for Women, Children, and Men.

beginning of the row, and work off as before. Repeat the second row, only in every succeeding row, and work the fancy stitch into the plain stitch of the previous row. Work this until it is square.

IMPORTANT POINTS.

The Lungs and Feet Should Be Protected.

When the chest and extremities are kept well covered the rest of the body is almost sure to avoid chills. Hence two recipes are given here, the one a chest-protector, the other a pair of boots and garters in combination for a child. The recipes are "Weldon's." For the chest-protector are required 6oz. of 3-thread best superfine fleecy wool, and a pair of No. 10 or No. 11 bone knitting needles, 3 yards of braid for binding, 1½ yards of narrow ribbon or tape, and 3 buttons. Cast on 60 stitches for the bottom of the back, and work forwards and backwards in all plain knitting for a length of 12in. For the next row, knit 24 stitches, cast the last stitch but one over the last stitch, knit 1, cast another stitch over, and so go on until 16 stitches are cast off, when knit to the end.

Proceed upon 22 stitches for the first shoulder for 6in., then cast on 10 stitches at the end of the row by the neck; work upon 32 stitches a length of 6in., when stop; and go to the other shoulder and knit that in the same manner. When it is the same length as the first cast on 10 stitches by the neck, and continue in plain knitting, but make 3 buttonholes, one in the fourth or fifth row from the neck, another about 2in. further down, and another at again 2in. further.

When this front is brought to the same length as the first, work all the 64 stitches upon one needle, and knit on till the front, from the neck, measures 11in., when cast off. Bind all round the protector as represented in the sketch.

The gaiter and boot in combination is intended for a child of a year, to be worn over his house socks and shoes. They encase the feet and legs, and come well up over the knees, thus affording warmth where most necessary.

Procure 1½oz. of white peacock fingering and a pair of No. 14 or No. 13 steel knitting needles. Begin at the top of the leg by

Warm Skirts Ward off Chills.

casting on 60 stitches. Knit 6 plain rows, always slipping the first stitch of every row. Work in ribbing of 2 stitches plain and 2 stitches purl for 10 rows. Knit 6 more plain rows.

For the next row, to shape the knee, slip 1, knit 51, and turn, leaving 8 stitches unknitted on the left-hand pin; slip 1, knit 43, and there will be 8 stitches left unknitted on the other pin; turn, slip 1, knit 42; turn, slip 1, knit 41; turn, slip 1, knit 40; turn, slip 1, knit 39; and so on, knitting one stitch less each time of turning, and, of course, therefore leaving one additional stitch unknitted at the end of every row, till you come to slip 1, knit 11, when there will be 24 stitches left at the end of each pin; then turn, slip 1, knit the 11 stitches back, and proceed to knit the 24 stitches to the end of the pin; turn, slip the first stitch, and knit the whole of the row, 60 stitches as at the beginning. Knit 10 plain rows.

For the next row knit 2, increase 1, knit 4, increase 1, knit 48, increase 1, knit 4, increase 1, knit two; now there are 64 stitches on. Knit 24 plain rows. With the next row you must begin to decrease the leg. Knit 2, knit

Easily Knitted and Very Welcome.

2 together, knit plain to within four stitches of the end, knit 2 together, knit 2. Knit 5 plain rows. Proceed as in the last six rows till six decreases have been made, when you will find 52 stitches on the needle. Knit for the ankle 20 plain rows.

For the next row proceed to make the holes for the ribbon. Knit 2, make 1, knit 2 together, and repeat from make 1 to the end; but if you do not care about a tie round the ankle you can knit this row as a plain row. Knit 6 plain rows. For the first row of the boot and instep, knit 33 stitches; turn, slip 1, knit 13, turn again, and slip 1, knit 13; and continue these little rows for the instep until 32 little rows are done.

For the 33rd row, slip 1, knit 2 together, knit 8, knit 2 together, knit 1. Knit 3 plain rows. For the 37th row, slip 1, knit 2 together, knit 6, knit 2 together, knit 1. Knit 1 plain row. For the 39th row, slip 1, knit 2 together, knit 4, knit 2 together, knit 1. Knit 1 plain row of 8 stitches, and break off the wool. Resume upon the right-hand needle, on which you have already knitted 19 stitches, pick up and knit on the same needle 20 stitches along the side of the instep, knit also 8 stitches at the top of the instep, and pick up and knit 20 stitches along the opposite side, and also knit 19 stitches off the left-hand needle, in all 86 stitches.

Knit 17 plain rows. For the 19th row, slip 1, knit 2 together, knit 35, knit 2 together, knit 6, knit 2 together, knit 35, knit 2 together, knit 1. The 20th row is plain. For the 21st row, slip 1, knit 2 together, knit 34, knit 2 together, knit 4, knit 2 together, knit 34, knit 2 together, knit 1.

The 22nd row is plain. For the 23rd row slip 1, knit 2 together, knit 33, knit 2 together, knit 2, knit 2 together, knit 33, knit 2 together, knit 1. The 24th row is plain. For the 25th row, slip 1, knit 2 together, knit 32, knit 2 together, knit 2 together, knit 32, knit 2 together, knit 1. For the 26th row, cast off. Sew up the back of the leg and the sole of the foot.

LADY CHARLOTTE.

ABOVE: A middle-class Victorian family.
BELOW: Women walking in Hyde Park on Sunday after church.

1900

The Century Opens

Despite the fact that 1900 was the 61st year of Queen Victoria's reign women in Britain and throughout her far-flung empire had benefited in only a small measure from having a woman in so prominent a position. In fact the Victorian era had seen the cultivation and acceptance of a curious paradox about the nature of women. While society and science nurtured the beliefs that women were less intelligent and weaker both physically and emotionally than men, women were also revered and elevated for their sensitivity and feminine virtue. Women had to be protected and cosseted from the brutal realities of the world. Such beliefs, held by women as well as men, meant many of the iniquities and inequalities such as the denial of voting rights could be justified on the grounds either that women were incapable of understanding or that they would be tainted by the experience.

However during the latter half of the nineteenth century there had grown a feminist movement in Britain with women such as Sophia Jex Blake, Josephine Butler, Millicent Fawcett, Emmeline Pethick-Lawrence and many others. The cause of women's emancipation took much of its inspiration from the eighteenth-century thinker Mary Wollstonecraft. Her book *Vindication of the Rights of Woman,* published in 1792, claimed women were equal to men and had caused much controversy.

By 1900 women had made some gains both legally and socially in that wives were no longer regarded as their husbands' property to the same extent as they had been in 1800. But many of the gains they had made were offset by other judgements. In 1870 women lost their right to retain their British citizenship when they married a foreigner. And as late as 1899 a court ruled in a case brought to trial that a man could not be found guilty of raping his wife if she refused to have sex with him, even if he was suffering from a disease (presumably venereal disease) of which he was aware but she was not.

As the century opened, in every sphere of life – education, employment, marriage, finance, legal and political rights, inheritance, social status – women had a long way to go before they could be said to be equal to men.

1900 POSTSCRIPTS

• The 1899 London Government Act was amended to allow married women to be members of Metropolitan Borough Councils. Initially the Act had excluded them.

March – Women in Germany petitioned the Reichstag for the right to sit State examinations and attend university.

• The government in France limited the hours women and children were allowed to work to eleven. In Britain, too, employment legislation invariably placed women and children in the same category, as in the 1848 Factory Act which limited their working hours to ten per day and the 1842 Mines and Collieries Act which barred them from working underground.

July – The second Olympic Games was held in Paris with women competing for the first time. They had been barred in 1896.

NO LADIES NEED APPLY

The Bethnal Green Board of Guardians proposed to appoint Miss Knowles as first assistant medical officer but the Local Government Board demurs, and gives as its reason that Miss Knowles would have to act as a medical officer sometimes and it is open to great objection that a lady should occupy such a position.
Daily Mail, 1 January 1900

Woman's Realm

LOOKING BACKWARDS.

Early Fashions Revived for Mourning.

The very simplest evening dresses for the home circle only, are now being made, and the dressmakers are mounting pin-spotted net upon silk for the purpose. Two illustrations of its efficacy are shown in this column. In one, beneath a soft cloud of black tulle, an embroidered white crêpe bolero and sleeves

A Simple and Effective Evening Gown.

in combination appear, and in the other all the trimming given the gown is gauging, with bunches of black and white violets on ribbon ends hanging from the décolletage.

Three-quarter length coats are truly elegant when well made and worn by the tall and graceful. The one sketched of crêpe cloth has an ermine collar and pair of cuffs upon it; it is lined with white satin and banded thrice across the front with black satin bars held by satin buttons. Military notions and ideas are being very much exploited in mourning models. A picture in the last column shows handsome jet and silk cord frogs upon a little tightly-fitting bodice of the coat persuasion sharply pointed in front. White braid lace is very effective upon a background of black or grey chiffon or satin, with a vivid contrast of black satin ribbon, and as a sketch in our fourth column will prove, it can be applied to a house gown of black cloth with excellent results, or of grey, when grey becomes possible as a mourning fabric. Picture millinery is prevailing at present; it is so much more becoming than the toque when a complete mass of effective black is wanted.

Point d'Esprit Gauged for Mourning.

It is noticeable how very remarkably we are pathetically and unconsciously harking back in our suits of woe to the fashions that prevailed when our late beloved Sovereign ascended the throne. A window in Knightsbridge the other day might almost have been taken for one sixty-four years ago, save for the fact that huge sheets of plate-glass were not in fashion then, for the panes of the period were very small and set in heavy frames. A long length of black net closely embroidered with dull jet beads, threw one's thoughts back more than half a century, and so did the great muffs with their wristlets of satin, puffed and gauged with flounces at the edge to fall over the hands. One button gloves, too, are in fashion again, and for the feet nothing is more modish in the house than heelless shoes, concerning which, by the way, Paris has more to say at present than we have.

In olden days with a black suit of mourning went a set of black-edged handkerchiefs, and here again we have an early Victorian vogue revived, but now the deep black band is less new than embroidered black edges on white lawn mouchoirs, and others spotted all over with black dots. It is modish again to wear a pocket handkerchief like this tucked among the furs of one's coat, so that it just peeps out from them.

The floral decoration of the moment is a big bunch of violets, purple having been chosen by the King as the colour for mourning drapery upon houses and shops. It is a beautiful idea, and strictly in accordance with precedence, for purple has always been considered the Royal mourning colour. The shops have looked very sad, and yet very beautiful. Some had their black boards tied round with purple velvet sashes and bows, others with crêpe and white ribbon. In London all the boards were merely of wood put in mourning by means of a coating of Brunswick black; but in Birmingham I hear that cloth was used to cover the boards, which made the effect much better.

Three-quarter Coat with Ermine Trimmings.

The new edged ribbons are very mourning-like and pretty. White, with a rim of black at the edge, and black, with a silver edge, are two forms that are available for neck wear and millinery rosettes. Girls who like to trim their own hats are able to buy huge crisp rosettes of black tulle, and a little later, when white is possible, they will find white powdered with black chenille spots available, or black net with a powdering of white a graceful choice.

It is a pity that aiguillettes, ferets, and tags have been exploited in so many unworthy metals. Nothing has a more common look than a poor finish of this kind upon a frock or rosette. On the other hand, really good and antique tags provide a distinguished and pretty appearance on a costume.

QUEEN ALEXANDRA'S TASTE IN DRESS.

How She Exercised Her Influence as Princess of Wales.

Throughout Europe, and, indeed, throughout the world, the name of the Princess of Wales has been synonomous with beauty of face, form, and character, and with faultless and exquisite taste in dress. The name of Queen Alexandra will, let us devoutly hope, continue for many and many a long year to arouse the admiration of all who hear it. The beneficial influence upon dress so quietly but powerfully exercised by "the Princess," as it was our joy to call her, has been marked in England ever since she set foot upon our shores. Never has she countenanced exaggeration in any form. Balloon sleeves and huge bustles she forbade. But she has taught the people the art of looking young and of dressing becomingly—two qualifications towards a lovely appearance that are indissolubly mingled with one another.

QUEEN ALEXANDRA'S PREFERENCE IN JEWELLERY.

One of the pretty stories that was told about the Princess at the time of her first appearance as a beautiful bride in England was that she had been taught as a little girl all the arts and intricacies of millinery, and that when she arrived at her future home she made the Queen a bonnet! With what sadness do we recollect, too, the Jubilee times and the charming tales that were told of the Princess helping the Queen to choose and order lovely bonnets for the two grand occasions. It was even said that

the Princess Herself

composed the beautiful lace, soft white feathers, and exquisite diamond ornaments into the bonnets worn at the Jubilees, and that she took special pains to ensure their being of a very light weight, so that her Majesty should not feel them heavy during the long hot hours of the processions.

Take a little thought, and you will observe that all the fashions Queen Alexandra has favoured have gained a direct and permanent hold upon us. The princess bonnet, for example, that closely-fitting little shape with its smart upstanding lace coquille or ostrich plume and the narrow strings tied beneath the left ear, shown n the small sketch, worn by the august lady whose name was given to it for many years, was the precursor of the toque, which, of course, is quite a national possession among us, and has made many another face, with regular features and a clear complexion like hers, look its prettiest and sweetest.

Then, again, there was the princess robe, a model that never came into fashion with any particular craze or zest and never will go out of fashion, for the simple reason that it only becomes those whose figures are as sylph-like and as exquisitely proportioned as is Queen Alexandra's, and that it is

Difficult to Cut

and fit. It will always be associated with the Princess of Wales, and particularly with the dress that she was wont to wear at one time cut after this model and trimmed upon the skirt with paniers such as the little picture shows.

At Court the Princess of Wales was ever the cynosure of every eye, and as Queen will continue so to be. It is scarcely sufficiently well known that she always took a special and intense delight in pleasing her husband's mother, our great Queen, in her dress, and that the Court corsage worn in the correct way with a deep point in front and a décolletage falling from her beautifully-formed shoulders was the pattern that found favour above all others in the Queen's eyes.

Her constant habit of wearing a broad velvet neckband closely fastened round her throat led to a fashion for pearl dog-collars that has never gone out and never will. It was she, too, who first started the great rage for ropes of pearls. Her portrait, painted with her little dog in her arms, in evening dress, with a rope of pearls round her neck, shown in the Royal Academy some years ago, was the precursor of the vogue, and another instance of the long life her preferences are given in the world of fickle fashion.

Her favourite colours of late years have been heliotrope and the delicate purple and filmy grey shades of rare orchids, when she has not actually been wearing simple black toilettes as mourning for the many near relations she has lost. At Sandringham she wears tailor-made coat and skirt costumes and a sailor hat or a Tyrolean felt, for one of the useful tenets she has taught Englishwomen is that occasions rule choice, and that to appear suitably garbed for each one is what we should all aim at doing.

As Princess of Wales she did not materially change the manner of coiffure arrangement that so well suits her, year in year out, choosing to keep her hair curled on and above her brow, and there raised rather high, and at the back coiled or curled, an arrangement her daughters, daughter-in-law, and thousands of Englishwomen have all faithfully copied.

❖ ❖ ❖ ❖ ❖

ROYAL DUTCH WEDDING.

Secrecy on the Subject of the Trousseau.

Sketches and details of the trousseau and wedding dress to be worn by the Queen of the Netherlands are likely to be apocryphal until after the marriage ceremony; for

The Princess Bonnet and Robe.

this simple reason Mme. Nicaud, of the Rue de Rivoli, Paris, made the trousseau, and though she was bombarded on all sides for information and permission to sketch the dresses she persistently refused to give either. This was in no way an act of discourtesy, for Mme. Nicaud simply acted on the express commands of the Queen, who wished all details of her gown and trousseau to be kept absolutely private. It was this dressmaker who made the coronation gowns for Queen Wilhelmina, which every one will remember were very simple in design though rich with glorious embroideries on the skirts and soft lace berthes and fichus. The National

Braid Lace Mounted upon Chiffon.

School of Applied Arts at the Hague had the honour of making the embroideries for the coronation gowns, and have been very busy over the exquisite ornamentation that will appear on the wedding gown.

VEILS UP-TO-DATE.

An Improvement on Those of Past Times.

There are one or two items very noticeable concerning mourning veils. In olden days they extended to the knees, and were made either entirely of crape, or of black gauze, edged with a deep band of crape.

The most beautiful veil sold for present mourning wear is of the finest black Brussels

Black Silk Cord and Jet Adornments.

net with a delicate tracery upon it, so arranged that it does not absurdly interfere with the features as some patterns will. Since it is no longer modish to twist the veil under the chin in a little knot, thereby making it veritably a bag over the countenance, the new veil is provided with a flounce of lace or with a hemstitched border, which is neat and excessively pretty. Less expensive veils are of white tulle with large spots of chenille upon them; and be it noted white veils, which were becoming so fashionable before the present period of sad black set in, are certain to have a vogue when half-mourning is worn.

There are some new veils of a double persuasion which many women have been wearing for a long time, though to the majority of people there is novelty in them. Rather fine open net is used for the outer veil, with black velvet or chenille spots upon it, while inside there is a lining of white tulle guaranteed to keep the complexion fresh and clean even though the weather be foggy and smut-laden.

Brown was promised a following three weeks ago, and very wisely so with a fresh complexion behind it, seeing how well it accords with sable and other brown furs. It has, of course, departed, though it may come back again in a little time. It is

Picture Hats Prevail at Present.

most urgently to be hoped that purple veiling will not find a place among the grey and white nets that we may expect to meet a month hence, for if there is one colour that is more trying to the complexion than any other in the form of net it is purple, though for dresses and millinery there is scarcely any hue more universally becoming.

❖ ❖ ❖ ❖ ❖

A NEW MAGAZINE.

Realism in Fashion Plates.

A new way in America and in Paris for displaying fashions is to photograph the toilettes upon pretty women of ordinary build, some slim as the fashion now is for sylph-like femininity, some more rotund, as many people cannot help being. This plan is in direct contradiction to the one that used to prevail among fashion plate artists of idealising the figure, which in many instances was carried to an absurd extreme.

A very beautiful new production called "Les Modes," a magazine for women devoted to fashion and society, appeared last week, and is published by Goupil and Co., whose fine art work is so well known. The first number is absolutely beautiful. There are coloured pictures as well as black and white ones in it, and articles upon painting in portraiture, furniture, and interior decoration. For the present the magazine is only published in French, but even those whose knowledge of the language is elementary will find the sum of one franc fifty centimes a month well spent for the sake of the illustrations.

LADY CHARLOTTE.

1901

Women at Work

In 1901 there were few opportunities for women to earn money and mostly theirs were poorly paid, low-status jobs. Even where a woman entered a profession the very fact that she was a woman deprived her of the respect granted a male colleague. Although the 1901 Census revealed that there were 212 women doctors, two architects and a few women clerks and assistants in the legal, banking and insurance worlds, many professions were still closed to women. At the beginning of 1901 eighteen-year-old Margaret Hall had found a solicitor in Scotland willing to have her articled to him but was awaiting a High Court order granting her permission to sit for an entrance exam.

Of the three and a half million women in paid employment 50 per cent were confined to jobs in domestic service. In certain areas of the country a tradition of female factory workers had developed and the textile industry alone employed more than half a million women who, despite being highly skilled, were paid low wages.

As purveyors of education the governesses of the nineteenth century remained but more women were turning to teaching as a means of finding better rewards for their skills – although not rewards equal to those of a man in the same job.

Nursing had begun to attract 'respectable' women after the tireless efforts of Florence Nightingale and others and in 1901 there were 68,000 nurses in Britain.

In 1901, 29 per cent of the workforce were women and most were single. Only ten per cent of married women worked outside the home. The convention was that a man should earn enough to keep his wife and family and, apart from a few areas such as textiles where a different tradition had developed, it was a source of terrible shame if the wife worked outside the home. That is not to say that the woman at home led a life of leisure. For the servanted classes time did hang heavy on the hands of the women but for the great majority of women life was a never-ending drudgery trying to cook, feed and clean for and give birth to large families.

ABOVE: *Lady Sarah Wilson who became the first woman war correspondent when she sent dispatches back to the* Daily Mail *from South Africa during the Boer War. She was at Mafeking while Baden-Powell was preparing for a siege and caused a sensation among the residents of the African kraals as she cantered across country in an area where women on horseback were rarely seen.*
BELOW: *A group of young Edwardians at Scarborough. A day at the seaside once or twice a year was something many of the working class could afford even if they could not afford holidays for a week or more.*

1901 POSTSCRIPTS

January – The death of Queen Victoria.

May – Norway enfranchised some women taxpayers for local elections.

July – Charlotte Sterry won the Ladies' Championship at Wimbledon for the second year running. She was reigning Olympic Champion having won at the 2nd Olympiad held in Paris in 1900.

LANCASHIRE COTTON WORKERS WANT FEMALE SUFFRAGE

The scene was suggestive of an allegorical picture – 'The Battle of the Sexes'. At one end of a committee room of the Houses of Parliament sat sixteen stern-faced, work-hardened factory women; at the other sat the frock-coated smiling Members, very sympathetic indeed. On the table reposed the petition, coiled up in a huge roll, bearing 29,359 signatures of factory women.
Daily Mail, 19 March 1901

WOMEN WHO HAVE FOUND NEW PROFESSIONS.

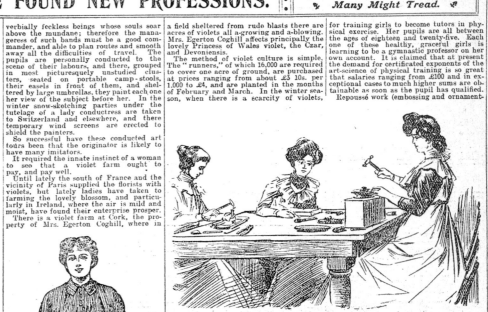

A lady professor who teaches her pupils to become instructors in physical training. Some of her students have been able to add considerably to their incomes by giving lessons in the art they have learned from her.

Specimens from the Studio of a Woman Metal Worker.

Women metal workers—an artistic profession in which there is room for many recruits.

A LADY POTTER WHO TURNS CLAY INTO GOLD. Miss Vulliamy at work in her studio making the "uglies" that have of late become so popular.

WHEN women set themselves to make incomes they do not invariably invade professions peopled by men, such as the medical, in which, as at Burnley the other day, they have met many rebuffs.

Shrewd enough are the cleverest among them to grasp the fact that a new calling when successfully engineered has more chances of becoming highly lucrative than an old one; hence of late there have been several prosperous callings invented by women workers.

One clever young lady, for instance, has discovered that there is a wide field in designing pottery, especially those knick-knacks that are known as "uglies." Miss Vulliamy, the lady-potter in question, not merely designs vases, tobacco-jars, and the like, but in common-sense fashion sells them at good prices. Her dainty little studio in Kensington is a splendid object-lesson in the go-ahead spirit which imbues the "new woman"—in the best sense of that ill-used term.

Her Majesty the Queen has shown her appreciation of Miss Vulliamy's art by purchasing a selection of her vases.

These articles of bric-a-brac are all examples of the use of the grotesque in design. Weird owls, bats, frogs, and demons are the basis of many of Miss Vulliamy's ideas; and it is mainly through so-called "lovely-ugly" pottery that she has made her reputation. Although it is given to few to own such genius as hers, there is no doubt that a comfortable living awaits those who try working on similar lines.

A lucrative employment for women with a love for travel is that of personally conducting sketching parties of girl students to all parts of England and the Continent.

In such centres of concentrated beauty as Sark and the other Channel Islands, Brittany, Italy, and Switzerland, these parties may frequently be met. Girl artists are pro-verbially feckless beings whose souls soar above the mundane; therefore the manageress of such bands must be a good commander, and able to plan routes and smooth away all the difficulties of travel. The pupils are personally conducted to the scene of their labours, and there, grouped in most picturesquely unstudied clusters, seated on portable camp-stools, their easels in front of them, and sheltered by large umbrellas, they paint each one her view of the subject before her. In the winter snow-sketching parties under the tutelage of a lady conductress are taken to Switzerland and elsewhere, and there temporary wind screens are erected to shield the painters.

So successful have these conducted art tours been that the originator is likely to have many imitators.

It required the innate instinct of a woman to see that a violet farm ought to pay, and pay well.

Until lately the south of France and the vicinity of Paris supplied the florists with violets, but lately ladies have taken to farming the lovely blossom, and particularly in Ireland, where the air is mild and moist, have found their enterprise prosper.

There is a violet farm at Cork, the property of Mrs. Egerton Coghill, where in a field sheltered from rude blasts there are acres of violets all a-growing and a-blowing. Mrs. Egerton Coghill affects principally the lovely Princess of Wales violet, the Czar, and Devoniensis.

The method of violet culture is simple. The "runners," of which 16,000 are required to cover one acre of ground, are purchased at prices ranging from about £3 10s. per 1,000 to £4, and are planted in the months of February and March. In the winter season, when there is a scarcity of violets, as much as 1s. 10d. is given in public auction for a nosegay of eight dozen blooms. But the supply is often much inferior to the demand, so the prospect looks promising for more cultivators.

There is now in London a German lady, Fräulein Wilke, who has founded a college for training girls to become tutors in physical exercise. Her pupils are all between the ages of eighteen and twenty-five. Each one of these healthy, graceful girls is learning to be a gymnastic professor on her own account. It is claimed that at present the demand for certificated exponents of the art-science of physical training is so great that salaries ranging from £100 and in exceptional cases to much higher sums are obtainable as soon as the pupil has qualified.

Repoussé work (embossing and ornamenting copper and silver in relief) has two great advantages. The artistic work is growing more and more popular, and the most delicate girl can undertake it.

One of the first schools to be established for teaching this branch of artistic handiwork was Miss Cristine Connell's, whose studio is at Stafford-place, Buckingham Gate. About twelve months are required for tuition, and a good worker may certainly largely increase her income by this work, £200 a year being by no means an outside figure.

THE PERSONALLY CONDUCTED ART TOUR.
A few enterprising ladies with a love for travel have lately organised sketching parties of girl art students, conducting them to all parts of England and the Continent. They smooth over all the difficulties of travel, and the idea has proved so successful that the pioneers are likely to have many imitators.

A LADY'S PROFITABLE FLOWER FARM.
This charming occupation has been found highly remunerative, and there are now in the United Kingdom a number of successful farms owned and managed by women. The above illustration shows the violet fields of Mrs. Egerton Coghill, in County Cork, Ireland.

1902

Legal Rights

During the second half of the nineteenth century women had been granted some rights in law but many laws only emphasized the inequality of treatment between men and women. A man could divorce an adulterous wife but a woman could not divorce her husband just for adultery, she also had to prove cruelty, desertion, bigamy or incest. Custody of the children in any divorce or separation was invariably granted to the father, although laws in the nineteenth century had undermined the father's automatic right to custody. Once divorced a woman had few means of supporting herself. Like most women at the beginning of the century lack of money directed a dependence on men.

It was less than 20 years since the Married Women's Property Act gave wives the same rights as husbands over their own property but as few daughters inherited few women married or single had property over which to have rights. The vast majority of women had no money and no right to any money. Unless they brought their own money and property to the marriage, everything legally belonged to the husband.

A husband was also legally responsible for any crimes his wife might commit in his presence. The assumption being that women only did, and were expected to do, their husbands' bidding and were incapable of autonomy of action when with them.

ABOVE: An outfit from the early years of the century . . .
BELOW: . . . and the corsetry required to give the finished silhouette.

1902 POSTSCRIPTS

February – An Imperial Decree in China abolished the practice of binding the feet of female children, although the practice was to continue for some years.

May – The government of Prussia, the principal region of Germany, denied women the right to form political associations, a ban which lasted until 1908 when the central German government, the Reichstag, lifted it.

October – The *Daily Mail* reported a proposal that lady correspondents should indicate whether they are married or not, perhaps with an M if married and S if single after their name, so that any reply could be properly addressed.

A HUSBAND'S PRIVILEGE

'I want a summons for abusive language,' said an applicant at Brentford Police Court yesterday.
The Magistrate: Against whom?
Applicant: Against my husband.
The Magistrate: You can't summon your husband for abusive language.
Daily Mail, 2 April 1902

Professional ❧ Nurses ❧ for ❧ Pets. ❧

Valuable animal pets are often as delicate as young children, yet few persons have any idea of nursing them back to health when they become ill, and in consequence every year thousands of owners bemoan the loss of some little friend of whom they have become fond.

Here, then, is an opportunity for women in search of a new profession. They should study the ailments of valuable pets. Then

subject for many years, and until recently superintended the entire work of a pets' hospital in Kinnerton-street, S.W. In Paris and New York the ladies who professionally attend to the wants of invalid animals have become quite a numerous body, and have found the work highly profitable.

The nurse must first learn how to deal with the ordinary complaints from which the domestic dog or cat commonly suffers.

Both animals are liable to colds, sore throats, and rheumatic pains. In some cases pills have to be administered, in others powders must be given, and in cases of rheumatic troubles the limbs of the patient may have to be swathed in flannel. If a dog is bad-tempered it is, as may be supposed, a difficult matter to persuade him to take a powder or submit his limbs to be wrapped in flannel; but the trained nurse must learn how to soothe the patient so that he will readily submit himself to her handling as he would never do even to his own mistress. Cats are

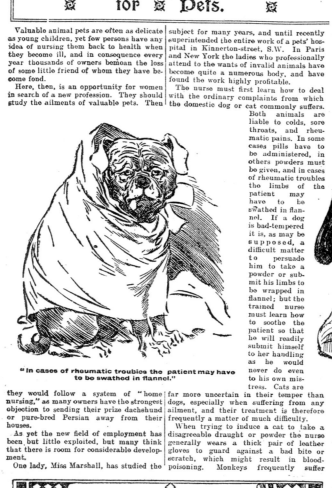

"In cases of rheumatic troubles the patient may have to be swathed in flannel."

they would follow a system of "home nursing," as many owners have the strongest objection to sending their prize dachshund or pure-bred Persian away from their houses.

As yet the new field of employment has been but little exploited, but many think that there is room for considerable development.

One lady, Miss Marshall, has studied the

far more uncertain in their temper than dogs, especially when suffering from any ailment, and their treatment is therefore frequently a matter of much difficulty.

When trying to induce a cat to take a disagreeable draught or powder the nurse generally wears a thick pair of leather gloves to guard against a bad bite or scratch, which might result in blood-poisoning. Monkeys frequently suffer

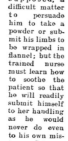

and while they will readily submit themselves to the management of one who loves them, they repel with equal readiness the attentions of those who either dislike or fear them.

Men who devote themselves professionally to attending to the ailments of different animals have, of course, to do work which would put the nerves of the gentler sex to rather a too trying ordeal. For instance, the manager of a London animal hospital may get a call to attend to an ailing zebra, as was actually the case a short time ago. The zebra is not by nature an evil-disposed or bad-tempered brute, but this particular specimen of his race had a fearful temper, in addition to being irritated beyond description by the pain from which he was suffering, caused by a sore on his knee. The doctor calmly examined the poor creature's wound, which he decided to operate on. As he was turning away the zebra suddenly made a savage rush at him, and it was only by the quickest of movements that the doctor was able to escape being badly bitten. Subsequently the zebra was drugged with cocaine and successfully operated upon. The manager of the Kinnerton-street Animal Hospital has frequently attended to ailing lions and elephants, and has even administered his healing hand to a camel. Of course, work of this character

would be quite beyond the scope of the ordinary lady animal nurse, whose ministrations should be confined altogether to the curing and healing of the ills from which the domesticated pet animal suffers.

At present the Royal College of Veterinary Surgeons does not recognise the lady animal nurse, though it is possible for a woman to attend a course of lectures until she becomes proficient. Her standing,

"When trying to induce a cat to take a disagreeable draught or powder the nurse generally wears a thick pair of leather gloves to guard against bites or scratches."

therefore, would not be that of a qualified nurse; but if she really has the knowledge and the necessary love for animals, she should find no difficulty in convincing clients of her ability.

She would, in fact, be in exactly the same position as the thousands of experienced women whose profession is that of attending ailing persons, and who, though well trained, have no letters after their names. Certainly there seems a wide field in the direction pointed out.

Monkeys frequently suffer from that most distressing of human ills—neuralgia, and to effect a cure is one of the most difficult problems the animal nurse has to confront.

from that most distressing of human ills—neuralgia. An ailing monkey is an extremely awkward patient to approach. Sometimes, in cases of extreme temper, it is necessary to put him under the influence of some drug, cocaine being the usual one administered. It can be readily seen that the animal nurse must possess a fairly extensive knowledge of the constitutions of various animals.

Should a nurse select to specialise, however, in attending to the ailments of any one particular animal, there can be no doubt that she would get plenty to do in London. A good parrot nurse, for instance, ought to find a large practice open to her. It often happens that a parrot will get

A Silent Fit,

during which it will refuse to utter a word despite all the blandishments of its master or mistress. This fit of silence may arise through the bird being really ill, or simply from a fit of bad temper. The nurse who understands her business properly will, however, promptly induce the parrot to resume its favourite utterances.

It may be at once stated that it is absolutely useless for any woman to take up nursing animals as a profession unless she be really imbued with a real love of the animals she proposes to devote herself to nurse. Without this affection for animals her skill or knowledge would be of little use. Animals of all descriptions, whether domestic or otherwise, seem to have an intuitive knowledge regarding this point,

A PATIENT OF IMPORTANCE.
The lady nurse finds it by no means an easy task to induce a St. Bernard to take the all-curing pill.

1903

The Women's Social and Political Union

In 1897 Millicent Fawcett, sister of Elizabeth Garrett Anderson, one of the first women doctors, formed the National Union of Women's Suffrage Societies. This brought together under a national umbrella all the associations that had fought for votes for women. The various groups had achieved some successes in the last quarter of the nineteenth century, gaining the vote for women householders in local elections and the right for women to be elected to Boards of Guardians, the bodies which administered the Poor Laws. They had also agitated for a change to the London Government Act which barred married women from membership of the Metropolitan Borough Councils. The National Union of Women's Suffrage Societies campaigned, as had its individual member societies before it, for constitutional change but despite the aforementioned limited successes no woman in Britain had the power to elect anyone to a legislative assembly. In fact, in 1903, the only women in the world with those rights were the women of New Zealand and Australia.

In 1903 a group of women in Manchester founded the Women's Social and Political Union. Their leader was Mrs Emmeline Pankhurst, a long-time campaigner for female suffrage and the widowed mother of five. She had been elected a Poor Law Guardian in 1895, and said her experiences there convinced her to think of 'the vote in women's hands as not only a right but as a desperate necessity'. Mrs Pankhurst's and the WSPU's motto was 'Deeds, not Words' and they chose to follow a militant course, pestering politicians and seeking publicity for their campaign to gain equal voting rights for women.

ABOVE: *Mrs Pankhurst being carried by a policeman from outside Buckingham Palace in the early years of the WSPU campaign.*
BELOW: *Millicent Fawcett pictured in 1928 shortly before she attended the House of Commons to hear the Royal Assent being given to the Bill to give women equal voting rights with men, more than sixty years after she had first become committed to the cause.*

1903 POSTSCRIPTS

January – The *Daily Mail* reported as 'quaint' the fact that in many towns and cities in Britain there existed charitable trusts which awarded dowries to poor women of good character.

December – Marie Curie became the first woman to win a Nobel Prize when, together with her husband Pierre and Henri Becquerel, she was awarded the prize for Physics.

WHY WOMEN FAIL

To the Editor of the *Daily Mail*:

The great number of women who are now finding their way into professions formerly monopolized by men must not be taken as an indication that women have really made up their mind that a life of toil is the highest feminine idea.

At heart the majority of women detest all work other than that connected with the home, which to them is only a labour of love.

This latent desire for the sheltered ease of home life accounts, in my opinion as a woman, for the surprisingly small number of feminine successes in directions which demand originality of mind and sustained mental or physical effort.

BA (Lond.)

Daily Mail, 14 May 1903

LIFE IN THE BABIES' HOTEL.
What They Eat and How They Play.

AS mentioned in a former issue of the "Daily Mail," one of the latest developments of modern life in England is an hotel for babies in London. Norland Nurseries, as the hotel is called,

milk pudding, whilst the world-worn veterans of eight are allowed biscuits and butter—a privilege on which they are most insistent.

Exercise is again taken in the afternoon, and tea, consisting of cake, bread and butter.

HOW THE NOSEGAY IS BEING WORN.
The old-fashioned nosegay in its revived form is cup-shaped, and is being used as the finishing touch of a Directoire costume or an Incroyable coat.

is a home for the children of well-to-do parents who are travelling, and is a scene of happy childhood, from little tots of one month to veterans of eight or nine.

From early morning until bed time the health and happiness of the children are the nurses' chief considerations, and, judging by an afternoon which the writer spent with the children, their lot is, indeed, an enviable one.

The daily menu is most carefully chosen, and, as far as possible, each child is given the food which is found most suitable to its constitution, but as a rule a plain diet suits every child.

Punctually at eight o'clock the children, fresh from their morning "tub," range themselves round the breakfast table, where they have an ample meal of either porridge, bread and milk, rusks, or eggs.

"I'se to have eggs to-morrow," remarked one toddling mite of five, "and Gwen's going to have porridge." "Who's Gwen?" ventured the writer. "Oh, Gwen's my sister, and I'se her sister," remarked the young lady—and forthwith the relationship was made clear!

After breakfast comes a period of play, and then, weather permitting, the children go out for a couple of hours' exercise. Half-past eleven is the signal for a siesta. Lunch consists of soup or fish, chicken and

ter, and jam, is served at 4.30, and then the children troop off to bed. The "veteran brigade," however, are permitted to sit up until the dignified hour of 6.30 or seven o'clock.

Lessons are a hardship only inflicted on the older members, for kindergarten exercises such as paper plaiting, clay modelling, or bead threading have been found to answer extremely well. When necessary nurses or governesses are engaged to initiate the "hotel residents" in the mysteries of addition and other elementary "horridnesses," as one young lady of seven termed her lessons.

A feature of each day nursery is a larder situated in the corner adjoining the window, in which the day's provisions are placed every morning by the housekeeper, so that the nurses are saved the trouble of having to go to the kitchen for each meal.

To see the children playing is a sight which would make the most trouble-stricken individual feel years younger. In a corner of one day nursery the writer watched three little children busily engaged in building a rather unsubstantial house on a miniature table standing only eighteen inches off the floor, so that to stand on a chair is a superfluous undertaking for the youngest resident. A rocking-chair is also a popular article, especially with the seniors. In

order that the children's well-being can be accurately ascertained, each child is weighed once a week, and it says much for the nurses' care that in not a single case has even the most delicate child lost weight, while one baby recently broke the record by increasing in weight over 8oz. in one week.

In the basement of the hotel is a laundry, where the greater part of the children's washing is done "at home," and, in fact, "luxury tempered with sound common sense is the order of the day in the babies' hotel." As the writer left the nursery one little girl aged six screamed out, "If you come to tea next Wednesday in Joy, you can have both jam, cake, bread and butter." The invitation was alluring, and "Joy" sounds an excellent name for a nursery. Forget-me-Not, Freedom, Dawn, Daisy, and Speedwell being the other quaint addresses in London—London's unique hotel.

AT PLAY IN THE BABIES' HOTEL

Seen in one of the nurseries where the children of the travelling rich are boarded at fixed prices.

★ ★ ★ ★
WOMEN AND HUGE BOUQUETS.
The Return of the Nosegay.

When the sky is draped with heavy clouds and the saddest season of the year is upon us, for we know that we have to endure worse climatic atmospheres than we have already known before we can expect better ones, what a joy flowers and foliage are.

Quite a speciality is now being carried out in the florists' shops for coat bouquets for women. The nosegays are cup-shaped, and are particularly appropriate as the finishing touch of a Directoire costume or an Incroyable coat, pinned on the left side of the corsage or tucked into the waist belt. The blossoms that are being principally used now are lilies of the valley, carnations of all colours, gardenias, white and tuber roses, the exquisitely lovely yellow and brown orchids which accord so well with the fashionable brown costume, and a charming mixture of violets and lilies of the valley, the violets used being those cultivated for their specially long stalks.

A chat with Mr. Goodyear, the Court florist, of the Royal Arcade, Bond-street, emphasises the fact that has already been pleasantly observable—namely, that smart men are endorsing the King's good taste by following his example and wearing buttonholes. The Prince of Wales is another votary of the little lapel nosegay, and is particularly fond of the modest violet or of the sweetly scented malmaison carnation.

What our French neighbours call the decorative flower of the moment is certainly the chrysanthemum with a huge ragged ball-shaped blossom and very long stalk. The freak chry-

santhemum is the green one, the flowers of which look just as if the leaves had been taken and twisted into the semblance of a bloom by hand; but the ones that are usually seen filling up the angles of halls, often right up to the ceiling, in company with rich foliage plants, are the bronze, the mauve, and the white varieties.

One feature of the Babies' Hotel for the children of the rich is that the little ones are weighed every week, in order to prove their pleasing progression in weight.

Among the fashionable foliage plants of this winter are the crotons, with their beautiful yellow and red shaded leaves, and the pandanas, all white and green with prickly edges to the leaves. It is still not too late for dwellers in the country to decorate their houses with the beautiful faded leaves of the beech, though, unfortunately, this foliage has an unpleasant habit of falling, forgetful that its autumn proclivities should not extend to the interior of a tidily kept house.

Hostesses with plenty of wall space

in the halls, and even in their drawing-rooms, are filling the angles and recesses with pots of blossoms and foliage. Among other lovely plants that are being used for this purpose are the white, pink, and red heather, tall lilies, that most decorative plant the begonia, of a beautiful rose pink, and cyclamens of the

utmost fragility and loveliness in white, mauve and purple, spiræa, and pink and white lancifoliums. Imagine a bank of apricot coloured mollis, azaleas in full bloom, or one in which the predominating motives are tubs of orange trees with their pungently scented blossoms, their foliage, and the ripe and green globes of fruit all on at the same time. Another very decorative adjunct which must not be forgotten is the Cape gooseberry, though better still is it to order the physalis, which is a large variety of this favourite plant, often familiarly called the Chinese lantern.

Though some of the most recent brides have elected to go to the altar without the customary bouquet, bunches or sheaves of blossom are usually ordered for that great occasion. The bride, of course, carries white flowers, and orange blossom leads the list. But sheaves of tall Harrissi lilies, borne in the crook of the left arm, so that the flowers tower above the shoulders, have been a good deal in request.

"Forget-me-not," one of the bed-rooms in the Babies' Hotel.

1904

Educating Girls

By 1904 some strides had been made in education for women and girls. The 1870 Education Act provided for elementary education for both boys and girls and also allowed women to sit on the School Boards responsible for carrying out the provisions of the Act. However, while girls were taught the three Rs, the elementary school curriculum for girls also included cookery, hygiene, laundrywork, sewing and infant care lessons. This was especially so after 1904 when a report on the poor state of the nation's health, revealed when trying to recruit soldiers to serve in the Boer War, blamed not poverty, poor housing, bad diet and lack of medical facilities but low standards of housewifery and mothering.

Even secondary schools for girls devoted time to educating their pupils in domestic skills. In 1904 there were a number of secondary schools for girls. Some like the North London Collegiate School and Cheltenham Ladies' College were for the daughters of the wealthy. Girls from the middle classes whose parents wished a secondary education for them would usually attend a Girls' Public Day School. These schools often offered scholarships to girls whose parents could not afford the fees but as books, uniforms and other items had to be paid for secondary education was out of reach of very many girls.

Attitudes to education for girls were changing but while the idea was fading that an education would hamper a girl's chances of marriage a new rationale had taken its place: elementary schools educated poor girls to be good wives, mothers and domestic servants, and secondary schools turned out more educated and accomplished wives for the rich and middle classes, or women who could earn a respectable living if they failed to marry. Many of the women providing the education sought to fight this rationale but it was there none the less.

Higher or university education for women was rare – there were women's colleges at both Oxford and Cambridge but while the women could attend lectures they were not allowed to sit for degrees, although the Scottish universities, London University and some of the English provincial universities did award degrees to women.

There were arguments that women were not suited to higher education and indeed many of those arguments were exactly those used against the education of girls in earlier centuries – namely that education damaged their health, fertility and attractiveness to possible suitors. The *Daily Mail* in July 1904 reported on a paper delivered by an American doctor which claimed that the health of American women was endangered by higher education because excessive education took blood to the brain and away from other parts of the body which then became diseased. He also claimed that highly educated women had fewer and weaker children.

ABOVE: *Some of the girls' public schools echoing the philosophy of boys' public schools included rigorous exercise on the curriculum.*
BELOW: *Emmeline Pankhurst* (second from left) *leads women in a suffrage demonstration.*

1904 POSTSCRIPT

November – A large increase in the numbers of people in receipt of poor relief was reported. In 1904 there were about 250,000 people in workhouses and more than 500,000 receiving aid without having to go into the workhouse. Women formed a very high percentage of those receiving poor relief.

Beauty's Secrets from a Beauty's Boudoir.

The Penalties of Frowning, Grimacing and Crying.

WHAT a difference there is in women! I allude now to the way in which they treat their looks. There are some who are beauties by inheritance, but who neglect their loveliness until it becomes marred and spoiled, and there are others from whom actual good looks have been withheld, who so cultivate comeliness that really they are more delightful to look upon than their so-called fairer rivals.

The woman who means to retain all the beauty she possesses, and intends to add to her stock of charms, loses no chance of improving her appearance. Every time she dresses she regards each little part of her toilet as a rite, and all day long keeps her aim in her mind.

I would say a word here upon the subject of grimaces, because they are a text upon which to base some forcible remarks. Do overcome such disfiguring habits as frowning and knitting the brows. Is it not worth while to have a pretty forehead—one that is white and clear, smooth and unlined?

To keep it so requires care. Let your forehead remain immobile and calm, so avoiding furrows on it. Don't raise your eyebrows with every other sentence, as so many women do, so that above them are formed a mass of wrinkles. Try to express nothing by your forehead. Do that by means of speech.

Of course, time will somewhat encroach upon the smoothness of your skin; but you can do much to detain its march. For instance, use massage and electricity, and try the following old recipe, handed down to us by

our grandmothers: Melt some white wax slowly. Then dip a cloth in it till it is thoroughly covered with the wax. Bind this cloth round the forehead on going to bed at night, and it will iron out the wrinkles. Be careful to have the forehead smooth when you put the bandage on, or you may iron the wrinkles in.

Above the brow clusters the hair. A fine head of hair beautifies a plain face, while it is, indeed, the crowning glory of the loveliest girl's physiognomy. Yet nine women out of ten do not know how to treat it properly, even for such a simple action as going to bed at night. Of course, it is brushed and combed; but are the tangles got rid of in the best possible way for the tresses?

The proper way to disentangle the hair of both children and grown up people, is to begin gently at the extremities with a large comb with coarse teeth far apart. If you proceed upwards you do not bring the tangles from above downwards in mere tangles, as most ignorant people are apt to do. If you come to bunches that resist, do not try to drag your comb through them, but use your fingers persuasively to reduce the tangles to smoothness. On going to bed at night be sure to shake your hair out thoroughly, and then plait it very loosely. Brush your hair always at least twice a day, and even if the hair comes out persist in this. It means stimulation and ventilation, without which no head of hair can be healthy. The hair should be thoroughly cleansed not oftener

The hair should be thoroughly brushed. Let the hair hang loosely now and then. Like the body it needs fresh air. If the hair is not strong, rub it with a pomade made of thirty parts of beef marrow, eight parts or oil of sweet almonds, two parts of sulphate of quinine, and fifteen parts of essence of lemon, and, if you want an excellent waver for the hair, get your chemist to prepare for you a lotion made of sixty parts of borate of soda and seven parts of gum arabic. Mix these ingredients together thoroughly, and add two quarts of boiling water to it. When the mixture is cool, add seventy-five parts of spirits of camphor and twenty parts of extract of heliotrope. Apply these at night to the hair, and put it into curl papers.

Perhaps you who read these lines are girls prone to all sorts of healthy outdoor exercise. If so, pray preserve your complexion from the rigours of change of temperature, which will otherwise deteriorate its beauty. The day when women were instructed to believe that wind and air were good for the complexion is over so far back. Any one who makes a speciality of beauty will advise them to protect their skins as much as possible from every change of weather.

Be out in the fresh air, but keep the air from your face. Wear veils, use powder, and protect the skin with a layer of good cold cream. A specially good one is made of three simple ingredients—thirty parts of oil of sweet almonds, eight parts of white wax, and the same of spermaceti. It is excellent for massage and for facial improvement generally, and will not encourage the growth of superfluous hairs as animal oils, such as lanoline, will.

I always find that the more simple the ingredients used in our cosmetics are, the better they suit the average skin. Take the three first mentioned as an example. They have been used from time immemorial, and are as worthy of our attention now as they were ages ago, for there is nothing in them that will harm the most sensitive skin.

Do you ever cry? Being a woman, I suppose you do. It is a foolish practice, for, though it may relieve the pent-up feelings, it inflames the lids, and makes the eyes look heavy and dim. I have heard a few tears recommended as a refreshing and brightening influence, but they should be only a few and be only very occasionally indulged in, to emphasise a scene between lovers, for example, when he proves unkind. For, of course, nothing moves some men more quickly and truly than the sight of a pair of pretty eyes suffused with tears. After the scene, repair to your room and bathe the poor eyes with salt and water, which will strengthen them after their trial. Sometimes you will wake to find your eyelids all swollen. Despair in the boudoir! "I know," says a well-known beauty, writing on this subject in the "New York American," every pretty woman has experienced these little miseries as well as ugly women. Don't make the mistake of thinking that only ugly women have their trials. Well, then, when your eyelids are swollen use compresses—hot compresses. But, like everything else, these must be applied correctly.

Make your compresses out of absorbent cotton. Apply them for six or eight minutes twice a day, dipped in an antiseptic lotion like boracic acid, dissolved in hot water in the proportion of one teaspoonful to a pint of water. Use it when tepid, and recollect that any lotion prescribed for the eyes is only good for them when absolutely fresh; so have small quantities made up and very often. Is it necessary to add that cosmetics should never be used near the eyes, nor should brighteners, like belladonna, be dropped into them? I have frequently been asked what to do for moist hands. Nothing can be more disagreeable to

than twice a month, but this does not mean that it should necessarily be washed.

Blonde hair, which is delicate and inclined to break easily, should be wetted as little as possible; whereas the brunette may use water or a prepared shampoo. If you are a blonde, when you want to cleanse your hair, don't wash it, but take the grease out with powder, dredging it into the hair and then brushing it out thoroughly. This is called a dry shampoo. The French use iris powder for the purpose, and very excellent it is. Pomades and oils are very good for the hair, particularly if it is dry and broken, but the mixtures should be fresh.

a day with a bit of linen dipped in the following preparation:—Seventy parts of eau de Cologne and fifteen of tincture of belladonna, and before putting on your gloves plunge your hands just for an instant into water mixed with alum.

BREAKFAST-TABLE PROBLEMS.

No. 406.—The Subtraction.

How can 45 be subtracted from 45 to leave 45?

Answer to No. 405.—Engine must proceed by Down

a dainty woman than to have hands that are over-hot in cold weather and on hot days are unbearably moist. I have heard this sort of drawback ascribed to constitutional weakness, and I dare say it is. Here is a recipe that is excellent for the afflicted in this way. Try it, and you will thank me for having given it to you. Rub the palms of your hands several times

Loop to truck "B," bringing it back and placing it up the main line beyond points "D." Then to points "C" up to Dead End "No. 2," and on to truck "A," setting that into Dead End "No. 1." Then to Dead End "No. 2," to points "C," up to points "D," up to truck "A," bringing it down to points "D," then back on to train, bringing trucks "A" and "C" to points "D." Then set truck "C" into Dead End "No. 1," next to points "D," and set truck "A" back on to train, into place. Engine must then proceed to points "D," fetch truck "C" from Dead End "No. 1," and leave truck "C" between points "C" and "D." Then engine must go to points "D"—to points "A"—"A" to "B"—"B" to points "C," and on to truck "C." Then to points "C" and "B" standing on the Main Line. Bring trucks "C" and "B" back to points "C." set truck "B" into Dead End "2," then back to points "C" and set truck "C" beyond points "D." Engine then to go by points "D" to points "A," and so along siding to "B" truck, and pull truck "B" back, leaving that in place. Engine then to points "A," down to truck "C." Then to points "C," and so up to Dead End "No. 1," leaving truck "C" in place. Then back on to train.

ABOVE: *Christabel Pankhurst.*
BELOW: *Annie Kenney who, unlike most of the members of the WSPU, came from a working-class background.*

1905

Men Hold the Purse Strings

On 8 August 1905 the *Daily Mail* carried an article which quoted a report in the magazine *Good House Keeping* that three out of four housewives must beg for money from their husbands. The *Mail* article pointed out that such a situation must obviously lead to marital difficulties and asked husbands to imagine how they would feel had they to beg for money from a relative.

While there were such pleas for understanding of women's financial position and for generous behaviour from men there was no belief that a woman had any right to money from her husband. A husband was supposed to support his family and whatever money he chose to give his wife was the only money she had, unless she was one of the ten per cent of married women who earned money. The Married Women's Property Act of 1882 had given married women the same rights over their own property as single women but if a woman saved money from the house-keeping money given to her by her husband it still legally belonged to him. This meant that she could only spend money on things approved by her husband.

There was no entitlement to any allowance from the State and it was to be another twelve years before Eleanor Rathbone was to make her call for family allowances. Any support for poor families came from the Poor Laws, the administrators of which handed out money after a means test or forced the family into the workhouse.

The workhouse or Poor Law relief was frequently the only recourse for women with children whose husbands failed to support them. A man might be unemployed or squander his wages or simply desert his family. A report in 1909 found a 33-per-cent increase in the desertion of wives and blamed it on higher living costs. It was possible for wives to sue for maintenance if they were deserted. However a loophole which meant the husband did not have to pay maintenance when in jail was an option pursued by some.

1905 POSTSCRIPTS

May – As supporters of women's suffrage gathered outside Parliament the Women's Enfranchisement Bill proposed by Bamford Slack was 'talked out' without a vote.

October – Christabel Pankhurst, eldest of Emmeline's five children, and Annie Kenney were the first suffragettes to be imprisoned when they refused to pay their fines imposed for assaulting a policeman at a political meeting.

November – Universal suffrage was granted in Austria.

December – Austrian Bertha von Suttner was awarded the Nobel Peace Prize.

WOMAN'S REALM.

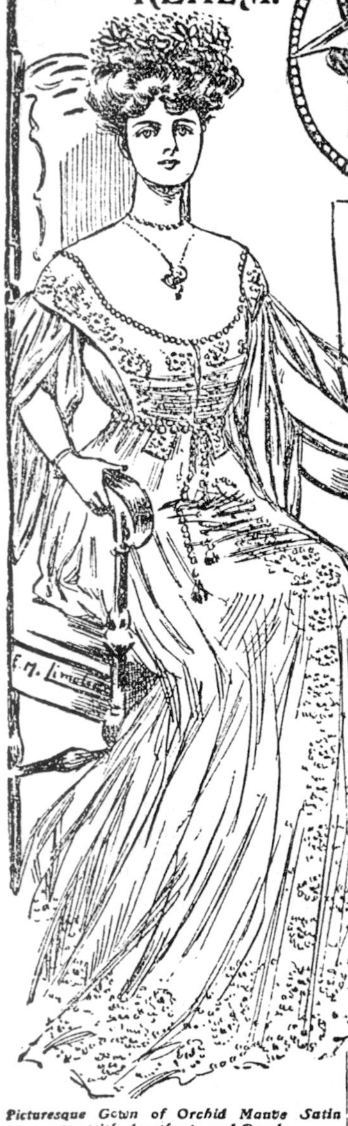

Picturesque Gown of Orchid Mauve Satin sewn with Amethysts and Pearls.

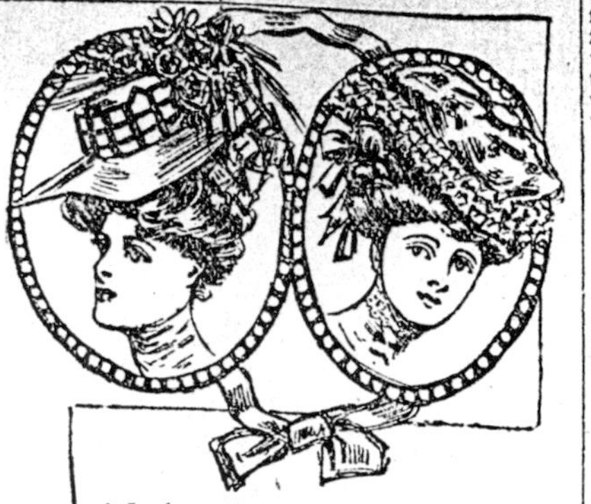

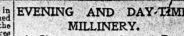

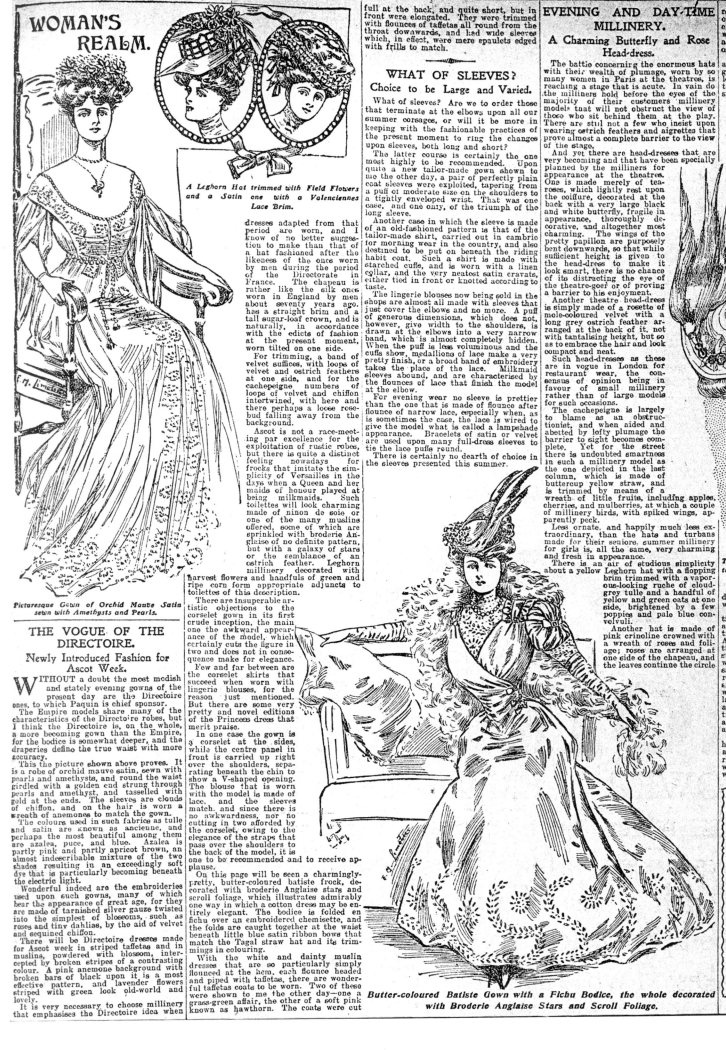

A Leghorn Hat trimmed with Field Flowers and a Satin one with a Valenciennes Lace Brim.

THE VOGUE OF THE DIRECTOIRE.

Newly Introduced Fashion for Ascot Week.

WITHOUT a doubt the most modish and stately evening gowns of the present day are the Directoire ones, to which Paquin is chief sponsor.

The Empire models share many of the characteristics of the Directoire robes, but I think the Directoire is, on the whole, a more becoming gown than the Empire, for the bodice is somewhat deeper, and the draperies define the true waist with more accuracy.

This the picture shown above proves. It is a robe of orchid mauve satin, sewn with pearls and amethysts, and round the waist girdled with a golden end strung through pearls and amethyst, and tasselled with gold at the ends. The sleeves are clouds of chiffon, and on the hair is worn a wreath of anemones to match the gown.

The colours used in such fabrics as tulle and satin are known as ancienne, and perhaps the most beautiful among them are azalea, puce, and blue. Azalea is partly pink and partly apricot brown, an almost indescribable mixture of the two shades resulting in an exceedingly soft dye that is particularly becoming beneath the electric light.

Wonderful indeed are the embroideries used upon such gowns, many of which bear the appearance of great age, for they are made of tarnished silver gauze twisted into the simplest of blossoms, such as roses and tiny dahlias, by the aid of velvet and sequined chiffon.

There will be Directoire dresses made for Ascot week in striped taffetas and in muslins, powdered with blossom, intercepted by broken stripes of a contrasting colour. A pink anemone background with broken bars of black upon it is a most effective pattern, and lavender flowers striped with green look old-world and lovely.

It is very necessary to choose millinery that emphasises the Directoire idea when dresses adapted from that period are worn, and I know of no better suggestion to make than that of a hat fashioned after the likeness of the ones worn by men during the period of the Directorate in France. The chapeau is rather like the silk ones worn in England by men about seventy years ago. has a straight brim and a tall sugar-loaf crown, and is naturally, in accordance with the edicts of fashion at the present moment, worn tilted on one side.

For trimming, a band of velvet suffices, with loops of velvet and ostrich feathers at one side, and for the cachepeigne numbers of loops of velvet and chiffon intertwined, with here and there perhaps a loose rosebud falling away from the background.

Ascot is not a race-meeting par excellence for the exploitation of rustic robes, but there is quite a distinct feeling nowadays for frocks that imitate the simplicity of Versailles in the days when a Queen and her maids of honour played at being milkmaids. Such toilettes will look charming made of ninon de soie or one of the many muslins offered, some of which are sprinkled with broderie Anglaise of no definite pattern, but with a galaxy of stars or the semblance of an ostrich feather. Leghorn millinery decorated with harvest flowers and handfuls of green and ripe corn form appropriate adjuncts to toilettes of this description.

There are insuperable artistic objections to the corselet gown in its first crude inception, the main one the awkward appearance of the model, which certainly cuts the figure in two and does not in consequence make for elegance.

Few and far between are the corselet skirts that succeed when worn with lingerie blouses, for the reason just mentioned. But there are some very pretty and novel editions of the Princess dress that merit praise.

In one case the gown is a corselet at the sides, while the centre panel in front is carried up right over the shoulders, separating beneath the chin to show a V-shaped opening. The blouse that is worn with the model is made of lace, and the sleeves match. and since there is no awkwardness, nor no cutting in two afforded by the corselet, owing to the elegance of the straps that pass over the shoulders to the back of the model, it is one to be recommended and to receive applause.

On this page will be seen a charmingly-pretty, butter-coloured batiste frock, decorated with broderie Anglaise stars and scroll foliage, which illustrates admirably one way in which a cotton dress may be entirely elegant. The bodice is folded en fichu over an embroidered chemisette, and the folds are caught together at the waist beneath little blue satin ribbon bows that match the Tagal straw hat and its trimmings in colouring.

With the white and dainty muslin dresses that are so particularly simply flounced at the hem. each flounce headed and piped with taffetas, there are wonderful taffetas coats to be worn. Two of these were shown to me the other day—one a grass-green affair, the other of a soft pink known as hawthorn. The coats were cut full at the back, and quite short, but in front were elongated. They were trimmed with flounces of taffetas all round from the throat dowawards, and had wide sleeves which, in effect, were mere epaulets edged with frills to match.

WHAT OF SLEEVES?

Choice to be Large and Varied.

What of sleeves? Are we to order those that terminate at the elbows upon all our summer corsages, or will it be more in keeping with the fashionable practices of the present moment to ring the changes upon sleeves, both long and short?

The latter course is certainly the one most highly to be recommended. Upon quite a new tailor-made gown shown to me the other day, a pair of perfectly plain coat sleeves were exploited, tapering from a puff of moderate size on the shoulders to a tightly enveloped wrist. That was one case, and one only, of the triumph of the long sleeve.

Another case in which the sleeve is made of an old-fashioned pattern is that of the tailor-made shirt, carried out in cambric for morning wear in the country, and also destined to be put on beneath the riding habit coat. Such a shirt is made with starched cuffs, and is worn with a linen collar, and the very neatest satin cravats, either tied in front or knotted according to taste.

The lingerie blouses now being sold in the shops are almost all made with sleeves that just cover the elbows and no more. A puff of generous dimensions, which does not, however, give width to the shoulders, is drawn at the elbows into a very narrow band, which is almost completely hidden. When the puff is less voluminous and the cuffs show, medallions of lace make a very pretty finish, or a broad band of embroidery takes the place of the lace. Milkmaid sleeves abound, and are characterised by the flounces of lace that finish the model at the elbow.

For evening wear no sleeve is prettier than the one that is made of flounce after flounce of narrow lace, especially when, as is sometimes the case, the lace is wired to give the model what is called a lampshade appearance. Bracelets of satin or velvet are used upon many full-dress sleeves to tie the lace puffs round.

There is certainly no dearth of choice in the sleeves presented this summer.

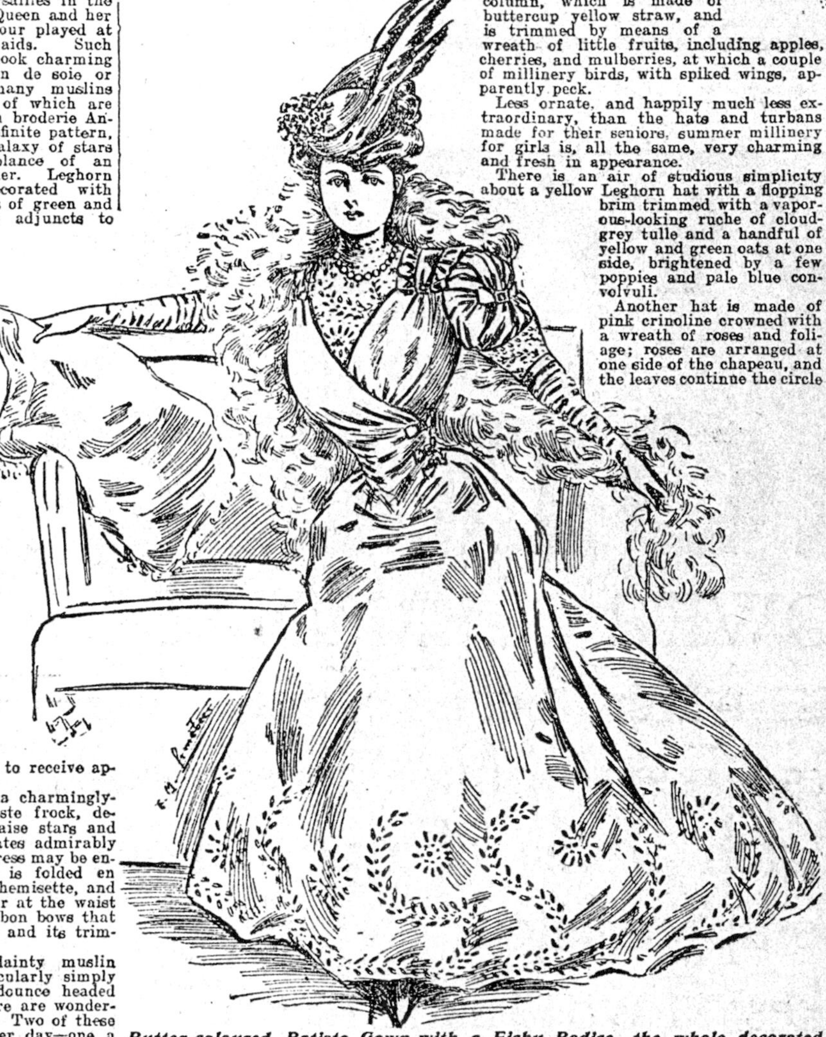

Butter-coloured Batiste Gown with a Fichu Bodice, the whole decorated with Broderie Anglaise Stars and Scroll Foliage.

EVENING AND DAY-TIME MILLINERY.

A Charming Butterfly and Rose Head-dress.

The battle concerning the enormous hats with their wealth of plumage, worn by so many women in Paris at the theatres, is reaching a stage that is acute. In vain do the milliners hold before the eyes of the majority of their customers millinery models that will not obstruct the view of those who sit behind them at the play. There are still not a few who insist upon wearing ostrich feathers and aigrettes that prove almost a complete barrier to the view of the stage.

And yet there are head-dresses that are very becoming and that have been specially planned by the milliners for appearance at the theatres. One is made merely of tea-roses, which lightly rest upon the coiffure, decorated at the back with a very large black and white butterfly, fragile in appearance, thoroughly decorative, and altogether most charming. The wings of the pretty papillon are purposely bent downwards, so that while sufficient height is given to the head-dress to make it look smart, there is no chance of its distracting the eye of the theatre-goer or of proving a barrier to his enjoyment.

Another theatre head-dress is simply made of a rosette of mole-coloured velvet with a long grey ostrich feather arranged at the back of it, not with tantalising height, but so as to embrace the hair and look compact and neat.

Such head-dresses as these are in vogue in London for restaurant wear, the consensus of opinion being in favour of small millinery rather than of large models for such occasions.

The cachepeigne is largely to blame as an obstructionist, and when aided and abetted by lofty plumage the barrier to sight becomes complete. Yet for the street there is undoubted smartness in such a millinery model as the one depicted in the last column, which is made of buttercup yellow straw, and is trimmed by means of a wreath of little fruits, including apples, cherries, and mulberries, at which a couple of millinery birds, with spiked wings, apparently peck.

Less ornate, and happily much less extraordinary, than the hats and turbans made for their seniors, summer millinery for girls is, all the same, very charming and fresh in appearance.

There is an air of studious simplicity about a yellow Leghorn hat with a flopping brim trimmed with a vaporous-looking ruche of cloud-grey tulle and a handful of yellow and green oats at one side, brightened by a few poppies and pale blue convolvuli.

Another hat is made of pink crinoline crowned with a wreath of roses and foliage; roses are arranged at one side of the chapeau, and the leaves continue the circle round to the back. Right across the crown of the hat and threaded through it at either side, is a band of blue satin ribbon, which is tied upon the hair at the back in a large bow, forming there a cachepeigne of moderate height.

The sailor hat, with its narrow brim and fairly tall crown, is less adapted to girlish needs than the boater, which has a lower crown and a wider brim, and is trimmed with rosettes of ribbon at one side, instead of the wired loops that usually decorate the sailor hat worn by grown-up women.

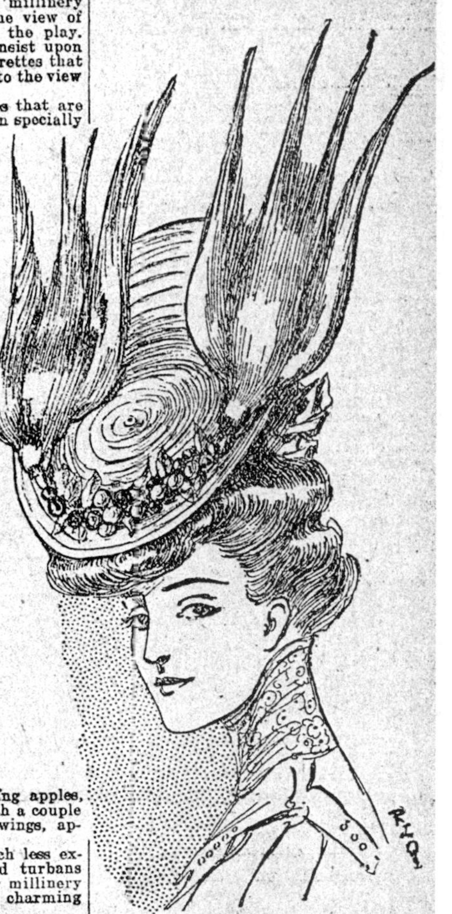

This Millinery Model was Sketched in Paris to Illustrate the Obstructionist Cachepeigne and Spiked Plumage.

Lingerie millinery abounds, and is particularly pretty this summer, ranging from a coarse crash model, embroidered with a trellis-work of stitchery and broderie Anglaise star centres, to a hat made entirely of Valenciennes lace frills, with strands of white muslin between, trimmed with a sash of pale blue or pale pink satin, and perhaps one large and one small rosebud mingling with the loops at the side. In the second column of this page will be seen a charming hat with a white lace brim and full pink satin crown, and adjoining it is a Leghorn model with a trellis-work of velvet upon the brim and a bunch of field flowers, wheat, and grass at the back.

Very little girls are wearing mushroom hats again, and almost invariably rosettes are placed beneath the brim with short ribbon streamers hanging from them, while the outside is trimmed with a wreath of simple flowers or sash of ribbon.

THE NOVELTY OF THE WEEK.

New "Boater" for River Parties.

For river parties there is a new "boater" to be chronicled, a hat made of stiffened Panama, with a wide brim, bordered by straw of a coarser quality. It is fashionable to trim such hats with dainty veils of a pale colour, honeycombed with open-work embroidery, and a white, trellis-like pattern meandering between the tinged portions.

The veil is quite loosely tied round the crown of the hat, falls far down at the back as well as at the sides, describing a series of pleats of graduated lengths, culminating somewhere near the waist. Green weed is introduced upon numbers of hats at the present moment, and frequently forms, with the addition of flowers, a very smart aigrette.

LADY CHARLOTTE.

1906

Sportswomen

Throughout September 1902 the *Daily Mail* had carried a great deal of correspondence on the linked subjects of women, beauty, health, exercise and sport following an article by a Mr H. B. Marriot Watson. Mr Marriot Watson argued in his article that the increasing vogue for women to take exercise or play some sort of sport would only create gaunt, flat-chested women who would be weak and prone to illness. Many letters totally refuted Mr Marriot Watson's ideas and spoke of the benefits of exercise to women's health and beauty. Other correspondents clung to the notion that it was ladylike to be rather frail and claimed that a woman's feminine grace was damaged by sport, while one woman suggested that the only exercise a woman need take was to sweep the house from top to bottom each day.

In 1906 the Physical Director at Harvard University suggested that sports such as lacrosse, hockey and netball might be physically damaging to women and girls. Sport was more widely participated in by both sexes in the USA although the curriculum of many British girls' secondary schools and colleges included sport. Elizabeth Garrett Anderson had suggested some form of exercise in girls' schools as an antidote to the objection that girls' health suffered from too much study.

However, many of the arguments against education for girls were transposed to women and sport. It was said sport would damage their health and, more crucially, damage their chances of having children, which in a country like Britain with an Empire to people and run would be a severe problem if it could be proved true. Even cycling was cited as dangerous but whether that was because of the exertion involved or the unladylike clothing and posture required for riding is unclear.

1906 POSTSCRIPTS

February – The *Daily Mail* published an article entitled 'Shall Women Have the Vote' by a Dr Emil Reich. In his article he claimed women should not have the vote, not on the grounds of intelligence or fairness, grounds on which he admitted they did have a claim, but on the grounds that women knew nothing of politics and if they had the vote logically they would have to be able to be MPs, a role for which they were eminently unsuited. But Dr Reich did not believe that women should have to stick to the kitchen. He thought they should go into Civil Service jobs to free men, especially university-educated men, at home and in the Empire for the work which their mentality and character more suited them.

April – The Independent Labour Party called for female suffrage and Labour MP Keir Hardy had a motion in favour of votes for women 'talked out' in the House of Commons.

However the Labour party's attitude to female enfranchisement was a little ambiguous. As there were a number of poorer male workers who still did not have the vote they felt that it was in some respects wrong to fight to enfranchise what they believed would be a group of mainly upper- and middle-class women.

June – The results of a census in the USA showed that of 303 occupations women worked in 300 of them ranging from blacksmiths to architects, undertakers to journalists, barbers to house painters. The *Daily Mail* reported it under the title 'Queer Trades For Women'.

November – Keir Hardy introduced another Bill for Female Suffrage which failed.

December – Suffragettes in Holloway Prison refused to eat Christmas Dinner.

Tennis player May Sutton who shocked Wimbledon with her short, loose-fitting tennis dresses in an era when some women still played sports in whalebone corsets.

DAILY MAIL, TUESDAY, FEBRUARY 12, 1907.

WHICH HAS THE BETTER TIME IN LIFE?

By GEORGE R. SIMS. A Man or a Woman? Why?

"IF I had a second time on earth I should like to come back as a man." It was a pretty woman who made the remark in my hearing. She was young, elegantly dressed, and appeared to be sauntering along the road of life by the rose-strewn way.

Not having the pleasure of this pretty, smiling young woman's acquaintance, I could not ask her reasons for desiring a change of sex in her next incarnation. So I passed along with a new question added to the many which nowadays furnish food for private thought and public discussion. Which has the better time on earth, the man or the woman? There is, of course, the point of view of "a good time" to be taken into consideration before the question can be particularly argued, but speaking generally I am inclined to think that so far as enjoyment of life is concerned the women of to-day have little cause to envy men. In spite of the rapid strides towards equality—I would if I were a bolder man say superiority—which the women of the Western civilisation have made, they have lost none of the privileges which were theirs in the days when they accepted the position of "the weaker vessel." To-day, though they have their clubs, in

which there are smoking rooms, though they revel in the "robustious" joys of athletic sports and country life, and join freely in discussions on subjects of which the mid-Victorian woman—the word was lady then—was kept in profound ignorance, the woman of to-day, though always asserting her strength, rarely fails to claim the privileges of her weakness.

In spite of the higher education of women, and the acknowledgment of the rights of the bachelor girl, the code of honour among men is still sterner than the code of honour of the fair sex. A woman may do with impunity many things that would cause society to look askance at a man.

In the matter of small debts she is allowed forgetfulness, and it is never called by a harsher name. The privilege of forgetting small debts must necessarily add to the enjoyment of daily life. To be reminded of them certainly interferes with the enjoyment of the ordinary man.

But these are, perhaps, frivolous points to urge. Let me take woman as seriously as to-day with the wars of the Suffrage raging she takes herself. Her home life is a joy denied to the average man. There is not one man in a thousand who finds in the domestic interior that joy of possession which animates women from morning till night.

The most loving father, the man devoted to his children, can only have a faint conception of what her children are to the loving mother. He knows that he idolises and that she idolises them; but when all is said and done, they only fill his leisure, and they fill her life.

Just as no black man can think white and no white man can think black, so the paternal instinct, which is the patriarchal instinct modified by the decay of the tribal system, cannot see eye to eye with the maternal instinct.

THREE GREAT JOYS—
ALL FOR WOMEN.

The home, the family, are women's joys, as they can never be man's. And love, which is the foundation of home and family—that, as the poet who knew has told us, "is of man's life a thing apart" but "woman's whole existence."

Love, home, family, are the three great joys of life, and in not one of them does the lot of man compare with the lot of the woman.

In the pleasures that pass man may, and often does, have the larger share; of the joys that remain from youth to age the woman is the chief possessor.

In friendship the man has a pleasure that is keener than woman's. David and Jonathan have thousands of modern prototypes. But the peerless depths of friendship are rarely sounded by women. Few of them understand the loyal, abiding, soul-knit friendship that to many men is a lifelong blessing. There are exceptions, but they prove the rule.

Every woman who has the smallest capacity for the enjoyment of life is man's master. It is only the dull woman who is his slave, and probably she is happier in her slavery than she would be in freedom.

A man may be a very great man in the City, where he has scores of clerks who tremble at his frown, but when he gets home he trembles at his wife's. Therefore, the woman has the joy of being the master of the master of many. The judge, the embodiment of the law, may rule his

court with a rod of iron. It is contempt to contradict him. But the women of his household rule him, and it is he who, when his wife lays down the law, contradicts at his peril.

It is in more senses than one that the hand that rocks the cradle rules the world, and whatever pleasure there is in absolute power, that pleasure is the woman's and not the man's.

A woman's strength lies in her tears. She can obtain all that man can bestow upon her by crying for it. Her tears are her tyrannies. A man's tears are his weakness. The pleasure of gaining his ends by a little weeping is denied him.

To woman's share fall all the joys of angelship—ministering angelship. She has only to smooth a pillow to be rewarded with a smile.

There are very few men who are allowed to smooth a pillow. If a man smoothed pillows all day long no one would dream of calling him a ministering angel.

£7.

A man's idea of real fun!

A woman's most exquisite pleasure is selecting a new hat—

On the lighter side of life the balance is all in the woman's favour. Her father or husband pays her bills and his own as well. What he buys for her in the shape of personal adornments is a pleasure to her. Every new frock, every new hat, every new piece of jewellery is to a woman a new joy.

Men, after their first youth, pass through life without feeling even a thrill of excitement in the ordering, trying on, or getting home of a new suit. Even her parasol is a pleasure in a woman's life. What man ever went to bed happier because he had bought a new umbrella?

"Shopping" is a perpetual joy to woman, from her childhood to her old age.

Shopping to most men is unattractive, not merely because it means outlay for which they see little return, but because stopping to look in at shop windows, going into shops, and struggling on special days from counter to counter mixed up with a never too well-mannered crowd, always bores them and sometimes irritates them.

Woman finds her dullest day brightened by a little shopping. To man the necessity of having to go to his tailor or his hosier, or to buy a present, is, as he curtly puts it, "a nuisance."

To try and make money is the ordinary man's task between his breakfast and his dinner. To spend it is the ordinary woman's occupation during the same period.

The making of money, which is man's daily occupation, is always associated with anxieties. The spending of money is only woman's change of pleasure from the pleasures of home and family.

And yet, though it is a common thing to hear a woman say, "Oh, I wish I were a man!" how many of us have heard a man exclaim, "Oh, how I wish I were a woman!"

—But, just imagine a man having a good time choosing a hat—that's the difference!

[Correspondence is invited on this question. Letters should be addressed to the Editor, Magazine Page, "Daily Mail," London.]

A Dish for To-Day.

THE following ingredients will be required to make the batter for ordinary pancakes:—A quarter of a pound of flour, half a pint of milk, one egg, a level quarter of a teaspoonful of salt, one lemon, three ounces of lard or dripping, and some caster sugar.

The flour and salt should first be mixed in a basin, then make a hole in the middle of the flour and break the egg into it. Be sure that it is a good one.

Now add about two tablespoonsful of milk to the egg and stir it in smoothly with a wooden spoon, and when this is as thick as thick cream, add some more milk to it till all the flour is mixed in with half of the milk. The whole mixture should then be beaten for five minutes. Next stir in the remainder of the milk. If possible the batter should be allowed to stand for two hours.

When ready for the frying process, strain the batter into a jug, and melt the lard or dripping in a small saucepan, and pour enough out of it to make a thin coating of fat over the frying-pan. When a faint smoke rises from this fat pour in sufficient of the batter to thinly cover the bottom of the pan. Let this set over the fire, shaking it gently to see that it does not stick, and when it is a nice brown underneath toss it over to the other side.

When both sides are a nice brown colour turn the pancake over on to a piece of sugared paper and squeeze a little lemon juice over it, also a dusting of castor sugar. It should lastly be rolled up lightly and put on to a hot dish in a hot place while the rest of the batter is being made into pancakes.

When the eyes are red and inflamed they should be bathed two or three times a day with boracic lotion, drying them very carefully after the process if it is to do them good and not harm. The lotion is made of one ounce of boracic acid with a pint of boiling water stirred on to it till it is dissolved, and when it is cool it should be bottled for use. Pour a little of the lotion into a saucer, add enough boiling water to it to make it lukewarm, then use it for bathing the eyes. Make it fresh very frequently.

In the Invalid's Room.

AN ordinary tin bread box is easily converted into a temporary refrigerator for nursery or sick-room use.

Tapes are attached to the corners of a rectangle of flannel as large as the bottom of the box. These, drawn down beneath the box and then tied together, make a serviceable shelf of the piece of flannel.

It is surprising how much broken ice this flannel shelf will support, and how long it will keep if covered with another piece of flannel. The cover of the box can be closed and a cloth thrown over it to exclude the air.

A hole cut low down in the box and fitted with a cork, makes a practical overflow for the waste water. The cold space beneath the shelf answers admirably to hold bottles of milk or drinking water, and the medicines that must be kept in a cool place.

A metal bed is desirable in a sickroom because of its germ-proof qualities, but its open construction may permit a draught to strike the unprotected head and shoulders of its occupant. If the pillows are inefficient as a shield, or if the relative positions of the bed and door present a possibility of exposure to a sudden current of air and its consequent chill, a tall screen should be spread behind the head of the bed, or a coverlet hung over it to safeguard the patient.—From "Good Housekeeping."

The following method has been found excellent for the obliteration of wrinkles on the forehead. Beat the white of an egg well, then add to it a few drops of eau de Cologne, spread it on a soft rag, and bind it on the forehead when going to bed. Wear it till the morning, and then bathe the forehead with warm water.

A little skill in the choice of waistbands does much for the appearance of the waist. Take a yard and a half of ribbon about an inch and a half wide, the same colour as the blouse, then double it and fasten it into a clasp as though it was an ordinary piece of petersham. When it is on pull the ribbon at the back up and down and pin it securely. In this way it is wide just where it is needed, and the clasp pulls it into a narrow shape in the front.

1907

Family Planning

In 1907 the birth rate in Britain continued the fall begun in the late 1870s. In 1876 it was 36 per 1,000 of the population; in 1901, 28.6 per 1,000; and in 1905, 27.2 per 1,000.

In 1877 Annie Besant and Charles Bradlaugh were prosecuted for publishing 'obscene material'. The material in question was information on methods of birth control which was priced to enable working-class women to purchase it. The middle classes had had access to this knowledge for a few years and their family sizes, when matched against the families of the poorer classes not infrequently numbering twelve or more, indicate that at the end of the nineteenth century they were putting that knowledge into practice. Fewer years spent pregnant and fewer children gave middle-class women time and energy to turn their attention to issues and pastimes outside the home, be it charities to help the poor, sport, politics or the campaign for the emancipation of women. It is interesting to note that most of the suffragettes were middle-class women.

Methods of birth control available in 1907 were withdrawal, injections of alum and water, the vaginal sponge soaked in quinine, quinine pessaries, the sheath, and the Dutch cap which had been invented in Holland in the 1870s and although it was against the law to disseminate information about birth control some people did gain some knowledge. Many of these methods had been known throughout the world for centuries but in Britain few people had knowledge of them before the last quarter of the nineteenth century. Prior to that, infanticide and abortion were the only real options in family limitation, and remained so for many poorer women.

Suffragette Elsa Myers addresses a meeting.

1907   POSTSCRIPTS

January – The *Daily Mail* published a fulsome obituary of Josephine Butler who had campaigned vigorously in the 1860s for the repeal of the Contagious Diseases Acts which meant that any woman in an army or naval town suspected of being a prostitute could be imprisoned and medically examined, forcibly if necessary, for signs of venereal disease. The theory was that men could thus be protected from 'unclean women'. There was no censure of unclean men and that men used prostitutes was an accepted fact of life. Josephine Butler's campaign brought prostitution and all the attendant moral and social issues into the public eye.

May – The Finnish Parliament met following elections in March at which women had the vote. It was also the first Parliament in the world to have women MPs.

November – Florence Nightingale, 87, was awarded the Order of Merit.

THE COMING WAR AGAINST THE HOUSEFLY

Why it Must Begin in Winter.—A Remarkable Investigation.

How Flies Bring Disease into the Household.

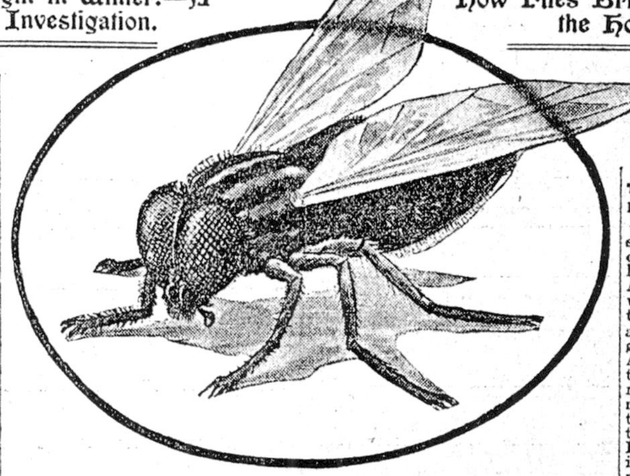

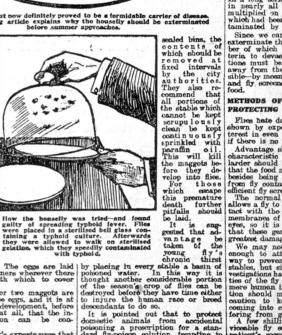

Long suspected but now definitely proved to be a formidable carrier of disease. The accompanying article explains why the housefly should be exterminated before summer approaches.

By H. H. RIDDLE, M.B. (Camb.).

THE common housefly, which formerly was looked upon merely as a nuisance and annoyance which had to be put up with during the summer, has lately come to be regarded in a new and more serious light.

Like the rat and the mosquito, scientists have proved that the fly is an active agent in the spread of many diseases, and must be exterminated or at any rate must be treated as a dangerous enemy of mankind.

When one considers the habits and the anatomy of the fly one is amazed that this insect's capabilities as a microbe carrier have not been more fully realised long ago.

Experiments have lately been made which show that the fly has a most voracious appetite and an almost limitless thirst. It is not a simple desire to cause torment that makes the fly choose the face of a sleeping person for his exercise ground. He is attempting to satisfy his hunger and thirst, and as he is decidedly omnivorous he wanders about in search of organic matter he can steal.

Getting little sustenance from the skin, he works up to some mucous membrane where he finds dampness and perhaps thrown-off and worn-out mucous membrane cells and mucus secretions.

HOW THE HOUSEFLY INFECTS YOU.

These he will find at the edge of the nostrils and the corners of the mouth and eyes. It is in these locations that flies will collect when an invalid is too ill to brush them off.

Unfortunately, in nearly all infectious diseases the mucous surfaces are the chief breeding grounds of the bacilli, so the fly in his search for food is almost sure to become contaminated if his temporary host is suffering from an infectious bacterial disease.

Then the insect, moving on to some healthy individual, carries the bacilli straight to those tissues which are most suitable for their reception and growth; that is, to mucous surfaces.

Under the microscope over one hundred thousand bacteria have been counted on the legs and mouth of a single fly. It has been estimated that in one summer there will be twelve generations of flies, the sexes being about equally divided, and that each female will lay about one thousand eggs.

These figures show that extermination during the summer would be practically an impossibility, so some other means must be found for protection against these microbe carriers.

In New York a committee on this subject has just handed in its report giving some very valuable suggestions as to the best way of handling what is now recognised as a very serious problem of preventive medicine.

While utterly impossible to exterminate them in the summer, the report states that certain precautions taken now in the late winter will do much to keep these pests in check.

Investigations made recently by the United States Bureau of Entomology show that more than 95 per cent. of the flies in a city are bred in stables. The eggs are laid in damp, dark corners wherever there is any refuse with which to cover them.

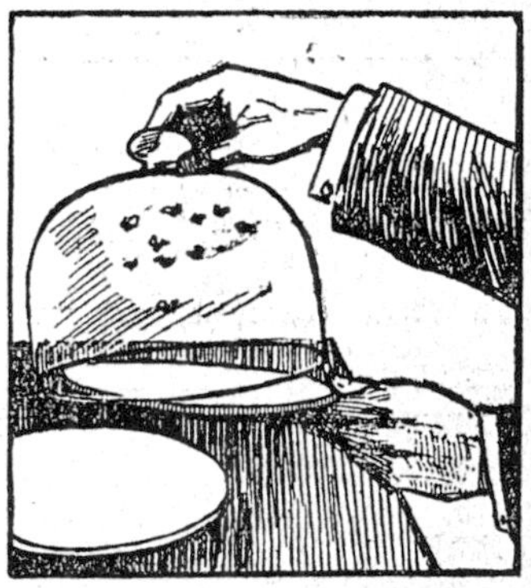

How the housefly was tried—and found guilty of spreading typhoid fever. Flies were placed in a sterilised bell glass containing a typhoid culture. Afterwards they were allowed to walk on sterilised gelatine, which they speedily contaminated with typhoid.

Within a day or two maggots are hatched from these eggs, and it is at this period of its development, before it is really a fly at all, that the insect's multiplication can be controlled.

The Government's experts urge that all stable refuse be kept in tightly sealed bins, the contents of which should be removed at fixed intervals by the city authorities. They also recommend that all portions of the stable which cannot be kept scrupulously clean be kept continuously sprinkled with paraffin oil. This will kill the maggots before they develop into flies.

For those which escape this premature death further pitfalls should be laid.

It is suggested that advantage be taken of the young fly's chronic thirst by placing in every stable a basin of poisoned water. In this way it is thought another considerable portion of the season's crop of flies can be destroyed before they have time either to injure the human race or breed descendants to do so.

It is pointed out that to protect domestic animals from accidental poisoning a prescription for a standard fly-poison solution, tempting to flies but unsavoury to animals, should be issued by the local health authorities.

The guilt of the fly in thus disseminating disease germs is not merely a supposition, but has been proven by actual experiment.

THE GELATINE EXPERIMENT.

Flies have been placed in a large sterile bell glass under which a small dish containing a gelatine culture of live typhoid bacilli has been put. After waiting until the flies have walked about on the typhoid culture this has been gently withdrawn and a dish containing carefully sterilised gelatine has been inserted in its place. After the flies had walked about on this sterile gelatine the dish was removed and put under conditions of moisture, temperature, etc., suitable to the growth and development of typhoid bacilli if any were present. In a long series of such experiments, in nearly all cases, bacilli grew and multiplied on the gelatine medium which had been quite sterile until contaminated by the flies.

Since we cannot hope absolutely to exterminate the species, a single member of which can carry enough bacteria to devastate an army, precautions must be taken to keep the fly away from the sick as much as possible—by means of fly poison solutions and fly screens—and also away from food.

METHODS OF PROTECTING FOOD.

Flies hate darkness, and have been shown by experiment to lose all interest in even the most tempting food if there is no light.

Advantage should be taken of this characteristic of the fly, and the larder should be in such a location that the food may be kept in darkness besides being thoroughly protected from fly contamination by the use of efficient fly screens.

The normal healthy person rarely allows a fly to come into intimate contact with the easily infected mucous membranes of his mouth, nostrils, or eyes, so it is by food contamination that these germ-carriers do their greatest damage.

We may not be public spirited enough to attempt in any practical way to prevent flies breeding in our stables, but since recent scientific investigations have proved the possibilities of the fly as a disease carrier the mere human instinct of self-preservation should make us take every precaution to keep existing flies from coming into contact with people suffering from germ diseases.

A few shillings would pay for serviceable fly screens for the typhoid patient's room and for the kitchen and larder as well.

Advertising by Samples.

The Enormous Cost of the Gift in the Letter Box.

SOME time ago a number of men who were delivering samples of a certain article from house to house reached a street just as a number of "samplers" employed by another firm were leaving it.

The men who were departing, being novices, had carelessly stuck the samples into the letter-boxes in such a way that they could be easily abstracted from outside; so the newcomers, in delivering their own "tasters," took out those of the other manufacturers, getting altogether so many that they were able to exchange them round the corner for refreshment.

"Sampling," as it is called, is carried on so largely nowadays that a number of firms keep staffs not only in London, but in every centre in the three kingdoms, who do little else but deliver samples, of which in the metropolis alone some of them give away a million and a half yearly.

GRATUITOUS COCOA.

A million and a half! The housewife who gets a gratuitous packet of cocoa occasionally may gasp at the figures; but for all that they are accurate. Greater London contains about three-quarters of a million houses which are considered worth "sampling"—that is, excluding those which are too big, as the mansions in the West End, as well as those which are too little, like most of the dwellings in Stepney and similar parishes. The two extremes are generally left alone, though one commercial firm recently delivered expensive samples to large houses in Kensington and the West End generally. Since, then, the firms which "sample" on a large scale go over the ground twice a year, they give away in Greater London alone about one and a half million samples per annum. That, in fact, is the actual number distributed by the houses which regularly practise this method of popularising their wares.

On exactly the same scale are provincial towns "sampled," with the exception of those with a population of less than 3,000.

Yet, notwithstanding the enormous number of samples which certain firms distribute, people try to get more out of them on all manner of pretexts. Two or three years ago, for instance, a well-known provincial firm received an application from a so-called "nursing home" in London for a quantity of samples, which, the "manageress" stated, should be distributed "for our mutual benefit" with some circulars she was going to send round in the neighbourhood. Told off to make inquiries, a representative found that the "nursing home" was a private house, and that the "manageress" had a large number of samples of meat extract, cocoa, etc., the whole enough to feed a regiment.

The cost of sampling aggregates many thousands of pounds. The mere distribution is a big item, notwithstanding that it is undertaken by charitable institutions for the comparatively low price of 3s. 6d. per 1,000; but distribution, with carriage, supervision, excluding packing and the manufactured commodity, costs one big firm 6s. 6d. per 1,000 in London.

Nevertheless, "sampling" pays, especially when it is preceded by bold advertising.

'Daily Mail' Grand Tour.

CANDIDATES AT WORK AGAIN.

AFTER a brief interregnum the candidates for the tour are resuming their efforts to secure a place among the twenty who next August will be the guests of the Editress of the Magazine Page in the free three weeks' holiday through Europe.

Candidates who were far behind in the first "count" are pursuing votes energetically, and it is pleasant to notice that so few of them have lost heart. They have made fresh plans, organised new campaigns, and some, it is clear, will have taken a great stride upwards before the figures are published again.

New candidates between the ages of 18 and 35 can still be nominated for the tour, and nomination forms, which must be signed by two householders, will be forwarded on application.

By signing the nomination form the candidate accepts the conditions governing the tour. The Editress of the Magazine Page of the "Daily Mail" reserves the right to be the sole arbitrator in any question of interpretation that may arise.

VOTING BY COUPON.

A voting coupon appears at the top of the front page of the "Daily Mail," and can be used as soon as you have been properly nominated. Filled up with the name of the candidate one voting coupon will count as one vote.

Voting coupons will not be available after dates named on them. They should be forwarded from time to time in quantities, a slip being attached stating number enclosed. All voting coupons must be sent to—

Continental Tour Department, "Daily Mail,"
17, Bouverie-street, London, E.C.

Those readers of the paper who wish to use their voting coupons, and yet do not know the names of their local candidates, can obtain a complete list on application.

VOTING BY SUBSCRIPTION.

Bear in mind that there are two methods by which you can poll votes for a candidate:

1. By filling in the voting coupon every day. This method is explained above.

2. By subscribing in advance for the "Daily Mail" or the Over-Seas "Daily Mail," as described below.

By paying a subscription to your newsagent you can obtain votes on the following scale:—

Three months' subscription at usual rates entitles you to 250 votes.

Six months' subscription at usual rates entitles you to 500 votes.

Twelve months' subscription at usual rates entitles you to 1,000 votes.

By this method the subscriber pays his newsagent and obtains a receipt.

The newsagent's receipt for the money paid to him, with a penny stamp enclosed to cover acknowledgment, must then be forwarded at once to the Continental Tour Department. In return subscribers will receive a ballot paper filled in with the votes they are entitled to, and this ballot paper, when it has been filled in with the name of the person voted for, must be forwarded to the Continental Tour Department, "Daily Mail," 17, Bouverie-street, London, E.C.

In those cases where newsagents are not available, and subscriptions are sent direct to "Daily Mail," Carmelite House, London, E.C., with instructions to forward the paper by post, the ordinary rates will be charged as follows:

Three months' subscription with postage, 6/6, entitles you to 250 votes.

Six months' subscription with postage, 13/-, entitles you to 500 votes.

Twelve months' subscription with postage, 26/-, entitles you to 1,000 votes.

Some readers may desire to subscribe in addition to the Over-Seas "Daily Mail," weekly copies of which at their order can be sent to friends resident abroad.

For a subscription for twelve months to the Over-Seas "Daily Mail," costing 7/-, you get 350 votes. Newsagents cannot be subscribers.

"Woman" versus "Lady."

A MISAPPREHENSION EXPLAINED.

WHY do so many women object to the term "woman" and insist upon being designated as a "lady"?

The word "woman" has a far nobler and more sacred meaning than "lady," although both came from the Anglo-Saxon.

"Woman" is derived from "wifmann," a compound of "wif" or wife, and "mann," and if we consider that the root of the latter word is "man"=to think, cognate with German and Goth "man," Icelandic "madhr," Latin "mens," and Sanscrit "manes," it is easy to see that the term "man" with its feminine equivalent "woman" could only be applied to rational beings or persons possessed of high intellectual capability.

"Lady" is derived from Anglo-Saxon "hlaf-dige," loaf-kneader, the feminine form of "hlaf-weard," the loaf-keeper, the term applied in Anglo-Saxon times to the mistress of the household when she did not disdain to perform household tasks herself, though, on the other hand, she was considered somewhat in the light of a household chattel. The original meaning of "lady," however, has been lost sight of, till in later times it was used as a title of complaisance to those higher in rank, consequently "woman" came to be looked upon as correspondingly inferior.

Where women object to be called "women," I can only conceive they are hankering after the epithet "lady," thinking it implies they are intellectually or socially the superior of those around.

The term "lady help," again, is all wrong. If she be a lady, "hlaf-dige," naturally she will help, so what need of the suffix?

"Woman" is a term far to be preferred. Can anyone conceive of Wordsworth writing, "A perfect lady, nobly planned"; Shakespeare, "Frailty, thy name is Lady"; or William Watson, "Her lady's heart for me"? The effect is too ludicrous. The sensible woman must surely see that the term "woman" has been held in greater reverence than "lady"; while to-day what greater praise can a woman wish than to receive, and deserve, the epithet "womanly"?—V. L. W.

The Female Form

Much of the debate about 'athletic women' concerned how it would affect their physique. The flat chests and thinness said to result from the taking of exercise were frowned upon in Edwardian Britain. What was admired were full bosoms and bottoms and a certain plumpness which suggested that a woman was well nourished and consequently well provided for by the men of the family.

Clothing and fashion emphasized the bust and bottom. Corsets pulled in the waist which accentuated the bosom and the fashion for bustles made the bottom another focus of attention. Fashion further dictated a pale skin unaided by any form of cosmetics which meant women had to shelter from the sun either by staying out of it or under parasols.

A pale skin, and the voluminous and heavy clothes and corsets which women from all walks of life wore, were in themselves a way of limiting women's lives. It is very difficult to move freely, let alone run, play games or take part in many outdoor activities in tight corsets, wearing clothes weighing more than ten times the weight of women's clothing today and having constantly to shade your face from the sun.

Even poorer women followed the general fashion trends although with perhaps only one or two outfits, nowhere near as many as a wealthy woman might have in her wardrobe. Rather in the way children dress dolls, women from the upper and middle classes who had servants to run their homes, would spend their days changing from one outfit to another depending on the time of day, the season, the proposed activity and whether in the town or the country.

ABOVE: *Fashions on display at Epsom in 1908.*
BELOW: *Beach fashion.*

1908 POSTSCRIPTS

● Hoover introduced their first vacuum cleaner, although the cost meant that it could only be afforded by the wealthy for use by their servants.

May – Following the passing of the Qualification of Women Act in 1907 which enabled women to stand for county and borough councils and to be elected Mayor, Elizabeth Garrett Anderson became the first woman Mayor in her home town of Aldeburgh.

June – The largest suffragette rally to date when 200,000 women and men gathered in Hyde Park.

September – The *Daily Mail* quoted Mr Herbert Elvin of the National Union of Clerks who said, 'The undercutting by women clerks is a grave evil.' In 1908 male clerks earning 32s to £3 were being replaced by women being paid between £1 and 30s.

WHAT WOMEN WANT

Many people are still under the impression that we claim the vote for every woman, but this is not the case. On the contrary our demand is the essentially moderate one that women occupying a position and fulfilling the responsibilities equal to those of a male voter shall be placed on the roll of electors. Are married women to vote? is a frequent enquiry, to which our reply is that we do not expect to obtain votes for married women unless they happen to have a distinct qualification of their own. If the house is taken in the husband's name he will have the vote; if it is in the wife's name she will have the vote.

Extracts from an article by Christabel Pankhurst
Daily Mail, 13 June 1908

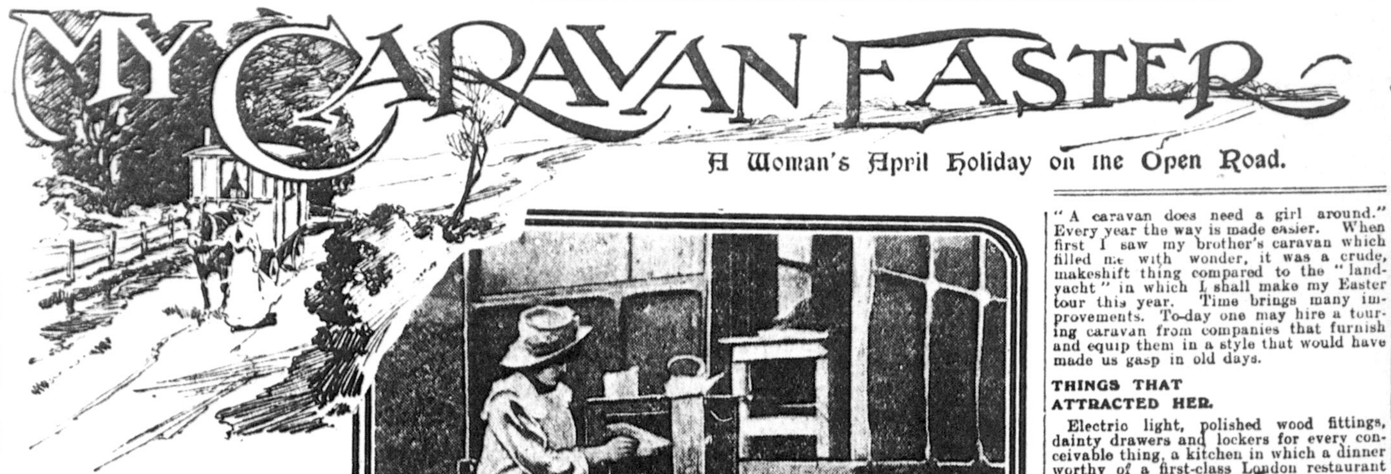

MY CARAVAN EASTER

A Woman's April Holiday on the Open Road.

MY first caravan tour—I remember it. It was Easter-time, and that year the sun was kindly, woods were already green and starred with primroses. And violets—why, in our first enthusiasm we almost filled the van with them.

It is long ago, but the first "pitch" on a Down-sheltered heath in Sussex, the first dinner in the new holiday house and the first night under the stars after seven months of London—those memories do not fade. They are as unforgotten as first love.

My brother had invited me. "Of course, you're a duffer at this sort of thing, and you'll probably growl over cleaning out the stove, but it's not half bad fun, really," he had said.

Also he made it quite clear that he only asked me because he had been disappointed by a man friend who "knew the ropes, you know," and "could make an eight-course dinner out of three sardines and an egg, by Jove!"

Even the genial speech of the road was as Greek to me then, and before that short holiday was over I had realised that my previous education had been wasted. I had not learned how to live before. I did not know how coffee tasted at dawn or how the woods smelt when the level sunbeams first shot through them.

A LOVABLE LITTLE HOME.

I remember that my brother met me at a tiny Sussex station, and that his first remark was, "You won't mind hefting this oil-can, will you, if I tackle the fish?"

I perceived then that he was surrounded by parcels, and I think he showed consideration for my feelings by gently pressing the oil-can upon me in preference to the fish parcel which was unpleasantly damp.

In the lea of a spectral copse of silver birches the caravan at last loomed into sight.

Looking back now over the years, I realise that I loved that little home on wheels at first sight.

Light was shining cheerfully through little white-curtained windows, and when the door was opened I saw an interior as luxuriously cosy as a yacht's cabin.

Dinner was laid on a table which, besides perfectly polished silver and glass, contained a big bowl of flowers. Another member of the party came out of a tiny kitchen to be introduced, and then rapidly served dinner.

Of that meal I only remember that we began with anchovies and olives, and that the excellent soup was followed by a succession of courses. We finished with coffee, and then some of the mysteries were explained.

"ROAD-WISE" PEOPLE.

My brother and his friend were old caravaners. They had toured over a large portion of England and Ireland, and both were very "road-wise."

They explained that the ideal "crew" consisted of three, that each must take his share in the work, and that each man should be able to perform any duties so that none should have the monotony of always having to do the same things.

Skill in cooking they said came by prayer and fasting—especially fasting, for a hungry man thrown upon his own resources made rapid progress.

I remember my surprise that evening when I saw the beds. I had been prepared to "rough it," and had no hope of comfort. What I actually found was a perfectly made bed in the dearest little bedroom imaginable. The pillows and bed clothes were just what any good housewife would provide in her house.

I slept that night as I have only slept in caravans.

We were up soon after dawn, and breakfast was ready before the spring sunshine gleamed through the muslin-curtained windows. I remember the first breath of morning air as I stepped out on to the heath, the delicious sense of having left all cares behind, the distant views of the Downs, and the diamonds on the grass.

A WOMAN CONVERT.

Many times since then I have seen such a morning. I have never thrilled with purer enjoyment than I did then. That morning made me a caravaner for life.

Yes, it all happened years ago, but to-day I know that there is no life like that of the road. At heart we are all wanderers. We must travel somehow, even if we have to do it in trains—the worst possible way. The caravaner is the only nomad who travels in his own house, and who takes as much or as little of civilisation as he pleases. For a woman who loves the open air, as I do, the life is ideal. Worries are left behind before the first "pitch" is made. From the moment a start is made and towns are left behind all the little troubles of life seem to vanish. There are no servants to think about, no callers. There are no fixed times for meals. Cooking, when done in this picnicky way, is just fun. All help, and generally every-one is in good humour.

"Housekeeping" in a dainty little caravan for three is the most amusing game in the world, and one of the nicest aspects from a woman's point of view is that the men of the party keenly appreciate her little contrivances to add to the general comfort.

Even my brother, who is not, as a rule, given to flattering, has been heard to say "A caravan does need a girl around." Every year the way is made easier. When first I saw my brother's caravan which filled me with wonder, it was a crude, makeshift thing compared to the "land-yacht" in which I shall make my Easter tour this year. Time brings many improvements. To-day one may hire a touring caravan from companies that furnish and equip them in a style that would have made us gasp in old days.

THINGS THAT ATTRACTED HER.

Electric light, polished wood fittings, dainty drawers and lockers for every conceivable thing, a kitchen in which a dinner worthy of a first-class London restaurant can be cooked, bunks like those in a first-class liner—those are but a few of the attractions.

One which cost £2,000 was travelling in England last year, and, as an interesting comparison, it is worth while to point out that many really comfortable ones have been built by their owners for £40, or even less. The modern ones which may be hired grow more comfortable each season, and it may be hinted that they offer not only the most pleasant possible method of spending a holiday, but also the cheapest.

Some enthusiasts, who every summer spend about eight weeks in one, and travel through the fairest of English counties in the comfort that only perfect independence can give, estimate that their holiday expenses rarely exceed £1 10s. a week each.

Naturally, one may make the expenses what one chooses, but, since caravaners are presumably lovers of the simple things of life, and avoid big towns from the day they enter their moving homes, the caravan holiday must always remain the cheapest possible, in spite of modern luxuries which were undreamed of by the pioneers. F.

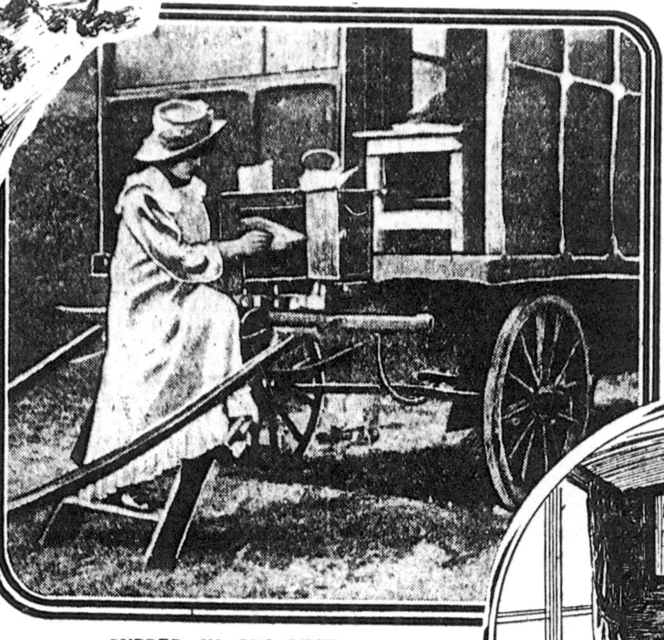

SUPPER IN PROSPECT.

From a woman's point of view one of the great charms of a caravan holiday is found in the freedom from complex domestic worries and the absence of servants. Meals, if simple, are easily prepared.

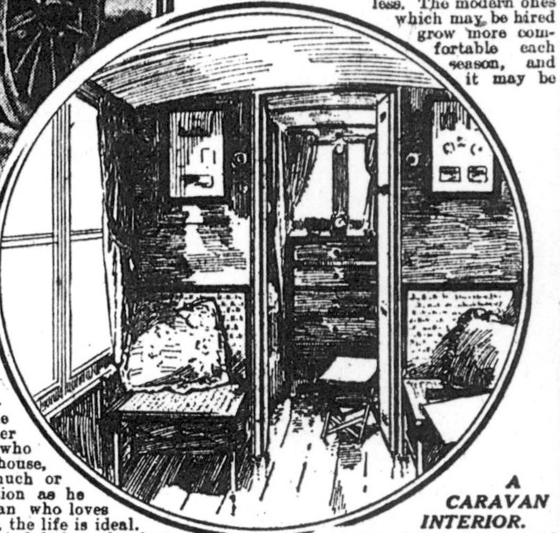

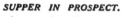

A CARAVAN INTERIOR.

[From "The Whole Art of Caravanning."]

Playtime Story

FOR THE LITTLE ONES.

No. 116.

APRIL 7.—Queen Victoria had quite a number of boys and girls of her own, and her eldest girl was known as the Princess Royal of England. She was awfully proud to have that title, and I do believe she thought herself the most important little girl in the world.

Like all her brothers and sisters, she had a little garden of her own, and one day she was putting in some plants when her mother, the Queen, came to watch her.

Now, what do you think? If the little Princess Royal had not on a pair of quite *new* kid gloves, to protect her hands from the dirt!

Her mother did not like that, of course, so she said, "When I was a little girl, I always did my gardening in old gloves."

"Yes, mother," replied the little girl, tossing her head proudly, "but you weren't born Princess Royal of England!"

NEW SPRING SALADS.

Dainty Recipes Worth Trying at Home.

AS every spring comes round the craving is a natural one for the wholesome salad, and now a day's vegetables, nuts, and fruit are combined in such unusual and amusing ways that they quite repay the study of the epicure.

The following recipes, which are new and original and culled from various sources, have been tried and pronounced excellent:—

TOMATO SURPRISE.

Cut in halves round, even tomatoes, but do not peel them. Scoop out the inside and fill with small dice of cucumber, well salted and mixed with mayonnaise. Make the tops even, spread with a coating of mayonnaise. Lay two anchovies crossed on top and serve on lettuce.

ROQUEFORT CHEESE SALAD.

Separate slightly a white head of lettuce that has been dried after it has been laid in ice water. Arrange among the leaves some bits of Roquefort cheese, using two tablespoonfuls to a head of lettuce. Surround the whole with watercress and pour over it French dressing. Serve wafers of thinnest toast with this. Asparagus, always excellent in salad, should be served very cold. It is good merely cooked and covered with a dressing, and is better in combination with cucumber.

RICE SALAD.

To two cupfuls of carefully boiled rice take one cupful of deep-red beets, finely chopped, and one cupful of chopped celery. Do not mix together until just before dressing, then combine with a French dressing and serve in cup form on blanched lettuce leaves.

MACARONI AND EGG SALAD.

Bring several quarts of salted water to a rapid boil. Gradually drop into the water a dozen stalks of macaroni, holding them until they coil, instead of breaking. When tender, drain and stand in a bowl of cold water until ready to use, and then dry on a cloth. Cut into inch pieces, sprinkle with a French dressing and let stand about half an hour. Cut three hard-boiled eggs lengthwise into quarters. Wash and dry a head of escorol or lettuce and arrange it on a platter.

Heap on the macaroni and arrange the quartered eggs in a circle round the base. Pour over the French dressing and serve.

GRAPE FRUIT SALAD.

Good with duck and wild duck. Carefully cut out the quarters from a large grape fruit, and with a sharp knife or scissors remove all pith. Pour a French dressing over the fruit and the finest of chopped parsley.

CHEESE ICE SALAD.

Take one pint of cream cheese, mash until perfectly smooth. It is best to mash it through a fine sieve. Add one quart of rich cream; put into a freezer and freeze like any other ice.

Lay five lettuce leaves on individual plates. Put a small cheese ice the shape of a heart in the centre of a circle of leaves on each plate, and sprinkle all over with finely chopped walnut meats and a little pepper and salt.

Eat with thin brown bread and butter or slices of thin pumpernickel—i.e., German black bread.

TOMATO ICE SALAD.

Cook a quart of tomatoes soft; strain and season with salt, grated lemon peel, a little grated nutmeg and sugar and paprika. Freeze until firm, preferably in round apple-shaped moulds.

Put each ice in a crisp lettuce leaf, pour mayonnaise over, lastly some chopped olives, and serve at once.

PINEAPPLE SALAD.

Get two pineapples; one big and one small one. Peel the large one, and with a silver fork pick it up into good-sized pieces. Take the whole inside from the smaller fruit, leaving the shell. Wipe it dry, and make it cold.

Arrange the pineapple pieces all round a dish on lettuce leaves, and in the middle put the pineapple (the smaller shell), filled with mayonnaise; pass the dish with a little silver ladle as well as with the usual salad-spoon and fork.

SPINACH SALAD.

Wash well half a peck of spinach, and steam it in a covered saucepan until there is enough juice to cook it in, using no water.

Make the spinach perfectly smooth by passing it twice through the meat chopper, season with salt, cayenne, and lemon juice. Press into little moulds, leaving a space in the middle. When cold fill the cups with mayonnaise made stiff with a level spoonful of gelatine dissolved in water, added to a cup of the dressing.

Turn out and serve on lettuce, with a little riced yolk of egg on each.

RED CABBAGE SALAD AND DRESSING.
(A German Recipe.)

Shred the red cabbage very fine, chill, drain, and serve on lettuce leaves with this dressing. Heat one cupful of cream, add one level tablespoonful of butter, a small teaspoonful of dry mustard, another of salt, and a pinch of cayenne.

When hot, add three well beaten egg yolks, stir until thick; but do not let it boil. Take from the fire and beat with an egg beater, adding gradually, as the mixture cools, two tablespoonfuls of vinegar.

A SALMON SALAD.

Utilise left-over cooked salmon by flaking it daintily and mixing it with mayonnaise or a plain dressing an hour before serving.

Cut walnut and other pickles or olives or pimolas are good in conjunction with this salad, if lightly and sparsely heaped on top.

SWEETBREAD SALAD.

This is as good as chicken salad and less expensive.

Soak sweetbreads in salt water overnight, boil until tender; cut into dice; add chopped celery or nuts or pickles; cover with rich mayonnaise.

BANANA SALAD (A Sweet Salad).

Cut bananas in two lengthwise, and then halve them, lay in a dish, and pour over some clear (bottled) raspberry or currant juice well sweetened. C. B.

1909

Suffragettes

In the six years since its foundation in 1903 the Women's Social and Political Union had succeeded in bringing the cause of women's enfranchisement much publicity. Newspapers debated the issue and published articles on both sides of the argument. The *Daily Mail* appears to have been somewhat ambiguous on the matter believing that female enfranchisement would come but that women were not quite ready for it.

WSPU supporters believed the time was right for women to have the vote and organized mass rallies throughout the country and protests at the Houses of Parliament and to individual political figures. When the police tried to break up their meetings the women refused to move. Many who believed they had been roughly handled by the police found themselves in court charged with assaulting the police. A policy of refusing to pay fines imposed by the courts led to the imprisonment of Christabel Pankhurst and Annie Kenney in 1905. Many more women were to follow them and soon after the first suffragettes were imprisoned some began to refuse food.

Panicked by the thought of a suffragette dying on hunger strike and in an effort to assert authority the government sanctioned the practice of forcible feeding. 1909 was the year in which the policy of force feeding suffragettes on hunger strike really came to the attention of the public with Keir Hardy asking questions in the House of Commons.

The following year in 1910 there was a public outcry against the policy when it was revealed that Lady Constance Lytton who suffered from heart disease had been force fed. Upper-class women were given preferential treatment in prison on health grounds. Lady Lytton knew this and dressed as a seamstress to lead a demonstration through Liverpool. When arrested she gave her name as Jane Wharton. She was imprisoned, went on hunger strike and was force fed without a compulsory heart test being carried out. When she vomited while being force fed the prison doctor hit her. As a result of her treatment in prison she was permanently injured and suffered a degree of paralysis for the rest of her life.

A woman chained to the railings outside Downing Street – this was another popular suffragette tactic as it meant they could not be removed bodily from the scene of a protest.

1909 POSTSCRIPT

June – The first British performance of the opera *The Wreckers* by composer and suffragette Ethel Smyth.

The Coming Lace Year

Why Mechlin is Sometimes More Becoming than Brussels.

The Cutting and Keeping of Valuable Laces.

THIS is to be a year of lace. All the filmy materials with which lace agrees so well are the mode not only for evening wear, but for the afternoon too. Already the dressmakers are teaching us that the more filmy the frock is, the smarter will be the effect, and as the weather grows warmer the transparencies will monopolise the attention of the woman of fashion, to whom will appeal such fabrics as the many varieties of the genus crêpon, the mousseline voiles, the ninons, crêpes, and chiffons and lace.

NEEDLE-RUN LACES.

There is ample reason, therefore, apart from the sovereignty of lace, for its appearance at this moment, and more than usual fervour is being shown in its honour owing to the fact that the embroidery craze of the immediate past caused lace to be relegated to a temporary background.

The charms of "baby" Irish, a fine guipure, are being recognised again by the coutouriers, who are using it for insertion purposes upon the lingerie blouse, as a ruffle upon the fashionable jabot, and even upon the hat, as a crown and brim insertion.

Not for two centuries past has point de Venise, raised or rose point, stood higher in favour in the fashionable world than it does now. It is so different from all other laces that its massive structure with padded outlines raised in double and triple tier are quite unmistakable. Fine design and variety in the fillings where or-

A very beautiful tunic made of Mechlin with a border of heavier lace, which can be worn with any dress requiring such an addition.

A fan of modern Honiton guipure, made in Devon. Above is a fine specimen of old raised Venetian point, a variety which has been known to fetch a guinea a square inch.

namental stitches are used are its distinguishing beauties.

Net embroidered with a pattern run on with a needle is in extremely good repute. The modern run laces have little in common with the old examples, for now heavy and conspicuous effect is aimed at, as with the embroideries on satin and other thick textures, rather than the delicate, light patterns of old.

In Paris such laces as hand-made Mechlin and Valenciennes are never out of fashion, for their creamy tint is more becoming than the dead white of Brussels and Devonshire lace. But when Brussels and Devonshire are of the appliqué types, they are laces that will wear well, and when the net on which they are mounted is torn the motifs can be easily and inexpensively remounted, or even readapted, without difficulty.

The owner of seven yards of Honiton appliqué flouncing, much out of repair, recently had the border and sprigs remounted on a two and a half yard scarf of net, with excellent results. Of lace it may be said that it is a thing of beauty and a joy almost for ever, if it be properly cared for by its possessors.

SHAKEN OUT IN THE SUNSHINE.

More good lace has been destroyed by injudicious dressmakers than by all the other destructive agencies in the world. Never permit the cutting of any piece to make it fit in; no corner must be mitred; the trimming must be so adapted that the lace when soiled can be removed intact.

After the dressmakers it is want of air and damp that are the worst enemies of fine lace. Much seventeenth and eighteenth century lace of the finest quality for ecclesiastical purposes has been ruined by being kept in damp sacristies. Lace should be kept on rollers and shaken out in the sunshine occasionally to keep it in good order.

It is a good plan to buy half a dozen wooden rolling-pins and to cover them with linen, padding them slightly to prevent their being too hard.

Then roll the flounces and entre deux on to them with a wisp of tissue paper between the layers, just as ribbon is rolled in a shop.

Infinite are the possibilities of lace utilisation! The happy possessor of a length

of black Chantilly lace, of a long scarf shape, cannot do better than utilise it in accordance with the suggestions afforded by one of the illustrations on this page, as a drapery wound about the figure in the manner now approved by fashion.

White net, spotted with black, built over a white silk foundation (a newly resuscitated though old fancy on fashion's part), forms the toilette, and seen beneath the net, upon the corsage and sleeves, is a background of Milanese lace, with which beautiful production the important-looking white silk buckles are covered.

ECONOMY OF VALUABLE LACE.

The Mechlin lace tunic with a deep border of heavier lace, shown by our artist in another sketch, is a noticeable feature in this year's dress repertory, and is a useful possession in that it can be worn with two or three different skirts that need an overdress.

As an emphasis of personality in dress old lace has no equal. The woman who owns a fine old Brussels veil or shawl has in her possession the means of making her Court train distinctive, while a yard or two of early Valenciennes relieves an evening gown of the uniformity such a toilette is apt to display.

If it is not given to everyone to possess fine Venetian point, yet it is possible to procure a few lengths of old Mechlin or dainty Court lappets of Flanders. It is sound economy to buy old lace as long as it is in good condition, for it can be used over and over again.

E. N. J.

The use of a black Chantilly scarf is here indicated, a conspicuous feature of a black and white spotted net dress.

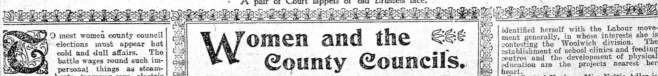

A pair of Court lappets of old Brussels lace.

TO most women county council elections must appear but cold and dull affairs. The battle wages round such impersonal things as steamboats, tramway-cars, electric lighting, and lunatic asylums, and, spite of all the brave talk of both parties, the one clear, emergent fact to woman's practical mind is that rates move up never to come permanently down.

Even the possession of the municipal vote has hardly dispelled the air of slightly disillusioned resignation with which woman listens to the arguments of friend and foe alike.

But a new note of peculiar and individual interest has been added to the county council elections which take place to-morrow in many parts of the United Kingdom, by the appearance of eight women as candidates.

ELECTED BUT DISQUALIFIED.

It is twenty-one years since Lady Sandhurst and Mrs. Cobden Unwin were elected members of the first London County Council and subsequently disqualified on the ground of sex, a barrier which was not removed till 1907 by the passing of the Local Government (Qualification of Women) Act, which enables unmarried or widowed women ratepayers to sit on all local governing bodies in the whole of the United Kingdom, and extends the same privilege to married women in London, Scotland, and Ireland.

The present general elections for county councils are the first that have taken place since this Act came into force, and although only eight feminine candidates have come forward, every one of these is so well qualified by years of good public work that all will make a strong claim on the votes of their constituents of various parties, and if returned may be relied upon to exercise a distinctive influence in affairs.

In London, where five of these women are offering themselves for election, two are standing as Municipal Reformers, one as a Progressive, and two as Labour candidates.

Miss Susan Lawrence, the Municipal Reform candidate for West Marylebone, has an attractive personality and is an excel-

Women and the County Councils.

THE FIRST CANDIDATES UNDER THE NEW ACT. TO-MORROW'S ELECTIONS.

Hon. VIOLET PENNANT, a candidate for South Islington.

Miss SUSAN LAWRENCE, who is contesting West Marylebone.

lent speaker. She has been addressing well-attended meetings in her district, and her supporters are confident of her success.

For four years she represented Marylebone on the old London School Board, and after its abolition became a co-opted member of the London County Council Education Committee. She has also been a school manager for nine years.

South Islington also possesses an excellent Municipal Reform candidate in the Hon. Violet Douglas-Pennant, who since 1905 has been a member of the Finsbury

Borough Distress Committee and a co-opted member both of the Central London (Unemployed) Body and the Central London Old-age Pensions Committee. She has also proved herself an able school manager, and is much interested in the work of friendly societies.

The best known of the candidates is perhaps Miss Margaret Bondfield, whose activity in connection with the Shop Assistants' Union has made her name familiar to Londoners.

She is an excellent speaker, and has

identified herself with the Labour movement generally, in whose interests she is contesting the Woolwich division. The establishment of school clinics and feeding centres and the development of physical education are the projects nearest her heart.

In Central Hackney Miss Nettie Adler is fighting the Progressive battle. She has done a great deal of work in connection with girls' clubs, and is a co-opted member of the London County Council Education Committee.

Miss Adler is keenly interested in the development of trade schools, and advocates the establishment of domestic schools for training girls for domestic service.

Another feminine Labour candidate is standing in North Kensington. As a medical practitioner of fifteen years' standing, Dr. Ethel Bentham takes especial interest in questions of hygiene, the feeding of school children, and infantile mortality.

RETURNED UNOPPOSED.

In the provinces one woman has already secured a seat, Miss M. E. Noble having been adopted without opposition for the Askham division of Westmorland. She had previously done good work on the board of guardians and rural district council.

In Essex Miss Courtauld has come forward for the Hedingham division. She is accustomed to public work, having been school manager and a member of the local sub-committee for old-age pensions, as well as on the education committee.

Miss C. Cochrane, who is standing as independent candidate for the Grantchester division of Cambridge, has the support of the Cambridge County Woman's Local Government Association, a newly formed society.

Varied as are their political creeds and interests, all the women candidates have in common a thorough knowledge of the needs, educational and physical, of the growing generation, and in this, perhaps, they will find their strongest claim to support, and their most useful field for activity; but woman's habit of economy and of carefully sifting details of expenditure give me some ground for hope that her influence would tend to keep the claims made on me for rates from mounting higher.

A. M. DOUGLAS.

1910

Girl Guides

ABOVE: One of the first Girl Guide Troops.
BELOW: A London Guide Troop returning home from a day camp in Buckinghamshire.

Lord Baden-Powell had founded the Boy Scouts in 1907. His experiences during the siege of Mafeking had determined him, once back in Britain, to begin a movement for boys which would teach outdoor skills such as tracking and firemaking as well as first aid and lifesaving techniques. The Boy Scout movement would above all aim to promote good citizenship, discipline and a sense of duty. There was never any intention that there be a parallel movement for girls. However there grew a demand from girls, attracted by the adventure they sensed in scouting, for a similar association.

The girls' demands were finally met in 1910 when Lord Baden-Powell and his sister Agnes, who became the association's leader, formed the Girl Guides. The aim of the Girl Guides was to encourage obedience, health and resourcefulness. Girl Guides, like their brothers in the Scouts, were taught first aid but most of the outdoor skills taught to the boys were replaced by indoor skills. Badges, such as the Little House Badge, were awarded for various domestic skills such as sewing, cleaning and cooking. The adventurous camps of the Boy Scouts were limited to day events for Girl Guides. Even today, when steps have been taken to offer an equal curriculum to both Guides and Scouts, Brownie Guides do not camp out under canvas like the Cub Scouts.

1910 POSTSCRIPTS

July – Chancellor of the Exchequer Lloyd George said reform of the House of Lords would have to take priority over women's suffrage. The power of the House of Lords to veto any legislation passed by the Liberal government was creating a constitutional crisis.

November – 'Black Friday' the 18th, when 119 suffragettes were arrested attempting to rush the House of Commons. The following day Home Secretary Winston Churchill ordered that charges against 100 women be dropped. Mrs Mary Clarke, sister of Emmeline Pankhurst, and Cecilia Wolseley Haig both died as a result of 'Black Friday'.

December – By the end of 1910 the first women had qualified as a Chartered Accountant and another had qualified as a Banker.

LADY LYTTON – IN PRISON UNDER AN ASSUMED NAME – SUFFRAGETTE STRATAGEM

Lady Constance, our Liverpool correspondent states, was met by her sister. She was in an exhausted condition and refused to discuss her escapade, except to complain in a weak voice that she had been forcibly fed since Tuesday last and that she had had to suffer gross insults at the hands of some prison officials.
Daily Mail, 25 January 1910

"The Men We Love and the Men We Marry."

Romantic Ideals and Their Disillusion

Loving a Husband into being what He Should Be.

I HEARD a woman respond to the toast, "The men we love and the men we marry." She began like this: "The men we love and the men we marry are no more alike than the lives we live and the lives we dream." There is here a strong commentary upon the evil of dreaming, which is certainly one of the great mistakes of womankind.

We have no right to "dream." Life is before us full of beauty, full of suffering, full of joy, full of sorrow—if we are not big enough to cope with it we must not lay the blame upon the other fellow.

True, the other fellow may be in a sense "to blame," but the deficiency of a fellow mortal, even though that fellow mortal be our nearest and dearest, is never a valid excuse for our failing too.

Often that which a man has to offer to the girl he marries is only "love"; and the girl declares that she will be satisfied with it, then discovers that love was not like she had imagined it, and that life has cheated her into a bad bargain.

THE SIGN OF LOVE.

It would be very well for girls if they were taught from infancy something about their real station in life, what they may expect, what they have a right to hope for, and that in marriage they take up a profession for which they need a special training.

I know a number of women who are merciless in their demands upon the men they have married—and then, too, I know a lot of men who are merciless in their demands upon their wives; it is, perhaps, about evenly divided.

But let us take the case of a woman who is suffering through thinking wrongly about the man she has married. Maybe she is a little ashamed of him. Many women are ashamed of their husbands. This is a pretty good sign that they love them.

There is a great humiliation in seeing the object of one's affection fall short of one's ideal.

THE HARD STRUGGLE.

If a woman is going to live with a man at all she might as well be the wife of whatever he is. You are called to be the wife of the man you married, not the wife of the man you thought you married when youth and the little god had somewhat blinded your eyes.

No tare ever grew faster in a field of good grain than does the thought, once admitted, that maybe after all we do not love the man we married. There is a sort of literary twang to such a thought that tickles the fancy and seems to chime with the last novel we read. Here indeed is food for thought. Pernicious thought, that should at once be banished in favour of plans for winter bazaars or children's wardrobes, or the work that lies nearest. Of course you love the poor fellow though he spoke unkindly to you, though he seemed selfish with his money and unreasonable in his demand upon your strength. Life is a hard struggle. You may not know just how hard—for woman's life is sheltered when she has a "man," even if only poorly, and she may not know when he is staggering under his load.

HER ROMANTIC IDEAL.

I grew up with my romantic ideal of love, and I married. The pathetic part of my romantic ideal was that I believed fully and firmly that there was some mysterious power in love that would henceforth glorify every moment of my life.

True, some of my friends had tried to explain to me that there was a "glamour" which would "wear off," but I laughed at them.

I insisted that I was not at all sentimental, that I knew we were poor, that I was quite willing and anxious to work—and that I was going to be happy!

Well, I have been happy, strangely happy.

Possibly I may be wrong, but it is a theory of mine that few men spend much time and thought on the business of making their wives happy. The wife, more than any other creature, has to make her own happiness. Her world is made by her way of thinking, and her way of thinking about the man she marries is the keynote of their mutual happiness.

The great failing of some women is their dissatisfaction with the things they have. A woman has a longing and a desire for something beyond her reach, and frets because the man she has married cannot give it to her. Then begins a general dissatisfaction all along the line, and finally she comes to regard herself as a fine creature full of high tastes, yet wedded to an inferior who can never satisfy those tastes.

This is a very unjust attitude on our part, and one that, after a few minutes' thought, we should relinquish.

WOMEN WHO HAVE GREAT TRIALS.

In the first place it is not good taste that makes us long for things; it is bad taste. Good taste is the quality that enables us to make beautiful and harmonious the things we have.

It is probably mere incapacity that leads us to the discouraging conclusion that in other circumstances we might have "shone."

There is never anything but personal lack of fineness to keep one from being fine. Remember this. Do not set it down to his carelessness or lack of energy or unkindness or injustice. None of these need affect your personal fineness. To be sure there are many women who have great trials in the men they live with, and vice versa.

The story of the man who has a great disappointment and trial in the wife he marries is not so common only because men do not talk. With true manly philosophy they try to make the disappointing wife "do"—and they succeed very often. I know lovable men who have simply loved their wives into seeing what they should be, and wives who have done the same for their husbands.

J. V. S.

The Erratic Feather.

A MILLINERY FANCY OF THE MOMENT.

THE vagaries of the feather continue to prove one of the most absorbing topics of interest in the millinery world. No extravagance seems too great to be acceptable by those who value the bizarre in hat adornments, and the fresh appearance of the Gourah plume adds another possibility of eccentricity to the many schemes already made manifest.

The Gourah is a feather dear by fits and starts to women, and in Paris it is now a re-established joy.

To cause the plume to wave right away from the hat, as if it were almost a detached affair, is one of the resources of the designer. Such a method a picture on this page displays.

It is the despair of the concert habitué even more than of the theatrical devotee, because at the theatres its removal would be demanded, if it were not conceded without a request in accordance with the rules of the management; whereas in the concert hall there seems to be no obligation of the kind.

To shut the eyes is the only resource of the plume-maddened enthusiasts under such conditions, and then the joy of following the score or of watching the orchestra at work must be foregone.

Fashion is ruthless, however, and at this moment she deals out nerve irritants of this type with no sparing hand.

If the feather is not set at an absurd angle such as this it is equally obtrusive in another form, waving out at the back of a bonnet or rising abruptly from a mass of plumes wound modestly round the crown of the hat.

"DONKEY'S EAR LOOP."

A toque made of velvet has what is called the donkey's ear loop at one side, or both ears are shown in velvet, branching away from the swatheries of material. This is one among many trimmings of a plume-like effect, among which may be reckoned the knitted quill, the one composed of beads, and the spun glass "brush."

The fast approaching Durbar is bringing into fashion's domain the high upstanding "brush," rising from an ornament of magnificent splendour, the accompaniment of a turban made of gold or silver tissue damasked with a colour less blatant than its prototype of some two or three winters ago, for the trend of fashion now is towards gravity instead of garishness.

A black velvet model of the new shape, half hat, half bonnet, trimmed with a crimson feather.

Another design, more bonnet than hat, is made of lemon tinted mousseline and mahogany brown velvet, with masses of shaded uncurled ostrich plumes at the back.

1911

Women as Scientists

ABOVE: *Marie Curie.*
BELOW: *Dr Elizabeth Garrett Anderson and Mrs Emmeline Pankhurst (right) pictured when they arrived to lead a suffragette deputation to Parliament.*

At the beginning of 1911 the Académie des Sciences in Paris voted, rather than have a woman member, to admit Jean Becquerel. The woman proposed for membership of the Académie was Marie Curie, who ironically became the first person ever to win a second Nobel Prize when she received the award for Chemistry in Stockholm in December of the same year.

Science was a male preserve throughout the world and any contribution women had made in the past had been suppressed. In the ancient world, Hypatia, a professor at Alexandria University, is the only known female mathematician but it is difficult to accept that she was the only female scientist as many history books would have us believe. What is more likely is that her murder by Christians, incensed at the heresy of her teachings, has assured her a mention in history.

Many other women scientists throughout history worked with fathers, husbands or brothers whom the world credited with achievements while their female 'assistants' remained hidden. One of the clearest examples of this is the Herschel family. William Herschel, a musician and later astronomer, was credited with doing much to forward the science of astronomy in the eighteenth and nineteenth centuries. His sister, Caroline, was described as his housekeeper and helper. In fact William worked in partnership with her. Caroline built the telescopes he designed, edited the information from his observations, did all the mathematical calculations and recorded the results.

Self-education or learning from male relatives were the only ways for women to gain scientific knowledge, although in Britain women were not barred from studying science as they were in some other European countries. In fact in the sixteenth century science was seen as a suitable topic for women to study as it was regarded as a far less important subject than the classics, which dominated male education.

Girls' schools did not teach science and women did not have access to universities before the mid-nineteenth century. And soon after science was included in the curriculum for girls, a new subject, domestic science, appeared. Subsequently, girls' schools that did not offer this subject lost their state grant.

A further obstacle in the path of women scientists was that many women's skills, and knowledge such as the ability to heal with home-made medicines and remedies, were not accepted as scientific skill but dismissed and persecuted as witchcraft. In some countries and centuries women were actually banned from studying science. Maria Agnesi, daughter of the Professor of Mathematics at Bologna, became a celebrated mathematician herself in the eighteenth century despite the fact that in Italy women were not allowed to study science or mathematics. Women had also been banned from many of the trades and professions that had a scientific base. Before the seventeenth century there were women working as surgeons, doctors and brewers until men forced them out, citing their lack of scientific knowledge as reason for doing so.

1911 POSTSCRIPTS

March – Norway's first woman MP, Anna Rogstadt, took her seat in Parliament. Women did not have an equal franchise to men but there were women voters and women could stand for Parliament.

November – In Britain more than 200 women were arrested following angry demonstrations when Parliament voted to extend the male franchise. Hopes had been high that PM Herbert Asquith might accept some limited female franchise.

'Now it is to stem this gigantic evil,' said the Bishop, 'that I summon the forces of the Church today. The Roman Church, all honour to it, has never wavered in condemning such practices [birth control] as a sin, and it would ill become the Church of England to condemn less clearly the practice which, if it continued, must eat away the life blood of our country. Let teaching be given in suitable ways and at suitable times on the responsibility which married life entails, on the glory of motherhood and the growing selfishness which first thinks of creature comforts, of social pleasures, and then of the primary duties and joys of life.'
Daily Mail, 1 December 1911

The Chances of Marriage.

WHERE THEY ARE BEST AND WORST. TOWNS AND COUNTIES WHERE MEN ARE MORE NUMEROUS THAN WOMEN.

If marriage is every woman's chief ambition the Census Returns now being issued must be very doleful reading. Probably very few women will care to examine these millions of millions of figures, and yet they contain matter of great feminine interest, for they tell exactly where a woman has the greatest chances of getting married, and where, on the other hand, the chances are more strongly in favour of her dying unmarried.

The first important fact we come across is that every year women are increasing in numbers proportionately to men.

A long time ago, in the year 1821, there were only 1,036 females of all ages to each 1,000 men; at present there are 1,068. Thus, for every thousand women who may find husbands 68 must remain unmarried.

THE REASON WOMEN ARE MORE NUMEROUS.

In England and Wales there are no fewer than 1,179,276 females for whom there are no corresponding males. Even if women died faster than men there would at least be widowers available. But they do not. The contrary is what happens.

Nature never intended that this female excess should obtain. Considerably more boys are born every year than girls. But boys are difficult to rear: they die faster than girls in infancy. The same happens in adult life, and to make matters worse men emigrate in larger numbers than women.

WOMEN SCARCER IN SMALLER TOWNS.

Then the distribution of the sexes throughout the country is very unequal. Women seem more dissatisfied than men with country life. They flock to the large towns, and especially to what may be called the pleasure towns.

In the smaller towns, say from two to ten thousand population, a woman's prospects of marriage should be very good, for in these the sexes are fairly equal in numbers. In many of the smaller towns there is an actual scarcity of women, and this is especially the case in the mining districts.

But in London, Manchester, Birmingham, and all the large cities, women are so numerous relatively to men that tens of thousands of them have no chance of finding husbands, while in such places as Bath, Brighton, Bournemouth etc., the excess of women is enormous.

It is not practicable to give the very long list of all the places where women are in excess, and where they are in equal or small numbers than men. But the following facts form a useful guide.

WHERE THERE ARE MOST WOMEN.

The counties in which women most preponderate and where, therefore, the chances of marriage for a woman are at their lowest are:—

Sussex (East)	1,256	females to	1,000 males.
Cardiganshire	1,224	" "	1,000 "
Surrey	1,166	" "	1,000 "
Cornwall	1,164	" "	1,000 "
Somerset	1,153	" "	1,000 "
Middlesex	1,144	" "	1,000 "
Gloucestershire	1,143	" "	1,000 "
Isle of Wight	1,139	" "	1,000 "
London	1,127	" "	1,000 "
Sussex (West)	1,117	" "	1,000 "
Westmorland	1,112	" "	1,000 "
Carnarvonshire	1,106	" "	1,000 "
Devonshire	1,102	" "	1,000 "
Worcestershire	1,101	" "	1,000 "
Cheshire	1,100	" "	1,000 "

In the best of these, for each 1,000 women who can find husbands there is an excess of 100 for whom there are none: in the worst 256 women must remain unmarried to each 1,000 who can marry.

In many counties, however, there is a shortage of women. The following is a list of these counties:

Monmouthshire	908	females to	1,000 males.
Glamorganshire	925	" "	1,000 "
Brecknockshire	952	" "	1,000 "
Rutlandshire	973	" "	1,000 "
Isle of Ely	980	" "	1,000 "
Durham County	986	" "	1,000 "
Radnorshire	992	" "	1,000 "
Derbyshire	993	" "	1,000 "

These are the figures per thousand. Of course, the actual numbers of women in excess or deficiency are very large. For instance, there are 269,000 too many women in London and nearly double that number in Greater London. In Sussex there are 66,000, in Surrey 59,000, in Middlesex 75,000, in Devonshire 35,000 too many women.

On the other hand there is a shortage of 44,000 in Glamorganshire, of 19,000 in Monmouthshire, of 10,000 in Durham. Wales as a whole has room for 43,000 women to equalise the sexes.

Without going further into tiresome figures it may be said that in a good many towns there is a shortage of from one to several thousand women. Among these are Coventry, Aberdare, Colchester, Alfreton in Derbyshire, Abertillery, Barrow-in-Furness, Burton-on-Trent, Doncaster, Grimsby, Middlesbrough, Pontypridd, Rhondda (only 69 women to 83 men), Erith, Sheerness, and Andover.

The sexes are fairly equal in Maidenhead, Isleworth, Wantage, Basingstoke, Winchester, Arundel, Newhaven, Shoreham, Chichester, Faversham, East Grinstead, Abingdon, Reading, and Staines.

But women are greatly in excess of men in Folkestone (100 to 70), Hastings (150 women to 100 men), Oxford, Scarborough, Southend, Tunbridge Wells, Leicester, Nottingham, Bexhill, Blackpool, Bournemouth, Brighton, Bristol, Bromley, Cheltenham, Croydon, Kingston, Richmond, Chislehurst, Herne Bay, Ramsgate, Margate, Whitstable, Hastings, Eastbourne, Hove, and Bath.

In and around London the places are Kensington (105 women to each 66 men), Chelsea, Paddington, Fulham, Hampstead, Lewisham, Ealing, Wimbledon, and Barnes.

T. F. M.

Dressing the Girl of Fifteen.

THE PROBLEM OF HER HATS.

Josie must have some new hats. That is a point that has been decided definitely by Josie's mother. She must have a closely fitting fur cap that will be comfortable in the car and for very cold days out walking, and she must have a more frivolous chapeau because she is going to be bridesmaid.

Yes, and for the twelfth time in her little tally of only fifteen years!

Josie's mother is not superstitious or she would have refused her girl's services after her second appearance in that capacity, seeing that she has not the slightest desire to have a spinster daughter.

But she does want the hat Josie is to wear to be useful afterwards, and so is very glad that it has been decided that the bridesmaids are to have laurel green velvet "mobs" gauged upon the brim and hemmed with deep écru Malines lace.

ROSE OR OSTRICH FEATHER TRIMMING.

Trimmings of frost-bitten pink and apricot-tinted roses are to be added, for which can easily be substituted later the sweeping white ostrich feather that Josie longs for with all the ardour of her age.

It is a sealskin cap with a white tailless ermine crown that Josie eventually decides is her choice, and, happily enough, the child's grandmother is at hand to press gold into the peltry monger's hand in exchange for it.

Her grandmother has never yet been known to resist Josie's truly bewitching appearance in a "good" hat, and cherishes the tenet that anything less than her definition of the word good is not worthy to sit upon her little maid's head. Happy Josie and very happy grandmother, the one to receive and the other to give!

FAGGOT STITCH EMBROIDERY.

The cap must have a trimming and the wheel of fortune seems to be a happy choice for the purpose, made of white velvet pleated round a centre of tailless ermine, over which a faggot-stitch embroidery of a bright green shade is disposed.

Grandmother agrees with Josie that the girl of fifteen must be very careful indeed not to grow up. Most careful, they both say, with intense emphasis.

Josie has no wish to say farewell to her short frocks and long hair days, and so the velvet paletots she is to wear this winter only reach to her boot tops, and her dresses are shorter, showing in the house a very pretty vision of slender silken-clad ankles and shoes of the daintiest description.

H.

Cap made of sealskin and tailless ermine with the wheel of fortune rosette at one side. [Fairyland.]

A laurel-green velvet mob for a girl bridesmaid, with a lace border and a trimming of frost-bitten roses.

1912

Militant Suffragettes

Despite the fact that the Women's Social and Political Union had since its formation gained much publicity for the cause of female suffrage, votes for women, even with the limited franchise the WSPU demanded, were in reality no nearer than they had been in 1903. In 1911 the male franchise had been extended which meant that virtually every man in Britain over the age of 21 had a vote. This measure had been passed by the Liberal government which was still split over the issue of votes for women, Asquith the Prime Minister being anti female suffrage. There was also in the all-male House of Commons a majority against female enfranchisement. In the face of this political opposition the WSPU embarked on a far more radical route to their objective.

In 1912, despite the fact that the Labour Party Conference committed the Party to votes for women, the WSPU broke their affiliations with Labour and all other similar organizations. The WSPU had decided on a course of militant action. With the aim of getting insurance companies to pressure the government into accepting the WSPU's demands, they began a window-smashing campaign. Armed with stones and hammers suffragettes, in groups and individually, smashed windows in shops, post offices, labour exchanges and other government buildings. Damage was also caused to well-known paintings and works of art.

Throughout 1912, 1913 and into 1914 suffragette tactics became increasingly more violent with arson and bomb attacks on pillar boxes, churches and the homes of politicians. Mercifully no one was badly injured in any of these attacks and indeed that was not the intention which was only to damage property and gain attention for their cause. In April 1913 Mrs Pankhurst was sentenced to three years in jail for a bomb explosion at Lloyd George's newly built golf villa.

By the end of 1912 the WSPU was virtually an underground organization as police raids on their offices forced the decision to move their headquarters to Paris where they remained until the outbreak of the Great War in 1914 brought a dramatic turnaround in the policies of the WSPU.

The results of this increased militancy are difficult to judge but the 1912 Women's Enfranchisement Bill was defeated by fourteen votes on its second reading in March 1912 and the government withdrew, it claimed on technical grounds, its own Franchise Bill in January 1913 which was what largely provoked the bombings and arson attacks. A number of men both inside and outside Parliament, who had perhaps been not wholly committed to the idea of female suffrage, found the militancy and violence a good excuse, or perhaps were genuinely horrified by what they saw, and withdrew their support. But the militant campaign did keep the issue of votes for women at the forefront of public imagination and the political agenda.

ABOVE: *Millicent Fawcett* (standing front) *and the National Union of Women's Suffrage Societies continued their peaceful campaign in parallel to the WSPU.*
BELOW: *A crowd of suffragettes who took part in a window-breaking raid pictured waiting patiently for Bow Street Police Court to open.*

1912 POSTSCRIPT

November – The Royal Commission on Divorce recommended that the grounds for men and women seeking divorce should be the same and it also suggested that divorce be made easier to obtain.

The *Daily Mail* published a Leader supporting the minority report produced by the Commission which, while accepting that grounds for divorce should be equal for both parties, refuted the idea of easier divorce, claiming that there was no public demand.

Garden-Party Dresses.

RETURN OF THE PLEATED PETTICOAT. FASHION FOR BOWS.
THE TUNIC AND THE DRAPED SKIRT.

CALLED by the generic term of garden-party dresses are the pretty frocks in which we appear for the various afternoon functions of the season. They are the toilettes that arrive with the strawberries, and are summerlike and airy in design and construction.

A dress for a débutante's wear on such occasions designed by Miss Bessie Ascough is sketched by her in this page. It is made of patterned crêpe de Chine, of a soft café au lait shade, sprinkled over with pale pink roses, and the draped waist-belt is of a stronger tint, the rich glow of its petunia colouring giving character to the whole and agreeing with the crêpe rose which decorates the white straw hat.

In keeping with the newly aroused feeling for the tunic, the skirt is vaguely draped at the back, though in front it is quite simple. A white tulle chemisette is added and there is a flopping lace "tucker" at the throat.

Draped Skirt Variations.

Concerning that newly aroused feeling, what a chance it provides for variations of the draped skirt! I see, creeping in with it, the pleated petticoat, a filmy but determined rival of the slit seam, whose hours, it is said, are numbered, and a fitting opportunity for the use of lace and ribbon-run net.

But the petticoat in its present interpretation must not be regarded as the rightful owner of that title. It is simply a part of the gown instead of being a separate affair worn beneath the gown. Yet who knows? It may come to pass that from being a travesty only the petticoat, having set up a claim to its heritage, may be restored unto its own again.

Conjecture apart, it is certainly with us, this peep of dainty lace and pleated chiffon, filling up the hiatus that would beforetimes have been left a void, and in consequence its début must be chronicled.

One of the prettiest little garden-party frocks I have seen was an elegant trifle composed of blossom mousseline, lace flounces, and accordion-pleated chiffon.

The lace flounces, each headed by a crisp quilling of tulle and a garland of flowers, were arranged above the petticoat so that nothing detracted from its glory, and where the mousseline was parted to disclose the petticoat a bunch of blossoms was arranged.

Buskin Shoes.

The new buskin shoes are regarded with mixed feelings. Some people will dance in them, but will not admit their suitability to day-time appearance. Others are so frankly in love with them that they adopt them for all occasions.

Already ingenious devices have been discovered whereby the ribbons that bind the ankles can be kept in their place. One demands specially concocted stockings, with button-holes that can be attached to buttons concealed in the ribbons, a practical notion that saves much anxiety but cannot be very salutary for the stockings, especially when they are of the modern filmy description.

Everything is filmy nowadays with the exception of the waist-belt. It is a more substantial attribute of the costume than any other part of it.

This assertion has ample testimony in the broad bayadère sash, even when it is made of thin-patterned silk, and is still more newly displayed in the case of those girdles that are finished at one side with a huge floppy bow.

Bows are a great feature of the afternoon frock of the moment. One dress noticed recently was draped like an apron in front and then drawn up to the back, where it was tied (or apparently tied) in an enormous bow just below the waist, showing a petticoat beneath.

There are bows on our shoes and bows on our hats made, as a rule, of soft ribbon. That which is used for millinery purposes is extremely broad and demands very cleverly constructed supports to keep it at the desired angle.

Full Value of Tulle.

The débutante who realises the full worth of tulle as an accessory of the summer toilette is a wise damsel. Perhaps her mother or some sympathetic aunt may have sung its praises to her, remembering their own day of allegiance to what was called "illusion," but was frank fact in its powers of beautifying the face and neck.

It is used immensely for ruffles and bows, and for the brims of the "halo" hat, which is again a favourite choice, and its possibilities in the form of kerchiefs, neck and wrist ruffles are practically unlimited.

But it is in ways of their own devising that clever and artistic girls use it most potently. One beautiful young creature keeps lengths of various colours for which she cuts cloud-like scarves to drape her pretty shoulders at the Opera and upon occasions to bind her bonny hair.

But she never overdoes the effects she seeks to convey, and she uses—dare I hazard the guess?—miles of tulle for her deft machinations.

M. H.

[Copyright in U.S.A., 1913.

Dress for a debutante of pale brown crepe patterned with roses, with a petunia-coloured belt the same shade as the rose in the white straw hat. The skirt has a folded effect at the back, but in front is quite simple.

Lace Collars.

PRESERVATION OF VALUABLE LACES.

EVERY woman knows the fascination of good lace, and the more delicate and gossamer-like that morsel of fragility may be the more admiration it receives.

But real lace—or very fine, good lace which may not be real—requires great care.

A jar of soapy water—rain water, if possible—is prepared, and in this the lace should be steeped. The jar is vigorously shaken up and down until the lace is clean.

Careful rinsing to remove any soap follows, and next must come the stiffening process. Starch is unthought of. Its substitute is gum-water. A quarter of a pound of gum arabic, melted in one quart of boiling water and strained, makes gum-water, and the average proportion used is a tablespoonful to a gill of water.

With white lace a little blue should be added to the gum-water. Dip twice to enable it to stiffen. If gum-water is not to hand, rice-water or sugar-water may be used.

For tinting lace that has lost its colour through washing, an infusion of tea, coffee, or hay mixed with the gum-water may be used.

After the washing and stiffening follows the pressing. A glass bottle covered with flannel is a good old-fashioned method. The lace is wound carefully round and round the bottle and left to dry. When dry it appears to have been ironed.

Elaborate patterns may be pinned carefully on a piece of flannel, wrong side up, and a heated punching-iron used carefully over every part.

The pinning out is quite a business. The selvedge edge must be placed near the edge of the board and the pins must lie parallel with the edge of the lace. If there are points they must be pinned separately and to the right length.

In the case of piece lace it should be pinned out over flannel, then left to dry. A moderately heated small iron should then be passed along the middle; next remove pins and iron selvedge; lastly press out any points.

A lace collar is pinned out to dry with pins around the neckband and in every point. The ironing process starts with the centre and ends with the points. J. K.

The Handicap of Sport.

CHARM *versus* GAMES—
A WOMAN WHO FOUND HERSELF UNPOPULAR.

I HAVE made a great discovery. I feel as proud as though I had come across the horn of a unicorn or stumbled upon the nest of a dodo. For in the pages of a daily paper I have found a man who owns to liking the masculine girl. He writes in praise of her collars and ties, he admires her sensible shoes and her rough tweeds with their large "poacher" pockets; further, he says he should consider himself lucky to marry so sporting a damsel.

Frankly, I did not know such a man existed. He is a greater "find," I am sure, than the egg of a dodo. True it is that once upon a time—years ago, alas!—I set out from a finishing school equipped with tailor-mades, sport hats, shooting boots, and a covert coat. And I joined a tennis club and a cricket club and a golf club, and "took up" fencing and swimming and hunting. And I married and "lived happily ever after."

Inherited Charm.

But truth compels me to own that there was an element of luck about the affair, that I got my share of romance in spite not because of my athletic feats.

I fancy my husband was attracted by the exceedingly feminine glances which I have inherited from an Early Victorian mother, and not by the muscle which I had developed by my own efforts. I do not fancy he married me because I can bowl overhand, keen as he is on the national game.

For the average man delights in a woman who contrasts vividly to himself. The better he is at games the less he values her prowess at them. Six foot three and broad in proportion, brown as a berry and strong as a bull, his ideal is a tiny pink and white thing with dimples and a lisp.

A Liking for Frills.

"Throw away those beastly collars—and what on earth made you buy those blouse things that look like one of my shirts? I like frilly things, with lots of lace." So said my husband, surveying the garments which I thought would specially please him because they were neat and business-like, and therefore seemed suitable for a country honeymoon.

I have learnt wisdom since then. Nowadays, if I must needs don a short, thick skirt for a country walk, my blouse keeps its frills; if my hat has to be close-fitting because I am going to motor it still has an alluring air about it. I give up my games and my love of out-of-door life for no man; but it is not by them that I expect to fascinate.

Because he adores me in silks and satins my husband tolerates me in sporting tweeds. He looks on my fervent desire to reduce my handicap as an absurd whim, not to be taken seriously, whereas he can quite understand me being really annoyed when a dress does not fit.

By the same token he laughs indulgently when I scream at a mouse, and thinks none the worse of me for my inherited terror of such small deer, but he becomes testy when I slice a ball or serve two faults. On such occasions he has been heard to mutter that "women *will* play games and always spoil them."

In the Playing Fields.

Certainly women get no quarter in the playing fields. In drawing-rooms you can tease and torment your men-folk as you please; you can run them into debt and worry their lives out, and (provided always you "have a way with you") they remain your humble slaves.

But I have never known a man so fond of feminine society that he would not cheerfully do without it at his favourite sport.

I have known a man do without his favourite sport for the pleasure of my society—but that is another story; he never cared for the two things mixed.

No! The average man is not attracted by Sportswoman. He puts up with her, he makes the best of her, he marries her, but only because he must.

She never guesses that her fascination lies in some attribute which she has inherited from the dear, dead women of long ago—those tender, absurd, dainty creatures who never broke records although they sometimes broke hearts, and who never wanted to excel but only to be loved.

B. TELLING.

Water Ices.

Lacking the richness of cream ices, water ices are very cooling for hot weather, and they are essentially easy to prepare.

VANILLA WATER ICE.—Take ½ pint of water, ¼lb. of sugar, a tablespoonful of vanilla essence.

Boil the water and sugar till the latter is dissolved. Strain. Add the vanilla essence. Freeze.

BLACK CURRANT WATER ICE.—Take ¾lb. of black-currant jam, ¼lb. of caster sugar, ½ pint of water, lemon essence.

Boil the water and sugar. Strain. Heat the jam and mix with the sugar syrup. Strain. Add a few spots of lemon essence. Freeze.

LEMON WATER ICE.—Take 6 lemons, 2 oranges, 1 pint of water, ½lb. of caster sugar.

Boil the sugar with the water and the grated peel of two lemons. Strain, then mix with the juice of all the lemons and oranges, and freeze.

GRAPE WATER ICE.—Take 1 lemon, 1 orange, 1 pint of water, ¼lb. of sugar, and ½ pint of grape syrup.

Strain the juice from the lemon, grate the orange peel, mix both with the sugar and water, and boil till the sugar is dissolved. Strain, and mix the grape syrup with the liquor. Freeze.

TORTURING WOMEN IN PRISON

VOTE AGAINST THE GOVERNMENT

ABOVE: A WSPU Poster.
BELOW: Suffragettes mounting a vigil around Emily Davison's coffin and funeral carriage at Victoria Station.

1913

'Cat and Mouse'

Since the case of Lady Constance Lytton had come to attention in 1910 there had been much public disgust at the practice of force feeding hunger-striking suffragettes. The government had been severely censured both at home and abroad with allegations of torture being levelled, particularly at Prime Minister Asquith. With increased suffragette militancy bringing increased numbers of hunger-striking women into jail public pressure on the government increased. The government responded by passing the 'Cat and Mouse' Bill.

This bill allowed for prisoners to be given temporary release from jail on the authority of the Home Secretary if he felt that their health was in danger. This meant that hunger-striking suffragettes were no longer force fed. A hunger striker was allowed to become very weak and then she was released subject to various bail-style conditions. When she was well enough she was simply re-arrested and continued to serve her sentence. A single prisoner could be released and re-arrested many times before her sentence was completed. It was likened to a cat playing with a mouse with the cat always winning in the end, hence the name 'Cat and Mouse' Act. This absolved the government from the charge of torturing women and to a large extent satisfied the public's anxieties over the treatment of suffragettes in prison.

1913 POSTSCRIPTS

January – The first sickness and maternity payments were made under the new National Insurance Act. The Act had been passed in 1911 but had to be amended in 1912 because the original terms did not allow for illness as a result of pregnancy or childbirth for women workers under the scheme. Even amended the Act did very little for most women. True, it ensured the family of an insured worker had an income if he was off sick but while her husband had access to free or assisted medical care a wife and her children did not. There was not even medical care during pregnancy and childbirth.

June – Emily Davison, an active member of the WSPU, died as a result of injuries sustained when she tried to seize the reins of the King's horse in the Derby to draw attention to the cause of female suffrage. Her death was to become one of the symbols of the suffragette movement.

• Emily Dawson was appointed the first woman magistrate in Britain.

• The Norwegian Parliament granted women equal electoral rights to men.

October – Sir Almroth Wright published his book *The Unexpurgated Case Against Woman Suffrage* in which he claimed from his standpoint as a medical man that the case for female suffrage was put only by women whose minds were warped and made abnormal by bitterness and jealousy of men.

A TRIAL OF PATIENCE

The last of the seven suffragette conspirators sentenced on June 17 to lengthy terms of imprisonment was released yesterday under the 'Cat and Mouse' Act. At first sight these offenders might seem to have worsted the law. But if the Act is applied with patience and firmness – if, that is to say, all offenders who 'hunger strike' are reincarcerated the moment they have recovered health – the law will sooner or later triumph. The suffragettes are only punishing themselves by their resistance to it, and have only themselves to blame for the unpleasant consequences.
Daily Mail Leader, 27 June 1913

HOW TO MAKE THE WOOLLEN BELTS AND SOCKS.

The Gift from the Queen and the Women of the Empire

"GIFT to the troops at the front, from the Queen and the Women of the Empire." So runs the superscription at the head of the printed directions for making the gifts, which can be obtained on application to The Lady in Waiting to the Queen, Devonshire House, Piccadilly, London, W.

The gifts required are socks and woollen belts. The socks, made with heels and toes of the usual kind, should be woven or hand-knitted with No. 13 needles and 4-ply super-fingering or wheeling in grey, Lovat's mixtures or natural colours.

The lengths of foot asked for are 10in., 10½in., 11in., a 11½in., and the largest number required are those measuring 10½in. and 11in. in length.

For sizes 1 and 2, 64 stitches should be cast on in the first instance, and for sizes 2 and 3, 68 stitches.

 WIDTH AND LENGTH

The woollen belts should be of natural colours, woven or hand-knitted, and the width at the edges when folded should be as follows: Size 1, 9in. wide and 12in. long; Size 2, 10in. wide and 12½in. long; Size 3, 11in. wide and 13in. long. The belts are not to have either buttons or tapes.

Take Nos. 16 and 10 needles (four needles of each), and use 4-ply worsted fingering of natural shades. The amount required will be from 2oz. to 3oz. The directions for knitting the belts are these:

HOW TO PROCEED.

SIZE 1.—With No. 16 needles cast on 234 stitches, knit 1 plain, 1 purl, for 3in. Now with No. 10 needles, knit 1 plain, 1 purl, for 6in. Now again take No. 16 needles and knit 1 purl 1, for 3in.

SIZE 2.—With No. 16 needles cast on 260 stitches, knit 1 plain, 1 purl, for 3in. Now take No. 10 needles and knit 1 plain, 1 purl, for 6½in. Now again take No. 16 needles and knit 1 plain, 1 purl, for 3in.

SIZE 3.—With No. 16 needles cast on 286 stitches, knit 1 plain, 1 purl, for 3in. Now take No. 10 needles, knit 1 plain, 1 purl, for 7in. Now again take No. 16 needles and knit 1 plain, 1 purl, for 3in.

Each belt must be marked with its size and all parcels containing the belts are to be marked "Woollen Belts," and addressed: The Lady in Waiting to the Queen, Devonshire House, Piccadilly, London, W.

All parcels containing socks are to be marked "Socks" and addressed as above. The size should be marked on each sock.

The value of the belts every soldier knows. They are wonderful resisters of chill and prevent many of the illnesses incident to the fighting line.

Presents that keep the men in good health, as warm belts and well-fitting socks help to do, could not be excelled in merit as offerings to our brave soldiers from their Queen and the women of the Empire.

SOME SAVOURY DISHES.

An excellent Welsh rarebit requires one egg, two tablespoonfuls grated cheese, two tablespoonfuls milk, a tablespoonful ale (the older the better), a teaspoonful Worcester sauce, a pinch of salt, the same of pepper, cayenne to taste, half a teaspoonful mustard (dry), two ounces butter.

Method: Use a double saucepan, unless you have someone in the kitchen who can stir the mixture and prevent it burning. In a teacup put salt, pepper, and mustard, mix with the milk to a paste, then add the remainder. Next stir in the ale and Worcester sauce. In the saucepan place the butter, and when dissolved stir in the beaten egg, stir till it thickens, then add the cheese, and lastly the mixture from the cup. This can remain in saucepan till ready, then spread on slices of hot buttered toast and serve on hot plates.

⊙ ⊙ ⊙

Roe on toast can be made of the soft roes from fresh herrings or bloaters for breakfast. Half a roe is sufficient for each person. It needs to be heated through, then placed on a small slice of hot toast, set beneath the grill for three minutes, with a dash of cayenne and a half-teaspoonful of anchovy or other sh sauce added for piquancy. The secret of serving this to perfection lies in the fact that the roe must be heated through before it is placed on the buttered toast, otherwise you get really hot toast and merely warm roe, and the roe must be piping hot to be appreciated.

⊙ ⊙ ⊙

Kidney toast is a familiar savoury and needs no comment, save a reminder that the kidney should be dropped in boiling water and skinned before being grilled. Minced kidney, if there be a cold one left over from breakfast, is good served on buttered toast. M. K.

MILLINERY NOTES.

From a French Correspondent.

 WHILE everyone at Biarritz, including the Spaniards who are there, works her and his hardest to alleviate the sufferings of the wounded, the branch establishments of the famous Paris houses of the Rue de la Paix are doing well.

The dressmakers and milliners are showing their new models and executing orders. It is all a splendid example of "keeping on as usual."

The new autumn hats are specially attractive, free from exaggeration and subtle in colour.

Black and white remains first favourite, and all the pastel shades of grey and grey-blue are in great demand. In a recent article I spoke of the popularity of soft felt and of silk beaver. Some of the new shapes in velvet felt are ideal for October wear. They are small enough to be comfortable on a windy day and yet are quite picturesque in outline.

OLD ROSE VELVET FELT.

A charming little model was made of old rose velvet felt, with a simple trimming which consisted of a loose scarf of printed silk in dull shades of blue, black, and grey. The brim of the hat was flat, after the manner of a sailor model, and the scarf was lightly wound round the crown, the ends being tied at one side and allowed to jut out over the brim.

I have seen this model copied in pale powder-blue felt, with a scarf of black and white printed silk caught down by a buckle made of dark blue enamel. I have also seen it carried out entirely in shades of golden brown, with an effective touch of black in the printed design on the scarf.

One of the newest ideas of a very famous Paris milliner is the close-fitting shape made of velvet and trimmed with clusters of fruit—the latter being placed all round the crown at regular intervals. Artificial grapes, black and green, are once more fashionable, and bunches of these are mingled with peaches or with realistic apples, cherries, or tangerine oranges.

In the early part of this year I saw this idea tentatively launched at Monte Carlo. Some particularly smart hats were trimmed with clusters of small oranges and lemons, branches of orange blossom being mingled with the golden fruit. Just now artificial grapes are the favourites.

FLAT-BRIMMED HATS.

Flat-brimmed hats covered with a heavy make of black satin will be fashionable all through the winter. A little later on these hats will be trimmed with a band of skunk or fitch round the crown, and these fur bands will be fastened at one side with a handsome buckle or clasp.

An air of elegant simplicity seems to rest on the hats of this autumn. They are almost all becoming, and none of the models present difficulties to those clever girls who like to trim their own shapes at home.

In the millinery world the two favourite colours of the season are Fragonard blue and the splendid purple known as violet de monseigneur. All the soft brown tints are also in favour, and, of course, blue in every known shade.

A closely-fitting black velvet hat trimmed with clusters of peaches and black and green grapes.

The New "Daily Mail" Feuilleton Begins Next Week.

Women in the Home

In 1914 almost exactly half of the 15 million women in Britain were either married or widowed and at home looking after children. One and a half million single women were also involved in looking after homes and families. When a mother died, most commonly in childbirth, it was often the case that the eldest girl or girls had to take over responsibility for the upbringing of younger brothers and sisters and the running of the home. Many of these girls missed out on the chance of marriage if they then found themselves looking after fathers or other elderly relatives. A further one and a half million women were employed in 'keeping home' as domestic servants. Of the remaining four and a half million women some were employed in work outside the home but even then often in family businesses, some few were students, others were retired and others were living off private means.

Although things were beginning to change, for the vast majority of women 'home' was their world. Most women did not have time for interests outside the home, all their time was consumed feeding and caring for their family. Even relatively wealthy women who had servants to work for them tied themselves to the home in the belief that it was their duty to 'manage' the running of the home and its servants. They might spend some time in charity work and other 'womanly pursuits' such as music, sewing and visiting friends but generally it was not expected that any woman, whatever her class, would be interested in anything outside the home.

Poster parades, especially outside the homes and workplaces of politicians, were a popular suffragette tactic.

1914   POSTSCRIPTS

● Iceland awarded the franchise to women.

August – The outbreak of the First World War put on hold all claims and possibilities of women's suffrage. The WSPU suspended their campaign, changed the name of the campaign paper from *The Suffragette* to *Britannia* and pledged full support to the government and the war effort. Some of the WSPU's supporters believed this to be a betrayal of the cause and left to join the pacifist movement. Sylvia Pankhurst was one of the supporters to leave. A rift had already opened between Sylvia and her mother. Sylvia and her East London Women's Federation had split in early 1914 from the WSPU basically on the issue of the WSPU's cutting its ties with the Labour Party.

CHEQUE BOOK FOR WIVES
Bank Manager's Plaint – Women a Plague

'For goodness' sake,' he said, 'don't encourage the idea. You can't conceive of the amount of trouble which married women's accounts give us. We have a number of them of course and I can only think of three or four women among them who have any sense of business at all.

'The most amusing client I ever had complained bitterly when she was told she had overdrawn her account. "Why," she said, "I have lots of cheques left in my cheque book. How can I be overdrawn?" That, I admit, was exceptional stupidity but a great many come pretty near it.'

Daily Mail, 1 April 1914

ABOVE: *Women of the WRAF at work on an airbase. At the outbreak of war the Royal Air Force was called the Royal Flying Corps.*

BELOW: *The serious shortage of doctors during the war meant greater responsibility for medical students like these women at the Royal Free Hospital.*

1915

Women at War

Throughout history and its many wars women had been involved to varying degrees with 'front line action'. The camp followers and Service wives of the Napoleonic wars had, like many women before them, tended the wounded, removed the dead from the battlefield and helped feed and care for the active soldiers. During wars in the nineteenth century women had been moved further back from the front line as the army organized more of its own provisioning and medical care.

The First World War saw a new departure in the role women played at war. Initially the Women's Legion was formed in 1915 and women were engaged as auxiliaries to the men's Services but in 1917 women's corps were formed – the Women's Army Auxiliary Corps (WAAC); the Women's Reserve Naval Service (WRNS or Wrens); and the Women's Reserve Air Force (WRAF). The Women's Land Army was also formed to help with food production. There was never any conscription for women in the First World War and all the women in the Services were volunteers. Their job was principally to free men for the fighting. Women staffed the administration of the war both at home in Britain and nearer the front in continental Europe. When war ended, the temporary nature of the women's corps, inherent in their titles, 'reserve', 'auxiliary', was emphasized by their disbanding.

The women closest to the front line, on some occasions even working among the men in the trenches, were the various corps and groups of nurses. The British War Office turned down the offer of help from groups like the First Aid Nursing Yeomanry, Dr Elsie Inglis and the Scottish Women's Hospital units who went instead to work with the other Allied Armies at the fronts. There were nurses working for the British Military and these came from a variety of sources – the Voluntary Aid Detachments (VADs); the Territorial Force Nursing Service; Queen Alexandra's Military and Naval Nursing Services. The War Office deployed some of these nurses abroad and some to care for the wounded when they returned home to Britain. The War Office also changed its rules about women doctors and in 1915 did employ them but only as civilians; they refused to give women doctors commissions.

Many of the women who joined these volunteer corps were middle class, and had led sheltered lives protected from many of what were considered to be the more unpleasant aspects of life. For them the war took them out of their close circle of family and friends, introduced them to men and women from other countries, classes and backgrounds and gave them a degree of freedom and independence unimagined only a few years earlier.

ABOVE: British nurses played their part in the terrible retreat from Serbia, tending the tragic number of wounded.
BELOW: British Red Cross nurses working close behind the firing lines in Flanders had to learn to wear gas masks in case of gas attacks.

1915 POSTSCRIPTS

● Women in Denmark were given the vote.

March – The government appealed to women to register for war work at their local Labour Exchange.

October – 10,000 people attended a memorial service for Edith Cavell, a British nurse working in Brussels who was executed by the Germans for helping Allied soldiers to escape.

'A lady porter at Marylebone station dragging along one of the trucks much to the admiration of two of the men that she supplanted.'

A woman blowing a lamp at the Osram Works.

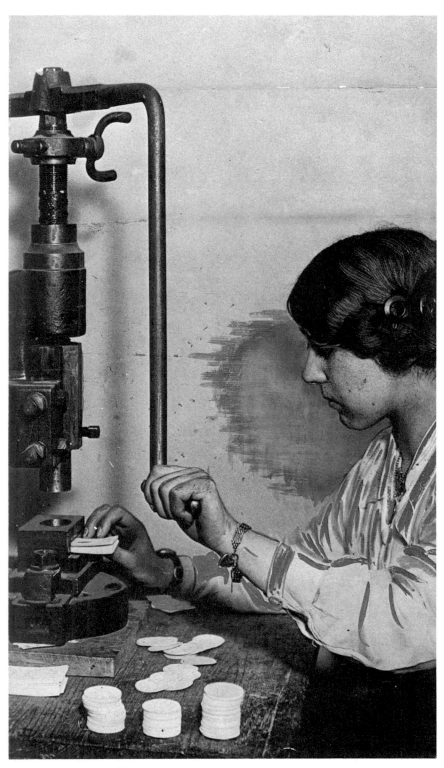

A women worker making watches at Ingersols where by 1916 all the work was done by women. Before the war the entire workforce had been male.

A woman working a cinema 'lantern' at a North London picture palace.

1916

Women Working for the War Effort

While thousands of women volunteered to join the Military and Nursing Services thousands more women were working in war industries and taking over men's jobs to free more recruits for the fighting. Four hundred thousand women left domestic service and more than 750,000 entered paid employment for the first time in response to calls for workers to help the war effort.

Despite the hostility of employers and the male-dominated trade unions women were willing to take on any job. Many middle-class women took on jobs in offices of the Civil Service, businesses, banks, insurance companies and other institutions, drove ambulances, and joined the newly formed women's police patrols. Working-class women took on a wide variety of jobs in industry – from munitions workers, wearing special clothing and with every item of metal removed to reduce the chance of a spark when handling highly explosive substances like cordite or TNT which turned the workers yellow, to non-munition factory workers making anything from light bulbs to paper.

Women also took on a vast selection of semi-industrial and service jobs which previously only men had been thought capable of and allowed to do. It was not unusual to see women roadsweepers, postal workers, railway porters and ticket collectors, window cleaners, even road-mending teams and the newspapers were full of pictures and reports of the newest area of work to be colonized by women. One of the most popular of these types of job was as a bus or tram conductress after the government allowed women to apply for licences as conductresses in October 1915. In some areas outside London women were also allowed to drive buses and in February 1917 the government gave permission for women to become taxi drivers.

All these jobs, however, were for the duration only and when the 'boys' came home women found themselves out of work. All the temporary legislation and bending of the trade-union rules were revoked and, as the title of the 1918 Restoration of Pre-War Practices Act suggests, things were back to how they had been in 1914. But for the women who had taken up paid work or volunteered to run canteens, administer war charities, collect salvage or supervise welfare schemes, life was not exactly as it had been in 1914. They had experienced earning their own money and had the knowledge that they could achieve what they never would have dreamt of before the war.

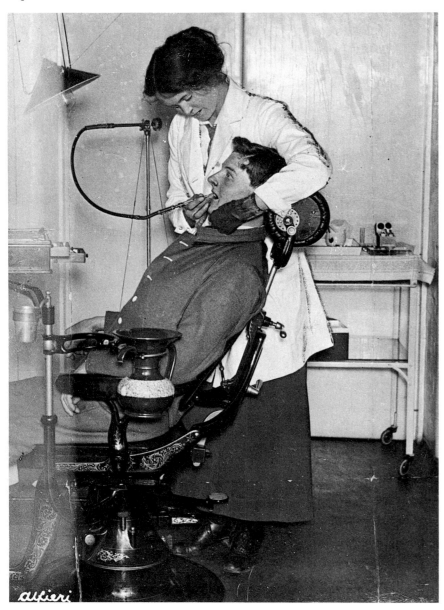

A postwoman.

A woman dentist.

1916 POSTSCRIPTS

September – US President Wilson, attending a women's suffrage rally, pledged to give women the vote.

October – Ethyl Byrne and Margaret Sanger opened the first birth-control clinic in the USA. They were later arrested and convicted for running the clinic.

November – Jeanette Rankin from Montana became the first woman member of the US Congress.

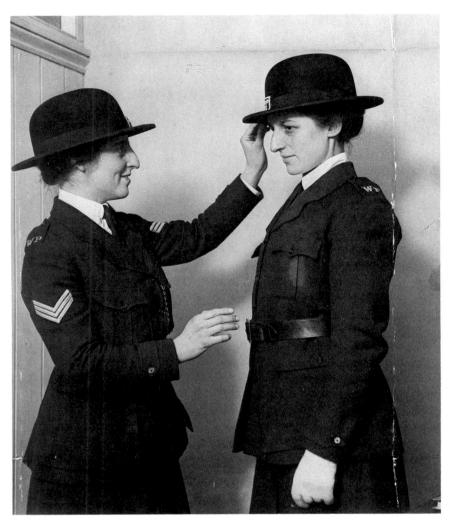

Two of 300 women constables recruited to 'guard women workers and prevent carelessness' try out their uniforms.

Two women guards on London Tube trains.

Women making paper at a mill at Purfleet on the Thames.

1917

The Benefits of Marriage!

By the end of 1917 the position of some six million married women in society had changed. Married women over 30 who were also either a householder or the wife of a local government elector were given the vote in national elections.

Women's performance during the war was to be rewarded with this limited franchise. Even Herbert Asquith a long time opponent of female suffrage had changed his mind in the face of the evidence of women's abilities and the knowledge that Britain might well have not been able to win, or won only at great cost, the war against Germany had women not left their homes and staffed industries, services and offices throughout the country.

However the advantage of a married woman over 30 being able to vote was counterbalanced by the fact that married women, even in wartime, were in most cases not allowed to have a job. Virtually every profession and public institution demanded that women leave their job when they married. Even in jobs where there was no hard and fast rule about employing married women, women left when they married. It was simply not expected that a woman would work after marriage. She left to take care first of her husband and home and then any children they might have.

One of London's first women taxi drivers.

London County Council began recruiting women ambulance crews in 1917.

1917 POSTSCRIPTS

● Following the Revolution women in Russia were enfranchised on equal terms with men.

● The Family Endowment Council was established by Eleanor Rathbone to campaign for family allowances.

December – Elizabeth Garrett Anderson died. After studying medicine at home in the 1850s and '60s, because women were barred from studying at any of the established British Medical Schools, Elizabeth Garrett was awarded a medical degree in 1870 by the University of Paris and became the first qualified woman doctor in Europe.

MARRIED WOMEN NOT WANTED

Women, and particularly married women, have risen so well to so many big occasions during the past few years – so many wives have prevented wreck and ruin by slipping into their husbands' business shoes when they have had to put on khaki – that it is surely time for it to be recognized generally that matrimony does not necessarily kill a woman's natural ability and that there is no sane reason why she should be deterred from keeping or taking a job just because she is married.

Extract from an article by H.M.K.N., *Daily Mail*, 17 September 1917

Women tar-spraying roads in Westminster.

Women setting up type.

1918

Equal Pay for Equal Work

A survey in 1906 by Edward Cadbury showed that the great majority of women believed that it was right that they should receive lower wages than men. In 1906 the average man's wage in industry was 30s while women textile workers, who with a long tradition of trade unionism were among the best-paid women workers, earned on average 18s 8d. Most other women in industry earned between 9s and 10s.

There had been agitation for better pay and conditions in the few industries where women had a strong showing in the workforce but this was not for pay equal to that of men in the same industry and it was seldom organized. Women had been excluded from most trade unions during the nineteenth century and when they were allowed to become union members they found that rather than fighting for equal pay for their few women members the unions sought only to promote the interests of their male members.

During the First World War women were given many promises of equal pay from government, employers and trade unions. Promises were seldom honoured, although after strikes on the trains and buses the unions negotiated deals with the employers which ensured equal pay for women workers. The war also brought equal pay to the fore as an issue in a way it had never been before. Before the war there were many jobs which had been seen only as 'men's jobs', no one would ever have thought that these jobs could have been done, let alone done equally well, by a woman. Necessity, during wartime, proved to women themselves that they could do many 'men's jobs' and they began to press for equal pay.

Women forestry workers.

A woman controlling train signals in Birmingham.

1918   POSTSCRIPTS

● The Maternal and Child Welfare Act was passed enabling local authorities to provide services such as welfare clinics and health visitors.

● Dr Janet Campbell reported to the War Cabinet Committee that women's health had improved due to better nutrition than in the pre-war years. Probably the extra money women earned and the setting up of workplace canteens aided this improvement in women's diet.

January – Rosa Luxemburg was murdered by members of the State Police in Germany. A committed communist and strong believer in women's equality Rosa Luxemburg, 'Red Rosa', had spent most of the war in prison for her agitation against the fighting and post war had led a communist uprising in Berlin with Karl Liebknecht.

July – Marie Stopes published her controversial book *Married Love*, which suggested that sex could and should be a pleasure for both sexes. As a sex instruction book *Married Love* became a bestseller overnight.

October – The House of Commons passed the Parliament (Qualification of Women) Act to allow women over 21 to stand as Parliamentary candidates.

● A women's employment committee at the Ministry of Reconstruction suggested there would be many new jobs post war for women as midwives, home helps, health visitors, nursery helpers, child welfare workers, women police and probation officers – all jobs as carers.

December – On the 28th the first general election in which women could vote and be candidates took place. Of the 1,600 candidates only 17 were women and only one was elected. She was Constance Markiewicz who stood for Sinn Fein and refused to take her seat in the House of Commons.

FOR OUR WOMEN READERS

GAMES FOR GIRLS.
PRACTISING GOLF.

THE world of sportswomen, taking to golf as an outlet for the active spirit born of the war, is discovering that there is something in the game which did not appear previously to exist.

There was an interesting article in this journal last week concerning the difficulties of girl beginners on the links. It pointed out that these enthusiastic novices, finding the pastime less easy than they had imagined it, were apt to retire crestfallen and embarrassed when they realised that, owing to their failure to propel the ball with reasonable accuracy round the course, they were hindering other players.

There can be no doubt that too many novices still approach golf in the frame of mind of the irresponsible individual whose motto is, " Here's a ball; let's hit it."

But on the links there is a correct way of hitting the ball, and it is because the girl beginner who has had no instruction thinks that any way will do that she brings so much harassment to herself—and to other people.

SOLO PRACTICE.

For a month, or even more, the best way for the beginner is not to play a match at

DAILY MAIL MENUS

LENTEN LUNCHEON.
Cod's Roe Cutlets.
Brown Bread and Butter.
Creamed Macaroni.
Nut Jelly.

NUT JELLY.

Ingredients: 2oz. of almonds, 2oz. of walnuts or any nuts, 1½ pints of milk and water, two tablespoonfuls of sweetened condensed milk 1½oz. of gelatine, half-gill of water.

Method: Melt the gelatine in the water, blanch the nuts and put them through a mincer or nut mill, or chop them finely. Boil the milk and water, pour it over the nuts, strain the gelatine and add, mix and beat well add the condensed milk and a little sugar if not sweet enough. When cold pour into a mould rinsed out with cold water and leave it to set.

all. She will be much more profitably employed practising shots in a quiet corner of the course.

An hour's teaching by a competent professional is worth a thousand hours of self-guided efforts. But, assuming that the professional is not always available, there are certain points which may be laid down for the direction of recruits to the game.

THE FATAL SWAY.

Of primary importance is the point that you must avoid the common error of drawing away from the ball as you take the club back and swaying forward again in the down swing as you hit.

There is only one true golf swing. It is founded on the principle that the body must turn on its own axis—it must not sway backward and forward. It must be governed by a turning at the hips. Harry Vardon says—and the declaration carries conviction—that the swing will not go wrong if you remember to keep your head absolutely still. Doing this, the only way to swing the club back will be to allow the body to turn at the hips—to let the arms wind up the body, and in the down swing unwind it.

That is the art of golf in a nutshell. Even though the swing shortens for the shorter shots—as, for instance, with the mashie—the same principle obtains. The mashie pitches of 60 or 70 yards are very interesting to practise, and the point to remember is still this turning of the body at the hips. With these shorter strokes the feet—like the head—should be as nearly still as possible. All the evidence of champions goes to show that with the mashie the turn of the body begins at the knees; there is no pivoting at all on the feet. From the knees the turn diffuses naturally to the hips, the correct turn of which is the secret of every successful swing. R. E. H.

NEW USES FOR STRAW.

STRAW for our heads and straw for our feet, made manifest in new ways too. For there is nothing really stirring in the thought of an ordinary straw hat, and as for straw to walk upon there are still some people left who can remember the horrid swish of it upon the floors of omnibuses, and have no wish to perpetuate in that manner the customs of prehistoric times.

No; the new ways with straw are artistic and prove both a novelty and an economy.

BASS AND RAFFIA.

In the form of headgear we find bass and raffia used this spring. Garden lovers gazing in the shop windows of millinery artists, at charmingly becoming-looking turbans and tams, will wonder why there is a familiar aspect about some of these delightful objects. Presently the fact dawns upon them that they are made of bass of the soft pale natural yellow shade, patterned with coloured designs of the prettiest pastel shades. Raffia, used for making flowers, is quite a welcome addition to the gauze, crêpe, velvet, satin, and other materials used for the purpose. It is seen in wreaths and clumps upon the hats of the spring. But the newest mode of presenting it is in strands and balls of a very novel aspect, at first sight easily to be confused with ostrich feathers treated in the same way.

THE DUTCH MAT.

These strands are highly glossed and look neat as well as smart wound about a tailor-made hat's crown, or, as I have said, massed in large conical balls, sometimes as many as three appearing in front of a hat above the " poke " brim.

The new departure in straw for the floor is the Dutch mat that comes from Holland. It has been perforce absent for so long that it is quite a stranger in our midst, and arrives at a most opportune moment, with carpets as expensive as they are. The mats are made in goodly sizes, and interwoven with the natural colour are stripes of purple, green, or orange. Oval shapes are much admired and look well on highly polished floors. M. H.

From Paris.

One of the smart and easily made tunics now so fashionable in Paris. This model is of Egyptian blue fringed with blue and with a rose embroidered in crimson, green and dull gold threads.

HOUSE DECORATION.
HOW TO WHITEWASH A CEILING.

DESPAIR enters into the heart of the housewife, for the ceiling of the kitchen is sadly dirty, she sees no prospect of securing the services of a professional whitewasher. There is no help for it—she must whitewash it herself! It sounds a difficult undertaking, but if it is set about in the right way it is comparatively simple. In order to be able to spread the whitewash evenly, it is as well to practise on the ceiling of the scullery or a small bedroom before attempting that of a larger room.

First of all, prepare the room and gather together the necessary materials and plant. Either short trestles or two pairs of steps and a plank strong enough to bear a person's weight are required; two pails, two sponges, and a distemper brush. The sponges can be made by filling a bag of Turkish towelling with broken pieces of sponge. If the towelling wears out a fresh piece can be put over the old one.

EMPTY THE ROOM.

Take all the pictures, ornaments, and furniture that can be moved out of the room, cover any heavy furniture with dust sheets, and leave as much space as possible for moving the scaffold quickly from place to place.

If the ceiling alone is to be distempered and the walls untouched, the latter must be protected. Fix, with drawing pins, sheets of newspaper on the walls as close to the ceiling as possible; the lower part may be covered with old sheets.

Should there be any splashes on the paper when the whitewashing is finished rub them off gently with a little dough, and remove as soon as possible any spots that may have fallen on the paint.

Before beginning to distemper the ceiling the old distemper must be washed off. Place the scaffold, which is made by laying a plank on the trestles or steps, in position and dip the distemper brush in a pail of water. Mount the scaffold and wet the ceiling to remove the old coating of distemper. Clean as much as possible with the brush and finish with the sponge. Let the brush be fairly dry when rubbing near the edges of the wall-paper and the sponge pressed to as sharp a point as possible. If there are any bad cracks in the ceiling clear the distemper out of them with an old knife and fill them with cement. Wet the cracks or bad places; then press the cement in well.

A SIMPLE PREPARATION.

A simple preparation for whitewashing a ceiling can now be bought quite inexpensively at any oil shop, and does away with the first coating of size, which would otherwise be necessary. It is mixed according to the directions with cold water. Make ready a quantity of this preparation in a pail. It is better to prepare too much than too little, and the surplus can be always utilised to whiten the inside of a cupboard or larder. Before beginning, close the doors and windows of the room in order to keep the surface of the ceiling as wet as possible when working. It is best to work towards the light, although when a room is not square it is sometimes advisable to take the narrowest width of a ceiling.

Work from one end of the ceiling to the other and try to keep the edge wet, or when the ceiling is dry the marks where the brush overlapped will show.

The whitewash must be applied quickly, to avoid the edges drying, and care must be taken not to miss any part, as the ceiling cannot be retouched afterwards without showing. When the whole ceiling is finished open the windows and doors to allow it to dry quickly. M. W.

Within the dim, five-windowed house of
  sense
I watch through coloured glass
  The shapes that pass.
Soon I must journey hence
To meet the great winds of the outer
  world
And see
  (When God has turned the key)
The true and terrible colours of His
  scheme
Which now I dream.
        Lieut. F. W. HARVEY.
        (A Gloucestershire Lad).

1919

Women in Public Life

'A person shall not be disqualified by sex or marriage from the exercise of any public function, or from being appointed to or holding any civil or judicial post, or from entering or assuming or carrying on any civil profession or vocation, or from admission to any incorporated society.' So opened the Sex Disqualification (Removal) Bill which became law in 1919. However many spheres of life were not covered by the Act. The Church, the Stock Exchange, the House of Lords were some of the areas outside the scope of the Act. There were other areas of life which although they were covered by the Act did not see any wholesale changes. For example one clause said that university rules and statutes could not exclude women from being admitted to membership of the university. Oxford University acted quickly and changed its rules in 1920 but it was not until after the Second World War that Cambridge allowed women to sit for degrees.

The Sex Disqualification (Removal) Act did however mean that women had a greater chance of pursuing a career or taking jobs that had previously been barred to them. The legal profession was one of the areas opened to women and on 30 December, one week after the Bill became law, Helena Normanton was admitted to Lincoln's Inn as the first woman student at the Bar. Women could also become judges, magistrates and Justices of the Peace, and gradually over the next years women began to fill these posts in lower courts, although it was to be another 46 years before the appointment of the first woman High Court judge. For women as citizens the Act was also important as it allowed them to sit on juries in the criminal courts.

The Civil Service came under the aegis of the Act but it also allowed the Service to organize its own rules for entry. Women were barred from some posts including overseas postings with the Foreign Office, obliged to resign on marriage and in most cases received lower pay than men. These conditions lasted, in the case of the marriage bar and overseas postings, until 1946. Equal pay, to which the Civil Service committed itself in 1921, did not come fully until the Equal Pay Act came into force in 1976, although a partial victory was won in 1955.

ABOVE: In July Suzanne Lenglen won Wimbledon and amazed the crowds with her short and sleeveless tennis dresses.
BELOW: Nancy Astor pictured after being elected to Parliament.

1919 POSTSCRIPTS

● Italian women were allowed to become barristers and solicitors but not to sit as judges.

September – By the end of September all women conductresses on London omnibuses were replaced by returned soldiers and given a certificate, but no offers of jobs, in appreciation of their work.

November – Nancy Astor won the by-election caused when her husband was raised to the peerage and had to give up his parliamentary seat. On 1 December she became the first woman to sit in the House of Commons.

● Women in France voted for the first time in a general election. As in Britain it was not on a franchise equal to men. French women had to wait another 25 years for an equal franchise.

THE FIRST WOMAN TO SIT IN THE COMMONS

In this country our women have proved under the stern test of war that they can face the grim facts of life without flinching; and the gifts of intellect, energy and courage which they displayed in such varied directions have won them the confidence of the public. So much so we anticipate a large increase in the number of women Members, where there is so much legislative work for which they are peculiarly qualified waiting for them to do.

Extract from a Leader, *Daily Mail*, 2 December 1919

Looking Glass Reflections: An Important Aid to Beauty.

HAVE you ever noticed that there are some quite pretty girls who are not attractive—at least not so much so as they ought to be—and we sometimes find girls quite unblessed by actual beauty who nevertheless are really attractive? There is something about them that attracts the eyes to them. Without being beautiful—without even being pretty—they are pleasant to look upon. They are admired—although they are plain? Why is it?

Well, in the great majority of cases it is simply a matter of *dress*, of care, or of carelessness in choosing and putting on garments!

TOO PRETTY TO CARE!

There are some pretty girls who are " so sure of themselves " as it were, on account of their beauty, that they think they need not trouble about their raiment. They look at themselves in the glass and are so satisfied with the reflection therein that they feel there is no need for troubling about dress. They can dress as they please. " I am so pretty that everything becomes me!" cried a girl of my acquaintance as her eyes turned to the mirror over my mantelpiece. As a matter of fact she was wrong. She was not so pretty as she thought she was. She could, with care, have looked ever so much better than she did look. She was very, very fair—of that flaxen fairness that needs care in colour to do it justice. She wore colours that were just too faint. They gave her that " washed out " look that takes the edge off beauty. The pink in her cheeks was of the faintest. Her choice in colours was for the very palest hues—and they did not become her. Her blues had a faded look and made her eyes look faded too. Her whole appearance gave one the idea of something that had been out in the sun too long! Poor Trixie, she was too sure of herself; too vain, if one put it bluntly. She thought she could not be improved upon, and that is a great mistake for anyone to make. No one is so beautiful that she can afford to neglect the " becoming " note in colour or the style that best suits her figure. A certain amount of vanity is natural, but there is such a thing as being too vain.

TOO PLAIN TO CARE!

And—the plain girl. She makes the mistake sometimes of thinking that because she is plain " there is no use in bothering " about what she wears. There is every use. Becoming dress can often make a plain girl pretty!

ONLY CHILDREN.

Are They Robbed of Childhood?

THERE is one great danger which confronts mothers of only children —the danger of robbing the little ones of their most precious possession—the gift of childhood.

Children may be robbed either physically, mentally, or morally of childhood. Some poor mites are deprived in all three ways, but naturally a mother never robs her precious bairn on purpose—she simply errs through ignorance or lack of thought.

MISTAKEN KINDNESS.

We all know the mother who robs her boy of childhood—physically. She feeds him like his father and then wonders why he is never well. She keeps him up late at night, takes him into crowded and unhealthy places, and always dresses him unsuitably.

The child who is robbed mentally generally has a lonely mother. She makes a companion and a confidant of him—treating him always like a " grown up." Consequently the lovely little childish mind is overburdened and overdeveloped. The boy

Worldly Wisdom.

To be a woman of the world is not necessarily enviable. Worldly wisdom usually only comes through experience—and that is not always pleasant. Commonsense is far more valuable, and even if that be coupled to innocence it will carry many a girl forward upon life's highway to honour and success.

constantly says smart things and is considered " clever and advanced."

But what is cleverness compared with the whole world of childish wonders that are lost to him—the delicious frankness, the charming simplicity, the sweet innocence that once driven out can never come back?

Lastly comes the mother who robs her child morally. Thinking she is making him happy, she always indulges him. She never checks his faults, never teaches him control, but brings him up to behave as if everybody and everything were simply created for his selfish pleasure. Unless such a child is soon removed from this well-meaning but dangerous influence, he will eventually become one of the world's wasters.

IN LARGE FAMILIES.

The mother of many does not often rob her children. She has learnt how to look after them properly physically; she does not rob them mentally because they lead their own nursery life in each other's company; and she brings them up to be unselfish and self-controlled because otherwise the home life would be impossible.

But it may often mean much denial for the mother of one to see that her child *always* has plenty of fresh air, sound sleep, simple food, and the constant companionship of other children for which he naturally craves. Her reward will be the lasting health and happiness of her little one, while she will find that other mothers will give her helping hints and a helping hand. For there is a bond between mothers that few ignore.

A becoming and easily made matinee jacket of eggshell-blue printed silk lined with shell-pink tussore is here depicted. A paper pattern (No. 28063) may be obtained in 22, 24, 26 and 28 inch waist sizes from "The Daily Mail" Paper Pattern Department, 291a, Oxford Street, W.1. To cut the jacket allow 1⅜ yards of 40 inch wide fancy material and an extra ¾ yard of 27 inch wide plain material.

The Toilette for Breakfast in Bed.

WHICH one among us does not enjoy an occasional breakfast in bed? And then it is we wish to look dainty and fresh. It is a safe rule that bed-jackets should be very short and full. Perhaps one of the prettiest materials to use is voile-lined voile or flannel-lined voile.

DIFFERENT COLOURS.

I have seen lovely bed-jackets—for summer wear—done with two short lengths of voile in different colours. For instance, white lined with mauve, with mauve ribbons tying the small garment together at neck and sleeves. An excellent model may be made from one yard and a half of wide-width material, with one yard and a half of another colour for lining. On the garment I have in my mind there is practically no making. The two materials are stitched together, then doubled over evenly like a sheet of letter paper, and a straight slit is cut for the head to pass through and ribbons are added at the sides to tie and form a kind of sleeve. The neck can be decorated according to the individual taste of the wearer, either with a collar or a halter, or merely embroidered. Materials *must* be supple, but they may be quite inexpensive, for everything depends on the colours chosen.

A fascinating little bed-jacket—very much like that illustrated—was made of lemon-yellow crepon, with a lining of white cotton crepe. The collar and cuffs were turned back with the white material, and just over the left breast there was an embroidered flower—a long-stalked marguerite with palest green leaves. White crepon lined with white flannel makes an ideal bed-jacket, the borders worked over with a coarse blanket-stitch in some bright colour, and a monogram or favourite flower embroidered at one side. These embroidered motifs are in great favour with the Parisiennes.

A POPULAR NOVELTY.

For special occasions one can have delicious little breakfast-in-bed-garments made of fine nainsook, and inset with insertions of Valenciennes lace. Plenty of pastel-tinted ribbons should be added at the breast and loose sleeves. This year we have had a run on pale lemon-yellow—for bedroom, boudoir, and ballroom. In Paris they are showing dainty lingerie made of palest yellow cotton crepe, piped with white and embroidered with white and *dark blue* washing silks. This is one of the most popular novelties of the hour. V.

CROCHETTED RAG MATS.

I HAVE been most successful in turning to account a collection of old clothes. I cut all the woollen pieces into strips about half an inch wide, and joined each colour into one continuous length, rolling it into a ball just as one would do with wool. Stocking legs I cut around and around the leg, making a continuous strip of stocking material. This was also wound into a ball. When I had completed the cutting into strips of the whole of the material I procured one of those large wooden crochet needles used for working double Berlin wool some years ago.

HOW TO START.

First I made a strip of chain about 12in. long, and then I worked along one side with double crochet, turning the end of the chain with enough extra stitches of double crochet, so that the whole would lie flatly when placed on a flat surface. It is impossible to give the number of extra stitches, as it depends upon the tightness

Food Accessories.

Just as the success of a dress depends to a great extent upon its finish, so the success of a dish depends somewhat upon its accessories, the way it is served, the sauce and the garnishing. You cannot fail to become a successful cook if you study " The Daily Mail " Cookery Book, price 3s. 6d., on sale at all newsagents, or obtainable from the Book Publisher, " The Daily Mail " E.C. 4; or from " The Daily Mail " Branch Office, at 130, Fleet-street, London, E.C. 4, price 3s. 9d. post free.

of the work, some workers making tighter stitches than others, and the thickness of the material has also to be taken into account. The double crochet must be fairly loose, however, so as to allow the material to set nicely. Experience will teach this point better than any amount of written explanation. Work along the other side of the beginning chain, placing a stitch into every chain, until the end is reached, then add the same number of extra stitches that were added at the other end. Continue working around and around, taking the stitches completely under the top chain of the double crochet, and adding extra stitches at the ends, distributing them carefully so that the mat lies flatly when straightened out. The colours of the rags should be varied to form borders and strips until sufficient has been done to make a large enough oval for the mat. This can be of a size suitable for a doormat, or to be used as a covering for quite a large space. The mats can be mounted upon a strong foundation or not, as liked, and require no edging.

ROUND, SQUARE, OR OVAL.

The length of the beginning chain must be varied to suit the size of the oval mat required. Twelve chain is a good number with which to commence an oval mat to place in front of a small dressing-table or wash-stand. The mats can be made either round or square, or worked from end to end, but in the latter case a final row of double crochet should be worked all around the edge of the mat to give it a neat finish. H.

1920

The Nineteenth Amendment to the US Constitution

ABOVE: *Women queueing to collect unemployment pay. More and more women were being forced to give up their jobs to returned soldiers and the country's economy began to decline after the war, failing to create any new work.*

BELOW: *Voluntary Aid Detachment nurses returning to Britain from France where they continued to be needed to tend the wounded long after the war had ended.*

In Britain men like John Stuart Mill, who attempted to gain the vote for women in 1867 by introducing an amendment to the voting Reform Act by substituting the word 'person' for 'man', fought to change the inequalities in women's position. In the USA, the cause of female emancipation was hampered to an extent by the anti-slavery movement. While some abolitionists linked the causes of women and slaves, most channelled their energy into defeating the more obviously iniquitous and cruel practice of slavery.

Susan Anthony, who was to become a figurehead of the American women's movement in the nineteenth century, came from an anti-slavery background. Her father had been a strong campaigner for the abolition of slavery. Susan Anthony too became involved in the abolitionist movement while campaigning against alcohol on the slave plantations. In the 1850s when she was in her thirties she turned her attention to the cause of women's rights. In the early years of the twentieth century she founded the International Women's Suffrage Alliance which gave support and encouragement to women like Emmeline Pankhurst.

Women's rights campaigners in the USA had been fighting, and continued to fight throughout the nineteenth and early twentieth centuries, for a female franchise state by state. In 1869 Wyoming was the first state to enfranchise women and by the beginning of the First World War several other states, mainly in the western USA, had given women the vote.

Susan Anthony, however, had always insisted upon a federal amendment to the constitution rather than working for changes to the franchise state by state. In 1912, six years after her death, two women, Alice Paul and Lucy Burns, broke from the National American Suffrage Association whose policy was to fight to enfranchise women state by state. With first-hand experience of the militant suffragette movement in Britain, they formed the Congressional Union, later the National Women's Party, to campaign, as Susan Anthony had done, for a federal amendment to the constitution.

In August 1920 the Nineteenth (Women's Suffrage) Amendment became part of the constitution of the USA.

1920 POSTSCRIPTS

May – Women professors at Oxford were given equal status to their male colleagues.

October – At Oxford the first 100 women were admitted to study for degrees.

Composed of cyclamen pink brocaded crepe de Chine, this charming negligee is bordered with swansdown and tied with Nattier blue ribbon. The cap is made of net and Malines lace, with a cluster of flowers in the front and finished with a Nattier blue ribbon.

New Design by Miss Bessie Ascough.

This negligée could be easily made at home by any girl with clever fingers, especially as a paper pattern (No. 353) may be obtained, price 1s. post free, from "The Daily Mail" Paper Pattern Department, 291a, Oxford-street, W. 1.

The Care of Children's Clothes.

Some Hints Mothers will Appreciate.

THE cost of clothing three or four children nowadays is not a light one, but garments of all descriptions can be made to last longer and look fresher if care is bestowed on them by mother or nurse.

BOOTS AND SHOES.

A little castor oil should be warmed and rubbed into children's school boots before they are worn. This oil not only softens the leather and prevents it from cracking but it will keep out the wet. Boots so treated will not blacken very well for a few days, but when the oil has sunk in they will take a good polish. An excellent plan to make the soles of boots or shoes wear longer is to give them a coat of clear copal varnish, and this should be quite dry before the boots are worn.

Children often return from school with straw hats soaked with rain; if the ribbon is not discoloured it should be removed at once and wound round a bottle until dry, when it will look like new. The hat itself should be placed flat on a table and books with covers of little consequence placed round the brim to keep it in shape.

Some children fidget with the buttons of their coats until one gets lost, and an odd button cannot well replace it; and to save buying a new set the other buttons could be covered with a piece of good velveteen to match the material of the coat—only a tiny length will be needed—and an odd button could be used to replace the lost one.

All socks and stockings worn by children will last longer if they are darned lightly at the heels and toes when bought, and to prevent ladders being started by suspenders the hose should be stretched out to their fullest extent and machine stitched with the same coloured cotton round the leg just below where the suspenders will grip.

The fingers of children's gloves are so small they often shrink and curl after being washed unless they are pulled into shape, or have glove stretchers placed in them, and they should not be dried too near the fire.

WHEN DAMP.

Children should be taught to hang up their clothes as soon as they remove them; it is crumpled and creased garments that look so shabby, and damp clothes should have special attention in this direction, as the creases are doubly pronounced if allowed to dry in their folds.

NOTES ON NOTEPAPER.

WOMEN excel as writers of notes, and therefore notepaper is to them of paramount importance. Notepaper fashions vary with the times, and always have their devotees.

We are most of us favourably impressed or otherwise by the notepaper which a stranger uses in writing to us for the first time. It influences our estimate of the social standing and character of the writer. Some women have a special fancy for particularly good notepaper, perhaps partly for this reason.

MADE IN ENGLAND.

It is good to know that the best notepaper is of British manufacture, the finest white being made in Kent, while Scotland is famed for its wonderful bank paper. Women of taste are often conservative in their choice, and use the same paper for years. Considerable thickness used to be an essential quality, but at the time of the royal visit to India for the Durbar the most exclusive stationer in the West End put on the market a lighter weight paper, which was immediately taken up by all the other firms, and has been used ever since.

The same firm has recently issued a new idea for stamping the address, using instead of a die a copper plate with some charming old French design. Another delightful notion is to have a medallion in the left-hand corner with the initial handpainted in various enamelled colours and afterwards stamped in gold or silver.

At present azure is the colour most used for notepaper, and in fancy papers buff, mauve, and delphinium blue are the popular shades. There are also some very pretty bordered French papers, pale blue edged with a dark blue line, buff with brown, mauve with purple, accompanied by some beautifully tissue-lined envelopes.

FRENCH STATIONERY.

Just at the moment there is a passing fancy for some very gay French stationery in futurist colours, such as tango paper, the envelopes lined with paper patterned with green leaves and purple flowers. Then there is pale green paper with striped peacock blue, and green lining for the envelopes, and purple with envelopes lined with purple and yellow stripes. Quite a number of women are having their envelopes stamped before being sent from the stationers to save the trouble of sticking on the stamps.

A BREAKFAST DISH.

STEWED KIDNEY ON TOAST.

Ingredients.—½lb. of ox-kidney, 1 tablespoonful of flour, 1½oz. of dripping or margarine, ½ pint of boiling water, 1½ tablespoonfuls of mushroom or tomato ketchup, 1 tablespoonful each of minced onion and chopped parsley, salt, pepper.

Method.—Wipe the kidney with a damp cloth, remove any skin or core, and cut it into small pieces. Blanch it by putting it into a pan of cold water, bring to the boil, strain, and rinse in cold water and dry with a cloth. Mix the flour, ½ teaspoonful of salt, and ¼ teaspoonful of pepper, on a plate, dip the pieces of kidney in this. Melt the margarine in a pan, add the onion, and fry lightly, add the kidney, and brown, then gradually stir in the boiling water, and simmer gently until tender from three-quarters to one hour. Add the ketchup, season if necessary, and serve on toast Sprinkle the parsley over. If the kidney is tough add one dessertspoonful of vinegar to the water in which it is stewed.

Note.—This can be cooked the previous day, the ketchup added and the kidney reheated in the morning. This makes a good luncheon dish served in a border of boiled rice, macaroni, or mashed potatoes, with the addition of 3oz. of bacon.

VARIETY IN VEILS.

THE veil of the moment is not merely a covering for the face, it is a most necessary hat trimming. The variety of ways in which lace veils may be utilised in this connection is almost unlimited. Our artist, however, has depicted below three styles which are both new and becoming.

First there is a satin shape trimmed with Spanish lace, draped somewhat in the manner of the "yashmak," worn by women of the East. In the centre is a straw toque with a lace veil so arranged as to form a most effective ornamentation; and finally a lace veil used in conjunction with velvet ribbon, on a close-fitting straw shape and giving a "mask" effect, is a suggestion which many a home milliner might like to follow.

GIRLS, BOOKS AND CHARACTER.

NO wise mother allows her daughter to make friends indiscriminately, because she knows what good or what evil friends can work. But so can books, those friends one picks up at will and which make one forget a while worry, sickness, or sorrow. Their influence, though insidious and often difficult to trace, is immense, as mothers and teachers can testify.

Most mothers take care that no coarse book should fall into their girls' hands; but they are not sufficiently aware of the harm the trashy novel does, even though it ends by the villain's downfall and the reward of the just. Many mothers have complained to me of the growing girl's intractableness, her sulkiness, her idleness at home, and her at times almost hostile attitude. Believe me, this kind of novel is usually at the root of the trouble. She takes the printed word for truth, and, in comparison with the exciting adventures which fill the life of the heroine of a novel, home life made up of cooking, darning, and lessons seems intolerably dull.

FATAL ILLUSIONS.

The wise mother should object to the novelette because it fosters illusions about life. A child should consequently not see the world only through the spectacle of "nice" women writers. If she has been reading a sentimental book it is best to talk it over tactfully with her without scoffing. Thus her sensitiveness will not be hurt. She should be carefully told how different things are in reality, how ridiculous a man and woman would be if they behaved so in real life, and she should be shown how a great writer has treated the subject. In this way a girl's good sense is developed and an impetus given to her future happiness.

HOUSEHOLD ECONOMIES THAT COUNT.

"MY housekeeping expenses are much higher now than they were during war-time, yet our menus are much the same and prices are supposed to have gone down." So a harassed housewife as she sighed over her weekly "books."

UNCONSCIOUS SLACKING.

And many a housewife is confronted by the same problem. The reason is not really far to seek. It is simply that, the war being over, almost unconsciously little economies of the past are being dropped. Now that it is no longer so difficult to obtain certain commodities, we have grown imperceptibly slacker and we have become so accustomed to high prices that our standard of values has gradually changed.

For instance, we use perhaps more firewood than hitherto and have dropped lighting the fires with folded newspapers; also, we no longer bank the kitchen fire with rubbish folded in damp paper and wet slack when the day's cooking is done. Neither do we continue to sift the ashes and use them for cleaning saucepans and steels—instead we employ expensive cleaning materials. We are not so careful with the scraps; we perhaps do not bother to utilise the washed peelings and trimmings of vegetables for stock; we throw away stale pieces of bread as well as small portions of "left-over" dishes instead of transforming the latter into dainty little savouries. Also, we have grown careless about clarifying fat and utilising ends of soap by making them into soap jelly with which to wash kitchen rubbers.

Small economies may be tiresome, but they count in the long run. The Scotch truly say, "Mony a mickle mak's a muckle."

"A Cheerful Wife—

is the joy of life." She who feels that eventualities are more or less provided for is bound to be more cheerful. To achieve this she should fill in the forms in Page 3, and so qualify both herself and her husband for "The Daily Mail" Free Travel Accident Insurance benefits.

1921

Mother's Clinic

In March 1921 Marie Stopes opened her Mother's Clinic in Holloway which was the first birth-control clinic in Britain. Marie Stopes had become interested in birth control through the study of female sexuality and a belief in eugenics.

Marie Stopes was a palaeobotanist who became the first woman lecturer at Manchester University. Despite her education and learning she was, like many women of her day, ignorant about sex. After five years of marriage she set about trying to find out why she had not become pregnant and discovered that in fact the marriage was unconsummated. She then read everything she could in English, French and German on the subject of sex and in 1918 published her book *Married Love* which suggested that both men and women had a right to enjoy sex. She also saw that sex was difficult for women to enjoy when continually faced with the possibility of pregnancy.

In setting up her Mother's Clinic Marie Stopes was not only trying to remove the fear of unwanted pregnancy from the women who attended her clinic, she had another and less altruistic motive. There was a belief at the time that unless the lower classes could be encouraged to practise birth control the stock of the nation and the race would be diminished, watered down by the unchecked reproduction of the mentally and physically less fit members of society. Middle- and upper-class families had been limiting the size of their families for several decades by this time but working-class families of ten or more were not unusual. Eugenics were not at the time as reviled as they were to become after Hitler's attempts to create a master race in the 1930s and '40s. Nevertheless there was a strong working-class feeling against birth control because it was an idea promoted by eugenicists and was seen as a way of keeping the masses in their place.

However women did come to the Mother's Clinic for advice and help. The main method of birth control offered to them was the cap. The efforts of the Mother's Clinic and other clinics set up by people like Dr Helena Wright and Norman Hare were hampered by both the law and popular prejudices. Any printed material about contraception was deemed by law to be obscene so the dissemination of information about birth control was difficult. And many people, mainly men, feared that contraception would give women too much freedom, making them less willing to follow the route of marriage, home and family.

ABOVE: *Policewomen on duty in London parks were referred to as 'park mothers' in the* Daily Mail *caption to this photograph.*
BELOW: *Some of the 1,000 women awarded degrees at Oxford in 1921. These women passed their degree exams in the first 20 years of the century but because the university would not allow women to graduate they had never had formal recognition of their achievements.*

1921 POSTSCRIPTS

● Helena Normanton became the first woman barrister at the English Bar.

January – The first women undertook jury service in a Divorce Court.

July – A survey showed that of the eight million women in paid employment in the USA 87 per cent were in teaching or secretarial work.

August – Official figures showed there were two million more women in Britain than men; 1,096 women to every 1,000 men whereas the ratio had been 1,068:1,000 in 1911.

DEPENDENT HUSBANDS

The St Pancras Borough Council is to advertise for an assistant medical officer of health to replace Dr Gladys M. Miall Smith, who had recently under the rules of the council to vacate the position in consequence of her marriage.

The Parliamentary and General Purposes Committee agree that the principle of terminating the appointment on marriage should still be enforced but at the same time, they think that the council would desire to make it clear that they are prepared to consider applications from married women with dependent husbands.

Daily Mail, 20 December 1921

GIRLS & SECRETARIAL WORK.

How It can be a Stepping Stone to Success.

THERE are three points of view from which we may regard secretarial work. First the parents', since they must pay for training in shorthand and typewriting; then that of the aspirant, and last but not least the employers' point of view. Parents are often informed on good authority that the supply of shorthand-typists exceeds the demand, that many attain only mediocre ability and that few become mistress of the craft. Thus the average parent naturally thinks twice before deciding to pay for training in shorthand and typewriting, which takes at least six months and costs anything from £5 to £50.

If a girl has marked ability in other directions, the parents' hesitation is perhaps wise, but for the ordinary well-educated girl who is all-round at everything, but has no particular ability, shorthand and typewriting offer a definite career, not so much a career in itself, but as a back-door entry into professions not open to women by the front door.

OPENING FOR OTHER PROFESSIONS.

Just as every private carries a field-marshal's baton in his knapsack, so does every shorthand-typist carry the key to success in her notebook. A competent secretary holds all the keys, though at first the keys of her typewriter absorb her vision. For is not the correspondence of her firm its very centre? By keeping her eyes and her ears open she can pick up the technical terms and a practical working knowledge of the business in which she is engaged, and this could be strengthened by systematic study of its theory during leisure hours. Many are the typists who have risen to managers' posts, many are the authors' secretaries who have learnt to write books of their own.

Shorthand and typewriting, in the opinion of successful business women of to-day, who began as stenographers, provide an opening to other professions, and secretarial posts may be considered as stepping stones to success.

Viewed from this angle, parents may see possibilities in the work, but may doubt their daughters' ability to profit by them. Here I maintain that the secretary has to use her brain in so many other ways besides actual shorthand and typewriting, that if only she is interested in her work her general mentality develops and in time she becomes a capable business woman.

LOOKING TO THE FUTURE.

Looking at it from her point of view, she must formulate her ambitions and try to realise the romance of typing, disregarding its disagreeable and sometimes backaching effects. There will come a time, generally in the early thirties, after spending years with her nose to the typewriter, when she will no longer be content to remain the channel for the expression of the ideas of others; she will want to give vent to some of her own.

TO MAKE A WATER BOUQUET.

A CHARMING table decoration can be made by submerging a bunch of wild flowers in water. The best kind of bowl to use for the purpose is one made of paper; but a soup plate and a plain glass bowl—a small sized goldfish bowl, for instance—can be used quite successfully.

White or yellow blossoms should not be chosen; one of the chief attractions of this pretty device is the gathering of tiny glistening drops on every petal and stem, and these are not visible unless displayed upon a rich background of colour. Scarlet, purple, or pink blossoms should be used.

SIMPLE DIRECTIONS.

Arrange the nosegay in the band, tie it round with bass, and cut the stalks rather short. Then attach the stalks (invisibly if possible) to a flat, heavy weight. Place the bouquet in the middle of the soup plate and lower both to the bottom of a bath of cold water. The water in the bath must be more than twice the depth of the glass globe, as the success of the bouquet depends upon the exclusion of air, and this can only be brought about by manipulating the globe entirely under the surface of the water.

Fill the globe to the brim with water, lower it into the bath, turning it upside down over the bouquet in the soup plate. Lift the whole out of the bath, keeping the plate quite steady and allowing the overflow of water round the rim to remain. The globe must be absolutely full of water.

Wreath the rim of the plate with ferns and place the bouquet where it is to remain. In about twelve hours the flowers viewed through the magnifying medium of the clear water should be a picture of dazzling dewdrops.

If there are any loose petals on the flowers selected they should be removed, otherwise they will spoil the whole appearance of the nosegay. Do not allow any of the flowers or foliage to touch the glass; arrange them so that they stand erect and clear in the middle of the plate.

The Adaptable Cape-Apron.

Silver-grey charmeuse and lace of the same tone combine to give two aspects to one gown. The cape, when not required in that capacity, can be tied at the low waistline to form one of the fashionable lace "aprons." The long, loose lace sleeves are detachable.

QUEER QUILLS.

A BOUT this season of the year the milliners begin already to introduce autumnal "touches" into their hat designs. Quills always feature on holiday headgear, and this time they are decidedly erratic in appearance and behaviour.

In one case the crude ends of the quills are not concealed at all; in fact, they are given a prominent position, being placed well to the front and high up, and often with the plumage drawn tightly to the back of the hat.

STRANGE FASHIONS.

Pinions bunched into a crude rosette droop over the narrow brim of a windy-day felt hat, and—rather grotesquely—organdie quills are used to trim many of the latest summer transparent hats of lace and fine crinoline. Made of white organdie, long, narrow, sharply pointed, and piped with black or a colour, the "quills" are as light as thistledown and give just the hint of autumn that feathers are always able to bestow.

Raspberry & Red Currant Jam.

Ingredients.—To each pound of raspberries allow 1 gill of red currant juice and 1lb. of preserving sugar.

Method.—To extract the juice from the currants remove the stalks and put them into a jar, cover and place in a pan of cold water. Bring to the boil and boil until the juice flows freely. Strain through a cloth tied to the legs of a chair inverted over another chair. One quart of berries should yield about half a pint of juice. Remove the stalks from the raspberries, weigh and put them into a preserving pan with the red currant juice. Bring to the boil and boil for 10 minutes. Warm the sugar and add, stir until it melts, then boil the jam fast until it sets when tested by putting a little on a plate and left to cool. Keep the jam well skimmed. Put into pots and cover.

VARIETY IN THE HOME. *Useful Suggestions for Housewives.*

THERE is, of course, a good deal of monotony about ordering meals, week after week and month after month, but it is possible to bring variety into home life without adding to one's labour.

Why not attend a good course of cookery? It will not only give you ideas for new dishes, but it will arouse new interests in the culinary side of housewifery.

Sometimes the men folk absolutely refuse to accept anything but the stereotyped bacon and eggs for breakfast. But most of them will not object, at any rate, to the addition of a few fried potatoes in the delightful Devonshire fashion.

Then with cakes women are in the habit of using recipes for one or two kinds only, yet there are many delicious varieties that can easily be made at home. Try, for instance, an orange cake with icing on the top, or round shortbread biscuits with chocolate icing between them.

Even a few new dishes in which to serve food will make a delightful change. For example, there are all sorts of different shapes for stewed fruit to be found in cut or moulded glass.

TO WIDEN THEIR INTERESTS.

Even in the choice of topics for conversation at the dinner table is there not often a singular lack of variety? Young people should be encouraged to get up debating societies, book clubs, or art study circles, and to go to see plays of interest, especially Shakespearean productions, which they generally love, in order to widen their interests in every possible way.

STUDY YOUR APPEARANCE. *Puffy Eyes can be Improved.*

A PUFFY condition of the eyes, whether it be merely a slight puffiness of the lids or bagginess of the skin beneath the eyes, adds years to a woman's appearance and completely spoils the attractiveness of her eyes, however large and bright they may be.

The cause of this puffiness is either eye-strain, insufficient rest, or possibly excess of uric acid in the blood, and before any local treatment is attempted the cause must be discovered and removed—or at least reduced.

For outward application an astringent lotion applied to the skin beneath the eyes every night will be of great assistance, and a simple harmless one may be made at home by dissolving two drachms of powdered tannin in one ounce of eau de Cologne, together with an ounce of pure glycerine. This should be painted on the skin beneath the eyes with a fine camel's-hair brush, and allowed to dry in. In the morning the skin round the eyes should be sponged with very cold water, which will improve the relaxed skin and assist in bracing up the muscles near the eyes.

A course of mildly aperient salts taken regularly every morning, and a lithia tablet dissolved in a little water and taken about fifteen minutes before dinner, will be most beneficial. The amount of sugar taken should be reduced to the minimum and very acid fruits avoided. Oranges, however, may be taken with advantage.

CAREFUL DIETING.

The right kind of diet is of extreme importance, and red meat should be avoided as much as possible, also beer, stout, and the majority of fizzy drinks.

1922

Business Girls

For many working-class women who were not needed to help in the family home it had long been accepted that they would take a job, mainly as domestic servants, before they married and had a home of their own. Only a few middle- or upper-class women ever did paid work before the First World War but by the 1920s there was a growing number of women, 'business girls', working as clerks in a variety of businesses and institutions.

Women proved willing and able to use typewriters which were becoming an increasingly common piece of office equipment. However the fact that employers were able to pay women less than the male clerks was probably more of a reason than their skills for the increasing number of women clerks. This lower pay for women led to a great deal of ill-feeling on the part of the male clerks and, instead of fighting for equal or better pay for women, the clerks' unions decried women for taking men's jobs.

Outside business, there was an increasing number of women in professional jobs such as medicine, nursing and teaching and the first women had been called to the Bar. However the number of women qualified or aspiring to be doctors, lawyers, accountants or aiming to follow a high-level career in business or the Civil Service was infinitesimal in relation to the number of men in those areas. A report in the *Daily Mail* in 1924 revealed that there were 25 women acting as, or qualified as, barristers; eight women qualified or admitted as solicitors; 30 women trying to qualify as accountants; a few women working as auctioneers; and a slowly increasing number of women as analytical chemists. The fact that, in most jobs, there was a stark choice between marriage and a career severely limited women's horizons.

ABOVE: Published in November 1922 this Daily Mail *picture showed 'how the women law students who are being called to the Bar will be dressed'.*
BELOW: An office scene from the early 1920s.

1922 POSTSCRIPTS

● Rose Witcop, a socialist and women's rights campaigner, was prosecuted and found guilty of producing an obscene work when she published US birth-control pioneer Margaret Sanger's *Family Limitation*.

February – Marie Curie was elected to the French Académie des Sciences.

May – Parliament passed the Separation and Maintenance Orders Bill which ensured that maintenance to a wife and family would be continued even if the husband was in jail. Previously, for some men jail for non-payment of maintenance was seen as an alternative to paying up.

August – Following the first congress of the International Federation of Feminine Athletes a one-day Olympiad for women athletes was held in Paris. Great Britain won with 50 points, USA came second with 31 points and France third with 29.

September – The US Congress passed a bill giving women equal naturalization and citizenship rights to men.

October – Mrs W. H. Felton of Georgia became the first woman Senator in the USA.

MOCKING AT MARRIAGE

To the Editor of the *Daily Mail*:

Women are now taking the place of men in almost every sphere and like the *nouveaux riches* their new interests are intoxicating them and they have not found their true perspective. But the one thing they did stand for – finely and simply – the honour and sanctity of home, has been trodden down more ruthlessly by them than by men.

May Atkinson

Extract from letter to the *Daily Mail*, 23 November 1922

FROM PARIS.

Smart Millinery which will be Worn in the Sunny South of France.

BUSINESS GIRLS AND COLD WEATHER.

"WHAT a miserable, raw morning!" exclaimed Marion as she came into the office. "How I dislike the winter! I suppose I shall get my usual crop of chilblains and be thoroughly unhappy until spring comes again."

There are many business girls who really suffer in winter weather and are quite unable either to work efficiently or to look their best when a severe spell of cold or wet is in progress.

A Doctor's Advice.

The advice recently given by a woman doctor to a business girl of this type may be of assistance to others.

"Get up in good time every morning," advised the doctor, "have a brisk sponge down in hot water, followed by vigorous friction with a rough towel, and one or two simple Swedish exercises. Dress quickly and eat a good warming breakfast at leisure. Then walk part of the way at least to the office so that you arrive in a glow of healthy exercise."

The doctor was also very emphatic about suitable winter clothing for business girls. Rubber-soled brogue shoes, warm stockings, a reliable mackintosh for wet weather, a warm winter coat, and pure wool " undies " she regarded as essentials, with the additional recommendation of woollen gauntlet gloves for girls who suffer from chilblains.

The doctor, in addition, condemned the habit of the " tea and cake " luncheon. She suggested cheese sandwiches and a cup of cocoa; a bowl of good soup followed by a steam pudding, or scrambled egg and a glass of malted milk, as nourishing yet inexpensive luncheon menus. The business girl cannot hope to keep fit in winter time if she does not eat a sufficiency of sustaining food.

Proof Against Chill.

The problem of how to keep warm during office hours has been successfully solved by a business girl who used to suffer from constant chills and chilblains. She kept her hands warm by wearing deep cuffs knitted in rabbit wool.

She wore double brown paper socks in her shoes with some dry mustard sprinkled between the layers, to prevent her feet from becoming chilled.

The business girl needs a brisk walk during her luncheon hour, so as to get the blood well circulating through the body again between her spells of sedentary work. Moreover, she would find great benefit to her health in winter time if she joined a hard court tennis or a Badminton club for regular exercise.

TABLE DECORATION.
A Floating Bulb Garden.

PROCURE some flat pieces of cork, and with a penknife cut out holes big enough to hold snowdrop bulbs. The underside of the bulb must reach the level of the cork, which will touch the surface of the water, when floated in a bowl.

The bulbs should be fairly close together, and when all are inserted in position, grass seed should be thickly scattered on the cork. The bowl in which the cork is floated should be shallow, and if it is intended for the nursery some floating celluloid ducks will make the island of cork still more fascinating.

A piece of charcoal should be added to the water in order to keep it sweet.

An Attractive Choice.

Scillas make a charming floating bulb garden, as do also Chionodoxa, or Glory of the Snow. For a large island, or series of islands, crocuses are attractive. The smaller tulips, if used for a floating garden, are better surrounded by wheat or oats rather than ordinary grass seed.

FRIED CAMEMBERT.

Cut the crust from a Camembert cheese very carefully, and divide the cheese into small triangular portions. Brush over with beaten egg, roll in breadcrumbs, and fry in hot fat in a deep frying pan. Drain on soft paper. Dish on a lace paper on a hot dish, and garnish with fried parsley. Serve hot.

THE small cloche has taken a new lease of life. On the Riviera the small cloche hat of uncommon material and original trimming—if trimmed at all—is one of the necessities of life—or rather, of dress—this season. It is always " just right " for any occasion.

Patchwork Models.

I have seen several delicious patchwork cloche hats which have been made for the Riviera, with bags to match.

A novelty which is likely to be worn a good deal is the little flower-pot hat nearly covered with brilliant embroidery; dangling from either side, completely covering the ears, are flat plaques of jet. One model of this kind accompanied a wonderful black silk-jersey coat which had the hem thickly covered with wool and silk embroideries in vivid colours. It was full knee-length with bishop sleeves caught in at the wrists by black moiré bands, and a black fox skin laid flat—in rug fashion—across the back of the shoulders.

Two Original Designs.

Two Riviera hats are depicted in my sketch. On the left is a pagoda toque of dull gold tissue surmounted with gold ornaments. Baby leopard composes the crown of the other hat, which has a brim of puce and silver glacé taffetas.

MASS CANVASSING.
Election Time Work for Women.

"NUMBERS of women who come to offer their services during the election say they would like to canvass, but that they are too nervous to attempt the work," said a girl who is assisting a woman candidate in one of the constituencies.

"We explain to them that canvassing need not be a *dreadful* ordeal—as they express it—but still a large number declared they could not set out and ' tackle ' electors. We have overcome their difficulties by mass canvassing. This is what we do.

" Union is Strength."

"During the day we go in a party—as many as ten or even twenty of us—some in a car, some on foot, arranging to meet in a street in a poor part of the district, choosing the neighbourhood where a properly organised meeting is to be held in the evening. One of the party is an experienced canvasser, but the rest, for the most part, are making their first acquaintance with election work. We reach the appointed place, and when the whole of the party is together we ring a hand-bell. All the canvassers scatter and go to the various doors in the street and knock while the bell is ringing, and tell the women who open the doors that a short meeting is going to be held then and there, and request them to come to listen.

"Sometimes we get quite a chilly reception for the first few minutes—not even a dog barks at us!—but gradually a window is flung up over there, a door, which was first shut against us, is slowly opened. One by one, attracted by our enthusiastic clatter, women approach the car. We no longer speak to the empty air. We have an audience, which quickly grows bigger and bigger. Men returning to their dinner or tea stop to listen. Our crowd numbers more than fifty.

"In our speech we touch upon points which the candidate for this constituency will deal with in his or her programme.

An Earnest Discussion.

"Enthusiasm is catching. An inexperienced canvasser, emboldened by the interest shown among the audience, engages in an earnest discussion with a voter. Another girl does the same. On the way back several of our helpers recount how they ' found their tongues.'

"Again and again, after such an outing, a girl will tell me that she believes she is a born canvasser; in fact, she is eager to go out after that by herself. The ' bogey ' which she has conjured up has disappeared. She has seen enough to gain confidence and has learnt that the *human touch* is the canvasser's surest asset to success."

Ornaments of Coloured Glass are Fashionable.

NECKLACES, earrings and bracelets of glass are obtainable in really artistic tones. Many of these delightful ornaments come from Russia and China. Sometimes they are in plain colours and blown into intricate forms. Many bangles have a central coloured core of twisted threads, resembling some Venetian glass. Others are combined with metal. Large links of glass form necklaces and bangles.

1923

Divorce on Equal Terms

The 1923 Matrimonial Causes Act granted women the right to divorce their husbands on the same grounds as men could divorce their wives. Eleven years before, in 1912, the Royal Commission on Divorce had recommended that the grounds for divorce should be equal for women and men. The Commission and finally the 1923 Act were the result of pressure against the inequality of the 1857 Matrimonial Causes Act.

Before 1857 divorce could only be granted through a Private Act of Parliament the expense of which meant that it was a recourse only for the very few. The 1857 Act allowed divorce through the law courts but the grounds for divorce were not the same for men and women. A man could divorce his wife for adultery but a woman had to prove not only adultery on her husband's part but also bigamy, desertion, incest or cruelty.

The fact that the 1923 Act still relied on proving the adultery of the other partner meant divorce was still regarded as unacceptable to most people as in order to be divorced you had to have been involved in some way with an immoral act. If neither partner was guilty of adultery but the marriage had simply broken down and they wanted a divorce one or other of the partners would have to furnish evidence of adultery, even if it meant fabricating that evidence.

At the time of the Royal Commission on Divorce less than one in 500 marriages ended in divorce. Divorce was only the remedy of the desperate. Divorcees, whether the 'innocent' party or not, were shunned by society, and indeed barred from the Royal Enclosure at Ascot.

*ABOVE: The eight women MPs returned in the 1923 general election:
(L–R) Dorothea Jewson; Susan Lawrence; Lady Astor;
Mrs Wintringham; the Duchess of Atholl; Mrs Hilton Philipson;
Lady Terrington; Margaret Bondfield.*
*BELOW: Women training at Paddington Recreation Ground for an International
Women's Olympiad.*

1923 POSTSCRIPTS

February – A bill was passed making married women responsible for any crimes they commit in their husbands' presence. Previously husbands were deemed responsible for offences their wives might commit in their presence on the assumption that the wife was coerced by her husband into acting criminally.

March – The actress Sarah Bernhardt died. She had gained a degree of freedom as an actress she would never have achieved had she not gone on the stage. She earned enough money of her own to buy a theatre which she named after herself.

April – The Académie Française, an association of 40 French scholars and writers, admitted its first woman member, Mme Alfred Mortier.

June – Mussolini approved a bill to give Italian women the vote in local elections.

November – Stanley Baldwin, soon to be Prime Minister, stated in an election campaign speech: 'The discrimination between men and women contained in the present franchise cannot be permanent.'

SUCCESS IN GAMES:

The Choice and Care of Implements.

A COMMON error made by girls when taking up a sport in which they are quite inexperienced is to choose a heavy implement in the belief that it will enable them to hit with great power.

It sometimes happens that the weight stamped on rackets, billiard cues, and so on, is not always accurate. In any case balance is far more important than nominal or actual weight, though a woman should not choose a lawn tennis racket which exceeds 14oz.—many experts would say 13½oz., or even less—and a billiard cue not more than 15oz. Hockey sticks vary in weight with the player's position. A range of from 18oz. to 22oz. or 23oz. should suffice.

An ill-balanced implement usually proclaims itself, but a racket or cue may be tested by placing it across a finger or other suitable "edge." The racket should balance at a point between 13in. and 13½in. from the end of the handle, and the cue, about the points of splicing.

Instinctive Judgment.

Closely allied to balance is the "feel" of the implement. Do not be in a hurry to make your choice. Keep on trying different samples until you pick up one that somehow or other you *feel* is the one for you. In nine cases out of ten this instinctive judgment will prove correct, but there is a tenth case. Out of a dozen, or, for that matter, fifty bats, rackets, clubs, identical in make and dimensions, perhaps only one will have a "soul." Instinct will generally detect this invaluable quality, but sometimes it takes actual play to reveal its presence or absence.

Unbleached, undyed gut is the strongest. Usually grain should be regular and neither very close nor open, but much depends on the nature of the wood.

One turns now to a few necessary general hints on the care of your new bat or whatever it may be. Pure linseed oil is the best lubricant. This must be used sparingly and well rubbed in.

Among various implements the cricket bat needs oiling most, and more so than ever owing to the fashion of white blades, which are white merely because contrary to former practice they are not oiled while seasoning. Some cricketers favour castor oil.

When Not to Use Oil.

Oil should never be applied to racket frames. Whether it be used for golf club shafts is debatable. Certainly a new club does not need oiling, but probably the "veteran" will be none the worse for an occasional rub with an oily rag.

A hockey stick will bear oiling once a week, or twice if the grain be wide, but oil must not be applied to the binding.

Oil is the best preventive of rust. Anything that has got wet must be carefully dried before oiling, for oil keeps water in as well as out.

A head cover and press are, of course, essential for the well-being of a racket not in use and its strings should be treated with gut preservative.

Many implements, especially rackets, are ruined by being strapped to bags when travelling. Never leave any "tool" leaning against a wall or table. It should lie flat or be kept in a suitable rack or stand. Damp, extremes of heat or cold must be avoided.

A new implement should be used lightly and sparingly until it has had time to acclimatise itself and settle down. This precaution is absolutely essential in the case of ivory billiards balls, which should be left untouched in their box for two or three weeks after being brought into the billiards room.

MILLINERY CONTRASTS.

Small and Wide Brims.

THE best of the new hats run to extremes; they are either very small or very large. The cloche outline remains practically the same, but the narrow brim is given a coquettish twist that suggests something quite new without doing away with a popular favourite.

This coming summer 1880 hats are going to be immensely popular. They will be worn with fitted coat-dresses and with tube-frocks. These hats have very high crowns and very narrow brims—the latter curled up at the sides.

Hat strings are coming into fashion

ROSE CAKES.

INGREDIENTS.—Genoese pastry or sandwich-cake mixture, 4oz. of almond paste, pistachio nuts, carmine or cochineal, apricot jam.

METHOD.—Just before baking the cakes, colour the mixture pink with cochineal. Bake in shallow tins lined with greased paper. When cooked turn on to a sieve to cool. When cold stamp into rounds with a two-inch cutter. Roll out the almond paste, which must be pink, and cut it into small rounds about the size of a sixpence. Rub the jam through a hair sieve and paint it over the top of the cakes. Place the rounds of almond paste round the edge of each cake just overlapping each other, press them down in the centre with the point of a wooden skewer, place a second row of almond paste "petals" inside the first one, and in the centre place a piece of skinned pistachio nut.

again; chin-straps are already with us; some are made of lace, some of velvet.

Fascinating mask-veils are shown on many of the best models—large and small hats alike. The latest mask-veil just clears the tip of the nose and then spreads out into wings at either side; it is a clever combination of two favourites—the mask veil and the floating veil.

Hiding the Hair.

We have a wide choice as regards the size, shape, material, and trimming of our new spring hats; in the manner of wearing them we have no choice at all. Large, medium, or small, they must be pressed down on the head to cover the brows and the hair; to this rule there is no exception. VILLIERS, Paris.

From Paris.

A charming summer hat of almond green rice straw trimmed with silver tissue ribbon.

A FLOWER WEATHER BALL.

A FLORAL weather ball which pleases children and is also quite a good indicator of conditions can be made with a small rounded sponge to which is tied a piece of string so that it can be suspended. A number of dandelion flowers should be gathered, choosing those that have newly opened. Nip the stalks from the flowers, leaving only about an inch. Then make the sponge damp and push the stalks of the blooms into the holes in the sponge. Put in as many dandelions as possible until the sponge is practically covered.

Hang up the "ball" in a room, and the dandelions will open when the weather is likely to be fine and close at the coming of rain. If the sponge is kept damp the flowers will last for a week at least. It is to be noted that the dandelions will close, of course, at nightfall no matter what the weather may be and must not then be regarded as indicating coming rain.

THE HOUSEHOLD ORGANISER.

EVERYONE learns by experience, if not by her own, then by taking advantage of someone else's. Various women have realised this and made it their profession to place their experience and common sense at the disposal of others.

A New Profession.

One of the latest developments in this line is the expert household organiser—a woman who from actual experience knows all there is to know on household matters and is anxious to use her knowledge for the benefit of others as well as herself. She will entirely organise a

Do You Know—

That when you wish to boil an egg that has a crack or a hole in it you can keep the contents from coming out in this way? Turn the egg over and exactly opposite the first hole make another one. Then, at once, put the egg into the boiling water. None of the contents will emerge, because, with the two holes, the pressure on the egg is equalised.

home—find it, furnish it and staff it, or she will reorganise the running of a house and place it on a practical, "smooth-sailing" basis. She will give advice in the apportionment of incomes, and recently, for a young couple who were getting married on an income of £500 a year, she secured a flat for a moderate rental, completely furnished it, and started the youthful housewife in the straight and narrow way of successful housekeeping.

Then she undertakes to arrange entertainments of every kind, to draw up menus, and to give advice on all questions of catering. Women living in the country find her a "friend in need," and she executes monthly shopping orders for a small annual fee. She is surely a pioneer in a profession which should offer splendid opportunities to the woman who possesses the necessary qualifications.

1924

Dying to Give Birth

Three thousand women died in childbirth in 1924. To give birth to a child was four times more dangerous than for a man to work down a mine, the most dangerous job of the period. Countless other women were disabled or damaged by the process of giving birth or from the infections which spread through the increasingly commonly used maternity wards.

Following concern at the poor stock of the nation's manhood and the high infant mortality rates which deprived the state of fit soldiers during the Boer War at the turn of the century, efforts were made to cut the infant death rate. In 1900 for every thousand babies registered alive there were 154 which were stillborn or died soon after birth. By 1919 when the Maternal and Child Welfare Act came into force and the Ministry of Health was set up the infant mortality rate had been cut by 42 per cent to 89 deaths per thousand live births. In the same period of time the reduction in the maternal death rate was less than 25 per cent.

It was again a war which prompted the government into action to try to improve women's health generally and reduce the cost, in terms of death and disablement, of childbirth. The need for women workers in wartime showed that women's health, and that of working-class women in particular, was in a poor state. The Maternal and Child Welfare Act was passed partly in response to these findings and partly in respect of the fact that a proportion of women were now voters. Prior to 1919 there was no statutory requirement to provide education, supervision or medical care for a woman during pregnancy or childbirth.

The Act, however, made few inroads into maternal mortality. In 1929 the number of women dying in childbirth was still 2,787. Much of the reason for the failure to lower these figures was probably because there was an increasing tendency to encourage women to have their babies in hospital. Even though the reason for more hospital births was because of the appallingly unhygienic state of housing for many mothers, the risk of infection and puerperal fever was much higher in hospital as it would spread from one mother to the next if extremely rigorous disinfection procedures were not followed. The fact that obstetrics and gynaecology were looked down upon even by the medical profession itself meant there was a serious shortage of doctors with any training or experience in these areas which further hampered efforts to reduce the maternal mortality rate.

ABOVE: Ethel Muckelt, a British Olympic skater.
BELOW: Wales versus England in an international hockey match at Merton Abbey.

1924 POSTSCRIPTS

January – The first Winter Olympics were held at Chamonix – but women were only allowed to compete in figure-skating events.

February – A bill to give all women the vote at 21 was given a second reading but this bill was never to become law.

THE SUBJECTION OF MEN

. . . though we may doubt if at any date married women were really treated as slaves or chattels by the British husband.

Since then a whole host of Acts of Parliament has removed woman's real or fancied disabilities, she has obtained the vote, and she is shortly to receive it on the same terms as men, which means that as she preponderates in numbers she will gradually dominate the electorate. Women have the right to sit in the House of Commons. They can practise at the Bar, and as solicitors, as doctors, as surgeons. They may act as Justices of the Peace. They can take university degrees at most of our universities, including Oxford, though not yet at Cambridge. What is more they appear to be dominating certain of the English Universities . . .

If there are disabilities in marriage today they attach to the mere male. The unfortunate husband can be sued if his wife is guilty of slander, libel or assault. He has to pay the penalty, and according to an excellent legal authority, it is doubtful whether he has any remedy against his wife's property. Divorce is now to be obtained by either sex on identical grounds. The subjection of women has certainly passed for ever, and it seems almost as if the subjection of men might be beginning.

Extracts from a *Daily Mail* Leader, 17 June 1924

Furniture for Modern Needs.

"OUR clients often suggest new designs for furniture," said a salesman at a large store where original and practical pieces are often to be found. "People give orders for certain furniture to be made to fit a special purpose, and as it works out cheaper for our clients we have several pieces made at one time, putting the rest into stock."

That was probably how a delightful oak bedroom chest was made. Unlike the ordinary chest, which is merely a box inconveniently deep for everyday use, it is made with two small top drawers and a long lower one. In small bedrooms there is often space to spare in the middle of the room at the end of the bed, and this is where the chest is kept, or it can be put under a window with a loose cushion on it to form a seat.

To Save Space.

Most modern designs in furniture are influenced by space-saving ideas. A delightfully commodious and compact bedside table, for instance, made in walnut and on cabriole legs, has three little drawers one over the other, and the hinged sides let down. When closed in this way it takes very little room, and when open it affords generous accommodation for a breakfast tray, books, and so on.

Corner wardrobes in mahogany and walnut are now being used a good deal in small bedrooms, and it is becoming usual for a bedroom suite not to include a washstand. Tallboys are increasingly used because, on account of being double the height of an ordinary chest, they hold twice as much. They are now made in white enamelled wood for nurseries. A piece of furniture which is nowadays much in demand is the chest of drawers with a millinery cupboard on the top.

Very convenient is the cheval glass which has been revived of recent years. But the original design is too wide to find a place in many modern bedrooms, so it is being made in walnut with a narrow panel mirror such as is generally used for hanging on the wall.

For the Business Woman.

The up-to-date woman's writing table has accommodation for a typewriter. One of the most interesting pieces of furniture exhibited in the British section of the Paris Exhibition is a writing-table specially designed by a well-known architect for his wife. It is in gilded mahogany with an ebony top.

A typical modern addition to the comfort of a room, especially at this season, is a pouf stool, which has now developed into a definite piece of furniture by being raised on an oval or square lacquered stand.

Coat of Blue Velour and Squirrel Fur.

Parisian dressmakers are using huge cuffs and very wide hems of fur on the new winter wraps.

Clifford

Women and Wireless.

By N. W. Fraser.

ALTHOUGH women are deeply interested in wireless and form the majority of this country's listeners-in, it must be admitted that their contributions to wireless progress have so far been unimportant. This at least appears to be true of the inventive, scientific, and engineering sides, and the Wireless Exhibition, held last week at the Royal Horticultural Hall, did not reveal any discoveries or improvements due to feminine research and ingenuity.

Opening for Lecturers.

Many women are finding careers of one kind or another in wireless as entertainers, accompanists, speakers, and lecturers. There are openings as lecturers for women possessed of expert knowledge of matters of particular interest to their sex. The field, however, is somewhat restricted by the fact that women's voices are generally inferior to men's for broadcasting purposes, although, as a broadcasting official pointed out recently, this may be the fault of the microphone, not of women's vocal organs.

Working for the microphone, however, is usually a temporary and part-time occupation. Apart from clerical work women hold whole-time posts as chief organisers and organisers under the British Broadcasting Company, but at present there are practically no vacancies.

The Chief Organiser.

At every B.B.C. centre there is a chief woman organiser, Mrs. Fitzgerald being chief organiser for London and also exercising general supervision over all provincial women chief organisers. The duties of a chief organiser vary with the importance of her station, but in every case she is directly responsible for the "Afternoon Talk," originally known as the "Woman's Hour." At a large centre she supervises the "Children's Hour," as well as the "Afternoon Talk," and she may also have to act as accompanist.

The main qualifications for a chief organiser, apart from organising gifts, are a good education, a suitable voice, and musical ability. Organisers are salaried, but just now there are many more candidates than vacancies. At the same time wireless is always developing and fresh centres springing up.

There is no official bar to a woman's obtaining the Postmaster-General's certificate of proficiency as operator or watcher as required by the Merchant Shipping (Wireless Telegraphy) Act of 1919, but no woman has yet been appointed as wireless telegraphist or watcher on board ship.

CABBAGE AS AN ENTREE.

SAVOY SCALLOPS

One medium-sized savoy, 3oz. of rice, 2oz. of margarine, salt, pepper, ¼ of a nutmeg, grated, 1 gill of stock, 3oz. of grated cheese. Wash the rice in several waters, slice the cabbage into fine shreds, remove all stalk, wash and drain. Put the rice and cabbage into a pan of boiling salted water and simmer for one hour. Strain. Melt the margarine in a pan, add the rice, cabbage, salt, pepper, and nutmeg. Stir over the fire for ten minutes, but do not brown. Add the stock and simmer gently until quite soft. Fill some greased scallop shells with the mixture, sprinkle with the grated cheese, put a few pieces of margarine here and there over the top, and brown under a griller or in the oven. Serve hot.

CABBAGE A LA BOURGEOISE.

One medium-sized savoy, veal forcemeat, stock, 1 onion, 1 carrot, a bunch of herbs (parsley, thyme, marjoram, and a bay leaf tied together), salt, pepper.

Remove all outside leaves from the cabbage and wash well. Boil in salted water for 15 minutes. Drain and put into cold water. When cold, drain and squeeze dry in a cloth. Open the leaves carefully and put a little veal forcemeat between each. Tie up with tape, put the cabbage into a pan or casserole with enough stock to cover, add the herbs, carrot, and onion, peeled and sliced, and simmer gently until tender. Lift up the cabbage, strain, remove the tape, cut the cabbage in half, place on a hot dish, and keep warm. Thicken the liquor in the pan with an ounce of flour, boil well, add a few drops of browning if too pale, then strain over the cabbage.

ABOUT THE NEW BOOKS.

THE DANCER'S CAT. C. A. Nicholson. (Holden, 7s. 6d.)

A clever study in contrasts. The Russian dancer is the exact antithesis of Lady Glenforsa, her future mother-in-law. One stands for art and freedom and class friendship, and the other for class distinction and the old order of things. Even good will and good breeding could not bridge the gap.

SIMON THE COLDHEART. Georgette Heyer. (Heinemann, 7s. 6d.)

A well-written and most interesting tale of mediæval England. Simon's choice fell on a lady as brave as himself, and untamed and imperious to boot, and his wooing began characteristically—at the point of the sword.

THE NOSE OF PAPA HILAIRE. Kenneth Macnichol. (Blackwood, 7s. 6d.)

A series of short stories as told by a little French journalist. They are well written, and to each has been given an original twist which makes for entertainment.

FAME. Micheline Keating. (Putnam, 7s. 6d.)

The authoress was only eighteen when she finished this story of a great actress, who rose from the gutter, and her daughter who eclipsed her triumphs. At times the hand of the novice can be detected, but most of the writing is so mature in conception and reflection that it is difficult to believe there are so few years behind it.

THE LOVE RACK. Cecil Roberts. (Heinemann, 7s. 6d.)

Tortured by the fear that she may lose his love, Madame Fauvette conceals from her son the unhappy secret of his birth. The mother's devotion and the boy's rise to fame as a violinist lead to situations which are forcefully handled.

1925

Custody of the Children

In 1839 an Infant Custody Act was passed which for the first time gave mothers some rights of custody over their children under seven. The courts could grant custody to the mother if the Lord Chancellor agreed and only if the woman was judged to be of good character. Despite these restrictions it was a major step forward and almost entirely due to the efforts of one woman.

Early in the nineteenth century Caroline Norton's alcoholic husband deserted her and took their three children with him. He then denied his wife access to the children, not even allowing her to see one of the children as it was dying. Caroline Norton had no recourse to the law as the law assumed that the father alone had rights over his children. Caroline Norton fought on to have the law changed even though by the time the changes came one child was dead and the others were too old for her to benefit.

A further law in 1886 again eroded some of the automatic rights of fathers to custody of their children. The Act stated that the welfare of the children should be taken into consideration when deciding on custody. It also allowed for a mother to become a child's sole guardian or to be joint guardian with a partner of the father's choice when the father died.

It was not until 1925 when the Guardianship of Infants Act was passed that the law gave fathers and mothers equal rights over their children. So, for example, a minor who wished to marry would require the consent of both parents when they were living together. When the parents were separated or divorced, consent went with custody and mothers were entitled to be considered equally with fathers for custody.

ABOVE: *Josephine Baker. In 1925 she was the talk of Paris for her performances at the Folies Bergère. She became a member of the French Resistance during the Second World War. After the war she and her French husband adopted a number of children from all over the world which she called her 'Rainbow Family'. She also had a long and highly praised career as an entertainer.*
BELOW: *Miriam Ferguson reading her inaugural address.*

1925 POSTSCRIPTS

● The Widows, Orphans and Old Age Pensions Contributory Act was passed giving widows a pension of 10s a week from January 1926.
January – After her election in November 1924 as Governor of Texas 'Ma' Miriam Ferguson was sworn in as the first woman State Governor in the USA.
March – Universal suffrage was granted to men in Japan.

AIR WOMEN.

Feminine Traveller Who Slept Above the Baltic and Wrote Letter over the Channel.

WOMEN who travel a good deal—particularly those rather lonely figures who spend half their lives flitting from one hotel to another over the breadth of Europe—are taking to the air assiduously as a means of flitting more quickly and easily. Equally important, it gives them, for the first time or two at any rate, a new thrill.

For air travel to-day is unquestionably the simplest and least worrying means of travel for women who move about alone. No scramble or arguments with Customs officers at the *douanes*, no hectic searchings for or skirmishes with Continental porters. Instead of this milady becomes an individual traveller.

Difficulties Smoothed Out.

If she has made a trip of any considerable length the aerodrome officials meet her with a "And has madame had a good trip. . ." Frequently they know her name beforehand as well. She is led, almost by the hand, to the Customs and the passport office; her luggage moves about, almost magically, to exactly where it ought to be. Naturally she has to pay considerably more for these privileges and pleasantries.

A few days ago I flew from Copenhagen to London and all along that 10-hours trip there were as many women passengers as men. Most of them, I found, were women travelling alone.

Indifferent to the Panorama of the Baltic.

There were two American women from Copenhagen to Hamburg, hardened air travellers they must have been, for they read and slept steadily without troubling to glance at the Baltic panorama below.

A little Frenchwoman hopped in at Hamburg, hopped out at Amsterdam, and into the Paris express waiting for her a few yards away. She might have been changing at Charing Cross for the Hampstead line—only that probably would have given her a deal more trouble.

Better Air Travellers than Men.

Women, air officials say, are generally better air travellers than men. That may be because they try to amuse themselves so much more on the journey.

The American woman who had read over the Baltic that lovely morning was writing a letter as we flew Londonwards over the Channel the same afternoon!

St. J. W.

SERIAL.

HARVEY GARRARD'S CRIME.

By E. Phillips Oppenheim.

CHAPTER XXX.—Continued.

"I DON'T want to seem unreasonable," Fardale assured her, "but for heaven's sake, Mildred, don't carry this aloofness too far. It's getting worse with you. I haven't had even the iciest little kiss for more than a week. There are limits to this stand-off sort of business, you know."

She patted his hand. Even her fingers seemed to him very cold.

"My dear man," she reminded him, "the limit is about three weeks."

Then came the morning when the long-waited-for telegram arrived. She sat up in bed and opened it and read it word for word while her maid deftly arranged the coffee equipage by the side of the bed. It was handed in at London on the previous day:

I have received your very amazing letter and refrain from any comment under the circumstances. Owing extra

Fashions About Town.

Between-seasons Display in the Shops Colours and Fabrics for the Autumn.

BECAUSE this is "between seasons" in the shops there is naturally a great contrast in the window contents. In one, for instance, the sun shines upon a galaxy of summer frocks; in the next an array of felt and velour hats reminds one that the days of summer are numbered; while in a third, model evening cloaks in gorgeous tissues with fur trimming again emphasise the approach of autumn.

At a well-known store in Regent-street new fabrics in silk and tissue are arriving.

"Mulberry, wine, navy blue, grey, and soft shades of green will be among the most popular colours in the coming season," said the buyer.

Velvet that Does Not Show Creases.

"Tissues and velvets will be much favoured. We are stocking a special couché velvet. This is one in which the pile is not quite straight, and, in consequence, does not show crease marks easily."

Another novelty in this store concerns a double border tinsel which makes up very effectively in coats and cloaks, the border trimming the hem, cuffs, and collar.

An Uncommon Suit for the Autumn.

As always, Miss Isabel Jeans has pretty clothes in the new play at the Queen's, "The Way You Look At It." An outdoor suit, suitable for smart autumn wear, consists of short coat and skirt of elephant-grey velveteen, with casaquin blouse of crêpe de Chine, the little velvet hat being upturned with rust colour and having "flue brushes" of shaded rust plumage at the right side.

Spotted designs have been triumphant this summer and here is a model, which could be quickly put together, using an ivory foulard spotted in tea-tint. Rows of tea-tinted lace, of which there are heavy stocks in the shops just now, are placed between two bands of tea-tinted crêpe de Chine.

In the Shops.

OLD Dutch tiles are much liked for use as tea and coffee stands on polished tables. Tiles there are, too, in hand-made pottery in delightful designs and colours, and lined with heavy felt to prevent scratching polished furniture.

. . . .

Bath mats are made of red rubber, like sponges, and are very strong and comfortable to use. They are mounted on sheets of thick rubber, and have bands and ornamentations of black, white, and primrose colour.

. . . .

Much interest is being taken in an electric refrigerator that dispenses with the use of ice—with its consequent melting and dampness—and works on the principle of dry cold, the temperature of the air within the food-safe being reduced to freezing point, or below. The working is automatic, so that when the desired temperature is reached the electric current is cut off, being switched on again automatically should the temperature rise. Cubes of ice can be made by placing in the refrigerator a vessel on the style of a cake-tin divided into several little compartments.

Fruits which Combine Well for Jam.

APART from a few very old-established favourites such as fig and rhubarb, raspberry and red currant, blackberry and apple, and plum and apple, Englishwomen have not experimented much with mixed-fruit jams until comparatively recent years.

The juiciness of gooseberries goes well with red currants. Gooseberry and strawberry jam I had at a wayside inn when motoring the other afternoon and it was delicious.

The definite flavour of orange and ginger are great assets to rhubarb, heavy crops of which housewives often want to use. A rhubarb jam is, moreover, a good store jam, especially where there is a family of children. W.

FRUITS.	QUANTITIES.
Apple and blackberry, or elderberry, or plum, or damson.	Equal quantities fruits. ¾lb. sugar, ½ pint water to each lb. of mixed fruits.
Apple and lemon.	1 lemon to 1½lb apples. ¾lb. sugar, ½ gill water to each lb. of apples.
Apple and rhubarb.	½lb. rhubarb, ¾lb sugar, 1 gill water to each lb. of apples.
Melon or marrow with blackberry, or elderberry, or plum, or damson.	To each lb. melon or marrow, ½lb. of blackberries, elderberries, plums or damsons, with ¾lb. sugar to each lb. fruit. Rind of 1 lemon and juice of two to each 6lb. fruit.
Melon or marrow and pineapple.	Equal quantities of fruits. ¾lb. sugar. 1 lemon to each lb. of fruit.
Melon or marrow and lemon.	See apple and lemon
Rhubarb and green fig.	Equal quantities of fruits. ¾lb. sugar, ½ pint water, 1oz. of seed pearl tapioca to each 1lb. of fruit.
Rhubarb and date.	½lb. stoned dates to 1lb. rhubarb. ¾lb. sugar, ½ lemon to each lb. of fruit.
Quince and apple.	1lb. apples to each pint of quince pulp, ½ pint water to each lb. quince when stewing them. ¾lb. sugar to each lb. of fruit.
Gooseberry and raspberry.	½lb. of gooseberries to 1lb. of raspberries. ¾lb. sugar to each lb. of fruit.

Quaint and Colourful China.

"OH! what darlings," exclaimed a woman in the china department of a West End store. She was looking at a condiment set of brilliant yellow china ducklings which, to judge by their lack of good looks, might have been closely related to the Ugly Duckling —before its transformation—immortalised in the well-known children's story.

The Ugly Duckling's Confederates.

At the moment there is a decided vogue for quaint and colourful china. The more absurd in appearance the more certain it is of success both for ornament and utilitarian purposes.

"There is a big demand for these animal condiment sets," said a salesman. "Most of them are intended for use in the nursery." Grown-ups, however, admire them as much as the younger generation! The three rabbits illustrated on this page, for instance, are for salt, mustard, and pepper. On the salt container the ear of one of them acts as a handle.

For the luncheon table of older folk are salt and pepper containers in china

Animal Condiment Sets for the Nursery.

representing squatting Chinamen. The condiments are sprinkled through their perforated hats.

China Imitating Lacquer.

"Lustre ware is as popular as ever," said the salesman, "and another best-seller is china, coloured scarlet and gold which imitates Chinese lacquer. This is so brilliant that it is most effective used sparingly. Most customers like to have just one piece to give a note of colour to the room."

Fruit designs predominate in dinner, tea, and coffee sets. "All these are made by different British manufacturers," said the salesman, indicating a number of services, "but each one has introduced fruit in his design."

For Breakfast Out-of-Doors.

Tea-cosy and egg-cosies are covered in orange linen to match the china marmalade pot fashioned in the style of an orange. The buff cloth is checked in orange.

1926

Women and the Trade Unions

In 1926 there were around three million women working in industry. For men industry was the most strongly unionized area of the economy but for women the unions brought little advantage. Only in the textile industry, which had a long tradition of unionized women workers, did the trade unions offer any positive support to women. Most other trade unions discriminated against women, many even banning them from membership. Mary McArthur had founded the National Federation of Women Workers in 1906 to fight for better pay and conditions for women workers but inevitably the male unions within particular industries were far stronger and better organized.

Pay was the issue which most affected the unions' treatment of women workers. There was also an underlying feeling that women should be at home. That it was legal, and in fact accepted, that women would be paid less than men drove the unions and their male leaders to fight, not for equal pay for women, but to exclude women from as many jobs as they could. They campaigned for restrictions on women's working hours, often classing them in the same category as children. This was not just in Britain but throughout the world – in 1919 the USA brought in legislation banning women and 'young persons' from night work.

Arthur Pugh, President of the TUC in 1926, estimated that of the five and three-quarter million women in work only one-sixth were in a trade union. The attitude of male trade unionists was responsible in large part for this but many women were in jobs which were difficult to unionize. As unemployment began to bite, domestic service, still one of the main sources of work for women, was the only area of the economy to show an increase in workers. But it was difficult to organize domestic workers who often depended upon their employers for accommodation and food as well as wages, were based on widely scattered sites and had little time or opportunity to meet each other.

Women workers suffered greatly during the rising unemployment of the 1920s and '30s. Many had been removed from their jobs at the end or soon after the end of the war in order to give work to returning soldiers – an agreement negotiated between employers, unions and government. The postwar economy failed to produce jobs for the many women seeking employment. And despite the fact that women were cheaper labour than men, when jobs were cut women were often the first to go in the belief that men as breadwinners should have any remaining jobs.

ABOVE: Gertrude Ederle prepares for her attempt to swim the Channel. BELOW: Eton crops, very short hair, were the vogue of 1926. The style complemented the very 'mannish' style of dress.

1926 POSTSCRIPTS

● The Legitimacy Act was passed making a child legitimate if its parents married after its birth. Previously an illegitimate child was illegitimate for life – its status could not be changed. But the Act did not allow for children born as a result of adultery to be legitimized.

May – Women in India became eligible to stand for election to public office.

● The General Strike began and many women volunteered to help run essential services.

August – Gertrude Ederle, a 19-year-old Bronze Medal winner in the 1924 Paris Olympics became the first woman to swim the English Channel. Her time of 14 hrs 31 mins was two hours quicker than the previous record.

RADIOGRAPH SILHOUETTES

Slimness More to be Desired than Sunburn – Wispy Women who Keep on the Fashionable Side of Nine Stone – A Standard Outline for all Nationalities – Deauville.

Like a radiograph is the silhouette of the lovely women and girls now in Deauville. Their flimsy, exquisitely made frocks seem to contain only a shadow of a human form. How they have managed so entirely to standardize themselves is a mystery, for they are all outlined in the same pattern: French, English, Italian, Spanish, whatever the race, they all conform to the tyranny of fashion. And fashion absolutely refuses to countenance any plump, round contours.
Daily Mail, 20 August 1926

HOW OTHER WOMEN RUN THEIR HOMES.

Miss Radclyffe Hall, the Novelist, makes hers a recreation.

Miss Radclyffe Hall, author of "Adam's Breed," "The Forge," "The Unlit Lamp," and other writings.

"I LOVE my house," said Miss Radclyffe Hall. "My home is my hobby."

Coming from this business-like woman in tweeds and polo collar, with her fair Eton-cropped hair brushed straight back from her forehead, this was a surprising statement. We sat in her Spartan little study in the house in Kensington, which this year's Femina prize-winner shares with Una Lady Troubridge. There seemed to be nothing in the room but books and files. The very papers on the desk were meticulously ordered.

A Perfect Mania.

"Lady Troubridge sees to the food. I am not really interested in that side of housekeeping. There are various special dishes mentioned in 'Adam's Breed,' but I acquired that knowledge through my visits to Soho restaurants. My province is the house itself. I am a fussy housekeeper with a perfect mania for cleanliness.

When the "Seeing Eye" has to be Controlled.

"Except for feeding my dogs I have no routine. I often write for twelve hours at a stretch. If during that time I spy specks of dust I have to control my itch to remove them, for I have the housewife's 'seeing eye.' After that my housework comes as a relaxation. But I cannot let the house run itself—I must supervise it personally and do my accustomed 'chores.'"

We wandered through the rooms. I noticed that there were no mantelpieces, the gas fires being set into Old English red brick hearths.

"The only alteration I made in the house when I took it," said Miss Radclyffe Hall, "was to rip out all the mantelpieces. I dislike them almost as much as I do washstands. You see, there are none of these either—I prefer bathrooms.

Flowers Everywhere but in the Study.

"Flowers, though I never allow them in my study, are a pet extravagance of mine for the house, and I like to arrange them myself to tone in colour with the rooms. When I lived in the country, I worked a lot in my rose-garden. Here, of course. I have to buy my roses—and very expensive they are!"

The drawing-room walls were a rich glowing yellow, which set off to perfection the beautiful old oak furniture.

A Good Mural Colour.

"I think yellow is the best colour for walls," Miss Radclyffe Hall explained, "it's so warm and sunshiny. As for the oak. I have been collecting it for years. London, I find, is the best hunting ground. The English villages, which are mostly planted out by dealers, are the worst.

Polishing to Work Off a Jarred Feeling.

"The care of my treasures is the greatest of my household joys. The housemaid is allowed to help—only when she has been with me some time! And when I feel jarred and disgruntled, I work it off in a bout of polishing. "This I do with beeswax and turpentine, or with a made-up polish which I know does not darken the wood. For, of course, the value of old oak lies in its colour."

We were now in the dressing-room, where there was a toilet-table of that ashen grey tone cherished by collectors.

"'It ought to look like this,' she said, fingering the worn wood lovingly. "This other piece"—indicating a wardrobe—"has been made too dark and shiny by the wrong sort of polish."

In one of the bedrooms was Miss Radclyffe Hall's special pride—two beds of an early period with lovely linenfold panelling. At the foot of these stood a useful old German muniment chest, a boon in a small house for storing linen. Like every bit of oak in the house—which is almost entirely furnished with it—the great chest had been kept in excellent condition by its appreciative owner.

When the House Becomes a Vamp.

"Yes, I give a lot of time to my house." Miss Radclyffe Hall admitted, "but I never let it interfere with my writing. The minute my house begins to 'vamp' me—houses do become vampires sometimes—I run away from it. Somehow the household arrangements of an hotel don't clamour for my attention: that happens only in my own home.

"But it is seldom that my career and my home come into conflict. I usually manage to run them together."

HOUSEWIVES PREPARE FOR SUMMER.

Garden Furnishings and Labour-saving Devices are Chief Purchases at the Stores.

THE London shops are gay with brightly hued hammocks, picturesque sun umbrellas, beach mattresses upholstered in highly floral cretonnes, prettily painted garden furniture and other oddments with which we do "homage to the sun."

The sketch above shows a work-bag cushion, softly padded and made basket shaped, after the fashion of the familiar travelling-bag cushion. The basket part is sufficiently big to take a piece of needlework, newspaper, or a book which may be required in the garden or on the beach. It is in natural colour with stencilled design.

A semi-circular cushion, which is of striped pink, green and orange raffia, is a comfortable shape for putting under the head of a child when lying on grass or sand.

Raffia mats for the use of older people, or for those who fear rheumatism, are made in many styles and shapes. That above is in rug fashion, and being of grass-green raffia looks well in conservatory or on verandah.

To Keep the House Clean.

Although the spring cleaning season is drawing to a close, the labour-saving devices are still selling well. Women who had not such devices with which to do their cleaning are buying them now to facilitate their houses remaining clean.

At a well-known furnishing store in Oxford-street there is a special display of cleaning apparatus and kitchen and bathroom furnishings.

An electric vacuum cleaner which has been on the market only about a month interested me. It weighs only 10lb. and has a fixture which can be used to dry the hair after a shampoo and also will take the place of an electric fan for cooling a room.

"In one month the sales of this cleaner have averaged three months' sales of an older model," I was told.

Refrigerators, too, are selling well since the spell of hot weather. One model which is very popular can be worked by gas, electricity, or acetylene, so can be used by housewives in the parts of the country where there is no gas or electricity.

Fitments in a British Kitchen Cabinet.

A kitchen cabinet of British make which is having increasing sales dispenses with lids for the glass jars. There is a fixture which falls down on to the jars, keeping them airtight and therefore dust-proof. The porcelain ledge which acts as a table can also be used as an ironing board. The glass drawers for cereals have rounded corners, so the cereals do not adhere anywhere.

Apparatus for softening water is now very simple to manipulate, and some types are small enough to carry when travelling. With a water-softening apparatus displayed at this store, experiments have proved that it is necessary to use but a quarter the amount of soap used with hard water.

For the Garden.

"We are selling hundreds of garden cushions," said a salesman. Effective sets are cushions of casement cloth with sunshades to match.

Very amusing are beach bags of coloured towelling, finished with a doll's head at the top and her feet protruding from the base. The bags are very roomy, and will easily carry a bathing suit, shoes, and towel.

To Save Noise and Scratches.

Those who dislike unnecessary noise and clatter in their home will be interested in the rubber rims now being sold to fit on pails, jugs, coal-scuttles, bowls

and other household apparatus with or without a rim. These "protections" are of double flexible rubber, and save scratches on linoleum and polished and tiled floors.

When Making Up Parcels.

Everyone has experienced at some time or other the irritation of searching for scissors or knife with which to cut string. A solid metal gadget is intended to eliminate this, as the string is held across the top and pulled firmly down. It is a good plan to keep a box fitted with labels, both stick-on and tie-on, string, sealing-wax, and brown paper in some place such as a table drawer in the hall, where all members of the family will find it readily accessible when parcelling up is to be done.

How to Wind Wool.

When I was given the latest edition of "Woolcraft" (Patons & Baldwins, Ltd., price 6d.) I was told that no fewer than 2,000,000 copies of it have already been sold and the new edition consists of another quarter of a million.

Here are some hints from it:

"Wool should never be wound into a hard ball, as this takes away its nature, making it thin and poor. Wind loosely over three or four fingers, withdrawing the latter at frequent intervals so as to change the position of the ball and keep it symmetrical. Wool wound in this manner will retain its soft fulness."

Washing and Types of Knitting.

"Garments which have been knitted or crocheted too loosely are particularly liable to stretch. On the other hand, fabric which has been too tightly knitted is likely to felt in the washing, and especially so if subjected to rubbing. Never attempt to shrink the yarn before knitting. There is great risk in so doing of loosening the dye and taking the nature out of the yarn, while the possible advantages in the case of good wool, well manufactured, is practically nil."

A baby's bonnet, boy's cap, a shoulder circular bed wrap, cardigans, bootees and baby's mittens, and various kinds of socks are among the many "recipes" given in this handy publication.

The Housekeeping Expert.

Begin This New Serial To-day.

THE FORGER

By Edgar Wallace.

you? I want to speak to you very privately."

He left Jane momentarily bewildered. herself, have said, "How odd!" of an earthquake.

He made no other comment upon her

1927

The Changing Shape of Women

By the mid–1920s women were wearing clothes undreamt of less than 20 years before. The bosoms and bottoms of the Edwardian era were no longer the fashion. The period 1910 to 1919 had been very mixed years in terms of women's dress. The First World War saw many women in uniforms and other sorts of functional clothing. After the war there were some frills as a reaction to the severity of the war fashions but the general trend was for simpler, freer, more functional dress.

The war was not the only reason for this change. Women, mainly those of the upper and middle classes, were beginning to do more outside the confines of running the home, taking part in sports, some even having jobs. This busier lifestyle needed clothing to suit. Less use was made of corsets, and skirts became shorter as outfits became less fussy and heavy to wear. By 1919 clothes were much shorter and softer and the bust and bottom much flatter.

However the greatest revolution in women's dress was yet to come. The 1920s saw a rapid acceleration of the earlier trends. By 1927 women's clothing was almost tubular, hiding any trace of female shape. Slimming became popular to achieve the desired pencil-like shape. The bust, bottom, even the waist disappeared under dresses and suits cut to eliminate them and hemlines reached mid–calf to knee length.

The clothing of the 1920s was not the only way in which women's looks changed dramatically. Images of women drawn from popular Hollywood films made cosmetics more acceptable and there was a growing fashion for suntan and sunbathing. Hairstyles changed too. In 1919 most women had long hair which they wore up in some form or other but by the end of the 1920s short hair was more the norm than long. Shorter hairstyles as in the 'bob', the Eton crop and the 'shingle' were popular because they took less time to look after. They were also in a sense emancipating. Many men objected strongly to their wives and daughters having their hair cut.

The fashions of the 1920s reflected a growing sense of women's desire to be freer and to compete with men, so much so that in many respects the fashions denied women's femininity. And although most of the fashions were for middle- and upper-class women the hairstyles, shorter skirts and freer, more functional styles of clothing permeated all levels of society, revolutionizing the way women felt they could dress.

ABOVE: *'Two tasteful printed frocks among the new summertime modes seen in Hyde Park' was the caption to this picture published in July 1927.*

ABOVE: *Hair fashions changed frequently. This one, the 'clurl', was tipped to be the style of 1927.*

LEFT: *Towards the end of the 1920s 'pyjama suits', like this one in pink crêpe de Chine with silver quilted fur trimmed coat, became quite popular.*

1927 POSTSCRIPTS

● The birthrate in Britain was the lowest on record with a ratio of 85 births to every 100 deaths.

February – Revisions to the Book of Common Prayer, including the dropping of the word 'obey' for women, were proposed. However the House of Commons rejected the changes and none of the revisions was made.

May – Prime Minister Baldwin said the government would extend the franchise to all women over 21.

'A woman of 30 may serve on a jury, she may be a doctor of medicine, she may decide on a question of life and death where an operation may take place, but there are people who say she is not fit to vote. That is rather difficult to defend in public.'
Stanley Baldwin addressing 2,000 women union delegates at the Albert Hall, as quoted in the *Daily Mail*, 28 May 1927

Rollers for Reducing Our Feminine Curves.

Twenty-one Varieties at One Counter.

"WE have no fewer than 21 different types of roller in stock for slimming," said the woman manager of a West End surgical department. "Far from finding that the craze for slimness is abating, I count it bad trade if, as it occasionally happens, as few as six rollers are sold in a day. Sometimes as many as three dozen of one kind alone are bought in that time.

From 5s. to 10 Guineas.

"The cost varies from 5s. for the cheapest chin-roller to 10 guineas for a big electric one, and they come from seven different countries—Britain, America, France, Sweden, Switzerland, Austria, and Germany.

"Except for the papier-mâché model, one of the first to come on the market, the rollers are all of rubber.

"The latest one is made on the suction principle, so that the fatty oils are drawn out and the tissues broken up and rolled away at the same time by four or five little wheels set with slotted rubber. For this there is such an enormous demand that although the profit on it is relatively small, we make more from it than all the others put together. It costs 19s. 6d. and 25s. 6d. according to size, a small face or ankle model made like a photographer's squeegee costing 7s. 6d.

"Another 4-roller rubber type is made in England, and at 12s. 6d. is the cheapest body-roller I have. The rubber is cut in shallow slots, so that a certain suction effect is obtained with this too. The suction idea is embodied in all the newest rollers.

Easily Washable.

"One, however, that I would personally recommend as being very efficient is an English-made single roller of solid rubber, slightly 'dimpled' to squeeze the fatty tissues. It has the great advantage of being easy to wash thoroughly, the acids from the body deposited on the roller making this a hygienic necessity.

A Very Determined Client.

"It was with this roller that an important and very enthusiastic client reduced herself from 12st. to a lath-like slimness in six months. So energetic was she that the steel pin on which this, like most of the other rollers, revolves had to be renewed three times! She now claims that as our roller is responsible for her complete transformation the firm should undertake to alter all her dresses, which, she complains, are quite impossible to wear now.

"Another English-made roller consists of four solid rubber balls, about 3in. in diameter, grooved diagonally. A popular one specially made for hip-reducing has its six rubber-spiked rollers set on a flexible metal spiral so that it can curve round the body.

With the Aid of Electricity.

"The electric model has two long metal rollers covered with a hygienic bandage that can be renewed easily. The electric battery attached to it sets up a slight vibration and a comforting heat.

For Chin and Ankle.

"A clever idea from Switzerland is a wooden handle, 12in. long, with a grooved rubber ankle-roller at one end

At the back, beginning on the left, are two models of the latest suction rubber type, a British-made solid rubber roller, another of the suction varieties, the English one which is the cheapest of its kind on the market, the familiar coloured papier-mâché type, and a French flexible roller for the hips. The ten-guinea electric model is shown in the centre, together with smaller rubber examples for ankles and chin.

and a smaller chin and arm roller at the other. Various small rollers for chin and ankle massage are on the market, many being smaller editions of the kinds used for the body.

Men are also Roller Enthusiasts.

"My advice to roller enthusiasts is—go slowly and steadily! A quick roll-over at night, and not more than ten minutes' rolling in the morning, is all that is required. But if for any reason a day is missed the muscles harden and undo the work of many days. This was what a Mayfair doctor, who is himself a great user of a roller, told me. It is surprising, by the way, how many men go in for flesh reducing.

For Reducing During Sleep.

"A new English-made device for using in conjunction with roller-exercise has just come on the market, and I am unable to keep up with the demand for it. It is a chemise-like garment of red rubber, fastened by lacing up the side, and fitting quite loosely. It is worn all night, then the rolling exercise is done in the morning. This perspiration method, though it may not be specially pleasant, is certainly effective in banishing flesh."

STRAWBERRIES ARRIVE.

By a Harley-street Woman Doctor.

THE advent of the strawberry season brings with it delights and disappointments. To some this luscious berry is a forbidden fruit, while others can revel in them to their hearts' content.

The Reason for the " Rash."

The reason for any disagreement is not far to seek. Usually gouty or rheumatic people are the victims of the strawberry "bite," which appears as an angry and unsightly eruption. Apparently the large quantity of sugar the berries contain is responsible for their misbehaviour. However, in many people who do not suffer from either gout or rheumatism, strawberries are a poison, owing to some sugar idiosyncrasy on the part of the consumer.

As a Beautifier.

By reason of the sugar this fruit contains it is most nutritious, whereas its acid properties act as a blood purifier. Besides these internal values they have external uses. As toilette requisites they are much in demand. The French claim that the complexion, skin, and teeth are benefited by them.

Rub a strawberry all over the face and allow it to dry into the skin. Sponge it off with some softened water. Next rub over the face some slightly astringent lotion. Pure rosewater is useful for this purpose when there is nothing else at hand. The face feels like velvet. A month's treatment makes an appreciable difference in the texture of the complexion.

The French have a toothpaste made from strawberries. It is said that the great actress Ellen Terry indulged in it. A berry rubbed over the teeth has a whitening, cleansing, and astringent effect on teeth and gums.

Softening the Bath Water.

Extravagant as it may sound while strawberries are still scarce, they are nevertheless a useful adjunct to the bath when they are cheap and not good enough for table use or jam-making. A

Quite as much to be enjoyed as the strawberries is the wearer's hat of palest beige satin with the restraint of its braided trimming a little contradicted by a studding of topaz jewels.

pound put into a muslin bag and squeezed into the bath water is softening and has tonic properties. The bag should be dipped in the water, squeezed and re-squeezed, so that the skin may benefit by the tonic action to the greatest extent. Finally the body must be rinsed in fresh water. The feeling left by the strawberry bath must be tried to be appreciated. The chance will soon be at hand.

SERIAL

Can Women Forget?

By Florence Riddell

had been occupying a chair nearby, came forward to greet her.

"Mrs. Kinnaird, now that the others have left we are two lonely people to-night, I think. Would you give me the great happiness of dining with me?"

Elisabeth hesitated for a moment. But she could find no adequate excuse that would not seem a deliberate snub. And, as she was feeling so depressed, she decided that it would not be a bad idea to

Have You Got the End–seat Habit?

A Common Type of Nerviness.

MY sympathies were not always with seemingly pugnacious end-seat men, or women. I saw them as assertive, sometimes rude, and always very selfish. They *would* insist on a seat at the entrance to a row, be it theatre, music-hall, church, or even band concert at the seaside. What difference could there be between such a seat and one in the middle?

Take the cinema's continuous programme. If one sits next the gangway it may be necessary to rise a dozen times to allow the ins to get out and the outs to get in. A continual bobbing up and down, like a jack-in-the-box, is not conducive to good temper.

At The Theatre.

If one has booked an end seat at a theatre the only thing is to go a little late, giving the "insiders" a reasonable chance to pass along before one arrives.

In an omnibus I sat behind a middle-aged woman who simply would not take the inside seat. I travelled with her from Cheapside to Marble Arch. During that time she had to rise perhaps a dozen times to allow a passenger to get in or out, all of which might have been avoided had she sat next the window.

But I shall no longer be severe in my thoughts about these people. I realise now that many who are not exactly neurasthenics are yet quite unable to be comfortable in an inside seat.

What the Cinema Girl Said.

This I discovered in a casual conversation with one of the dapper electric-torch girls who guide you through cinema gloom to an empty armchair. I had previously noticed a couple get up from their seats about half-way in and take end ones when the chance offered three or four rows ahead.

So I asked the attendant if many people were similarly obsessed. "Dozens every day," was the reply. "Some will prefer to stand till the end of a row is vacant. Others will take an inside seat till an outside vacancy occurs, while sometimes they may change to a more

expensive seat if they can get it right on the end."

Talking this over in a mixed company I found that three women and one man present were afflicted in the same manner. "I cannot sit any length of time on the inside," said one, "without being mastered by an overpowering desire to get out."

It is largely, I gather, the complaint of the middle-aged and the old, though there are certainly exceptions. Some of its victims have also a hatred of crowds, detest being jostled, will not go up into heights of any kind, avoid lifts and upper bedrooms in hotels, and even walk invariably on the side next the kerb.

No Cure But Will Power.

The physician has no remedy for this mental impatience, if one may call it that. From the medical viewpoint it is plainly a symptom of claustrophobia. "Nerves," no doubt. But once acquired the end-seat habit comes to stay—not of choice, but of sheer necessity. There is no getting over it, I am told. The will weakens by indulgence.   J. O.

The Amateur Cook's Questions.

Why is salted beef so often hard and too salt?

Possibly it needed soaking before cooking. If it has been in brine over a week it will need at least twelve hours' soaking in cold water. Start it cooking in *tepid* water and simmer it very gently. Do not boil it.

How long should fish trimmings be boiled for stock?

A quarter of an hour is long enough. The stock is apt to be bitter if they are boiled longer.

How can I be sure of a Yorkshire pudding being light?

Beat the batter till bubbles form on the top. Make the dripping in the tin *very* hot, put the pudding into a sharp oven at first, then reduce the heat as it cooks.

1928

Equal Franchise

Ten years after the first instalment of the vote for women, the second instalment was delivered. Women at last had the vote on the same terms as men. Everyone over 21, regardless of their marital status, could vote. The Equal Franchise Bill was dubbed the 'Flapper's Vote' and gave the vote to six million more women. Flapper had come to mean almost any young fashionable woman but it was originally a pejorative term for women who adopted new fashions and conventions and were seen as loose-living, and derived from a German slang word for prostitute.

There were several reasons why it took ten years to secure votes for women on the same terms as men. First, the women's organizations which had been so vociferous before the war had to a large extent lost much of their momentum as a result of the war, and the fact that half the female adult population were given the vote in 1918 made it more difficult to argue a case of gross injustice.

Second, as many young women found opportunities to do things such as work outside the home, sports, go out to social occasions unchaperoned the fact that they had no political power seemed less urgent than if they had not had these new freedoms.

The fear on the part of men which existed before the first enfranchisement of women was the third and perhaps most overwhelming reason for the delay in bringing in an equal franchise. Men, and particularly those in Parliament, had feared that women would vote *en masse* for a woman's party, changing for ever the status quo and profile of the British political system. Ten years of women voting had shown that women distributed their votes fairly evenly among the existing political parties. While some men continued to argue that because there were more women than men giving women the vote was undemocratic and unfair on men, Parliament conceded that women should have the franchise on the same terms as men.

There had been positive benefits to women in the ten years since they had first been given the vote and had been able to be MPs. Between 1918 and 1928 sixteen Acts of Parliament which directly affected the status, health or rights of women had been passed. In the eighteen years prior to that only four such Acts had been passed. The vote had brought power to make changes, even if only limited, to women's lives.

ABOVE: *Emmeline Pankhurst's coffin leaves the church with nine of her old associates acting as pall bearers.*
BELOW: *A poster parade in support of the Equal Franchise Bill.*

VOTES FOR WOMEN

VOTES FOR WOMEN ON THE SAME TERMS AS MEN

1928 POSTSCRIPTS

● Radclyffe Hall's novel *The Well of Loneliness* was withdrawn after advice from the Home Secretary and much public controversy over its content. The novel deals with a lesbian relationship which was something unimagined, let alone talked about, by the majority of people in 1928.

May – A Leader in the *Daily Mail* asked for support for a manifesto published by the New Health Society which called for an improvement in the services to the 750,000 women giving birth annually of whom only 50,000 had access to a bed in a maternity hospital and who were served by only 800 antenatal clinics nationally. There was also a plea to cut the maternal death rate.

June – On the day the Equal Franchise Bill received its final reading in Parliament the funeral cortège of Emmeline Pankhurst travelled through the spectator-lined streets of Westminster, from the church of St John's, Smith Square, where her body had been lying in state, to Brompton Cemetery.

The Rush to Banish Wrinkles.

BRILLIANT spring light makes women conscious of their wrinkles.

The beauty salon of one big London store is treating about 30 "wrinkle cases" a day this week.

Mud packs of three different kinds are used. The newest, which is for very deep lines and furrows, is radio-active. Another, for less stubborn cases, is made of mud which is found in England.

After three or four treatments in the salon, many women buy the "mud" and use it at home. Dozens of packets of mud are sold each day. The radio active type costs 7s. 6d. the tube, which allows for four treatments. A 1lb packet of the British "mud," with enough for 6 or 8 treatments, can be had for a guinea.

With Mild Astringent.

Women are recommended to use a pleasantly mild astringent lotion as a stimulant for the skin after removing the caked mud-mask with warm, wet towels.

Sets of wrinkle rollers, made in different sizes for ironing out crows'-feet, and the lines round nose and mouth, are being sold in big quantities by one beauty specialist.

SOLUTION TO CHILDREN'S CROSS-WORD PUZZLE.

ACROSS.—1, Fight. 5. Rap. 8. Idle 9. Hose 10. See. 11. Feast. 12. Tankard. 14. Nib 16. Minster. 20. Aloft. 22. Ire. 23. Gale. 24. Anna. 25. Eye. 26. Otter

DOWN.—1. Fist. 2. Idea. 3, Glen. 4. He 5. Road. 6. ..ss. 7. Pets. 9. Herbs. 11. Faint. 13. Knife. 15. Sage 16. Mole. 17. Tint. 18. Erne. 19. Rear. 21. Lay. 24. At.

"CAN YOU GIVE ME SOME IDEAS for SKIRT DESIGNS?"

ASKS A CORRESPONDENT.

These skirts are all intended for the Newer Vogue of the Tucked-in Blouse and the Higher Waist.

AS soon as circular cuts, flares and godets began to be introduced into skirts made of tweed and the various types of "lainage," then was it possible to raise the waist-line and adopt the tucked-in blouse fashion which had been discarded for some years.

Two Reasons for Yokes.

Even so, dressmakers and tailors found they had to launch the idea carefully with some of their customers. That is one of the reasons why one quite often sees the yoke effect, which suggests both the high and the low waistline, another being that the fit round the hips must still be kept neat and trim.

The first skirt illustrated above is an instance of this, for it has a yoke a prettily shaped scalloped one longer at the back than at the front. The rest of the skirt is cut in circular fashion.

The second is of diagonal tweed in the yellow and mustard shades so vastly in favour at the moment. A dull yellow leather belt and buckle at the waist and at top of the pocket add interest.

Circular Skirt with Straight Panel.

The third is a skirt of circular cut, with a straight panel inset at the extreme left side. The fourth illustration shows a skirt of checked tweed viewed from the left side-back It has a straight front panel and yoke cut in one, the circular-cut back panel being cut with the pattern of the cloth going diagonally.

The fifth illustration reverts to the front view of the skirt—from the right. Into its scalloped yoke, which again suggests two "waist lines," are fitted circular-cut godets. The sixth skirt is made wholly of shaped gores, the seams stitched again on the right side, thus giving a pleated effect. A finely-plaited belt would look well with this type of skirt.

INVALID DIET *that is NOURISHING and ECONOMICAL.*

Suitable for Cases in which Swallowing is Difficult.

To the Housekeeping Expert.

Madam,—Could you advise me of a good and fairly economical menu that will be sufficiently nourishing for my husband, who has to have all his teeth extracted? What is necessary is a good nourishing diet, exclusive of all meat and suitable for one who works entirely with his brain

I was greatly interested in your helpful article "Meals for Two."—Yours truly, E. H., *Northampton.*

I AM often asked for this type of diet, for it is applicable to those with sore throats, mumps, tonsilitis, patients recovering from the operation for tonsilitis, and those who for any reason have difficulty in swallowing—*provided* there is no other constitutional complication.

When I was a V.A.D in jaw wards in No. 20 B.E.F. hospital at Camiers we used to feed the worst cases on egg-and-milk flips, flavoured, perhaps, with brandy, port wine, or beef tea. Milk, flavoured with very strong coffee, to give it character and mitigate the "milky taste, was given as both food and drink

Some Hospital Meals.

Those who could take it had milky porridge for breakfast, and chopped-up boiled eggs. Eggs lightly fried in good bacon fat would be tastier. Chicken or meat that had been passed through a fine mincer before or after cooking, mashed potatoes, baked custard, junket and soft milk puddings were among dinner items for those who could manage them.

Some of the patients liked "nursery" bread-and-milk, or bread-and-beef-tea, only soft bread, of course, being used. This acted as various meals. When necessary tea was scalded with milk instead of water to provide more nourishment, and coffee or cocoa made with milk for the same reason.

Soups Rich in Proteins.

Naturally the diet of a base hospital in war-time can be well augmented now. Lentil and pea soups are tasty and are rich in proteins. They can be flavoured with finely chopped young mint and young parsley which should be added at the last moment if the flavour is to be kept and not boiled away. Tomato soup besides having a definite taste is a good way of getting the patient to take milk, since it could be made with half milk and half stock, and flavoured with cloves or herbs.

Potato soup should have the potatoes thoroughly mashed. Onion soup should have the onions passed through a sieve; it is a good way of serving cheese too, and thus providing protein, as grated cheese is the right accompaniment to onion soup.

To Get the Value of Vegetables.

Mutton broth could be well simmered and then strained This would give much of the value of the vegetables without their having to be chewed. Vegetable purees are good also. Remember in making any of the soups to work on the principle of the consommé class—i.e., get as much nourishment as possible into the liquid, so *simmer* instead of boiling, and thus draw all possible good out of peas, beans, carrots, barley, sago, macaroni, or meat, where the latter is allowed.

Varying the Baked Custard.

Baked custard, though nourishing should be varied so that a sick person would not get tired of this delicious and useful food item Make it savoury by adding a little meat extract, a small quantity of pounded fish, a little sieved tomato pulp, or some minced parsley and mint. When it is served sweet alter the flavouring—cinnamon, nutmeg, vanilla, a little extra-strong coffee, a little pineapple juice, some grated chocolate, a little brandy, or some ground almonds—as used for almond icing—scattered in.

Blancmange and junket, while being good ways of getting the patient to take milk, could be served with mashed apples, mashed prunes, or a jam or fruit sauce to take on a little more interest. Prune jelly deserves to be more widely known and offered. Banana mash is a name that describes itself, except that strawberry jam, or bramble or black-currant jelly is mashed in with the fruit and cream added. Get the patient to take cream whenever feasible, as it isn't as extravagant as it sounds—you see there is no waste, and it is pure nourishment.

> I am often asked for this type of diet, so I am giving it in detail and cannot repeat it. Will those interested
>
> **PLEASE CUT IT OUT AND KEEP IT?**

When the Patient is Better.

When the patient can swallow more easily, or chew to some extent, don't neglect fish puddings, which can be so appetising when nicely made — well flaked or pounded, cooked fish mixed with bread crumbs, beaten egg and milk and flavoured, then put in a buttered mould and steamed. They ought to be spongy and puffy and "melt away in the mouth."

One reminder—in connection with soups, mainly. When celery is out of season a pinch of celery salt is a good flavouring agent.

THE WOMAN COMMERCIAL TRAVELLER

IN spite of the thousands of women whose daily cry is "I want change, variety, interest," commercial travelling as a career for women still remains comparatively unexploited. Yet it offers scope for freedom and enterprise.

"It is absurd to say it is not suitable work for a woman," declared a woman representative of a well-known house. "In many cases a woman is better fitted for it than a man.

"Baby Linen, for Instance."

"Take baby linen, for instance. A woman traveller can quickly create between herself and the buyer a bond of sympathy which must be an important factor in effecting sales. Millinery is another branch where women excel. Only a woman traveller can have that instinctive touch in putting a hat on a model's head, the touch which makes all the difference between making a sale and not making one."

There is an art in this work, as in any other, of getting the maximum of enjoyment out of it.

"Some women on the road," remarked another woman traveller, "make the great mistake of going to cheap hotels Even if I've had a bad day I always put up at a good hotel, where I am sure of meeting nice people and getting rest and quiet.

Not Lonely Work.

"I don't find the work lonely. One's route becomes as familiar as office equipment, and time and time again I meet old acquaintances I appreciate my week-ends at home, too, when there is so much to hear and tell."

Women "on the road" earn more money than the average office worker. Several of them are making incomes around the £500 mark It is usual for the firms they represent to pay expenses plus a salary and commission

The Rough as well as the Smooth.

It is not an easy post, however, and no woman should take up such a career unless she is prepared to put up with a good deal of incon enience and hard work. First calls on prospective buyers, I was told, must be made soon after nine o'clock, and representatives have to work hard until 11 to 11.30 After 11.30, except in small out-of-the-way towns, it is usually the policy of buyers not to see travellers again until 5 p.m.

At five o'clock the woman commercial traveller can start again and work until 6.30, then, according to her programme, decide whether to remain in town the night or go on to another destination. If she chooses the latter course, as indeed she often must, there follows a long drive by night or a long journey by train, possibly punctuated by cold and tedious waits on country stations.

So it is work with its rough as well as smooth side, but most of the women engaged in it are enthusiastic over its attractions.

The Basis of Success.

As in every other profession, "fitness for the job" is the basis of success. No woman should take up travelling unless she has adaptability, perseverance, the gift of making friends—and enthusiasm. With these qualities there is no reason why she should not find the post enjoyable and profitable.

M. W.

TEDDY TAIL'S GARDEN.

No. 4.—A Daisy Chain.

"Don't cut us, please," the daisies said,
"For that would cause us pain."
"'Twould be more fun to pick us, Ted,
And make a daisy chain."

Cried Dr. B., "That would be fun!"
We picked a few at that.
And danced a daisy chain, and one
Put on the doctor's hat.

POUR LES PETITS.

No 176.—
LE VENT.

Le vent m'a emporté mon béret par-dessus la falaise.

1929

Higher Education for Women

In 1921, 1,000 women gathered in the Sheldonian Theatre at Oxford to be awarded their degrees. Many of these women had sat and passed the university degree exams years before but had had no formal recognition of their achievements because Oxford University refused to award degrees to women.

The 1919 Sex Disqualification (Removal) Act prompted Oxford to allow women to sit for full degrees in 1920, hence the retrospective award ceremony. However the university statutes limited the number of places available for women students to one for every six male students. Cambridge University held out against awarding degrees to women until after the Second World War. Even among the non-Oxbridge universities where women had long been admitted they were not admitted in equal numbers to men.

The limited places awarded to women led to a distinct dichotomy in the way girls were treated in schools. Vera Brittain in her book *Lady into Woman* suggests that in many secondary and private girls' schools much time was wasted teaching girls of average and lesser ability 'accomplishments' rather than giving them a real education. The more able pupils, especially in the public school system, were rigorously schooled for examinations at the expense of developing social skills and personal confidence.

However, for many girls in the 1920s and beyond, the ability to attend school was often limited by the expectation that they would help out in the home. Girls' education was still seen as something which could be sacrificed for this or if there were boys to be educated when money was short. Few girls, especially those in the working classes, ever had the opportunity to progress beyond the elementary school to gain a secondary education and fewer still had access to higher education.

Scenes from girls' schools in the late 1920s.

1929 POSTSCRIPTS

● Following an enquiry and criticism by the League of Nations, the age of marriage in Britain was raised from 12 for girls and 14 for boys to 16 for both sexes.

● Obstetrics and gynaecology gained 'respectability' with the formation of the British College of Obstetricians and Gynaecology.

● Women were granted the right to sit in the Canadian Senate, Canada's second legislative chamber.

May – The first General Election in which women had an equal franchise returned 13 women MPs.

● Dr Linda Gage Roth published a report on the health during pregnancy and childbirth of over 1,000 graduates from Smith College, one of the USA's most prestigious colleges. Dr Roth found that those among the women who took exercise suffered fewer complications than those who did not, contrary to the prevalent view that sport damaged women's ability to bear children.

June – Labour Prime Minister Ramsay MacDonald named Margaret Bondfield as Minister of Labour. She was the first woman member of a British Cabinet.

October – The Stock Market on New York's Wall Street suffered the Great Crash and markets in London and around the world fell, plunging the world into the Great Depression of the 1930s.

GIRL TO BE IN BY 10
Magistrate Agrees with Father's Rule

A girl aged 20 complained to the Willesden magistrate Dr Lloyd Williams yesterday that her father had taken away her latchkey. He did not approve of her going to dances and insisted on her being home by 10 p.m.

Dr Williams: I think he is right. What business has a girl like you to stay out after 10 p.m.? That is quite late enough, and you must obey your father.
Daily Mail, 8 January 1929

HOUSEHOLD HINTS A.B.C.

HERE is a thoroughly up-to-date version of the "occasional" table that is so useful in drawing-room or lounge.

Carried out in nickelled metal and spray-painted wood, it makes an excellent Christmas present for the woman who likes restrained modern furniture.

The geometrical design on the parchment-coloured lampshade echoes the motive of the beautiful modern carpet, which is also shown in the photograph.

Compile an Invaluable Dictionary of Household Facts.

Cut These Out and Paste Them into an Indexed Book

ADHESIVE PASTE can be made for emergency use from a cold boiled potato. Rub it on to paper and it will make it stick quite well. This is excellent for fixing a dado or bordering of wallpaper that has become loose.

BRUSHES AND BROOMS will last longer and do their work better if they are washed every six weeks in a solution of two tablespoonfuls of household ammonia in half a gallon of water. Let the bristles stand in the solution for half an hour, then rinse thoroughly and dry in a cool place, away from the fire.

CREAM will whip more easily if the white of an egg is added to it. The addition of a few drops of glycerine often hastens the process, and for sweet dishes a little powdered sugar can be added. Stand in a draught, if possible, and use an egg whip.

EBONY ORNAMENTS for the dressing-table frequently become discoloured, but they can be revived by judicious applications of Indian ink. Apply the ink with a soft brush, leave to dry, then smooth with finest glass-

A WOMAN has invented this useful non-spilling filling gadget for hot-water bottles, oil lamps, and so on. Costing sixpence, it consists of a fitted float which is put into the ordinary household funnel. When the vessel is nearly full the float gives warning by rising.

paper. Apply the ink a second time, and, when dry, rub in a small quantity of linseed oil, using a little beeswax for a final polish.

FRUIT CAKES of the rich variety rise more evenly if, after the mixture is put into the baking tin, it is pressed into a slight hollow in the centre. If the cake is to be iced afterwards this often saves cutting the top off to make it even—a wasteful method which makes the cake liable to become dry.

HANDS should be rubbed over with damp soap, particularly round the finger-nails, before gardening or house work. Allow the soap to dry before setting to work. By this method the dirt will not become ingrained and will wash off easily.

JAPANNED TRAYS are best cleaned by rubbing them well with warm flour, afterwards polishing with a dry,

soft duster. If the surface is cracked, clean by polishing with a little furniture cream.

MARKING INK can be applied neatly and easily if the linen to be marked is moistened with cold-water starch, dried and ironed. This makes a smooth, stiff writing surface, and prevents the ink from running.

OYSTERS kept in a cool place—temperature of 40 to 50 degrees—excluded from air by a damp cloth, will remain fresh for five days. The shells should be flat side up. A sure sign of staleness is a shrivelled "beard" or fringe-like part of the oyster. When served, always insist on the oysters

being attached to the flat shells; when once they are freed from these and transferred to deeper shells much of the goodness is taken away.

Oysters that are "sandy" should be washed separately in clear running water. They should never be put into a basin with a number of others, for fear of any one of these being tainted in any way, as the oyster will quickly absorb impurities.

PEAT FOR FIRES is best stored out of doors and not under cover. This ensures slower but equally good combustion, resulting in most economical use. There is also less dust in burning.

RIBBONS used for lingerie purposes should be washed in warm, soapy water, rinsed in clear warm water, and then in cold water. Instead of ironing them wind them carefully round a clean glass bottle and leave there until quite dry. By this process the ribbons look almost like new, and are just stiff enough.

STARCH is useful for cleaning silver if used in a powdered form, and it will very often remove obstinate stains from wallpapers. A little starch added to the water with which windows are washed helps to remove the dirt, and if boiled starch is rubbed over newly washed linoleum and allowed to dry so that a skin is formed, it will be much easier to polish with beeswax and turpentine or floor polish.

TORTOISESHELL and horn-rimmed spectacles should be placed in a

drawer at night in frosty weather. If left on the dressing-table they are liable to snap.

WIRE BRUSHES are useful in a variety of ways. The unpleasant odour of burning fat which has spattered the grill of the gas stove when frying can be avoided by brushing the grill with a wire brush before using. Wire brushes are more effectual than sandpaper in removing paint, especially from crevices.

MANY business girls are using this metal safety-catch for attaché cases which have a habit of flying open. An oblong metal hoop, fitted to the upper edge of the lid, clips over the handle to keep the case firmly shut. The price is a shilling.

NURSERY NOTES.

THAT ODD STREAK OF "CRUELTY."

How to Deal with **A Difficult Problem.**

By **Len Chaloner.**

THE most difficult nursery problem to deal with wisely, and certainly the most distressing for the parents, arises when a child displays an odd streak of cruelty in his disposition. This may happen in a home where a child has never been unkindly treated, though occasionally it is to be discovered where he has been too heavily "snubbed."

Responsibility Helps.

It should be appreciated, however, that "cruelty" is different from the unintentional callousness of tiny children who take evident satisfaction in trying to catch flies on a window, and so on. Many little children pass through this phase just as they go through one of imagining quite unreal happenings which adults sometimes mistake for untruthfulness.

Deliberate cruelty is never cured by severe punishments, and these may even heighten what is in reality a peculiar and unhealthy "excitement" in cruelty. In particular, the type of punishment that inflicts on the child similar pain to that which he inflicts on others has the fatal error of being a directly personal punishment which arouses strong emotions of antagonism with more cruelty excitement.

The strange streak is sometimes due to the child having a strong feeling of power. A quiet delegating of responsibility may help such a child, though obviously we must be careful in the directions that we afford such an outlet, and the appropriate penalty for bad behaviour would be the suspension of the privileges.

A marked desire to bully springs from some excitement in cruelty. We must be particularly guarded in our emotions when dealing with such a child, remembering that cruelty is an acquired, not a natural, instinct, and if much marked we must face the fact that the child is in the grip of something which it has become beyond his power to control.

Nervousness.

Whatever such states may lead to in the adult in the child we must recognise them as definitely of nervous character, demanding highly specialised medical aid just as we would seek a surgeon for appendicitis, or an oculist for defective sight.

CLOTH-TRIMMED FUR COATS

And a **NEW FUR COLLAR.**

THE use of sleek cloths and flat-haired furs for the new coats is

1930

Competing with Men

In May 1930 Amy Johnson flew solo to Australia. She set off from the airfield at Croydon for the trip which was to take her 19 days in her tiny Gypsy Moth biplane. She became a heroine of the period, fêted by the press, even having a song, 'Amy, Wonderful Amy', to sing her praises. This flight was the first of many record-breaking attempts and achievements by Amy Johnson. The following year she flew from Britain to Japan via Siberia and in 1936 she set a new record for the flight from London to Cape Town.

Amy Johnson was only one of a group of women aviators of the 1920s and '30s. She, and later also Beryl Markham, were the darlings of the British public because they were home grown but there were other women pilots throughout the world. In 1928 the American Amelia Earhart became the first woman to fly the Atlantic. She went on to fly solo across the Pacific in 1935. Attempting, in 1937, to be the first person to fly solo round the world Amelia Earhart disappeared and no trace has ever been found either of her or her plane.

Women aviators were perhaps the most obvious sign of women's achievements in areas of life where men dominated or where women were thought incapable of competing but there were others. Gertrude Ederle had swum the Channel in 1926. She was the first woman ever to do so and cut two hours off the previous record set by a man. M. E. Foster won the King's Prize for shooting at Bisley in 1930. These were sports where women were competing against men and there was very much a feeling at the time that women had to prove themselves in a male environment if they were to be taken seriously.

Indeed much of men's arguments against women in the past had been that women had not the capacity mentally, physically or emotionally to take on, let alone succeed, in a vast field of activities outside the home. Many women throughout the 1930s worked hard in many spheres of life to dispel some of these ideas, achieving many 'firsts' for women, and broadening the horizons for many women to come.

ABOVE: *Amy Johnson pictured with her Gypsy Moth plane before her solo flight to Australia.*
BELOW: *Composer Ethel Smyth conducting the band which played as the Prime Minister, Stanley Baldwin, unveiled a statue to the memory of Emmeline Pankhurst.*

1930 POSTSCRIPTS

● Welfare Centres were allowed to give birth-control advice to married women.
● Mary Bagot Stack founded the Women's League of Health and Beauty to teach fitness through exercise and provide education on diet and hygiene.
January – Women Civil Servants voted in favour of compulsory retirement of women on marriage.

STILL MORE "CONFESSIONS."

Have You Tried This Victorian Game? Say What You Think—and Win a Prize.

By Mrs. C. B. Cochran.

1. *What makes life worth living?*
Keeping blondes out of my husband's way!

2. *What is the most lovable quality in the human being for whom you have the most affection?*
Tenderness.

3. *What is the most detestable quality in anyone you dislike?*
Vanity.

4. *What is the most attractive quality in yourself?*
Have not got one.

5. *And the most detestable?*
Mental laziness.

6. *What living celebrity (man or woman) do you admire most?*
King Alfonso.

7. *Is either sex superior to the other, and if so, why?*
Men, because of their superior physical strength.

8. *Which gives you most pleasure—a new frock, a new book, or a good meal?*
A new book.

9. *Do you dress to attract men, to compete with other women, or to please yourself? (Be very honest about this one.)*
To attract one man.

10. *If you could begin life again, what career would you choose?*
The one I have.

Evelyn Cochran

Mrs. Elinor Glyn.

1. *What makes life worth living?*
Having a definite aim and thinking first of others before yourself.

2. *What is the most lovable quality in the human being for whom you have most affection?*
Understanding.

3. *What is the most detestable quality in anyone you dislike?*
Petty jealousy.

4. *What is the most attractive quality in yourself?*
Sympathy with the age.

5. *And the most detestable?*
Too many to enumerate!

6. *What living celebrity (man or woman) do you admire most?*
Mussolini.

7. *Is either sex superior to the other, and if so, why?*
Both are equal—the unintelligent ones in either think their own sex the superior.

8. *Which gives you most pleasure—a new frock, a new book, or a good meal?*
A new frock — because you choose that yourself, and the new book may be nonsense.

9. *Do you dress to attract men, to compete with other women, or to please yourself? (Be very honest about this one.)*
Entirely to please myself.

10. *If you could begin life again, what career would you choose?*
I should like to be the best portrait painter in the world.

Elinor Glyn

Hon. Mrs. Victor Bruce

1. *What makes life worth living?*
The humorous side of it.

2. *What is the most lovable quality in the human being for whom you have the most affection?*
Unselfishness.

3. *What is the most detestable quality in anyone you dislike?*
Injustice.

4. *What is the most attractive quality in yourself?*
Humour.

5. *And the most detestable?*
Contrariness. .

6. *What living celebrity (man or woman) do you admire most?*
Colonel Lindbergh.

7. *Is either sex superior to the other, and if so, why?*
Our sex is superior, because more husbands are afraid of their wives than wives of their husbands.

8. *Which gives you most pleasure—a new frock, a new book, or a good meal?*
A good meal.

9. *Do you dress to attract men, to compete with other women, or to please yourself? (Be very honest about this one.)*
I dress to please everybody, because, unfortunately, I am not rich enough to dress poorly.

10. *If you could begin life again, what career would you choose?*
Chancellor of the Exchequer.

Victor Bruce

Mlle. Alice Delysia.

1. *What makes life worth living?*
The pleasure of enjoying the company of real kind friends and their friendships, and doing where it is possible a good turn to the under-dog without advertising it.

2. *What is the most lovable quality in the human being for whom you have most affection?*
Charity.

3. *What is the most detestable quality in anyone you dislike?*
Greed.

4. *What is the most attractive quality in yourself?*
That I leave to others to find out.

5. *And the most detestable?*
That also I am content for others to find out.

6. *What living celebrity (man or woman) do you admire most?*
The Pope.

7. *Is either sex superior to the other, and if so, why?*
The word "superior" needs closer defining to answer fully this question. There are many duties performed by women which cannot be performed by men, and vice versa. Each sex has been endowed with certain powers which cannot be compared.

8. *Which gives you most pleasure—a new frock, a new book, or a good meal?*
A good meal.

9. *Do you dress to attract men, to compete with other women, or to please yourself? (Be very honest about this one.)*
Why, to please myself, of course, as do all women. If they dress to attract, that is to please themselves. If to compete, that also is to please themselves.

10. *If you could begin life again, what career would you choose?*
The lights, the applause, the friendships—is there anything else in the world I should like to be but an artist? No—a thousand times no!

Alice Delysia

YES, YOU CAN WALK.
Third Series of Exercises for Graceful Carriage.
By Mrs. BAGOT STACK.

THE exercises for the loose swinging of feet and hips, described in the last set of movements, should now be followed by exercises to loosen the knee joints. These should be practised very gradually, the knee joints being generally weaker than any others.

1. Sink as lightly as you can into the position shown in the first picture, keep- ing the back as straight and in line as possible. Now take eight tiny jumps forward and eight back.

2. When you have mastered these movements, try walking with tiny steps instead of jumping. Work to foxtrot rhythm.

3. Sit down, if possible, without using your hands and without bumping on the floor. If you can keep the rhythm try doing this movement to four bars of a waltz.

1931

The Morality of Birth Control

ABOVE: Jane Addams.
BELOW: The District Maternity nurse in North Devon pictured on her new motorcycle given to help her cover her 200 square miles of territory.

Throughout the 1920s the birth rate continued to fall, partly through the pioneer work of the few family planning clinics, although growing economic hardship and crisis was probably a greater reason for fewer babies being born. The 'great debate' about the forecasted chronic under-population of Britain by the end of the century due to the falling birth rate also brought information to many women ignorant of the facts, and the idea that it was possible to control the number of children born.

Few women avoided conception by the use of contraceptive devices; for most, withdrawal was the only method of avoiding pregnancy that was available or known to them. Apart from infanticide, induced abortion was the other way to limit family size. These abortions were mainly self-administered with a variety of instruments, or by taking any of a whole host of 'special pills', many of which contained dangerous chemicals such as lead or other abortifacients, home-made mixtures of chemicals, herbal concoctions, or strong laxatives.

The fact that the Churches condemned artificial birth control only served to make those women or men who used contraceptive devices feel immoral. Even if they could justify their actions to themselves, society could not accept their reasons. The women who attended clinics run by Marie Stopes, Helena Wright and others had to be either very strong-willed or else desperate.

In 1930 came a revolutionary encyclical letter on the subject of birth control from the Archbishop of Canterbury, Cosmo Lang. The letter followed much debate within the Church of England and stated that, 'if there is good moral reason why the way of abstinence should not be followed, we cannot condemn the use of scientific methods, which are thoughtfully and conscientiously adopted.' This was not a wholehearted approval of contraception especially as the letter went on to urge restrictions on its sale and advertising, and condemned most severely birth control for selfish gain and convenience. Nonetheless this limited acceptance by the state Church in England paved the way for a far more tolerant public attitude towards contraception, so that by 1939, when the various clinics throughout the country came together as the Family Planning Association with the slogan 'Children by Choice, not Chance', the subject was almost respectable.

Within six months of the Anglican Church giving limited approval to artificial birth control the Roman Catholic Church had reaffirmed its opposition to the practice. A papal encyclical issued in January of 1931 clearly condemned any attempts to prevent conception artificially.

1931 POSTSCRIPTS

● The results of the census showed that, including teachers and nurses, professional women outnumbered professional men by 389,359 to 356,762.

The census also showed that 200,000 more women were in domestic service than in 1921 mainly as a result of the Depression and the fact that there was no other work available.

December – American sociologist Jane Addams was awarded the Nobel Peace Prize. She had devoted her life to campaigning for the poor, women's rights and racial equality and had spoken out against the USA becoming involved in the First World War.

WOMAN AUCTIONEER   My Voice Will Carry

Miss Margaret Price of Rodenhurst, Oxted, Surrey, who has worked in the office of her father, an auctioneer, has gained second place out of 698 candidates, in the final examinations of the Auctioneers and Estate Agents Institute and is now a fully qualified auctioneer. She is the first woman to pass the examination with honours.

Miss Price said to a *Daily Mail* reporter: 'A woman's voice need be no bar to her acting as an auctioneer, mine would carry all right, I think.'
Daily Mail, 8 May 1931

This is the MOTHERCRAFT AGE

"Modern Girls" who Love Babies

THERE is still a vague idea that in their efforts to compete with men in the professional and business world young women to-day are losing interest in what is, perhaps, the greatest career of all—the care of their own and other people's children.

Older women who feel pessimistic about their daughters' capabilities in this direction should go, as I did, to one of the schools where modern girls learn to look after babies and toddlers. Watch them soothing the few-weeks'-old baby to sleep, bending over his pram in the shady garden; watch them ironing out tiny garments, absorbed in their task; watch then romping with the toddlers, encouraging the shy one to join in—and themselves playing as if they loved it

Look at the charts which each one keeps of the daily life of the baby in her charge—the care and interest with which they note the tiniest detail and the baby's reaction to any change of routine.

For this is the mothercraft age; never has there been such a keen young generation of baby-lovers as these girls of seventeen to twenty.

Keen and Young

The nursery experts who train these young girls, teaching them to cook, make clothes, and launder for the babies, as well as how to plan their diets and treat their small ailments, will tell you that. And their opinion is borne out by the fact that there are long waiting-lists of would-be children's nurses at the important training colleges. So many girls want to learn baby management that a big London centre is inaugurating a training for day-pupils. One college has every entry booked up to the middle of next year.

The matron of this college declares that the young girl of to-day tackles her job of training to be a nursery nurse

THEY LOVE THE TODDLERS!—Young nurses join in table games during sun-bathing hour at a London nursery centre.

with more intelligence than her predecessor of a few years ago.

She takes a keen interest in the theoretical side of child management. This is a branch of the training which in many cases is a new addition to the nurse's training, but already a well-known child specialist who examines the students before they leave a nursery training college says that young nurses now have a sound knowledge of food values and the scientific arrangement of children's diets.

A Charming Scene

And how tremendously enthralled these girls are with the business of looking after babies at the toddler stage! That is another new development, for in the old days the nurses seemed to be interested chiefly in the tiny infants.

I happened to look in on a charming scene in the nursery school of a big London college. The children, all under five, were beating time on toy jazz instruments to a tune played on the piano. On a small stool stood the baby conductor, wielding a baton nearly as long as himself. And the student nurses joined in the drum-beating as merrily as any of the children.

Conversation at Breakfast

During the year they spend at the college modern young nurses learn everything about babies, from charting their diets to encouraging their breakfast-table conversation.

Each baby has its own night nursery and a student to share it with him. So that each girl can get practical experience of running an average-sized nursery, the older children are divided into "families" of three or four, sleeping in a large, open-air night nursery with a student in charge. But before they even attempt to look after the youngsters these girls spend several weeks in the kitchens and laundry, and even in doing actual housework. They may never be asked to cook or scrub when they go out to their jobs, but they like to feel that they are learning not only to look after other people's babies but how to run the "home of her own" to which every one of them looks forward.

When these young nurses have their own homes and families I think the pessimists will have to admit that they were wrong in doubting their domestic capabilities. Molly Kyle.

Why Not International Fashions?

—asks Gabrielle Chanel *(the well-known dress designer)*

IT is not so easy as it used to be to distinguish a smart Parisienne from a smart Englishwoman or a smart Viennese or a smart American. A change in the mode flashes round the world as fast as a wireless wave will take it. Fashion is an international business.

We dressmakers will have to keep pace with this spirit of boundary-elimination. Instead of each European capital being a watertight compartment, as far as the dress industry is concerned, we will all require to get together. Everyone in every country, from the designer herself to the maker of the minutest button, will have to wake up to the advantages of working together.

Revolutionary!

Recently I made an attempt to revolutionise the dress world by smashing down some of the old-fashioned ideas that make a barrier between the dress interests of London and Paris.

I brought my collection over here, made up in all-British materials. Also, instead of taking the usual elaborate precautions against the copyists, I actually invited women to bring their dressmakers to see my show so that they could copy the models at will. These unorthodox methods gave,

naturally, a splendid fillip to trade. The show went some way towards bringing the French dressmaking world into direct touch with creative designers in London.

But, after the rigid exclusiveness of the usual showings of models to buyers from the various shops, what a shock of surprise it gave to adherents of the old, watertight-compartment ideas of people who imagine that, dressily speaking, Paris is Paris and London is London, and never the twain shall meet!

Sacred Conventions

No one who is not in actual contact with the exclusive world of creative fashion realises what a conservative, almost ritualistic, world it is, and how sacred are the conventions that have arisen in the development of this intricate art of dressing the women of every country in the globe.

My motives, after all, were not so very complicated and obscure. For years I have been struck, in the course of various journeys through Europe and America, by the lack of liaison between people doing the same work in different countries.

The results of this lack of understanding were felt when the Customs war became acute and the raising of each barrier inspired a reprisal.

The "haute couture Parisienne," which had been only too content to remain haughtily aloof, was among

the first industries to suffer from these conditions. Paris possesses, and has long possessed, a unique position as a centre for invention and design of women's clothes. There is no reason to believe that this position will change.

"Let's Be Friendly"

But it is up to the artists who have created it, and who benefit by its prestige, to do away with the aspect of dress snobbery which involves the exclusion of fashion elements from other countries.

As I am a textile designer, as well as a dressmaker, my first step towards the realisation of this idea was to offer my collaboration to a number of British textile manufacturers. The exhibition of models in British materials was a proof of good will. The result has been the formation of a small group of manufacturers who are now carrying out my designs with British materials and British looms.

Smarter Clothes

For such a scheme to reach its full importance, an international syndicate, upon which all the industries connected with women's clothes from every country were represented, might be formed. This would result in what every woman in every capital wants—clothes of last-minute smartness carried out in the newest and best materials down to every detail.

I do not pretend to have found a solution to the crisis from which the dressmaking industry is suffering, but I am hopeful that my suggestions may do something to attenuate its worst effects.

"Backless" Beauty

WOMEN who have bought "backless" pyjamas and bathing suits for their holidays find that they must pay serious attention to beauty exercises for the back and arms. A few minutes of these each day will work wonders.

To improve the too-thin shoulders and upper back, the arms should be raised shoulder high, with elbows bent, and the fingers of both hands clasped one within the other. Then move the arms from right to left, trying to pull the hands apart, but keeping the head and shoulders erect. The muscles between the shoulders will soon be tired when the exercise is first begun, but as days pass they will become firm and supple.

The line of the neck is often spoilt by a small protruding bone at the top of the backbone. This can be improved by pushing the head and chin forward and relaxing the shoulders, then pulling the head slowly upward with the chin in, resisting all the time with the back-of-the-neck muscles.

One of the best ways of breaking down fatty tissues on too-plump arms is simply to lie flat and to thump the arms gently on the floor.

Don't forget during the holiday the three principal needs of the skin—cleansing, feeding, protecting. Before dinner after a tiring day at sports, motoring, or bathing use a rejuvenating mask while dressing. It will dry slowly, tightening and refreshing the skin.

1932

Nursery Education

The 1918 Fisher Education Act which raised the school-leaving age to fourteen, had also recommended the setting up of nursery schools for children before the age of five. This idea had perhaps been rooted in the fact that during the First World War a limited number of nurseries had been set up to allow women with children to work. Although most closed at the end of the war the prospect of economic growth ahead and an increased need for women workers would have necessitated greater nursery provision. The economy never in fact boomed but became depressed so there was no pressure from employers or women themselves for more nursery places – the pressure was on women through the 1920s and '30s to stay at home.

By 1932 there were only 52 state nurseries, catering for only a tiny proportion of nursery-aged children. Not only had the economic situation made the establishment of nurseries or the adoption of existing nurseries difficult but the 1919 Maternity and Child Welfare Act had transferred responsibility to the newly created Department of Health. The Health Department laid down far more rigorous standards for nurseries than the Education Department and subsequently few nurseries could match the standards demanded.

There was little public outcry at this low provision of nursery places. Many jobs operated a marriage bar so most women would be at home and expected to look after their children. Many other married women found their workplace bringing in marriage bars in the 1930s or felt under intolerable pressure to resign as male unemployment grew. And just as society had encouraged women to go out to work during the war, it now told women that the best place for them, and if they were mothers the only place for them, was at home with their family. Further, in order to make the job of mother a coveted one it had to be seen as a job that only the mother could do and so home and not a nursery was said to be the best place for the child.

ABOVE: *'The good looks of a large percentage of the women students now at Oxford is commented on in* The Isis*' captioned this* Daily Mail *picture of women cycling to a lecture.*
BELOW: *Mildred 'Babe' Didrikson in the hurdles.*

1932 POSTSCRIPTS

February – The French government resigned after the Senate rejected plans to extend the female franchise.

May – Amelia Earhart became the first person to fly the Atlantic twice after which she said, 'I don't think it much matters who flies the Atlantic, men or women – it's all the same.'

August – At the Los Angeles Olympics, Mildred 'Babe' Didrikson won three medals, gold in javelin and 80m hurdles and silver in the high jump – she was only allowed to enter three events. She is the only person ever to have won medals for running, jumping and throwing in one Olympic Games.

WOMEN IN COMMAND

Why are we *Unpopular?*

THE hundreds of letters received in response to the recent article, " Women in Command," were sharply divided. Women bosses are ideal, according to some ; they a e quite impossible according to (we have to admit) the vast majority. About one-fifth of the letters were from men. Here are some of the viewpoints. Letters printed will be paid for.

I HAVE worked under women and I have worked under men, and for real conscientious performance and unsparing effort, the woman wins every time. The efficient woman manager is frequently unpopular, and for a good reason—she can see through humbug. And she is proof against the blandishments of her sex.

London. (MISS) BEATRICE BAKER.

WHEN working for a woman, I have always found that there is only one way to do a job, and that is her way—and woe betide you if you try to do it yours!

Gillingham. E. FORSTER.

I WORKED under the woman " head " of a big Government office.

An earnest and hard worker herself, just and loyal, she commanded the liking and respect of all those whose hearts were in their work, and drew the best from them accordingly. Those who sought only *little* work, *short* hours, *much* pay, found her intolerant, " bossy," and severe!

Eastham. (MRS.) E. M. C.

THE man I worked for was by no means out of the ordinary as employers go, and his outlook was naturally masculine. When anything was wrong he was perfectly unreasonable, abused me heartily, and ended with a smile—and that was that.

But the woman! When she had reason to reprimand she was NICE. She was reasonable. She was tactful. She

was SWEET. Her arguments were beyond reproach and without flaw. And I have left her presence with a burning desire to commit three crimes at once!

Burton-on-Trent. TYPIST.

IN my experience I have always found it the irritable or temperamental person who is unable to get on with a woman chief. Personally I have found women as easy to serve as

men. Although they have always insisted on the smallest detail being carried out efficiently, they are ready to give praise where it is due, therefore getting the best out of those under them.

Dover. (MR.) E. W. TAYLOR.

MEN will have the honesty to tell you they value your work and that it is good. While the great mass of women will *not*—they only mention your failings.

Worthing. B. P.

WOMEN are less just than men ; less able to see both sides of a question.

When they discover a fault, they admit no extenuating circumstances ; hence they seem intolerant.

Women work more assiduously than men, giving up their whole time to what men could do in half of it, though perhaps rather less efficiently.

Women insist on petty details when broad outlines are the need of the moment.

Women are proud of their authority, and are merciless in their use of sarcasm.

Women are incapable of that *camaraderie* which most men exercise almost instinctively.

Ashford. OBSERVER.

IF you ask a girl what her new chief is like, ten to one she will reply, " Oh, he goes off the deep end sometimes, but he soon gets over

'Daily Mail' Readers Argue It Out

it." Women do not " soon get over it." They harbour resentment far longer than men, and do not scruple to remind their juniors of past faults.

It is not women's ability that is at fault ; working alone, I believe them to be capable of better and more sustained work than men. But in command over others, their tiresome consciences create such a rigid atmosphere of worry and excitement that any job under the easygoing authority of a man seems in comparison an absolute holiday.

Wakefield. WOMAN SECRETARY.

I HAVE taught in schools under masters and mistresses, and I have always preferred working under a master.

I have even been in command myself, and I candidly admit that a man could have done the work better, especially where the training of big boys was concerned.

Nevin. E. W. J.

AFTER all, why worry about the particular type your employer, man or woman, represents? Try being detached yourself, get on with your job, and keep the personal element out of it. Sex prejudice and jealousy are extremely childish and time-wasting. Your fellow-workers and employer should, from a personal point of view, be no more to you than the office furniture. BE DETACHED.

Wembley Park. ANTARCTICA.

" IF you want a thing done well do it yourself ! " quotes the woman boss.

Accordingly she quits the bridge to attend to the deck-washing. And then she wonders that trouble ensues, sitting down ruefully to declare, " One can't be in two places at once ! "

She is a slave to uniformity. Men are rarely such abject followers of fashion as women.

London. A. E.

This Week's Fashion Note

Trimming the Shoulder

THE extreme simplicity of the new evening gown requires careful trimming accents. The tendency this season is to place the trimming on one or both shoulders according to the type of ornament or the silhouette of the dress itself.

The upper figure shows a huge velvet ribbon bow in deep crimson on a white, rough crêpe dress. The ribbon starts in the underarm seam at the waistline, and is drawn up to the shoulder through a slot.

The revival of the over-shoulder spray of large flowers is seen in the second sketch—in this case large pale yellow roses on the cowl bodice of a hunter's green flat crêpe dress. Deep green leaves nestle among the roses.

My Great Little "Boss"

A charming portrait of her woman chief by a "Daily Mail" reader

MY chief was not of the "new woman" type, but her very opposite. I can see her now, a dainty petite figure, with a look of serenity, a never-hurried, never-ruffled look.

Yet behind all this quietness was the magnetic personality essential to the successful ruling of others, whether in state, workshop, or home. We are all familiar with the statement, "I would do anything for her or him," and it is nearly always inspired by a person who can command love from others—one who brings out the best by giving the best.

My woman "boss" treated us strictly, insisted on punctuality, severely reprimanded us for faults, and yet we all loved and respected her. We realised that she cared for our well-being. She was absolutely fair, and never blamed for an accident so long as we reported it to her. After a deserved dressing down we were always met by an unchanged demeanour. Nothing was ever allowed to rankle.

This woman had started herself on the lowest rung of the ladder, and could do any job in any department. We never felt she asked us to do anything she would not do herself, and, having entrusted the job to us, she left us to it. There was no nagging supervision, consequently a word of praise from her was highly prized.

The men took their orders from her just as cheerfully as the women. So I have come to the conclusion that sex does not count: it is the spirit which matters.

London. MARY BACKHOUSE.

"Daily Mail" Women's Bureau

WRITE TO THE DAILY MAIL WOMEN'S BUREAU

HOUSEWIFERY—Jennifer Snow

HOW can I clean the rubber rollers of my wringing machine, which are rather neglected ?

Chester. K. M. P.

Give the rubber rollers a thoroughly good cleaning with turpentine once, and then keep them clean with a warm soapy water wash.

BEAUTY—Joan Beringer

I HAVE auburn hair, creamy skin with plenty of colour in my face. What

shade of powder should I use ?

Bridgwater. P.

With your creamy skin have a light rachel or cream powder. And as you have plenty of colour I should not advise your using rouge, but have a vivid mandarin shade for your lipstick.

COOKERY—Doris B. Sheridan

RECIPE for date jam suitable for children.

Tetbury. F. E. H.

Stone 3lb. dates and cut up small. Wash, scrape, and grate finely 2lb. carrots. Mix together and put into the preserving pan with ¾ pint water and boil for 20 minutes. Add a few drops lemon essence and 2lb. sugar, and boil fast until a little

of the mixture, tested on a saucer, will set. It is inadvisable to make large quantities of the jam at a time, as it will not keep indefinitely.

CHILDREN AND THE NURSERY—Sister Cooper, S.R.N.

SOME suitable toys for the first year.

Leicester. MRS. H.

A well-made celluloid rattle, empty cotton reels, a wooden spoon, brightly coloured *large* buttons and a box to put them in and out, a "posting box," any small soft, washable "cuddly" toy such as a rabbit or lamb. These should have leather eyes sewn in to avoid danger of swallowing.

INQUIRY FORM, May 2, 1933.

DAILY MAIL WOMEN'S BUREAU

Pseudonym (if desired).

Name ....

Address ....

Queries must be accompanied by a STAMPED ADDRESSED ENVELOPE and an inquiry form. Write the subject—whether dress, children, cookery, housewifery, or beauty—at the top left-hand corner of the envelope, and address it to " Daily Mail " Women's Bureau, Northcliffe House, London, E.C. 4.

1933

Women in Fascist States

Between the two World Wars much of European political thinking was affected by Fascism. The two most obvious examples are Mussolini's Italy and Hitler's Germany but Spain, Portugal, Austria and most of the countries of Eastern Europe all had governments with political affiliations to Fascism.

Fascism organized a nationalistic and militaristic society on authoritarian lines in a strict hierarchy. In Hitler's Germany it was the Jews who were at the bottom of the hierarchy, indeed excluded from it altogether. But women lost a great deal in Germany when the Nazis came to power in 1933. Unlike Italy where women had made few strides before Mussolini came to power, Germany had been the home of a strong women's movement from the mid-nineteenth century.

The Reichstag that convened in November 1933 was dominated by Nazis and devoid of women and Jews. This was despite the fact that women in Germany had had the vote since 1918 and up to 1933 there had been between 30 and 40 women in each of the postwar Parliaments. The Nazi party had no women candidates and even discussed rescinding women's suffrage.

Women in Germany consciously or unconsciously found themselves turning back into 'Hausfraus' in response to political pressure, propaganda and laws passed to encourage the idea that a woman's place was in the home. Marriage and child bearing were encouraged, unemployed fathers had priority over single men in job applications; taxes were cut so that the larger the family, the less tax paid; posters, radio and magazines all put forward the ideal of the perfect Aryan family with father out at work serving the Reich and mother doing likewise by staying at home to look after a growing family.

Women who did work outside the home found that their jobs were taken over by men. This happened in industry and the professions, and women found that there were only jobs for them where the Reich needed them because men did not want to do the work. So for example women doctors lost their jobs but not nurses. Even with the outbreak of war the position of women did not improve. There was no need for them in the economy as there was in the Allied Countries because Germany used 'guest' workers from Occupied Europe to keep the country running. Ironically the women of the Occupied Countries found that much of the burden of providing for their children, organizing resistance and keeping the country viable fell on them.

ABOVE: Film star Marlene Dietrich wearing the masculine style of clothing which she wore regularly around Hollywood. She visited Paris in 1933 wearing a man's suit despite the French law against women wearing men's clothing in public.
BELOW: Student typists learning their craft at the Students' Careers Association.

1933 POSTSCRIPTS

● The British Nationality and Status of Aliens Act allowed women who married non-British nationals to keep their British nationality, but only in those cases where they did not acquire their husbands' nationality (previously in such cases they would have effectively been stateless).

● The Federal government and several large employers in the USA decided they would no longer employ married women. During the Depression married women workers were seen as a primary reason for the massive unemployment throughout the world.

● Various women's groups formed a Women's Health Committee to investigate the state of women's health and campaign for improvements in provision, especially for married women who had no right to free medical treatment under their husbands' insurance schemes.

WOMEN ON INQUEST JURIES
'I enjoyed it,' says one

Women sat on a coroner's jury for the first time in London yesterday.

They were summoned for inquests at Battersea SW, and the coroner, Dr Edwin Smith, referring to the innovation said:

'In case it is thought that mothers and wives have been taken indiscriminately from their babies and domestic work, my officers assure me that this new procedure is welcomed in this district.'

Daily Mail, 16 September 1933

Treat Your Sun-tan *Tactfully!*

JOAN BERINGER shows you the way

THIS tanning and bleaching business must be an annual source of mystery to the masculine mind.

Women, while the short holiday season lasts, do all they can to look like bronze statues. In a few days after their return home they will rush to their favourite beauty parlour for bleaching treatment.

Unreasonable, I admit. But then women *are* like that. My only objection comes when I hear women demand to have their complexions changed in the shortest possible time.

For it is dangerous, especially to a sensitive skin, to bleach too quickly. Bleaching must be done by degrees.

That Cream-and-Roses Look

Ideally one would put oneself in the hands of a beauty specialist and take a course of six to twelve treatments. This is outside the reach of the majority of us.

But a bleaching course can be given at home with perfect success, provided we restrain our impatience to return to cream and roses and use our bleaching preparations with due care.

A new after-summer bleaching outfit for home use will be popular this autumn. It is simple to use, moderately priced, and is packed all together in a neat case.

After the neck and face, or whichever part is to be whitened, has been carefully cleansed with cream, a bleaching ointment which is the vital part of the treatment is spread over the skin.

This ointment has a stimulating action on the skin, and brings the blood quickly to the surface. The

From this—

eyes and lips, therefore, should be carefully avoided.

At the first treatment the ointment should be left on for two or three minutes only, the time being gradually increased as the course progresses.

In the case of a sensitive skin, a minute may be sufficient. Your individual reaction will quickly tell you.

The ointment is removed, not with water or cream, but with muscle oil. Another generous application of skin food, and a freshener with tonic, will complete the treatment.

A Bleaching Course

In the beauty culture department of one of the big stores, a mask is the leading feature of a six-treatment bleaching course.

To get the best results, the treatment must be taken twice weekly.

First the skin is cleansed and, in order to open and make more receptive the pores of the skin, a short massage is given. Then you receive a very thorough oiling before the bleaching mask is applied.

At the first treatment the mask will be left on for perhaps ten minutes, gradually increasing the duration until, finally, the twenty-five-minutes maximum is reached.

After the paste is removed, the skin is left to soak in a lotion that is redolent of marigold flowers; this is a bleach in itself, but has delicately cooling and healing properties as well.

Many women will be rushing to bleach and freckle cream as soon as they get back from their holidays. Here again a word of caution is necessary.

Don't leave the bleaching cream on too long. If the skin feels resentful and sore, mix your bleach or freckle cream with a little skin food or almond oil.

Despite an intensive education in tanning without tears, many women will find when they return home that the skin on the body, especially on the back and the legs, is scaly and dry.

The best means of getting rid of this unsightly appearance is, before

the bath, to brush on a mixture of skin food (or cold cream) and almond oil, working it well into the pores If preferred, a blend of olive and almond oils can be rubbed in. instead of cream.

Care After the Bath

See that the bath water is softened, dry very thoroughly and then rub in some more cream or oil. or use a soothing

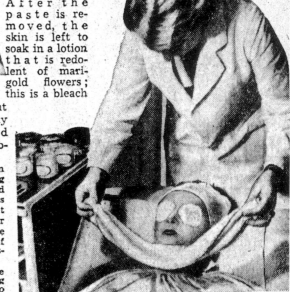

—to this!

hand lotion or jelly for the purpose.

A long-handled bath brush, provided the bristles are not too harsh, is an excellent medium for the application of cream to the back.

When available, buttermilk well blended with a good make of cold cream makes an inexpensive bleach for use on the body.

The cream should be warmed and the buttermilk added by degrees.

WAGING WAR *on* MOTHS

PUBLIC Enemy No. 1 in the house is undoubtedly the moth. Thanks to the hot summer that we have had, moths are still very much in evidence. Free your home from this pest with one of the useful insect sprays now on the market.

The actual damage to furs, feathers, and fabrics is, of course, the work of the moth grub, which hatches from its egg. Moth eggs are deposited in furs and skins, on the surface of closely woven cloths, and between strands of wool in loose material. As these eggs are very fragile, an easy method of moth control is by frequent shakings, brushings. and beatings of all garments and furnishings.

Before clothing is put away for any length of time it should be thoroughly cleaned, the

clothes moth grub makes directly for soiled spots. During the brushing pay special attention to coat collars, flaps of pockets, and other likely places.

After making sure that the garments are free from infestation, take steps to keep them so. Shut your clothes up in dress boxes and seal the lids down with adhesive tape, or place them in bags and seal the openings. You can also tie them up in parcels of strong brown paper, taking care to seal the joins in the wrapping.

In sealed containers

Place camphor, broken into small pieces. pyrethrum powder, flaked naphthalene, or crushed crystals of paradichlorbenzine, between the folds of the garments. These strongly smelling substances should be placed in closed and sealed containers or the fumes will escape.

Where an outbreak of moth has been discovered in upholstered furniture, treatment with paradichlorbenzine is recommended.

Crush the crystals finely, and scatter them liberally over the cover. Pay special attention to all crevices

in the back and sides of chairs and settees. Then wrap the furniture well in blankets to keep in the fumes of the chemical. Keep the room heated for several days' with the furniture wrapped up, and the moth grubs will be killed.

Save your carpets

Where carpets have been attacked by moth, the floor boards should be thoroughly treated with turpentine. Turpentine will destroy any clothes moth—egg, grub, or winged moth—with which it comes in contact. But, of course, it should not be used indiscriminately upon materials on account of staining. A reliable insect spray will not, however, harm fabrics or food.

Turn the carpet wrong side uppermost, and lay a cloth wrung out of boiling water over the affected parts. Press with a hot iron for steam and heat to kill grubs and eggs. Use the hot iron again over a dry cloth to make sure that no trace of damp is left in the carpet.

Repeat this treatment at intervals until you are sure that the carpet is free from moth.

Jennifer Snow.

1934

Slimming

'A woman can never be too thin or too rich,' was a famous saying of the 1930s, often attributed to Wallis Simpson, later Duchess of Windsor. Whoever first said it the sentiment expressed clearly the fashion and aspirations of the time. The Depression had made money short for a good number of people, especially the growing numbers of working-class unemployed. Hollywood, with its lavish lifestyle and its vast output of films, was becoming an important source for images of women and many fashions had their origins there.

The fashions of the 1930s were, despite the economic climate, many and quite varied. Trousers and shorts for women became acceptable as casual wear. Bathing costumes, including twopieces, became more recognizably modern. These casual clothes, together with the fashionable silhouettes of day and evening dresses, all demanded slimness, especially around the hips.

Slimming became a serious business for many women, and newspapers and magazines, together with a whole host of gadgets, all promised advice and results. Exercise was seen as a way of becoming slimmer and was a popular pastime in the form of golf, tennis and the like for the wealthy, while organizations like the League of Health and Beauty catered to a wide range of women who participated in exercise classes. Dieting too was important to maintain the right figure, rather an irony in countries like Britain and USA where many people barely had enough to eat because of the economic situation.

Around 1934 the shape of women's clothing began to change so that by the end of the 1930s the bustless, bottomless, waistless silhouette of the '20s had disappeared altogether. What replaced it was an altogether more shapely outline, padded shoulders or puffed sleeves emphasizing the classic hourglass shape of the Victorian era. But the outline was altogether slimmer than that of the Victorian women and dieting and exercise were usually necessary to maintain this shape.

Fashion trends in the 1930s were still mainly for the reasonably well off. There was more fashionable mass-produced and consequently cheaper clothing available but the economic situation meant that often working-class women struggled to afford anything, let alone anything fashionable, to wear. They had to be content to dream about the looks they saw in films or magazines and newspapers and hope to be able to afford a scarf, belt, fabric trim or hat to enable them to look a little more 'glamorous'.

ABOVE: *The new line for 1934 – a dress in black satin.*

LEFT: *A two-piece bathing suit from America.*

BELOW: *Members of the Women's League of Health and Beauty rehearsing for a display.*

1934   POSTSCRIPTS

July – Briton Dorothy Round won the women's singles and the mixed doubles finals at the first Wimbledon Championship in which women were permitted to wear shorts.

September – Evangeline Booth became the first woman General in the Salvation Army.

December – As part of a general 'Westernization' of the country, women in Turkey were given the vote.

WOMEN'S BRAINS ARE SMALLER – Not their Intellect

'Women have smaller brains than men, but do not run away with the idea that they are less intelligent,' said Professor Cyril Burt in a lecture at Kingsway Hall, Kingsway, last night.

He was speaking on 'The Psychologist's Measurement of Intelligence', and he declared that the size of the brain had nothing to do with the efficiency of the mind.

Daily Mail, 30 January 1934

Joan Beringer asks— Do You Look Your Best at the Wheel?

THE open sports car has captured feminine fancy.

Green, scarlet, white, blue as a kingfisher's wing, like the kingfisher the sports car flashes into our vision on its brief summery career. More often than not there is a woman at the wheel.

As she waves you good-bye, she looks a picture. Every eyelash curled up with mascara, vivid lips, beret tilted on piled-up curls. So far, so good. But the sports car driver hasn't gone a mile, let alone a hundred miles. And I shouldn't like to say how those lashes or that beret and curls will look at the end of the day's run!

Head comfort and the minimum of make-up are points for serious consideration when planning a run or a holiday tour in an open car.

There is nothing so smart as a beret worn at the right angle by the right person, but I cannot agree that it is the ideal headgear for summer motoring in the open.

A hat like a ski-ing cap—

actually I wear my ski-ing cap for motoring all the year round—is perfect. It protects the eyes from glare and the head from the rays of the sun.

If you cannot be parted from your beret, then you must wear a net, and should pin the ends of your hair closely to the head with invisible pins. The best kind of net is the invisible cap shape. It can be had in several colours, and really is invisible.

Powder Base is Important

For your motoring holiday, simplify your make-up as much as you can. Don't use a heavy, greasy powder base in summer, or after a few hours' motoring you will find a layer of grease over your skin that will attract every particle of dust that blows.

The ideal foundation for protecting the skin is a lotion and cream combined. If your skin is dry or sensitive give it a few moments' massage with skinfood before making up. Leave the skinfood on for five minutes, wipe off every trace of cream with a mild tonic, then pat on the semi-liquid cream.

Protect Your Eyes

This new powder base is available in every shade from peach to bronze. If you are likely to get tanned, take the bronze shade with you.

On a motoring holiday, eye make-up is, I think, best left at home or packed for evening wear only. I am sure you will not forget dark glasses and an eye lotion for cleansing and refreshing the eyes after the run, but you may forget to protect your eyelids. Even with glasses, the eyelids often get burned and painful under the hot sun. Grease them during the day and again at night if the skin round the eyes smarts.

Preventing Sunburn

Powder, if used at all, should be dusted on with a sparing hand, but the nose can have a double coat of powder over a foundation of sunproof paste.

When driving an open car I always wear a scarf or a high-necked sports shirt. If the shirt is left open, rub a sunproof paste well in and powder over fairly thickly.

Loose gloves are a comfort when covering big mileage. They protect the hands and nails from dirt, and if the gloves are powdered inside will keep the hands deliciously cool and fragrant. I always punch tiny ventilation holes in the backs of old loose gauntlets.

However tired you may be after the run, the face and neck must be thoroughly cleansed with a light cleansing cream or milk. At least three cleansings will be necessary to ensure getting out every atom of dust and grime. Soap and water should not be used after being out in the sun.

For Cleansing

Scalp as well as skin cleanliness is essential to comfort and beauty when on an outdoor holiday. When packing for your motor tour, then, whatever else you have to leave behind don't forget your cleansing cream or cleansing milk and a packet of shampoo powder.

I have recently discovered a shampoo that seems to have been made for the open-air motorist. It is non-soapy, therefore easily rinsed out, and is not affected by hard water. In a few moments the scalp is freed of dust and grime, and a quick rinsing leaves the hair bright and lustrous.

Sandals and Suntop— in LINEN or CROCHET

RENÉE MAUDE

NO beach outfit is complete without a sunbathing "top" and sandals. You can make these for yourself.

TO crochet the sandal you will require an old pair of rope-soled, calico-topped sandals; an ounce or so of left-over wool in two colours, and a little white silk thread.

The model is in navy blue, cherry and white.

Commence with navy blue wool. Make a chain of crochet long enough to stretch fairly tightly across the widest part of your foot; turn and double crochet into each stitch; repeat for six more rows. Then do two lines of double crochet in cherry wool and finish off with one row in white silk thread. This gives a firmer edge.

Cut the calico top away from each side. When you sew the crochet

pass the needle through the middle of the rope.

Measure Carefully

The heel is in three pieces. Put the sandal on and measure length of chain required for the strip which passes round the back of your heel. Proceed as before, using the blue wool for four rows, the cherry for two rows and finish off with one row in white silk thread. When sewing on, shape the strip so that the white edge is longer than the blue, as seen in the picture.

Measure the length of the two side straps and make these in the same way, but this time the blue edge is longer. Fasten with snappers, or buttons and loops.

If you want a sun-top to match the sandals you will require 3oz. of 3-ply wool in navy blue, 1oz. of 3-ply cherry wool and 1 ball of white silk thread of the same thickness as a 4-ply wool. A steel crochet hook size 1½.

To Crochet the Suntop

Work rather loosely to get six stitches and seven rows to the inch.

Commence with navy wool; make three chain; turn and double crochet into two stitches, turn with 2 chain, increase one stitch at the beginning

of each row by working 2 d.c. into first stitch. Continue working until the triangle measures 36ins. down each side from the top.

Now double crochet 3 rows in cherry wool to form a border all round and finish off with one row in white silk. At the corners put in 3 d.c. to keep the work flat.

To Make the Straps

For the 2 straps which tie round the waist, commence with 4 or 6 chain according to width desired, turn and double crochet into each stitch until each strap is long enough. Stitch one to each end of the long straight edge, cross them at the back and tie in front.

For the strap round the neck proceed in the same way but make it narrower, and use two colours. This can be fastened at the back with a loop and button, or it may be tied. The suntop is passed through the strap, then turned over to the right side and secured with a button.

Spotted Linen or Silk Suntop and Sandals

Rope soles and one yard of 36-inch material required.

Instructions for Suntop

Fold your material into a triangle and cut along the folded line. One triangle will make your suntop. The edges can be picoted or hemmed. If you prefer it, a double border of material in contrasting colour may be added instead.

You can make your sandals from the remaining triangle of material.

Instructions for Sandals

Place your foot on the rope sole and measure the length required for the two cross-over pieces over the widest part of the foot. Measure the length which you will need for the small side pieces, and measure round your ankle so that you will get the correct length of the little strap.

Make all the strips of double material. Attach them to the rope sole in the same way as the crocheted ones. If necessary you can use an insole to cover any roughness of the rope sole.

You can fasten the ankle strap with buckle, buttons, or ribbon ties.

FLOWER SETTINGS

Marigolds in a Grey Vase

MARIGOLDS are in full bloom now, and they make one of the loveliest, as well as the least expensive, flower decorations.

Here they are seen in a pale grey pottery vase designed by Keith Murray. Its shape is perfect for the arrangement of these somewhat stiff stems, allowing the flowers to branch gracefully.

If you want a different colour scheme, you can buy this Wedgwood vase in white, buff or light green.

1935

Married Women at Work

ABOVE: *Irène Joliot-Curie.*
BELOW: *Women in France were still fighting for an equal franchise and using many of the same tactics as the pre-war suffragettes in Britain.*

As the Depression and unemployment grew during the 1930s following the Wall Street Crash of October 1929, married women workers found their position increasingly difficult. The unemployed, men whose jobs were threatened, single women who had to support themselves saw married women who worked as a threat for a variety of reasons. Unemployed men and men whose firms were in difficult financial positions saw all women as a threat in the job market as the average woman's wage in industry was only 40 per cent of the average man's wage.

There was rarely any understanding that wives may have needed to work and no sympathy at all for wives who worked because they wanted to. Married women who worked were seen as greedy, working for pin money to buy luxuries for themselves when they already had a husband to support them. Single women earning their living often shared this view of working wives. And life was difficult for a single woman with no one to support her. While married women who were widowed became eligible for a pension, most single women in employment worked for years with no chance of a pension. Domestic service, a huge employer of single women in the 1930s, was not covered by unemployment benefit. An unmarried woman's only chance of providing for herself was to hang on to her job.

This, and the general public feeling against working wives, explains why often women themselves voted for, indeed insisted upon, marriage bars being imposed in many jobs. In 1930 women in the Civil Service had voted in favour of just such a ban. And the policy of excluding married women from work continued throughout the 1930s. In June 1935 the London and Home Counties Joint Electric Authority adopted a recommendation that women employees who married should be required to resign. The following month after a fierce debate the London County Council decided to remove the ban imposed in 1923 on married women doctors and teachers but this was a rare case and often where no rule existed there was a *de facto* ban on working wives.

In Britain the idea of a woman giving up her job on marriage had a long tradition but the idea grew even in countries where there had never been rules against employing married women. In 1933 the Federal government and many large employers in the USA brought in a marriage bar. And in the Fascist states of Europe the exclusion policy went even further, banning all women from most jobs.

1935 POSTSCRIPTS

July – At a National Conference on Maternity and Child Welfare, Minister of Health Sir Kingsley Wood called Britain's failure to cut the maternal mortality figures 'a great blot on the good health record of the nation'.

September – Women workers in Mexico were given the vote.

December – Irène Joliot-Curie, daughter of Marie and Pierre Curie, was awarded the Nobel Prize for Chemistry, together with her husband Jean-Frédéric Joliot-Curie.

GIRLS ARE SATISFIED

The Institute [of Industrial Psychology] reported that a large proportion of these [modern business] girls regarded their work as *a stop-gap until they attained their real ideal of marriage*. And why not? If every girl entered business determined to pursue a lifetime's career the employment market would become more crowded than it is today, and the prospect for homes of the future would be extremely poor.

Extract from a *Daily Mail* Leader, 1 July 1935

Your CHILD'S FUTURE depends on YOU

The Popular Novelist URSULA BLOOM Gives Outspoken Advice to Parents — in particular to Mothers

YOUTH should be the training time for life, but many parents forget this. They see the baby of to-day rather than the man of to-morrow, and, spoiling their baby, they spoil his future too, and leave him badly handicapped in the race for life itself. As he grows up they rob him of his greatest asset, a knowledge of how to live and how to get the most out of living.

A "Good Mother"

As soon as it was possible, my son was encouraged to do things for himself. It is the lazy parent who chooses to do everything for the child, believing that she is never sparing herself and being "such a good mother." It is maddening to watch a little boy's dilatory efforts to cope with the first knotty problems of dressing, but it should be dealt with.

Children can bath and dress many years before we allow them to do so.

I made my child buy his own sweets before he could talk properly, and he went alone, never attempting to cross dangerous roads or brave traffic heedlessly.

Early in life he learnt to appreciate honesty in adults. I never cheated and he knew it.

Even a babe respects truth and has a right to demand it. All young creatures need one person at least in their world on whom they can rely for sincere judgment.

His Own Risk

As he grew older I did not demand the implicit obedience which had been enforced in his infancy. I explained pros and cons, and left him to try things if he wished. If he tried them after I had warned him, and was hurt, then he got no sympathy, and his ventures proved to him very soundly that I was an unbiased judge.

At eleven he had a dress allowance which covered small details of his dress, and by this means I taught him responsibility and how to manage money. It is unfair to expect a youth suddenly to understand the tricky mysteries of buying and making money "do." At eleven

a boy is old enough to be serious on such points, and if he is one of the careless type who ruins his clothes, the fact that he has to replace them out of money which is not elastic, soon teaches him a wholesome respect for them.

Wasted Years

I try hard to impress on my son the immense value of to-day as compared with the minor importance of to-morrow. This is a lesson I myself did not learn until I had wasted thirty years of to-days, and it is the foundation-stone of making the most of life.

It is difficult to generalise on upbringing. So much has to be taken into consideration. Temperament. Sensitivity. The conditions under which you live. All these things must influence the methods that you employ. I have tried hard to be reasonable and normal, for I believe normality to be the greatest asset you can give a child.

I hope in that future for which I have tried to fit my son that I shall realise the rights he will have and respect them.

I want to say. "Here is your life, my son. Take it. I gave it you, I trained you for it, and it is yours. As your mother I cease to be. Let me stay now your friend. And pray God I'll be your very best friend always."

"A LATHER — from a Soapless Shampoo, Enid?"

"Ah, that's the AVA Secret."

Strange it is—but splendid abundant lather foams up gloriously from AVA SOAPLESS SHAMPOO . . , miraculously cleansing and clearing away every tiny vestige of dust and dandruff. And then—how simple and quick AVA is to use! No sticky after-film

HOLIDAYS AFLOAT

PAULA CATOR

describes Plans and Equipment for the Ideal River Holiday.

MUCH has been said about "life on the ocean wave" on board large and luxurious liners as an ideal holiday, but not enough has been said about the delights of a holiday afloat on rivers, lakes, and waterways on board much smaller but none the less exciting water craft.

A holiday of this nature is easily arranged for either a family party or a party of friends, or merely a couple

Let me place before your imagination an array of water craft in which you can take your holiday afloat.

Starting with the smallest, there is the canoe. Wet and rather perilous, you will think. Here you are wrong, for the latest touring canoe is safe, waterproof, and comfortable, and will hold one to three people as well as your camping equipment. Not only this, but it is also collapsible, packs into a canvas bag, and can be easily carried.

You can take your canoe anywhere, and it will take you anywhere where there is a waterway.

Women should find canoeing quite easy, as there is no strain attached, and, provided certain common-sense rules are observed, it is not in the least dangerous, although it is better that you should be able to swim. There is a British Canoe Association to which a great many women belong.

As an alternative, for the canoe holiday is not for everyone, a camping punt is good fun for a small party of two or three, who enjoy the simple life. This you can hire complete with cushions and mattresses, a table-board and large jar for water. There will also be a water-proof canvas cover which goes right over the boat at night and during wet weather.

River or Broads

Then we come to the more roomy and luxurious water craft, for parties of four to twelve. There is the wherry-yacht on the Broads, which you can sail or run with a motor, or the motor cruiser, launch, and houseboat available on the river.

Shorts or trousers are really justified for the river holiday, and these can be worn most of the time, varied by one or two changes in brightly coloured sports shirts, and, of course, have a warm sweater. A beret and a linen-brimmed hat is all the headwear you need, and for footwear a pair of plimsolls and strong walking shoes. Add a warm overcoat for chilly evenings, an oilskin and waders, and you have the main part of your outfit.

1936

Women as Homemakers

In 1936 most women's sole job was that of homemaker. Many women still never had a paid job outside the home between leaving the parental home and going to live with their husbands. And the vast majority of women who did have paid employment left as soon as they married.

The woman at home was defined in census information as unoccupied. This was despite the fact that for most women, without any servants or labour-saving devices, a life looking after a home and family was still one of unremitting toil.

All washing was done by hand often in water boiled specially for the job because there was no hot running water. There were no easy-care fabrics to lighten the load and in 1930 only a third of homes, rising to two-thirds in 1939, had electricity so that even ironing was a time-consuming process involving the heating of irons on an open fire or cooker before using them.

Cooking, too, took a great deal of time. Food had to be bought regularly, usually daily because there was no way to keep it for longer. A lack of convenience foods and the fact that many homes, a third even by 1939, still had ranges which had to be prepared and fuelled before cooking could begin added to the demands on women's time.

Even though Hoover had marketed the first vacuum cleaner in 1908, only 10 per cent of homes in Britain had one by 1939. In other homes the cleaning, sweeping and polishing was all done by hand and done regularly for there was a fierce pride in most women to have a spotless home. To be a good homemaker and a good mother were the goals most women were taught to aspire to.

The fact that women had no economic power, no money and no right to a share of their husbands' money, was the main reason why labour-saving devices were not more advanced in Britain in the 1930s. A woman would have to persuade her husband to buy an electric washer or vacuum cleaner and most men could see no need for such devices.

ABOVE: A kitchen with a range for heating and cooking.
BELOW: Beryl Markham is pictured here after she made a forced landing in Novia Scotia and sustained a minor head injury. Thirty minutes later she flew on to New York.

1936 POSTSCRIPTS

● The Soviet Union which had legalized abortion on demand after the Revolution changed its laws to make abortion less easy to obtain and aimed to give more support to mothers with large families, mainly as a result of the high death and injury rate caused by abortions. But many of these abortions were carried out in poor medical conditions and by unqualified staff.

February – The artist Dame Laura Knight became the first woman to be appointed to the Royal Academy.

May – Jasmine Bligh and Elizabeth Cowell joined the BBC as the first women television announcers but old prejudices remained, expressed in comments such as these by a letter writer to the *Daily Mail* in November: 'When women read prose or poetry in a radio broadcast their voices lack character and emotion.
'What is there more to be desired than the voice of a man?'

July – The Midwives Act was passed. This instructed local authorities to provide a service of trained midwives available to every expectant mother whatever her circumstances.

September – Beryl Markham landed in New York after flying solo across the Atlantic.

Dorothy Evans of the British National Association of Women Civil Servants speaking at the opening (of the Conference of the International Federation of Business and Professional Women) said, 'We do not want to be "women chemists", "women artists", "women teachers", we are chemists, artists or teachers. The argument that men must be paid more because of family responsibilities is not to be taken seriously. Arguments against the adoption of equal pay have never been sound, we women in the Civil Service are undaunted by our government's attitude. We intend to return to the attack.'
Daily Mail, 29 July 1936

Elizabeth Carlisle says
MEN really LIKE make-up

though sometimes they pretend they don't!

A MEDICAL officer of health recently insisted in a public report that "lipstick is repulsive," and condemned the use of cosmetics.

Most women, of course, will smile at the idea and proceed to experiment with the newest spring make-up. But what about the men? What do they say?

Some of them, if you ask them, may pretend they dislike make-up, simply because of an ingrained conservatism. Some of them will go so far as to acknowledge that they like a little—only a little, of course—nothing that looks artificial, please!

Two Viewpoints

But if a man says he dislikes his wife to make up (he's apt to call it "painting her face") it's probably only because he doesn't like seeing her do it. And an hour later he may, quite sincerely, admire a brunette who is, as the wife is furiously aware, "painted" with considerable skill.

So it seems that most masculine minds are divided on the subject.

Expert's Opinion

But what about the experts, the men whose work brings them into daily contact with lovely women? Well, curiously enough, they all say: "Make up, of course, but for heaven's sake, do it well."

C. B. Cochran, who has chosen so many lovely girls to appear in his revues that he has lost count of the number, likes to be completely deceived as to a woman's make-up. He says she ought to do it so skilfully that she looks as though she wore none at all. And as for scarlet finger-nails . . . he shudders at the thought, except when the fingers are white and tapering and perfectly shaped.

Well, what about a dressmaker? Norman Hartnell, for instance, who makes the Queen's clothes. No deception for him. For brunettes, he goes all out for "well-defined lips of the deepest pomegranate or carmine, soft brown eyelids, hair drawn off the brow and always gleaming."

And here's an interesting tip for blondes. He suggests that for two-thirds of the year they should remain "pale as a pink petal with just a suggestion of eyeshadow and rouge, gently marked lips and pale rose finger-nails." But in the summer he thinks they ought to wear a "beautiful shade of tangerine, with the colour of their lips deepened to poppy."

Photographer's Complaint

It isn't really fair to ask a photographer his opinion of feminine make-up. He sees too much of it. Captain Peter North, who has photographed most of London's loveliest women, even complains that he can tell at just which beauty parlour any woman in any smart restaurant has been spending the morning.

"Women ought to make up, of course," he says impatiently, "but why don't they learn the job properly? First at a beauty parlour, and then practising in front of the mirror until they become skilled workmen."

There was a time, somewhere back in the nineteen-twenties, when débutantes gloried in making up with slashing strokes of the lipstick and bold dabs of rouge. But not in 1937. The tide has turned. The average débutante to-day knows that she can manage things more cleverly than that.

Rex Whistler, the artist, thinks make-up is a good thing. "When I do see a pretty young girl looking pale and anæmic, I always think how greatly just a touch of lipstick and rouge would improve her.

". . . Pale lashes, too, annoy me—I long to see them darkened."

But this unusual young man likes freckles as well, that bane of six débutantes out of ten. So make up, but not enough to cover your freckles, is his advice.

And the lesson to be learned from our experts, it seems, is one which will for ever silence masculine criticism. First, to learn to copy nature with art—and then never to let anyone know.

Housewife's Diary

New form of strainer

I REALLY thought we had already been introduced to every possible form of juice extractor. But at a demonstration the other day I was interested in yet another which, besides squeezing and straining the juice from oranges, lemons, or grapefruit, can be turned over and used as an ordinary strainer, for sifting flour or sugar, or even for making just a single cup of tea direct into a cup. Made of rigid mesh which is rustless and stainless, this useful item costs a shilling.

Stainless steel skewers

STRAIGHT, stainless steel skewers with an exceptionally well-pointed end are a distinct improvement on the old-fashioned wavy variety. A set of five, in graded sizes ranging from seven to three inches, cost 7d. per card, and will be found of invaluable help by the cook.

Fluted blade knife

A NEW stainless steel knife just put on the market has a specially fluted blade which really does slice meat as thinly as you can wish, and it has the advantage that it can always be sharpened when required on an ordinary steel. A full-sized carving knife costs 5s. 9d., while a carver slightly smaller and lighter in weight, which has been designed for a woman's use, is priced at 4s. 6d. A small kitchen knife, having one of these practical blades with a handle so fitted that water will not penetrate between it, is being sold for 1s. 4d.

Labour saving board

A PARTICULARLY strong ironing table in a new design has legs so arranged that whole garments can be turned round on the board without any obstruction. Rubber feet keep the table absolutely firm, and besides a sleeve-board which swings out when required, one end of the table is specially shaped to facilitate the ironing of shoulders and collars.
—D. K.

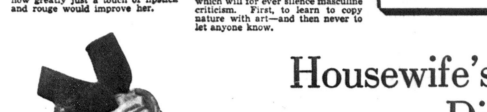

THAT you will probably be wearing a gaily coloured turban this spring is due to those Indian visitors of ours who came over for the Coronation.

Paris milliners are enthusiastic about them—they had time to study the intricate turbans worn by the Indian maharajahs and their suites who made a long stay in Paris before coming to London.

You can wear a turban pushed forward on to your forehead, if you like, on the lines of the Violette Marsan model shown here. In dull satin striped in grey and red, black and beige, it has a bow of black velvet ribbon sticking out of the back of the crown.

They are attractive things, these turbans, but if you want to wear one successfully you must remember several "Don'ts"; such as don't wear them with tweeds, don't forget to dress your hair to match, and don't forget that your face should be carefully made up.

RECIPE for TO-DAY

French Almond Tartlets

LINE patty tins with firm, rich, short crust pastry rolled out very thinly. Put a suspicion of jam in each. Mix scant 2oz. ground almonds with 3½oz. of castor sugar and add the white of one egg. Mix well, put the mixture into a small saucepan, heat and beat until it does not stick to the fingers. Beat another egg white stiffly (use the two yolks for another dish), and add to pan off the heat. Three-parts fill the prepared tins, and put two halves of almonds on top. Dredge with icing sugar before baking for about 25 minutes.

1937

Divorce Made Easier

In December of 1936 King Edward VII abdicated in order to marry the divorcee Mrs Wallis Simpson after it had been made clear by both the Church and government that they would not sanction the marriage of the King to a divorced woman.

Only weeks before the King's abdication speech, MP and writer A. P. Herbert had introduced a Bill to widen the grounds for divorce. The 1923 Matrimonial Causes Act, while granting women equal grounds for divorce, still relied on proving adultery by one of the partners. A. P. Herbert said of the 1923 Act, 'People are encouraged to choose between two abominations – adultery or perjury.'

Ironically Herbert's Bill had the support of much of the same Church and State that had condemned the King's proposed marriage and the Act was finally passed in July 1937. The new Marriage Act extended the grounds for divorce to enable either party to sue for divorce, for cruelty, for desertion after three years and for insanity after five years of marriage. This took some of the stigma out of divorce as it was not necessarily the result of an immoral act, although the Church continued to refuse to bless any remarriages.

Although divorce became a little easier to obtain with A. P. Herbert's Act it was still a drastic option for most women. As a divorce court judge warned wives in the same month the Bill was passed, they should not expect a third of their husband's earnings on divorce. He said there was no rule, as was commonly thought, that they were entitled to such a portion and that second marriages had to be taken into account. Divorce, then as now, brought financial problems to both parties but women, and especially women with children, fared worst of all.

ABOVE: Amelia Earhart
BELOW: Wallis Simpson pictured at Cannes with her pet terrier.

1937 POSTSCRIPTS

April – An article in the *Daily Mail* claimed that because two women secretaries had been appointed to two top government officials – one to the Director General of the Post Office, the other to the Minister of Labour – it had 'killed the reproach that women cannot keep secrets'.

June – Mrs G. B. Miller was the first woman owner to win the Derby with her horse Midday Sun.

July – Amelia Earhart went missing on her round-the-world flight.

MISSES WHO WANT TO BE MRS

Mrs Pethick Lawrence, one of the leaders of the Suffragist movement, wants to know why single women should be obliged to broadcast the fact by calling themselves 'Miss'.

Speaking at a luncheon of the Women's Freedom League in London yesterday she said it had always been her dream that women should not have to be divided into 'Mrs' and 'Miss' when there was no indication of whether a man was married or unmarried.

Daily Mail, 10 June 1937

Grey alpaca short-sleeved jacket over a tan-and-white spot voile blouse joined to a grey alpaca pleated skirt.

Bright yellow linen dress, dirndl-type, with vivid embroidery round the hemline.

Navy - and - white spotted brassière and pants outfit. Accompanying it, a white linen skirt which ties round the waist, then flies open.

Backless printed-linen sun and play-suit with a high-necked front to the shorts section. Over it goes a matching collarless dress.

Printed crêpe evening dress, cut on sleek, fitting lines, with matching bolero.

sketches by BENINGTON

CECILE LAVIGNE, *involved in the holiday spirit, advises you to*

TRAVEL LIGHT

—NONE of us wears everything that goes into the bag. The thing to do is to assemble holiday clothes on double, even triple, duty lines.

As for time, no more clothes are needed for a month's holiday than for a fortnight's, unless you are going to run into drastic changes of climate.

PACK TIGHT

Even the cleverest packing fingers, the most ingenious packing gadgets, cannot beat the old debbil crease.

So fill every quarter of an inch. Ruthlessly press your tissue-papered frocks one on top of the other. A little extra pressure might mean one case instead of two, which is my idea of travel pleasure. Creases shake out at journey's end, or you will take your travelling iron—they make them now to suit any voltage. If you are feeling classy, best things can be smoothed out at your hotel.

MCustoms of the Customs

MODERN luggage, with its clever pocketing and compartmenting, saves many packing headaches. Neat toilet cases prevent the minor tragedies of spilt lotions. Bottle and jar luggage has never been so varied, useful, decorative, inexpensive.

Anyway, whatever you do, there is always the Customs.

That exquisite irony of things whereby dozens of frequent 11 buses draw up while you wait long for an infrequent 96 ; until you need an 11, when 96 after 96 mock you as they pass, reaches its height in the Customs situation.

When I have packed with last-minute haste and casualness, thinking the Customs will muck things up, anyhow, I am never asked to open my baggage.

As sure as I see fit to pack like a careful spinster, uncaring Customs hands ravage everything.

So with me there is a temptation not to bother about packing carefully for abroad. Also a temptation not to declare. Yes, and I can imagine how my old friend Irony would treat that little caper.

—Holiday Abroad

The clothes discussed here are for any ordinary holiday abroad, which means, generally, some sort of Continental resort—sea, lake, river, or plain country.

Town, sight-seeing holidays, mountain holidays, cruises, or any specialised activity holidays need different outfits, of course.

Golfers, tennis-ers, fishers, riders, pack-on-backers, will obviously take their particularised play clothes.

Lots of people like to spend lots of their holidays playing their own games. For them, sports clothes should be incorporated into holiday kit.

Tennis can be played in ordinary beach suits, golf in what you travel in, or the culottes or bags that ought to go into every woman's bag. Riding offers no clothes compromise. Riding things are just plain extras.

Walking and fishing take in shorts, culottes or slacks again, and if anyone asks me what butterfly catchers wear, the answer is I haven't the faintest idea.

One garment I hate to economise on is a swim suit. I always take three, one for the current swim, one for to-morrow morning's swim, because I hate getting into a half-dry affair, and a spare in case I need an extra swim in the late afternoon.

Swim Suits

This year the quickly drying, silky telescopic swim suits are going to be a help, but for those who swim every day, I still think two swim suits a minimum.

One play suit is a must ; and, if it is backless, so much the better, because you do your sunbathing in it. Then when you want to take a cocktail on the terrace, or a quick look-see round the town, you put over it a matching, do-up-down-the-front frock Et voila.

Since you are abroad, there is no reason why you cannot be a bit oh-la-la about your beach clothes. If your body can take it, indulge in a brightly printed cotton bras-and-pants sunbather. You are sure to see plenty of women whose bodies cannot take it.

Over this wear a skirt that ties round the waist, then flies open. Or, à la Heim, a backless affair, starting with a sari top cut in one with the bodice part, then a wide corseletted belt, then a wide reach-the-ground skirt buttoning down front.

Holiday woollies should always be long-sleeved, high-necked.

If it's hot enough, a short-sleeved woolly is too hot.

If it's cold enough, arms and throat are where you feel it. Ours isn't the only country where it's hot enough for a naked outfit one minute, and the next so cold you wonder if you've really come to Greenland.

You will probably live and die in your swim, play, and sunning suits, plus-shorts, culottes, and slacks. But it is nice to have a frock or two by you. One might be of the dirndl type, which, this year, is at the peak of its popularity. Very pretty it is, too, in gay, printed, crease - resisting cotton, with a square-necked top, a full gathered skirt.

Another useful get-up is first in the row drawn above. The dress is schoolgirlish, with a bloused top, a pleated skirt. The coat is short, fitting, with short, turn-back sleeves, cutaway fronts.

Skirt and coat are grey alpaca. The blouse, joined to the skirt, is tan and white spotted, crease-resisting voile. The suit is grand for sightseeing and towning generally. On its own the dress looks all right for not changing for dinner.

Two evening dresses should be enough, one a frothy thing in lace, net, tulle, one a printed crêpe with a matching bolero which would go over the frou-frou dress too.

It all depends. If you want to shake 'em in the casino you'll probably need three or four dresses.

Hat boxes take, of course, a hat for every outfit. My idea of a holiday is no hat except a large flat one for the first sunbathing days, and the hat I travel in.

I can keep serene hair all day long with a little girl ribbon, rather wide, tying on top in a big bow, the rest of the hair tucked quietly into an invisible hair net which really is invisible.

Shoe Sense

Coloured handkerchiefs tying beneath the chin, peasant style, are inclined to make the chin ache. Tie them mammy style instead. It is newer. Best of all, let the hair loose to the wind and sun. Sure, it will take out your curls, but it gives your hair new life, new vitality.

Nothing benefits from a holiday more than the feet. They are unrestricted, happier than at any time in the year. A pair of the new unbelievably comfortable wedge-heeled type for travelling and odd expeditioning, one pair of heelless or flat-heeled fabric beach shoes, one pair of rather dressier linen or canvas shoes to wear with your dresses, and you are all set up.

You will travel in a suit, I suppose, and big coat. A shirt-type dress and blazer is an even better idea. Both come in on any holiday far oftener than a suit does.

BON VOYAGE.

TRAVEL *in a short-sleeved, square-shouldered grey flannel dress, belted at waist, with white pique behind the high curving neckline, and a chalk striped tan fitted cardigan jacket, which will go over practically any other dress.*

The top coat is a plumb-line-straight navy camel, unbelted, with patch pockets, a high neck. The hat is grey felt with a tan petersham band; shoes are white and tan, with wedge heels.

1938

The Abortion Laws Reinterpreted

A Ministry of Health Departmental Commission on Maternal Mortality which reported in 1932 admitted that around 45 per cent of the annual death toll was as a result of unskilled abortion. These figures did not reveal the numbers of women disabled or damaged as a result of self-administered or back-street abortions. Abortion was against the law and had been since 1861 when an Abortion Law determined that anyone, including a doctor or the woman herself, could be sentenced to imprisonment with hard labour for attempting or carrying out an abortion unless the mother's life was in danger.

Although the subject of abortion was not generally a topic for conversation or discussion there was growing support during the 1930s for a change to the 1861 Act. Many people favoured a change in the law to permit abortion in cases of rape and incest, and a few supported the idea of abortion for married women living in poverty and overcrowded conditions, and there were a few, very few, people like the socialist Stella Browne who advocated abortion on demand. In 1938 came a court case which brought the subject into headline news.

A Harley Street surgeon, Dr Aleck Bourne, was charged with carrying out an illegal abortion on a fourteen-year-old girl who had become pregnant as a result of an 'assault' (men could not be charged with rape until the late 1950s) by a Guardsman in Whitehall. Doctor Bourne had deliberately drawn legal attention to the case in order to test the existing law.

Aleck Bourne was found not guilty after the judge had directed that he thought that the law's definition of endangering *the life* of the mother could be interpreted as meaning *the health* of the mother and that if the doctor genuinely believed that the mother's mental or physical health would be severely damaged by the pregnancy it could be terminated. The outcome of the trial was to establish a precedent for future abortion practice. Subsequently a doctor could perform an abortion if he and another doctor believed the mother's sanity or physical wellbeing was threatened.

A *Daily Mail* Leader following Dr Bourne's acquittal described the verdict as a 'decision that will be endorsed by the great majority of the British public'. And although the change was generally welcomed the situation was still rather ill defined and depended upon finding two doctors willing to accept this interpretation of the law. Parliament did not change the existing law for another 29 years.

ABOVE: Helen Moody.
BELOW: Despite a growing awareness of contraception, large families, especially among the poorer levels of society, were still fairly common.

1938 POSTSCRIPTS

July – A Danish woman, Jenny Kammersgaad, became the first person to swim the Baltic Sea, she completed the 37 miles in 40 hours.

• Helen Moody won a record eighth Wimbledon Singles Final in 11 years.

December – The American writer Pearl S. Buck became the fourth woman to be awarded the Nobel Prize for Literature, following Selma Lagerlof in 1909, Grazia Deledda of Italy in 1926 and Sigrid Undset of Norway in 1928.

WOMEN ARE LOGICAL

'Women – are they logical or illogical?' was a point debated in the Court of Appeal yesterday.

'Your lordships know the sex of my client,' said Mr Gilbert Beyfus KC, 'and that logic is not the strong point of that sex.'

And here are the replies that the statement drew:

Lord Justice Greer: I do not agree with that as a general rule.

Lord Justice Claison: That won't do at all. It is a heresy.

Lord Justice Slesser: If you look at the university exam results you will find that women take very high degrees in logic.

Mr Beyfus: I withdraw my remark.

Daily Mail, 2 April 1938

PICK YOURSELF A NECKLACE TO-DAY

Just coloured dice on strands of bright wool.

THE pictures in this page have just arrived from New York, and seem to show that there, at any rate, the trend is "anything goes as a necklace." Screws, dolls' eyes, dice, corn kernels, nothing is too crazy—but remember they must be used with exceptional skill or they'll look just silly.

Well, why not amuse yourself, when you're out of doors to-day, looking for a necklace idea which you can really call your own.

Just as an illustrative suggestion —seashells. The tiny round shells are best. Thread them together on a coloured silk string or thin wire if they're soft enough to bore holes in ; if not, stick them on with sealing wax. And, remember, to bring out the lovely natural colours in the shells, soak them in vinegar first.

Or why not do something clever with flowers ? Garden flowers are best, as the wild ones don't last very long and usually contain so much pollen that they will leave yellow stains on your clothes. But small rose buds or tiny garden pinks (like miniature carnations) would last well and look good sewn on to velvet ribbon to wear round your neck or waist—or even on hair or belts. And if you're in a big hurry, simply thread the stems through the meshes of a gold chain or through a hair-slide.

The ideas are up to you, and you'll have lots of fun finding them.

You'd find this necklace useful if you sprang a ladder—it's made of darning silk spools hanging from a silk plait.

Remember your baby doll with eyes that could open or shut. Here those round shining eyes are clustered together on a velvet ribbon.

Polished metal screws and nuts, strung on twisted strands of wool. If the metal really shines this is most effective.

Here's one you could make yourself from scraps in your sewing drawer—red velvet strawberries stitched to a green wool plait.

ANN TEMPLE

I am getting married soon, and as my fiancé's amusements and mine are so dissimilar I am wondering how we can meet each other more in our leisure.

He always wants to be doing something, trying out gadgets and experimenting with wireless sets. He likes clubs, the cinema, playing cricket and golf.

Can you suggest how I can make him enjoy sitting by the fire sometimes with a book ? He says this does not appeal to him at all.
                                        A. K.

BUT that's a tall order, isn't it ? *Making* someone enjoy something ! How would you feel if he pushed the works of a clock into your hands and said, "Now, just you enjoy mending that " ?

To you, reading is necessary as one of your interests, but, to be honest, lots of people get through life very well without being very keen on reading. Many people who prefer action when they are young do arrive at reading later on in life. They usually begin by reading about their own hobbies.

So don't try to turn him into a sit-by-the-fire person. Let his home be for him a place where he can follow his interests happily. Then you will build up shared interests, and perhaps even come to take an active interest in those which are now dissimilar.

LOOK OUT TO-DAY

In order to get right away from my own problems and the noise of the world's problems and the wear and tear of city life, I am going to

person so affected ? Can you give me a reason for it ? Does climate really affect our disposition ?
                                        A. C.

ONLY the very, very healthy-livered are not affected by the East wind. Don't you know the proverb: "When the wind is in the East, It's neither good for man nor beast " ? and wasn't it Bacon who wrote : "To us in Britain, East wind is held for evil."

We are at our best when the organs and tissues of the body are kept *evenly* at work. The East wind blowing to us over wide lands (and therefore cold) makes a sudden call on certain glands to get busy. They in turn affect the liver—all this a bit of foresight on nature's part to make us feel more energetic in cold weather. With some people the liver rebels—it may have a congenital weakness that way—so they " snap and snarl."

The West wind coming over an ocean heated by the powerful Gulf Stream is warm, so the liver is undisturbed.

Undoubtedly climate affects us. Compare the temperament of a native of warm and sunny Andalusia with that of a native of the bleak and rugged coast of Scotland.

TALES IN PUBLIC

How can I cure my husband of telling little stories against me in public ? It does make me feel so horribly self-conscious.   F. F.

ONE of my readers told me that she had solved this problem in this way. She suggested to her husband that when he was telling

is made for you, not you for the rule. You have to adjust and adapt it. If you give the guest you know a blank stare just because you are making a bee line for your hostess— it's another *faux pas*. A pleasant smile as you pass is required of you.

It is permissible to have a different opinion from that of your host. But it is bad form to argue emotionally anywhere !

You will acquire control and poise if you keep your mind alert—by noticing what is going on around you instead of being concerned with your own reactions. Not easy—but that's the way to learn.

IN LOVE WITH LOVE

Two years ago we were great friends. He never told me he loved me, but his manner told me that he did. Then he went abroad and we did not correspond. Now he is back, and though he has not yet renewed the friendship, I still feel perfectly certain that he loves me. Can you explain this ?   PUZZLED.

NOW the last thing I want to do is to hurt your feelings, but so many girls send me this problem that I want to put all of you wise.

Just make up your mind that this young man does *not* love you. A man in love doesn't go away, forget all about the girl, come back after two years, and make no attempt to renew the friendship. Believe me, if he loved you he would have told you so. He would have written to you, and he would have hunted you up first thing on his return to tell you so again.

Women on the Eve of War

The Second World War began officially at 11 a.m. on Sunday, 3 September 1939. But throughout the first eight months of 1939 people in Britain continued to hope, as they had done for the past few years, that war would not come. As they hoped and convinced themselves appeasement would work the country and its people continued to prepare for war.

As early as April 1939 plans were in place to evacuate mothers with children under five, pregnant women, school children and other groups considered vulnerable, away from areas which would be targets for aerial bombardment. These people were to be billeted in the relative safety of reception areas. Here people were to share their homes with the evacuees.

Evacuation was one way of protecting the population from air attack but for the men and women left behind the Air Raid Precaution (ARP) system was essential. Many women volunteered as air-raid wardens. Indeed many women signed up to do Civil Defence work which involved a whole variety of jobs from ambulance drivers to fire-guard duty; staffing emergency control centres and first-aid posts to helping rescue parties. Despite an initial resistance to recruiting them, as the war progressed women's help in Civil Defence jobs became essential so that by 1943 one in four of CD workers were women.

The other major voluntary force in which women were involved during the war was the Women's Voluntary Service (WVS). The WVS, or one of many other similar organizations like the Townswomen's Guild, the Red Cross and the Salvation Army, were always there at the scene of a bombing to provide comfort, shelter, food and aid to the victims and the workers. The WVS also organized the collection of salvage; staffed rest centres; ran canteens in shelters, on the streets, anywhere they were needed.

Inside the home and within the family the effects of the preparations for war were clearly felt. The Military Training Bill which gave the government the power to conscript men into the Forces had been passed in May, so that women faced the next few months in the certain knowledge that should war come their husbands, sons, brothers and boyfriends all risked being called up.

Gas masks were distributed to everyone and drills held to make sure they could be donned quickly. Women with babies and young children faced the additional responsibility of getting their babies into gas-proof suits and helping youngsters put on their Mickey Mouse gas masks. Other protections against air raids involved the distribution of Anderson shelters or the preparation of some suitable cupboard or spot to shelter within the home if there was no access to, or wish to use, a public shelter. Windows had to be taped against the effects of blast and thin curtains lined or blinds made so that no chink of light could be seen during the Blackout.

Preparations for war within the home and within the various volunteer corps and organizations involved women in a great deal of extra work and the work increased as war became a reality.

ABOVE: *Midwives from Queen Charlotte's Hospital defied a ban by the BMA on midwives administering analgesics. They are pictured here going out on their auto-cycles carrying portable pain-relieving equipment.*
BELOW: *Women signing up for the Auxiliary Territorial Service in April 1939.*

AUXILIARY TERRITORIAL SERVICE

THE NEW WOMEN'S SERVICE

1939 POSTSCRIPTS

February – A Bastardy Bill was passed making blood tests compulsory in paternity suits.

May – Oxford appointed its first woman 'fellow' when Miss A. Bradbury became Bursar at Balliol.

The average woman does not want a career, has not the ability to carve one out, and would be a likeable, admirable creature if she stopped aping men, and made a job of the infinitely difficult business of becoming an attractive, practical, sensible and wholly adorable woman.
Extract from an article by John Aspland, *Daily Mail*, 4 January 1939

ABOVE: *These women making parts for bombers worked through the Air Raid Alerts, only stopping when a spotter on the factory roof saw real danger of a bomb dropping nearby.*

ABOVE: *A WVS canteen offering refreshments to workers after a night of bombing.*

BELOW: *Women tar-spraying in Hampshire. The accompanying caption suggests that it was the first time women had ever done such a job, ignoring completely the service of women in the First War.*

1940

Women of Britain 'Come into the Factories'

ABOVE: *Filling maritime distress flares.*

BELOW: *Women, or 'girls' as they were continually referred to in newspaper articles and captions, working on drilling machines making small parts for aircraft.*

Modern warfare demands a huge workforce not only to keep fighting men supplied with weapons but to keep the home country running as smoothly as possible. By 1940 Britain had three and a half million men in the armed forces. Nearly all of them had left a job behind and women were the only pool of labour from which to recruit.

In January 1940 Winston Churchill, then First Lord of the Admiralty, called for a million women to become munitions workers. This was only one of many calls for women workers up until December 1941 when women described as 'mobile', that is they had no pressing responsibilities in the home, aged 19 to 30, were conscripted to do essential war work either in the Forces or in industry. Throughout the war the ages for conscription were extended so that by 1943 nine out of ten single women and eight out of ten married women with children over fourteen were either in the Forces or in 'essential work'. Many thousands more women classed as 'immobile' took on part-time jobs outside the home or became outworkers and made or assembled small machine parts at home.

'Essential work' covered a variety of jobs. Munitions production was obviously a priority. As many of their mothers had in the First World War, women took on jobs they had not previously been thought capable of doing. During the Second War women were involved in a good deal of 'heavy' work, building ships, tanks, aircraft, barrage balloons and in fact generally extending the boundaries of what women could do even beyond those set by women in the First World War.

Munitions production also covered the production of bombs, mines and bullets. Many women were employed in producing the casings to such items which were then sent to be filled in other factories, usually sited out of town because of the risk of explosion. Women working with explosives wore a cloak and beret of undyed silk, rubber galoshes and had to remove jewellery, corsets, hairpins or anything metal which might cause a spark and set off an explosion.

Women workers were not only required in war industries but in the food and clothing industries. They were also needed to do many jobs essential to keeping the society running as normally as possible, jobs such as glazing broken windows, road mending and bus and taxi driving.

Food production was another area for essential work and the Women's Land Army formed the core of women engaged on that, although many other women factory workers along with school children, the Forces and men in reserved occupations could take a well-earned rest by having a free holiday on a farm providing that they helped out!

Women who did 'go into the factories' or into any other work during the war found their lives burdened. Women with a home to keep found the time especially hard. Compulsory overtime meant hours were long and it was usual to work at least a half-day on Saturday. Shops were closed by the time they got home from work, so, unless another family member could shop, the working housewife had to do it in her lunch hour. Queuing for everything took time and the lack of facilities for keeping food fresh meant shopping regularly. Sunday was often the only full day off in which to clean the house and do the washing, usually without the benefit of any mechanical aids.

1940 POSTSCRIPTS

January – In response to pressure from the public who believed that it was necessary to ensure a fair distribution, the government introduced food rationing – butter, sugar, bacon and ham were the first items to be rationed.

February – The government launched its 'Careless Talk Costs Lives' Campaign, often playing on the image of the gossip and Mata Hari stereotype women with lines like 'Be Like Dad – Keep Mum' and 'Keep Mum – She's Not So Dumb'.

October – The government of Vichy France which collaborated with Germany banned married women from working in the public services.

ABOVE: *'The munition grannies working on vital parts for aircraft cages for landing gear.'*
BELOW: *Women learning to be baby-minders for state nurseries.*

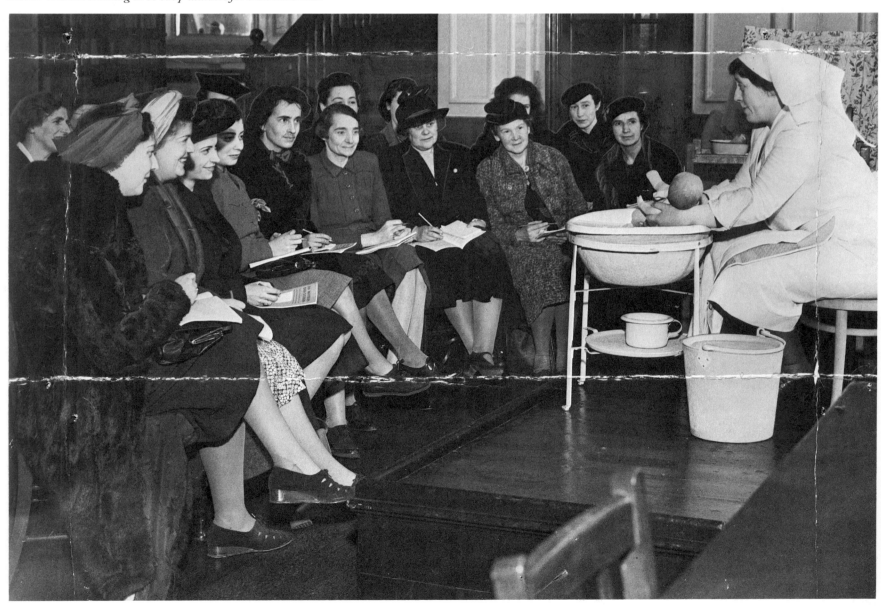

1941

Women in the Services

The National Service Act passed in December 1941 made women, for the first time ever in Britain, liable to be conscripted to serve in the Military Services. It was only unmarried women or childless widows who could be called on to join the Armed Forces, but the Act also allowed for other categories of women to be 'directed' to do war work in industry or on the land.

After the end of the First World War the women's auxiliary corps to the Navy and the Airforce had been disbanded. They had to be re-formed in 1939, the Women's Royal Naval Service (WRNS or Wrens) in April, and the Women's Auxiliary Air Force (WAAF) in July. There was also the Auxiliary Territorial Services (ATS) which had existed between the wars as a reserve of trained women to aid the Army in the event of war. Apart from the three main Services there were a variety of smaller corps which undertook more specific duties such as the Voluntary Aid Detachment (VAD) nurses; the Royal Observer Corps which staffed 24-hour watches in isolated lookout posts; the Air Transport Auxiliary Service whose ferry pilots delivered planes and essential supplies wherever they were needed.

It was stressed continually that women in the Services would be unarmed, serve only in non-combatant roles and always well behind the front lines. Aerial bombardment meant that the front line was Britain itself. Service women on duty in military command centres, barrack and air-base cookhouses, staffing anti-aircraft and searchlight batteries or driving bomb-disposal crews with their loads of unexploded bombs were all at risk of death or injury as a result of the bombing.

While on the whole not involved in policy decisions, women became crucial to the administration of the war. They were also important in maintaining the Services' transport and equipment including aircraft and torpedoes; feeding the men; staffing barrage-balloon sites and other defence posts. But women also undertook duties other than these, including some who parachuted into occupied Europe to help the Resistance movements and Wrens who served on warships as radio operators. By the end of the war of the 443,000 women in the three main Services, 624 had been killed, 744 wounded, 98 were missing and 22 taken prisoners of war.

ABOVE: *Women labourers employed by Islington Council to help clear air-raid debris break for lunch.*

BELOW: *Women from London evacuated to the country with their babies 'lend a hand on the land'.*

1941 POSTSCRIPTS

January – Amy Johnson the famous aviator of the 1930s was reported missing, feared drowned, when her plane developed engine trouble and she bailed out over the Thames. She had been working as a delivery pilot for the RAF transferring planes from aircraft factories to air bases.

March – The government announced a scheme to train baby-minders so that women could go to work happy that their children were left in good hands in state-provided nurseries.

June – Clothes rationing on a points system was introduced.

September – Two women clerks became the first women ever on the floor of the Stock Exchange when they sat and marked slips behind the Mining and Foreign Railway Counter.

More than a million women will be required during the coming months, and 100,000 of them are needed at once.

It is hoped that women between 18 and 25 who have no occupation will form the majority of the 100,000 who are required in the main for the women's Services and to be trained in Government Centres for work in industry.

Plans are being made to round up the women of leisure who, living in the comparative safety of reception areas, might try to avoid registration. 'Women who deliberately fail to register will be prosecuted and the penalties will be heavy,' a Ministry of Labour official told me yesterday.
Daily Mail, 24 March 1941

ABOVE: 'She-Navvies – Women can no longer be called the "weaker sex" for all over Britain they have answered the call and taken on jobs which were previously exclusive to men.'

BELOW: A Women's Defence Unit, similar to the Home Guard which only recruited men, is instructed in how to use firearms. Any such units were set up and funded privately as the government would not countenance the arming of women on any front. It was considered to be bad for morale.

ABOVE: *Anne Loughlin chairing her first meeting as TUC President.*

BELOW: *A woman bricklayer.*

1942

Vision of a Welfare State

In December 1942 the economist Sir William Beveridge produced his report which laid the foundations for a Welfare State after the war. The Report had all-party support within the coalition government and each of the major parties committed itself to its implementation post war. The public too were enthusiastic and 635,000 copies of the report or its official summary were sold. It became something to look forward to after the war.

The concept and implementation of a Welfare State which was to provide care and financial assistance 'from the cradle to the grave' was especially important for women. The proposed National Health Service would bring free medical care to millions of married women not covered by existing insurance schemes.

The Beveridge Report also suggested a number of financial benefits including family allowances, a state retirement pension and unemployment pay. These latter two allowances would be of great help to a large number of women who often worked in employment which had no insurance schemes to provide pensions or unemployment pay.

However, in many cases women would not receive equal allowances and pensions to men, much of the time because they would pay lower contributions. Again it was married women who had the worst deal. It was announced in September 1944 that married women would receive lower unemployment rates because they had their husband's earnings to fall back on.

1942 POSTSCRIPTS

● The TUC elected Anne Loughlin as its first woman President and pledged itself to the principle of equal pay for women.

April – It was announced that women of the ATS would staff the searchlights in anti-aircraft batteries – the most dangerous of all Civil Defence jobs.

August – The rules banning American soldiers stationed in Britain from marrying local women were removed, eight months after the GIs first arrived.

IT WAS WAAFS' FINEST HOUR AS WELL

The WAAFs in September 1940 had to stay put in trenches and wait for the bombing. Theirs were the 'after-the-raid' problems – attending to the wounded, stumbling into bomb craters, doing the unromantic jobs.

Examples as related to me yesterday:

At this Kent station after one heavy raid all but one cookhouse – the smallest one of the lot – were out of action.

Without water or light WAAF cooks had somehow to prepare meals for the whole camp. Water tanks were towed to the cookhouse, emergency lighting improvised and not a man missed a meal . . .

TAILPIECE: Once, during a heavy raid, an airwoman in the trenches shrieked so loudly that she was heard even above the noise outside. She had seen a spider!

Extracts from a *Daily Mail* article, 16 September 1942, celebrating the second anniversary of the Battle of Britain

ABOVE: *Recruits to the Women's Auxiliary Police Corps in Bedfordshire receiving instruction in Morse and Wireless Telegraphy.*

BELOW: *Women demolition workers resting from their work of pulling down a railway bridge in Wembley made unsafe by bombing.*

1943

Women and Money

For some women during the war it was the first time they had had to handle money other than the housekeeping allowance their husbands gave them. With husbands away in the Forces, sometimes earning less than they would in civilian life, women found themselves responsible for all of the family finances and often short of money; the soldier's pay would just not stretch to cover everything. Many of these women took on a job even if they had young children at home. State nursery provision for working mothers was dramatically increased during the war.

When she took on her job the working Service wife found like all other women during the war that she would be paid less than the man working at the same job. The trade unions, as they had before the war, did little to try to win equal pay for women although they did pledge themselves to the principle in 1942. A survey in 1943 found that women's average weekly pay at £3 2s 11d was only just over 50 per cent of men's pay which averaged £6 1s 4d.

The war did bring some financial freedom for some women. They were earning their own money even though there was pressure to donate at least a portion of it to the war effort and there was little to spend it on apart from basic necessities. However a legal case in 1943 emphasized just how little financial freedom married women had, especially those who stayed at home.

Mrs Dorothy Blackwell had saved £103 in a co-operative society – money she had saved from her housekeeping allowance and had earned from taking lodgers into the family home. Her husband claimed that the money rightly belonged to him and the Court of Appeal agreed with all the lower court judgements that Mr Blackwell was indeed entitled to the money and that a wife had no right to any savings from the housekeeping.

Even those married women earning their own money could not save money without their husbands' knowledge. As the husband was responsible for completing a tax return for both of them he risked prosecution if he failed to declare the interest on his wife's savings. This was a situation which was to continue for many years.

ABOVE: *Members of the WVS being instructed in unarmed combat.*

BELOW: *Wrens training to be torpedo mechanics regarded as one of the most highly skilled jobs in maritime engineering.*

1943 POSTSCRIPTS

February – A Commons committee recommended equal war compensation payments for men and women after women (and the men who worked alongside them at the scenes of bombings) protested that men received 20 per cent more for injuries sustained as a result of enemy action. A Personal Injuries (Civilian) Scheme was introduced but compensation was based on earnings and women earned less than men.

October – A report in the *Daily Mail* said that Sunday was now 'washday'. For many British housewives it was their only full day at home and they could not take advantage of laundries as many had closed because of shortages of staff and washing materials.

MORRISON HAS A CHARTER FOR MOTHERS
Happiest Homes Will Have Four Children

Mr Herbert Morrison, Home Secretary, yesterday outlined a charter of motherhood designed to clear away the obstacles to rearing families, and to the menace of the nation's falling birth rate . . .

He gave this warning: If the birth rate goes on at its present rate Britain's population will be halved by 1999. 'None of our long-term reconstruction plans will be more than pleasant dreams if we don't alter this,' he said. The plan for the attack on the evils that have caused families to dwindle is made under these heads:

Family Allowances.
Complete health service for all.
Pleasant homes for every family in pleasant surroundings.
Work for mothers only if they want it. They must not be forced to take jobs to support their children.
Nursery Schools for every child.

Daily Mail, 8 May 1943

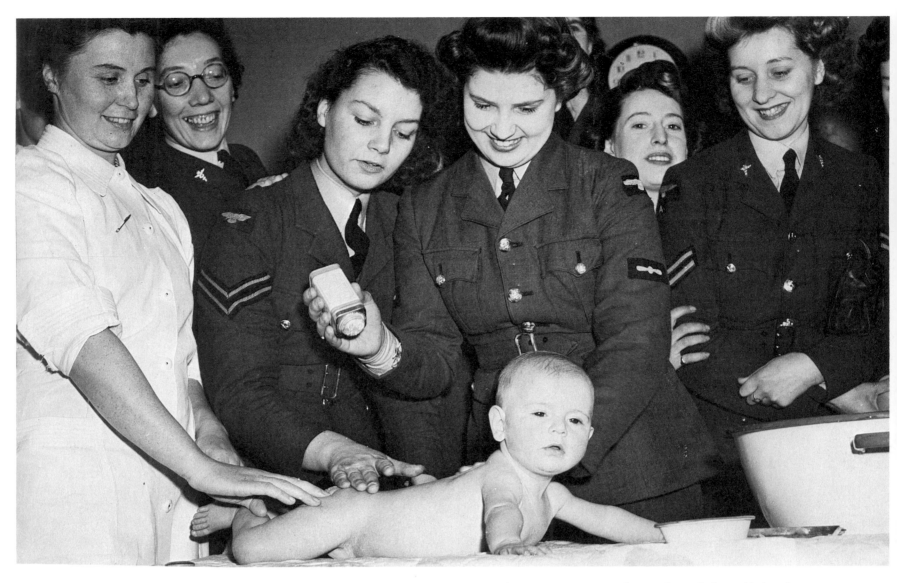

ABOVE: As the end of the war came in sight the country set its attention to the postwar society. These WAAFs are attending mothercraft classes 'designed to encourage among WAAF personnel an interest in the care and upbringing of children, both mentally and physically.'

BELOW: Wrens maintaining and repairing landing craft which were vital equipment during the D-Day Landings in June 1944.

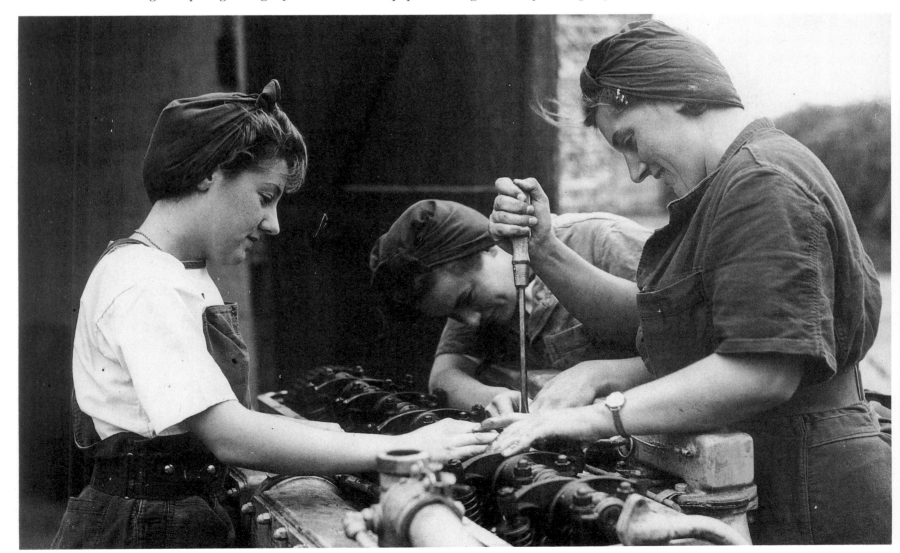

1944

Making Do and Mending

Britain's first production priority during the war was weapons. By the end of 1940 virtually all factories had turned to war production. A small amount of space in some factories was given over to making items for consumption on the home market. Cadbury's continued to produce some sweets and Yardley a limited line in cosmetics while the bulk of their factories produced shell casings and small parts for aircraft. It was necessary to maintain production of what were in effect luxuries in order to keep up morale in the country.

As the war progressed shops emptied of stock. Food had begun being rationed in January 1940 and in June 1941 clothes rationing was introduced and soap was rationed in 1942. But there were many things, such as crockery, cutlery, household furnishings, furniture, toys and cleaning products, which were not rationed but were in short supply. Some of these items were simply not in production at some periods of the war and if it was possible to buy them in the shops, or on the black market, there was usually little or no choice of style, colour or quality.

Women spent many hours during the war mending or improvising items which could not be replaced. Radio broadcasts, special classes, newspaper and magazine articles, government propaganda, even product advertising all urged the housewife to 'make do and mend'. Tips and instructions were given on how to make children's clothes out of unwanted adult clothing; turn shirt collars; unravel old woollens and reknit the wool into blankets or clothing; make rag rugs; repair shoes; patch towels; extend the life of bed linen by splitting worn sheets in two and stitching the less worn outer edges together; make a baby's cot from an old drawer; make polishes and cleansers for the home and face creams for the complexion.

The ingenuity of the advisers was endless but what they often overlooked was that in many cases it was difficult or impossible to find the ingredients or materials needed for repairs and renovations. Glue, sewing thread and needles, knitting needles, rubber for patching bicycle tyres or mending shoes were all in short supply. Salvage drives throughout the war netted many items of metal, rubber, paper and fabric that might have come in useful later on. Initially it was items that were unwanted and unused, although some no doubt donated a favourite pan or ornament in a spirit of patriotic fervour, but as the war progressed everything that could be recycled had to be cleaned and saved by the housewife ready for collection by WVS and other organizations. All salvaged material went into weapons' production and by 1944 British women and children had collected so much that 50,000 tanks could have been made from the metal alone.

ABOVE: *A WVS member collecting salvage.*

BELOW: *Wren signallers working on the British side of the Channel as they had done during the D-Day landings.*

1944 POSTSCRIPTS

March – R. A. Butler, the Minister of Education, said the ban on married women teachers working would be lifted as a reward for their 'great war effort'.

July – Servicewomen arrived in France to feed the troops following the D-Day invasion in June.

EQUALITY FOR WOMEN 'PERIL'
Warning by Churchmen

The way woman has used her newly won equality has created a danger to the state through the threatened decline in population, according to the report of a Church of Scotland Commission . . .

'There is little doubt that in the voluntary limitation of the family the woman's will largely prevails. It does so partly because she, in her days of economic self-sufficiency, has acquired standards of living which, naturally, she wishes as far as possible to preserve when she sets up home on her own.'

Daily Mail, 18 May 1944

1945

ABOVE: *After the war there were thousands of people to be rehoused. This woman pictured in her 'up-to-date' kitchen with two of her four children had just been moved into a new experimental house on the outskirts of London.*

LEFT: *A modern new cooker with automatic ignition to be fitted into the prefabricated homes which were an immediate solution to some of the housing problems.*

1945

Family Allowances

Eleanor Rathbone formed the Family Endowment Council in 1917 to fight for family allowances. The Council called for a weekly payment of 12s 6d for wives, 5s for the first child and 3s 6d for all subsequent children to be paid directly to the mother. Eleanor Rathbone felt it was important that the money went to the mother to ensure it was not squandered on beer by the husband. She saw, at a time when women had not yet been enfranchised, that the vote would not solve all of women's problems and that an improvement in the financial position of women was an important aim.

In 1945, after 28 years of campaigning, the newly elected postwar Labour government implemented the Beveridge Plan's suggestion for family allowances paid to the mother. But at 5s for all but the first child the payment was considerably less in real terms than Eleanor Rathbone had called for during the First War.

The first payments to mothers were made in 1946, the year in which Eleanor Rathbone died.

ABOVE: WVS members reinforcing the shoulder straps of uniforms for soldiers going to fight in Burma.

BELOW: Charity Taylor.

1945 POSTSCRIPTS

● Charity Taylor became the first woman prison governor when she took over at Holloway.

March – Women protested to the government about plans to close day nurseries at the end of the war, arguing they should be used for the under-twos once the new nursery schools for all children aged two to five were set up.

May – The war in Europe ended with the defeat of Germany.

August – Japan surrendered after the dropping of atomic bombs on Hiroshima and Nagasaki and the Second World War finally ended.

September – The government announced a census of 1,600,000 married women to gain information on population trends, including relative family size and the extent of childlessness.

UNWRITTEN LAW
Juries are Attacked by Wives
Life Cheapened

Protests that the two Old Bailey manslaughter verdicts, which have revived the 'Unwritten Law' controversy, cheapened the lives of mothers came last night from the Married Women's Association.

The verdicts were returned against two soldiers who had stabbed their unfaithful wives, and were given despite warnings by the judges that the men were guilty of murder.

Miss Juanita Frances, chairman of the association, told me:

'We are appalled that a mother's life should be held so cheaply by these juries.

'We identify ourselves with the statements of the judges and are horrified about the juries' verdicts.

'*If the women destroyed their husbands for similar reasons would the same juries acquit them of murder?*'

Daily Mail, 28 September 1945

ABOVE: *Preparing Sunday dinner in a communal kitchen. Until homes could be built for them many families had to share facilities in hostels.*

BELOW: *GI brides pictured as their ship docked in New York. Protests and demonstrations by some 50,000 British women married to American soldiers had forced the US government to speed up the processing of their papers.*

1946

'Not Worth Equal Pay'

During the war there had been a great deal of agitation by women for equal pay. The fact that in many cases women had been doing 'men's' jobs, and doing them well, often working alongside men doing exactly the same job but receiving far less pay than them, had forced women to rethink the argument that because men were generally the breadwinners they should earn more. Employers had many arguments against the women's claims: they required more training, created more waste and needed extra investment in terms of rest facilities. The unions paid lip service to women's claims for equal pay but were anxious to protect jobs for their male members when the war ended and many trade unionists feared equal pay would mean a reduction in men's earnings.

To accommodate the pressure for equal pay and examine all the issues the government set up a Royal Commission in 1944. The Commission of five men and four women reported in October 1946. Three of the women, including the trade unionist Dame Anne Loughlin, dissented with the report which came to the conclusion that women were not worth equal pay.

There were three main reasons for this conclusion. First, that women's performance justified lower pay, although the dissenters argued that women were often excluded from trades where they could be more efficient. Second, the Commission agreed with the argument that equal pay would mean lower pay standards for both men and women. The third reason given was that married men with families would become relatively the worst-off members of society.

The Report cited two linked factors of 'force of tradition' and 'economic factors' to explain how women were in the position which led the Commission to their conclusions. The Commission felt that women traditionally saw wage-earning as only a small part of their lives, working only until they married and had children. The fact that women's sick rates were higher was seen as an economic factor justifying lower pay, although the Commission also pointed out and seemed to accept as part of the 'force of tradition' that women were more poorly nourished than men. The report suggested that better feeding would improve women's health, reduce absenteeism and increase efficiency but offered no positive suggestions as to how to bring this about.

All in all the 1946 Commission on Equal Pay merely accepted and justified the status quo, with women in industry paid less than 60 per cent of the average male wage. Women teachers, local government officials and Civil Servants with rates of pay at 80 per cent of their male counterparts were the best-paid woman workers apart from those very few women who earned equal pay with the men in their professions.

ABOVE: *A family inside a quick-built temporary home.*

BELOW: *In the kitchen of a prefabricated home.*

1946 POSTSCRIPTS

March – The government removed the ban on women becoming diplomats but only if they remained unmarried. Monica Milne became the first woman to take up a diplomatic post.

May – For the first time ever bread was rationed – food shortages were even more severe than during the war as there were now 30 million people in Germany to feed, where the agricultural base had been destroyed.

WIFE LOST ALL CHATTELS

Judge Kirkhouse Jenkins, KC, decided at Melksham, Wiltshire, County Court yesterday that all the furniture acquired by Mrs Maud Elizabeth Shrapnell, of Beanacre, Melksham, out of household expenses, now belonged to her husband, William George Shrapnell, of Oakfield, Battledown, Cheltenham, a valet-chauffeur.

Mr and Mrs Shrapnell had separated under a court order after being married for 21 years.

The judge also awarded to the husband a tea service acquired by the wife, who paid 1s a week into a club, and also a cutlery set secured by the wife as a free gift in exchange for gift tea coupons.

Daily Mail, 13 April 1946

ABOVE: *This woman who cooked either on her kitchen range or an oil stove was unaffected by the fuel crisis despite the worst winter on record. In early 1947, domestic gas and electricity consumers were cut off from supplies for long periods during the day.*

ABOVE: *The 'New Look'.*

BELOW: *Ellen Wilkinson, Minister for Education. A committed socialist and fighter for women's equality Ellen Wilkinson died prematurely in 1947.*

1947

A Flood of Divorce

The government announced in March 1947 that it would fund bodies like the Marriage Guidance Council to try to help stem what had been described in a House of Lords debate the previous year as a 'tidal wave' of divorce. The aim of this funding was to try wherever possible to effect a reconciliation between the couple. The divorce rate was indeed growing at an alarming pace. From a figure of 10,000 divorce petitions in 1938, to 25,000 in 1945, rising to 38,000 in 1946 and 50,000 in 1947.

By May 1946 there were 50,000 divorces involving Service personnel outstanding and the Attorney General, Hartley Shawcross, appointed 35 legal teams to deal with them. The following month the period of time between the granting of a decree nisi and decree absolute was cut from six months to six weeks.

Real or faked adultery was still the main way of obtaining a divorce, despite the Herbert Act which had widened the grounds for divorce. In reality marital breakdown was the principal reason for the soaring divorce rate. Understandably, for there were so many points of possible friction. Six years of war had put a strain on everyone.

Soldiers at the front had obviously suffered the fear, mental and emotional stress, physical danger and actual injury connected with their role as fighters. Some men returned physically disfigured or mentally scarred by their war. Some were returned prisoners of war. The mere fact of having been away from home for so long in the company of other men made it difficult to resume a 'normal' life with their families.

The women and the men who had stayed behind on the home front had suffered too. They had experienced the bombing of British towns and cities, fear for the safety and welfare of their children and husbands, sons, brothers, loved ones serving in the Forces, as well as six years of sheer hard work to keep the troops supplied and their homes and families together. But the war had also given women some new freedoms and the confidence to do many things they would never have dreamt of doing before. For many women it was not easy to go back to living with a husband who made all the decisions, controlled the family finances and saw himself as head of the household when for several years they themselves had fulfilled all those roles.

1947 POSTSCRIPTS

April – As shortages increased the government banned the use of gas and coal fires – most families' sole form of heating – until September.

Spring – Christian Dior launched his 'New Look'. Nipped-in waists with peplums, slash pockets, and jackets flaring over the hips to accentuate the bottom; busts pushed up and out; skirts longer than for several years; clothes which unashamedly used yards of material were all a reaction to the austerity of wartime clothing and postwar shortages. The government in Britain called for women to shun the New Look out of a sense of patriotism, to save cloth in the face of the economic crisis. But few listened and very quickly Dior's new style was established in Britain as well as in the USA and throughout Europe.

June – Cambridge University finally agreed to award full degrees to women but they remained barred from the offices of Proctor and Esquire Bedell.

LONG SKIRTS TALK 'IS WASTE OF TIME'
Mrs Braddock Speaks her Mind

British women revolting against the longer skirt introduced by world fashion planners got support this weekend from Mrs Bessie Braddock, Labour MP for the Exchange Division of Liverpool. She described the trend as 'the ridiculous whim of idle people' . . .

'Most British women at present are glad to wear any clothes they can get hold of, and the people who worry about longer skirts might do something more useful with their time.'

Daily Mail, 22 September 1947

Fashion in the immediate postwar years, before Dior's radical, less austere line.

ABOVE: *Tenants of a newly built block of flats doing their washing in the basement laundry fitted with coin-operated washing machines.*

BELOW: *The District Nurse.*

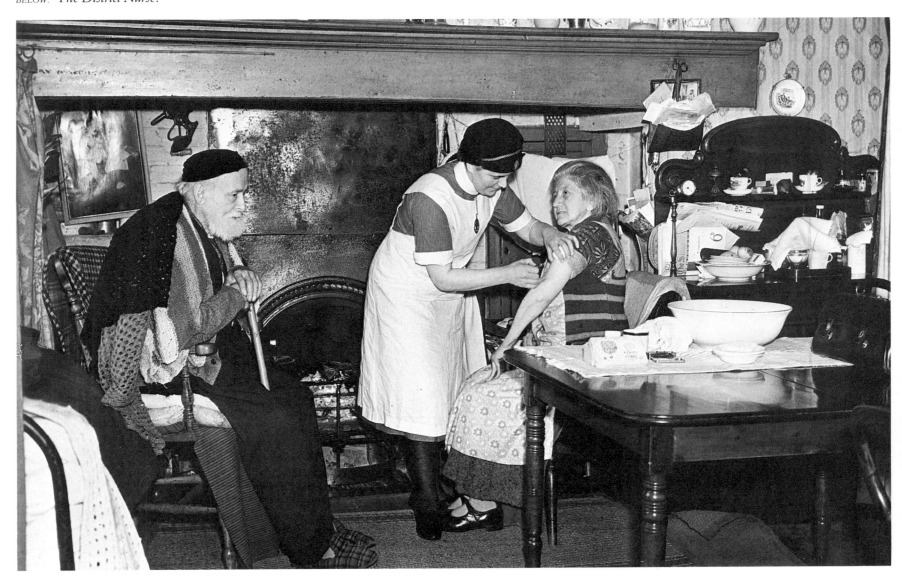

1948

Health Services for Women

On 5 July 1948 the National Health Service came into being It was perhaps the most momentous and revolutionary idea of the Beveridge Report and the 'crown jewel' of the 1945 postwar Labour government's welfare reforms. The National Health Service provided, for the first time anywhere in the world, access for every member of the population to a totally free system of health care.

For married women especially the new Health Service was extremely important. Before 1948 most working men and women paid into sickness insurance schemes through their jobs, which meant that they had the right when ill to free or subsidized medical care. Married women at home, and indeed a large number of working women who were in jobs such as domestic service which offered no insurance schemes, had no access to free medical care. The result was that most of the time if they were ill they did not seek medical help.

Women put up for years with a whole host of minor and less minor ailments – varicose veins, constipation and diarrhoea, gynaecological problems, problems with the menopause, thyroid conditions, toothache. Resorting to home remedies, over-the-counter preparations or simply ignoring the problem and carrying on were often the only way women dealt with their poor health. When the NHS started, doctors found a large number of women visiting a doctor for the first time ever, often with long-standing complaints.

Another benefit women derived from the NHS was the provision of a free national service for antenatal and maternity care. The Midwives Act of 1936 had allowed for local authorities to pay for a midwife, or a doctor if deemed necessary, but a national service was designed to remove any anomalies in the standard of provision throughout the country.

ABOVE: Mrs Barker of Middlesex pictured after winning a knitting competition sponsored by the Home Knitting Council together with Woman *magazine.*

BELOW: Fanny Blankers-Koen.

1948   POSTSCRIPTS

● A new Nationality Act allowed a woman marrying an alien to keep her nationality unless she took steps to change it.

● Margaret Kidd of the Scottish Bar became the first King's Counsel (KC) in Britain.

February – The Women's Service Bill provided for the ATS to become the Women's Royal Army Corps and the WAAF the Women's Royal Air Force and to be permanent corps, not to be disbanded as after the First World War.

August – Fanny Blankers-Koen, a Dutch athlete, was the star of the 1948 London Olympics when she became the first woman to win four gold medals at a single Olympics.

BRITAIN'S WIVES TOO TIRED TO THINK

By placing 61 women under a microscope and talking to others a woman doctor and a social worker have built up a picture of the housewife as she is today in austerity-bound Britain.

Dr Stella Instone, assistant physician at New Sussex Hospital, Brighton, yesterday published in the *Lancet* her findings on two groups of women – one whose husbands earn £5 a week, the other in the £500 a year group.

Of the first she says, 'The outstanding impression made by these housewives was their look of fatigue.' They suffered from defects of posture and minor clinical ailments which might have led to absenteeism in any other occupation.

In trying to answer the questions many women seemed incapable of thinking or speaking clearly, making such remarks as . . . 'I can't seem to remember anything these days.'

Daily Mail, 3 December 1948

ABOVE LEFT: *Mrs Violet Jones cooking some of the seven eggs the Post Master General persuaded the Ministry of Food to allow her after she broke seven eggs when she tackled two men damaging a phone box. Eggs, like many other foods, were still rationed and not easily replaced.*

ABOVE: *Gertrude 'Gorgeous Gussie' Moran scandalized Britain by playing at Wimbledon in lace-trimmed panties which could be seen under her tennis dress.*

LEFT: *Helena Normanton arriving at the House of Lords to be sworn in as a KC.*

COAT, LINED
18 to 16

TIES
1 to ?

RAINCOAT
16 to 8

SUITS FROM
CERTAIN MATERIALS
26 to 20

LEATHER
SOLED
SHOES
9 to 4½

The cost of men's clothing in terms of points before clothes rationing ended.

1949

Austerity

The ending of the war was not the end of rationing, going without and making do and mending. Indeed for a period after the war food-rationing became more severe, with even bread coming on to the ration.

Britain's economy had been shattered. It had borrowed, principally from the USA, to finance the war and now the debts had to be paid. Industry had to be turned from wartime to peacetime production in order to earn money to pay the debts. There was the task of rebuilding, repairing and refurbishing the thousands of homes affected by the bombing. The government had also embarked on a bold plan of restructuring and nationalizing many of the country's industries. It also had ambitious plans for establishing a Welfare State. All of these projects required the investment of money.

In 1949 Britain's balance of payments' deficit with much of the world was still drastic, the pound was devalued and the economic crisis severe. Although clothes rationing ended in 1949 this was the only hopeful sign for housewives who were exhorted by the government in speeches and pamphlets to save money, energy, food and materials, and to assume the responsibility for ensuring that the rest of the family did so too.

1949 POSTSCRIPTS

● Simone de Beauvoir published her book *The Second Sex* in which she said that, 'One is not born a woman, one becomes one.'
● Rose Heilbron and Helena Normanton become the first KCs at the English Bar.

May – Britain's first launderette opened in Bayswater, London, for a six-month trial period.

MORRISON PUTS NINE POINTS TO HOUSEWIVES

Mr Herbert Morrison gave these 'nine' commandments to housewives at a London rally last night:

1. Encourage those who go out to work to work with a will both for your family and for the wider family to which we all belong.

2. Shop carefully – make the money go as far as possible, and put off buying for the time being anything which is not necessary.

3. Beat unfair profit makers by not buying from them. If they are breaking the law, report it.

4. Watch for good design, service and good value, and praise it. Where you find shoddiness or slackness, overcharging or inefficiency, say so.

5. Remember your opinion is public opinion and public opinion is great and will prevail. Keep an eye on fuel and lighting meters. If you can put a bit aside in savings, even if it's only 6d a week, do so.

6. Keep an eye like a hawk on all extravagance, especially in public services. People who get away with joy rides in Health Service ambulances and unnecessary prescriptions are robbing your family's future standard of living.

7. Make home the best place to spend the evenings in – that's a sure help to the family budget.

8. Organize both spending and working. Get everyone in your family to share both – see that any economies you make fall on everyone equally.

9. Don't try and shoulder the lot yourself. And keep smiling.

Daily Mail, 3 November 1949

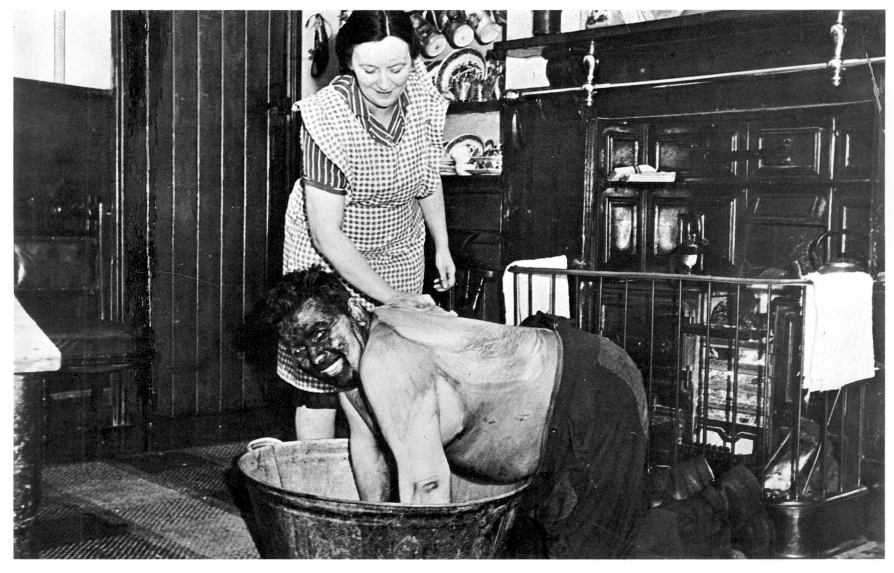

ABOVE: *Washing in a tin bath, like this miner being bathed by his wife, was still common.*

BELOW: *Mothers and babies at a child welfare centre.*

1950

Baby Boom

Cleaning the doorstep.

Just as the 1920s and '30s had seen a dramatic decline in the birth rate the '40s and '50s saw a 'baby boom'. So that while in 1927 only 85 babies were born for every 100 deaths, twenty years later in 1947 there were 121 births for every 100 deaths.

The low birth rate was blamed on the Depression but the economic situation during the war and for several years after was almost as bad. After 1952 the economy as well as the birth rate boomed. The rising birth rate from 1942 to 1945 seems to have been a direct result of the war itself as people sought not, as might seem logical, to prevent conception, but to reaffirm life in the face of death and destruction. Despite the austerity of the postwar years, the baby boom was fuelled by a powerful feeling of a brighter future ahead.

There were of course a great many unwanted pregnancies, especially during the war as people's passions overcame conventional morals and good sense. Although it was still expected that a woman stayed a virgin until marriage, there was a little more tolerance for those who did not. But for a woman to have an illegitimate child was a source of eternal shame. Many unmarried women who found themselves pregnant in the '40s and '50s were thrown out of the family home, asked to leave lodgings and their employment. Often there was nowhere for these women to go except charitable foundations where they could stay until they had the baby before giving it up for adoption. Women could even be committed to a mental home if they had an illegitimate pregnancy, and a survey in 1950 revealed that in 11 mental institutions there was a fair proportion of women whose only 'insanity' was that they had had an illegitimate child.

Birth control was becoming more widely known about and acceptable. It was however strictly for married couples. The Family Planning Association would only see, advise and equip married women with information and aids for birth control. To do anything other than exclude unmarried women from consultations would have risked the accusation that they were encouraging these women to act immorally.

1950 POSTSCRIPTS

May – Following the Communist takeover in China the new government began to bring in new laws, many of which improved the lives of women – laws banning polygamy; infanticide, of which girls were the principal victims; and child marriage, especially difficult for girls in a society where the wife left her parental home to live in the home of her husband's parents.

June – In Croydon grocer J. Sainsbury opened the first self-service store in Britain.

ABOVE: *Washing clothes with a scrubbing board.*

BELOW: *Domestic help was available to only a few.*

1951

The Average Housewife

A study by Mass Observation published in 1951 showed that the average housewife in Britain worked a 15-hour day, spending 25 per cent of her time in the kitchen. The study concluded that children and the preparation of meals were the two things which most restricted her freedom to organize her day.

It is not surprising that Mass Observation found a working day of fifteen hours for most women. Even vacuum cleaners, by far the most common labour-saving device, were only found in one in two homes and other surveys in 1951 showed that six per cent of British homes had no internal water supply; five per cent had no cooking stove, while 23 per cent shared a stove with another one or more families; 15 per cent had no toilet and 38 per cent no plumbed-in bath. Vera Brittain writing at just this period said in her book *Lady into Woman*: 'Foremost among the married woman's handicaps has been the primitive home still imposed upon her owing to the convention which still regards her as a domestic slave, and her own inexplicable failure to organize and protest.'

With hindsight it is easier to see why women failed to organize and protest. It was still expected and accepted by most women that this was their lot in life. Schools still trained girls in 'domestic science' and boys in woodwork. Girls were not supposed to organize and protest, even to express, let alone assert, their needs and desires. The images and ideals of what it was to be a woman were nearly all to do with working to make a home for a family. There were still only a handful of, usually single, women in positions of authority and power, to act as role models for other women.

With few women in any position to make their voices heard, houses, plumbing systems, labour-saving devices were all designed by men and did not always function to the best advantage of the women who used them. The individual housewife's lack of financial power meant that she still depended on her husband to purchase any of the equipment necessary to aid her in her working life. If she could not persuade him of the need for a washing machine, refrigerator or vacuum cleaner she would not get them. However as the 1950s progressed and the British people as a whole became more affluent there was a huge growth in the purchase of labour-saving equipment for the home so that by 1959 the average housewife's work was probably less physically demanding – but probably not less time-consuming – than in 1951.

1951 POSTSCRIPTS

● There were still 178,000 domestic servants working in Britain.

January – The BBC announced that all eight regular news readers would be men because, 'People do not like momentous events such as war and disaster to be read by the female voice.'

March – MP Eirene White introduced a Private Member's Bill to make it possible for a couple to divorce after a separation of seven years, in effect for a divorce to be granted because the marriage had broken down. It had a large majority on its second reading, but Eirene White withdrew her Bill when the government promised a Royal Commission to review the subject.

May – The government agreed to pay old age pensions from the age of 65 for men and 60 for women. This was because women, on average, were five years younger than their husbands and the age differential meant that married couples would be eligible to draw their pensions at the same time.

OLD GIRLS OF ATS JOIN UP
TO RECRUIT FOR WOMEN'S ARMY

Who are soldiers by day and civilians by night?

Former sergeants of the ATS and WRAC, whom the War Office has recruited as recruiters.

The girls (many of them now housewives) are enrolled for four years, given uniforms with sergeant's pay and allowances, and serve only in their home localities.

Qualifications are smartness, initiative and intelligence. The scheme brings the women's corps into line with the rest of the Army which uses pensioned sergeants for recruiting.
Daily Mail, 17 July 1951

A promotional picture of the new Hoover washing machine presents a smiling housewife in her immaculate labour-saving kitchen.

ABOVE: A cut in the meat ration prompted this butcher to put a display of mourning in his window.

BELOW: Children playing and resting in a nursery attached to the National Health's first purpose-built comprehensive health centre.

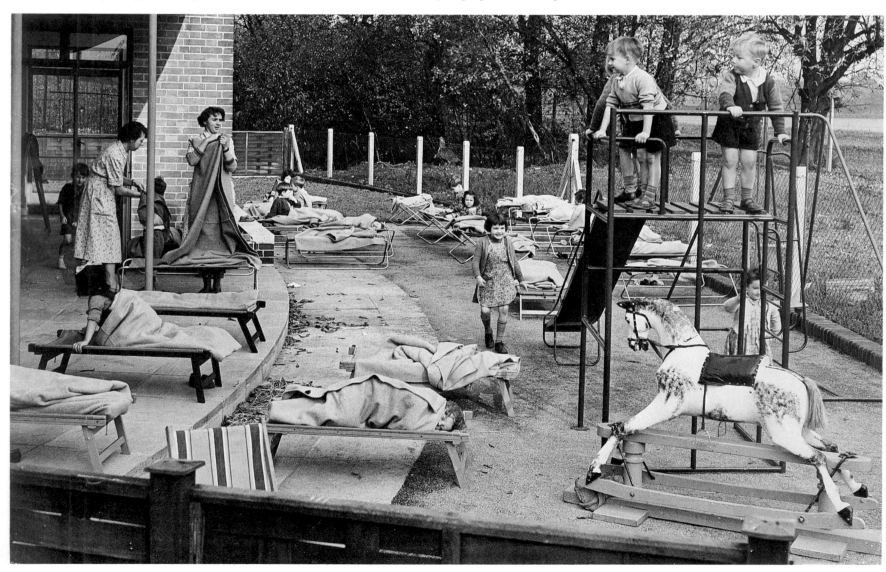

1952

Women's Disabilities

In 1952 one of women's major disabilities, as it had been before and still remains, was lack of money. Dr Edith Summerskill, who had been a Minister in the previous Labour government, recognized this fact and in April 1952 introduced a Private Member's Bill to try to ease the burden of worry about finances for some women.

Dr Summerskill's Women's Disabilities Bill ran out of parliamentary time before it could become law or make a real test of the House of Commons' opinion on the matter. The Bill proposed to give a woman whose husband had failed to pay a maintenance order the right to be paid the arrears directly by the husband's employer under a court order. The Bill also made provision for a wife still living with her husband to be able to take him to court for an order to be made for the payment of a reasonable housekeeping allowance. Failure to comply with such a court order would mean that property could be transferred into the wife's name. A further suggestion in the Bill was that a husband's savings could be divided equally on divorce.

In the same year, indeed in the same month, a row broke out within the Married Women's Association on the subject of women and money. Its President, Helena Normanton QC, resigned after being accused of insulting women by suggesting to the Royal Commission on Marriage and Divorce that wives should be given an allowance by their husbands provided they spent it sensibly. The Association said that this was contrary to their policy which was that the only way to give economic security to wives and children was to ensure that the housekeeping money was adequate and jointly owned by both husband and wife.

In Britain wives still had no right to any money they did not earn themselves unlike wives in some of the Scandinavian countries. Sweden had passed a Marriage Act in 1921 which made it a legal requirement for all income and property to be pooled and divided equally on marriage. In Norway, too, housewives had a right to share their husbands' income and property as a recognition that although they were not earning money they were making a contribution to the maintenance of the family. British wives had no such recognition. Apart from the State family allowance and their own earnings, they were dependent upon whatever their husband saw fit to give them and had no recourse to law should he choose to give inadequately or not at all. At least in Britain in 1952 wives had had for seventy years the right to own their own property and income; in France a husband could dispose of a wife's property without consulting her unless she had made a special legal arrangement with him prior to marriage.

ABOVE: Clocking on for a shift at the factory.

BELOW: End of a shift.

1952 POSTSCRIPTS

February – Princess Elizabeth is proclaimed Queen following the death of her father, King George VI.

May – Maria Montessori, Italy's first woman physician and a pioneer in the education of young children through discovery and less rigid organization, died at the age of 81.

• The House of Commons voted in favour of the principle of equal pay for women and John Boyd-Carpenter, a Treasury Secretary, said new pay structures would be introduced but it would have to be done in stages.

BEING A WOMAN IS SUCH FUN NOW

One of Them
May Become

BRIDE OF AKIHITO

From a Special Correspondent

FOR Japan's Crown Prince Akihito a surprise may be in store when he returns home this autumn : a girl to marry, chosen in his absence.

In the walled and moated palace at Tokio court chamberlains have been secretly engaged in "studies and investigations" to pick a bride for Akihito before the end of 1953.

The Prince is over 19 years of age, and sources close to the Imperial Household maintain that it is high time for court elders to plan his marriage.

Today, most young Japanese still marry not for love but by arrangement. Their brides and grooms are selected after careful negotiations by relatives. Akihito is unlikely to be an exception to this rule.

No mixing

THE higher the social status of a Japanese family the more difficult it is for its younger members to mix freely with boys and girls of their own age. Personal friendships between the sexes are unheard of in and around the Imperial Court, where "society" in the Western sense plays no part.

Akihito himself lives alone at his own residence far from the palace, surrounded by scores of male advisers tutors, and servants. His social life there is limited to sports with a selected number of his classmates at the Peers' College and to "stag" parties mostly at his own home.

He never goes to informal, mixed parties where he might meet girls of his own age. He seldom ever sees his sisters. Now, on his journey in Europe, he is behaving freely as a modern prince for the first time in his life.

The choice

BROUGHT up in such surroundings Akihito is naturally shy on the question of marriage. He is unlikely to fall in love with a girl of his own choice and say so. So the court elders in Tokio will decide for him.

They are members of Japan's most ancient noble families who still regulate life within the palace and keep court etiquette as strictly as it has been from time immemorial.

Who will be their choice ? The elders are now weighing the chances of half a dozen little Japanese girls in their early teens one of whom may one day share the throne with Japan's 125th Emperor.

The American occupation of Japan, and General MacArthur's "democratisation," have restricted their choice. When the

---

ANN TEMPLE

The woman he feared to marry—because he loved her!

I always thought love made people more kind and thoughtful. Now I don't know what to believe.

The man I was deeply in love with and who seemed equally in love with me, just left me flat without a word and, as far as I was concerned, disappeared. This after we had been going about together for six months. This was two years ago, and I heard nothing about him and was too proud to ask.

Recently we met by accident and he insisted on giving me an explanation. He said he broke off because he loved me. He found he could not marry me because he became involved in financial obligations.

Could a man really in love act in such a cruel way? Is it possible?—E. G.

IT could be. Always judge the motive of a man's actions by what you know of his character. Possibly it is consistent with his general attitude to problems for him to guard himself against his feelings.

He may have thought that explanations and argument would sap his resolution. He would probably argue that it was prudent for you both to take such drastic action.

A mistaken but not an uncommon masculine idea of kindness. The real kindness would be in trusting the girl to appreciate the position and understand. Nothing is more harrowing than to be left not knowing, always wondering why.

THE COPY-CATS AGAIN

HERE is a neat little pay-off to the Copy-Cats problem. It comes from a reader who was once a millinery designer. She says :

Having experienced the same annoyance as your correspondent I chanced one day to come across these lines of Kipling as I was browsing in a bookshop—

"They copied all they could copy

But they couldn't copy my mind

And I left them struggling and scheming

A year and a half behind !"

After that I made a game of it and had a lot of fun.—G. M.

TELEPHONE VOICE

I am told that I sound haughty and aloof on the telephone. I always try to speak clearly, and hate to find that I make such a bad im-

pression. What is the explanation?—X. Y.

JUST another case of telephone voice. You make an occasion of it, adopt a platform diction for clarity and so lose your natural voice. Any type of nervous consciousness makes a woman's voice sound hard and dictatory over the telephone and the radio.

Try to see your telephone at the other end. Smile and use the same facial expressions and gestures as you do when talking face to face. Talk to your listener, not just down a tube.

GI JOE

What is the meaning of the term G.I. or G.I. Joe? We know it refers to American soldiers, but how did it originate?—REGULAR READERS.

G. I. stands for Government Issue, meaning all the uniform and equipment issued to enlisted men.

As far as I know Joe has no significance—just used for sound effect—but I am open to correction. It is not the American equivalent of John Bull. Uncle Sam has that distinction. It is not quite the equivalent of Tommy Atkins, for Tommy is a private. G.I. Joe is any man of non-commissioned rank.

 HUMAN CASEBOOK

CONFLICT OF EMOTIONS

I was very interested in your reply to the good-looking girl who knew she was not attractive to men, but I wish that you had gone further with it.

The mental and emotional disturbances caused by the realisation of a "lack" with the desire still persisting for love and marriage, seem utterly opposed to a condition of contentment, so how can this "peace with ourselves," which you consider essential to the development of possibly dormant sex - attraction, be achieved ?—PONDERER.

THERE is, of course, a conflict in the awareness of "the lack" and the natural desire for love and marriage, but it is a conflict that yields to understanding.

About the natural desire nothing can be done beyond a determination not to allow it to dominate the whole outlook on life.

About "the lack," much can be done when it is understood that it is not a natural lack—a physical thing—but a psychological state brought about by conditioning in early training and environment.

Such understanding brings what I can only call a wisdom of the heart—a wisdom that can wait and so allow for the inner peace that you question.

FUN NOW

Those Infuriating Men in Toppers and Caps Are Ever So Nice

by SARAH LOVELL

WHAT fun it is, in a week of gold braid and yachting caps, of grey toppers and cricket caps, to be a woman in a country full of English males.

What fun, when they have the keen - as - a - ship's - prow good looks of the Duke of Edinburgh ; the surprising, superb presence of the Duke of Norfolk ; and the guileless schoolboy smile that no Englishman ever loses.

What fun, when they are constantly in love—with a cricket bat, a horse, a boat, a ball, or an engine of some kind. What fun—

Because it is satisfying just to look at them ; stimulating to distract them from whatever they think more important (watch the debs vying with the horses at Ascot) ; and blissfully comfortable to be married to them—for the women who have taken their measure.

Like the English weather, the English males are unique. They are passionately devoted to the elaborate conventions of their schools, clubs, and innumerable societies ; and sternly exclude women from this nonsense that any sensible girl discarded before she was ten.

★

THEY are impervious to acute discomfort when absorbed in games, racing, sailing, and on holiday. But if they find anyone in their favourite armchair they sulk.

THEY will wear magnificent clothes, elegant clothes, drab clothes, and clothes no woman would be seen dead in, all with an unself-conscious air of being absolutely right. But let a woman make one mistake, such as nylons with country tweeds or high heels in a boat, and their disapproval will shrivel her.

THEY will eat revolting food at their clubs without a murmur of reproach ; but look pained if the joint is overdone at home.

THEY will sit up all night with a sick dog ; but sigh ostentatiously if the baby wakens them from a doze.

THEY accept compliments as a right ; and offer them as if they were conferring a once-in-a-lifetime Knighthood.

THEY want their homes beautifully run, but don't want to hear about it. They wash up once and feel virtuous for a week. They can never understand why their wives can't be with them, cool and unflurried, for a leisurely hour before a meal is served.

They have seven ages :

"Mummy, you aren't going to wear that HAT ?"

"JANE, you—aren't—going—to —wear—that—H A T ?"

"Now, that's the kind of HAT I like, over there, on that rather nice-looking woman. Same as your black one? Oh."

"But you bought one last summer."

"Were you wearing a HAT, darling? I didn't notice."

"Really, Jane, I do think you ought to wear a HAT. It looks so slovenly to go without."

"HATS? I don't know why women make such a fuss about them. They're useless. But a MAN'S HATS are sensible."

And seven excuses :

"Sorry I'm late, Mummy. We didn't draw stumps till six."

"Sorry I'm late, Janey. I had a rubber of bridge at the club."

"Am I late? It was a long rubber."

"I'd better say 7.45, just to be safe."

"Don't wait dinner for me."

"I think I'll dine at the club."

"WHAT? You'll be out to dinner? What on earth am I to do?"

They are the most infuriating men in the world ; and quite the nicest.

SALUTE to the women who understand them :

WHO look entranced while hearing, for the 50th time, how they carried their bat for 73, did the hat-trick, holed in one, and made their contract.

WHO know exactly the kind of clothes they like, even to the seed pearls (because they're real), even to the spray of roses (because they're fresh), and who succeed in dressing well in spite of it all.

WHO manage, heaven knows how, to get home first, cook an admirable meal, change, and look as though they'd had all day to do it in.

SPECIAL SALUTE of 21 guns this week :

To the women who have weaned them away from sheepish loyalty to the tepid salmon, limp lettuce, and stiff prices of the enclosures at Ascot, and are packing a just-right-temperature lunch in a vacuum container.

NO SALUTE to the woman who can't think farther than a ham sandwich and coffee ; who can't enjoy the fun of coaxing a reluctant compliment out of an astonished English male.

Porpoise Was on the King's Menu

WHEN the Queen travels North next week for her visit to Scotland the royal progress will not cause so much anxious commotion and leave such mixed feelings in its wake as did some in the past.

A Coronation exhibition in the cathedral library at Durham, drawn from exceptionally rich collections and archives, brings to life the bustle of Court preparations that must often have been feared like visitations of locusts.

Charles I. in June 1633 received from the Dean and Chapter a red velvet cope heavily embroidered with gold and worth £116 8s. 1d. (multiply the sum 20 times to approach our values) and was entertained at a total cost of £232 18s. 1d.

And Charles rubbed salt into the wound by sending the next day a stinging letter of dissatisfaction about the condition of cathedral and close. He commanded that the letter be placed on official record.

Edward II. stopped a week on his way to Bannockburn in 1314. Thirty salmon and 2,200 herrings were bought.

Edward III. and Queen Philippa needed more 20 years later. The King dined with the Prior. Purchases included half a porpoise, 31 salmon, 287 chickens, 42 geese, and 2,400 eggs in two weeks.

As a guest of the Prior's successor, Dean Wild, I have just had the privilege of eating in the room where the future victor of Crécy consumed salmon caught below in the waters of the Wear.

Salmon are no longer caught because of river pollution, but Norman and Gothic cathedral, castle, and monastic buildings still dominate the magnificent landscape.

Pierre Jeannerat

PETER BLACK'S TELEVIEW

Why Do They Keep This for Women?

IT was pleasant to see "Leisure and Pleasure" once again on the evening programme. I wish I could report that it will appear as such regularly, but I cannot. We watched it only because its usual Tuesday afternoon spot was occupied this week by horse-racing from Ascot.

I believe that television planners make a great mistake in confining "Leisure and Pleasure" to afternoons merely because it happens to be designed mainly for women. In the first place it is produced by S. E. Reynolds, who is probably the most consistently successful producer inside Lime-grove. It is folly to cut him off from the great evening audience.

In the second place I resent and deplore the implied argument that what is good enough for women is not good enough for the rest of us.

I may be wrong, but I should say that the last thing Reynolds bears in mind is that his programme is designed for women only.

Having thus extolled him, it is now my painful duty to confess that last night's edition was not very good.

★

Equally, Hugh Newman's talk on butterflies was unrewarding except for Mr. Newman, who got a detailed plug for his forthcoming book.

Finally there was Arthur Dulay, bringing back memories of silent films with his piano. His piece illustrated sardonically the hopeless deadlock between TV and the cinema.

None of the films he accompanied will ever be shown again in the commercial cinema. But would the commercial cinema allow TV to use moving shots from them ? No. They made him accompany stills.

Razor keen

TV last night took viewers on a tour of H.M.S. Victory, Nelson's flagship. The ship's company dressed in the costume of Nelson's day. One of them, Colour Sergeant M. L. Eves, R.M., removes his moustache to conform to the demands of his rôle.

Good meals waiting

Ready and waiting to give you tasty, nourishing, easy to make meals are these good things by Maconochie's—and many more. They are food of the highest quality, of flavour assured by one of Europe's leading chefs.

Maconochie's PROCESSED Peas NET WEIGHT 10 OZ.

MACONOCHIE'S beans

Steak Puddings tender, high grade meat, savoury gravy, in a pudding

1953

Women in Parliament and Government

ABOVE: *Queen Elizabeth.*
BELOW: *Margaret Bondfield, the first woman Cabinet Minister, who died in June.*

Florence Horsbrugh became the first woman ever appointed to a Conservative Cabinet when her post as Minister for Education was promoted to Cabinet level in 1953. She was only the third woman ever to be given a Cabinet post. Margaret Bondfield was in Ramsay MacDonald's Labour government from 1929 to 1931 as Minister for Labour and Ellen Wilkinson was in the Cabinet as Minister for Education from the 1945 election of the Labour government until she died in 1947.

In 1953, of the 625 parliamentary seats available, only 17 were taken by women. They had been elected in the 1951 general election and they represented, more than 30 years after women had first become eligible, only three per cent of the membership of the House of Commons. In fact the number of women elected in 1951 was a reduction from the 21 elected in 1950 and seven less than the record number of 24 women elected in 1945. Before the war there were never more than fifteen women MPs.

Dorothy Evans, who campaigned vigorously to end discrimination against women, organized a pressure group, Women for Westminster, during the Second World War to try to encourage more women to stand for Parliament. She died in 1944 and the group did not last much longer but it undoubtedly had some impact as in the 1945 election there were 87 women candidates. These women had all had to overcome the selection procedure of their particular political party, a procedure dominated by men who were riddled with the fear that even in a safe seat many of the party's traditional supporters would refuse to vote for a woman.

Women's profile in local government, especially outside London, was only slightly better than in Parliament. On the London County Council about a third of the members were women in 1952 and this was the best ratio of women to men on local government councils anywhere in the country. In the same year only seven per cent of mayoral posts were held by women and in Scotland only three out of 106 Provosts were women.

In 1953 women were seriously under-represented at all levels of government and there was one further tier of government in which they had no representation at all. Britain's second chamber of government which still had considerable power to amend legislation was an all-male body to which women could not be appointed.

1953   POSTSCRIPTS

June – The Coronation of Queen Elizabeth.

August – Dilys Cadwaladr became the first woman to win a Bardic Crown at the Welsh National Eisteddfod.

December – Harold Macmillan, the Housing Minister, announced that 301,000 new homes had been built in 1953 – all part of the drive to replenish the housing stock following the losses during the war and to reduce overcrowding.

K Day and the Great Ballyhoo
SEX IS HERE TO STAY

Dr Kinsey solemnly reports that 50 per cent of married women sleep in the nude. He says, 'There is every indication that the percentage is still increasing much to the consternation of the manufacturers of nightclothes.'

Figures and alleged statistics dot the pages of the book, but the net effect is confusing.

How did Dr Kinsey and his associates reach their conclusions?

They say that they interviewed 5,940 females aged from two to 90 of various religions and occupations . . .

You don't often get 250,000 first printings of a book which sells at eight dollars a copy.

Sex is undoubtedly here to stay.

Daily Mail, 20 August 1953

A PROVOCATIVE POSER FOR AGE-ANXIOUS WOMEN

If a Man Can Be Young at 45, Why Lie about YOUR Age?

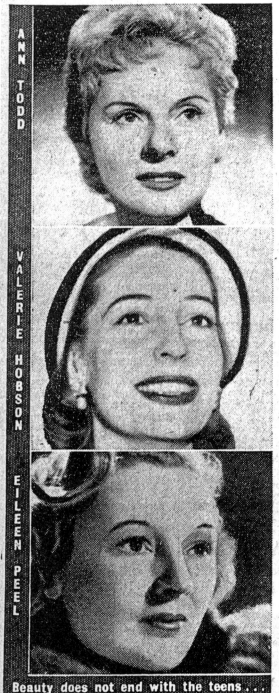

ANN TODD · VALERIE HOBSON · EILEEN PEEL

Beauty does not end with the teens . .

Hallo, Folks! by **IRIS ASHLEY**

MARIA HORNES'S courage after a catastrophe has led her to the secrets of beauty

NOT long ago I remarked in this column on the odd fact that you almost never meet a woman between the ages of 39 and 50. With a slightly nervous whinny a woman will often admit to 39 ; or with an " I dare you to comment " look in her eye she will announce a defiant 50. What happens in between is usually 11 years of hopeful lying.

Why not? you ask, since it hurts no one. The answer is : Because it is no longer necessary. We regard a man of 45 as still virtually in his flaming youth. " A remarkably young Minister," we read time and time again.

Proof

IN the prolonging of the expected span of human life women on average outlast men. Therefore it is reasonable to say that they can also reach the aspect of " middle age " as late or even later than a man.

To prove my point look at Ann Todd. She is starring this season at the Old Vic. She knocked the critics cold as Lady Macbeth, but in " Love's Labour's Lost " she swept the floor with the exquisite Virginia McKenna, who is only 23. Ann, who is 44, was enchantingly lovely. Make-up? No. I lunched with her in her suite at the Savoy when she sat facing the window with no other make-up than for her eyes and lips. She looked about 25. She looked any age—no age.

Two other great friends of mine seem like Ann to grow younger as they grow older. Gaining in poise and confidence and femininity they get prettier every year. It's fascinating to watch. One is Eileen Peel. Her daughter is 16. Playing the lead last week at " Q " Theatre in " Waters of the Moon " she had to remark that she was 40 and had " lost her looks." A voice behind me remarked dryly : " Well, I wouldn't half like to be 40 with those lost looks."

The other, Valerie Hobson, is not yet 40 it's true, neither is she 35 any longer, but she grows more attractive and beautiful each time I see her.

Of course, no one could leave Mrs. Susan Ward out of such a list. Her daughter was 19 on Saturday, but she is constantly cited as one of the great beauties of the day.

You might say these women are individuals of exceptional beauty. I would answer that they have certain things in common. They are all in or near what is known as " middle age " and they make the term absurd ; and they are all possessed of a fundamental gaiety which has left its imprint in charm upon their faces.

Can all this apply to you ? You bet it can. For a start, throw away that old convention of thought that accepts " A promising young man of 45 " and a " middle-aged housewife of 45 " in the same breath !

Then, come with me to visit Maria Hornes. I went to see her because last week I met a chum who is also a hard-working Press agent. " Good heavens ! Are you in love ? " I exclaimed. She looked ten years younger than when I last saw her some months ago. She said no, it wasn't love, it was Maria Hornes.

It turns out that Maria Hornes had a car smash and one side of her face became paralysed. Courage and patient continual exercise restored her facial beauty absolutely. She was so impressed that she decided to help other women to restore their sagging muscles. From that she developed a beauty business.

She teaches a series of brief but most effective movements which seem to obviate that telltale droop at the sides of the chin. She counsels a " pinching " massage *across the angle* of facial lines to promote circulation. She has evolved certain creams and facial masks which seem to do miracles to skin which is of an age to be rather faded.

Coincidence

I KNOW this because I have met three different women and after commenting in admiration upon their complexions was told (in confidence naturally !) that they had been given treatment by Maria Hornes.

The coincidence was too interesting to be ignored. I went along there myself.

When I came away I was skipping like a lamb and thinking happily " I am never, *never* going to be 40. . . ." And then I saw a man friend who is a dashing 46 and I promised myself that I would indeed be each year as it came along—and enjoy every second till I am 80 at least—a mere chit of a girl I'll be then.

1954

The End of Rationing

ABOVE: *A member of the Housewives' Association ceremonially tears up her ration book in Trafalgar Square to mark the end of rationing.*
BELOW: *Hans and Lotte Hass pictured underwater while filming one of their television wildlife programmes. Lotte Hass is described as 'taking shorthand notes on an aluminium plate'.*

Food rationing had first begun in Britain in January 1940 as a result of wartime shortages. Prices had begun to rise steeply and there was a public clamour for rationing and price controls to ensure that what food there was, was distributed fairly. The following year clothes rationing was introduced on a points system that allowed people to choose from the limited styles and items available how they wanted to 'spend' their allocation – although of course they had to pay money for the goods as well as points. The success of the points system, which was in fact copied from a German system, was extended to 'luxury' foods such as dried fruit, biscuits and tinned food later in 1941.

After the war, for a period, rationing became even more severe but gradually throughout the late 1940s and early '50s more and more items came 'off the ration'. Sometimes, as with sweets, rationing ended more than once.

Although rationing affected the whole of the population it affected women, in their role as homemakers, most. It was women who had to plan and prepare meals with a limited amount and variety of ingredients. It was women who were urged to save cooking and heating fuel in the home. It was generally women who queued for everything from basic rations to rare luxuries. It was women who patched, darned, sewed, repaired, cut down and remade clothing, tablecloths, towels, curtains and bedding. It was women who had to keep themselves, their children and their homes and clothing clean on rationed soap and cleaning equipment and materials in short supply.

Clothes rationing ended in 1949 and soap rationing the following year, leaving only a few items of food 'on the ration'. Problems with the balance of payments with sugar-producing countries meant sweet and sugar rationing did not finally end until 1953.

By 1954 only butter, margarine, cooking fat, cheese and meat were rationed on the domestic market. Gradually throughout the year the restrictions on their supply to the public were removed and on 3 July 1954 meat was the last item to come off the ration, almost exactly fourteen and a half years since rationing had first begun.

1954 POSTSCRIPTS

● Television was becoming an increasingly popular rival to radio. The ratio of applications for TV licences to radio licences fell from 5 to 1 in 1953 to 3 to 1 in 1954.

October – The Swedish Parliament approved the introduction of a National Health Service.

December – Divorce was legalized by Juan Perón's government in Argentina.

MEN . . . AND THREE MEN'S VIEWS ON WOMEN

'Marriage? It's Like Being Run Over by a Bus'

—SAYS ONE, BUT TWO DISAGREE

by CAROLE FINDLATER

Drawings by
FRANCIS MARSHALL

MARRIAGE, they say, is an institution heavily publicised by women but regarded with wary suspicion by the average male. Therefore, most women's magazine propaganda is directed at how to get—and keep—your man.

Are men really so reluctant to be caught? As an earnest seeker after this great truth, I have asked a bachelor, a "twice - married - and - never - again" cynic, and a heavily and happily married man.

Peter Bryant, familiar to all addicts of TV's Grove family, is one of the most eligible bachelors in his profession. Slim, fair-haired, he lives with his parents in a London suburb, readily admits that he would like to marry.

"The snag is if you leave it too long it becomes more difficult to choose a wife. You become too selective, too critical."

I asked for specifications for an eligible candidate.

"She must be intelligent. I loathe stupid women—heaven protect me from the dumb blonde. I don't agree with men who say that women talk too much—I'll listen for hours as long as they are saying something worth listening to."

Essential quality

WHAT, I asked, did he think was the most essential single quality his wife would have to possess. There was no hesitation. "A sense of humour, of course."

He looked idly across the bar, then added quickly: "She must also have good legs. That's the first thing I notice."

I wondered whether there was any one aspect of marriage which had kept him a bachelor for so long. There was.

"I have a dread of possessiveness, and, so often, wives do become possessive and demanding. I think a man must retain a measure of independence, don't you?"

Politely I agreed.

I asked twice-divorced big and burly American film star **Steve Cochran.**

In a red T-shirt, blue jeans, knitted socks, and no shoes, his black hair tousl'd, he slouched comfortably on a settee in his elegant London (temporary) home and gave me his strong and decided views on marriage.

Clever to be dumb

"MARRY again? Look, honey, a man can be run over by a bus once, even run over by a bus twice, but he'd be one heck of a fool to be run over by a bus three times.

"The trouble with marriage," he elaborated, "is that it's so dull. You know a girl—it's fun. You marry her—it stops being fun. You get dragged down by duty.

"Polygamy?" His toes curled reflectively. "Yes, I'm all for it."

Tentatively I asked how many wives he would suggest. He grinned. "I can't give you the exact number, but this I do know: one wife at a time is one too many—anything over, things improve."

"Do women talk too much? Of course, much too much." He became expansive. "You know, what you women think of as clever women aren't clever at all. The clever girl is the one who keeps her mouth shut — and that's just the girl that you all call dumb. Do you see what I mean?"

Mutely I nodded.

I asked **Rossano Brazzi,** fast and deservedly winning the title of the screen's most romantic male star.

I lunched with him at Shepperton studios, where, between shooting his new film "Loser Takes All," he let his meal get cold while he told me his views.

"Sometimes I feel that I was born married." he reflected. "I met my wife when I was a 17-year-old student; we've been married for 16 years. At first I was too busy trying to make a career to think seriously about my marriage. I made pictures, worked hard—and I am still married.

"I think the main reason a man marries is because he fears loneliness." He looked sad. "Loneliness—now, there's a terrible thing. Also, he has in him always a trace of the little boy, and every woman has in her a maternal instinct."

On respect

HE warmed to his subject. "Where people are wrong is to think of marriage as love. It begins as love but marriage is really a very special relationship between two people which is created over the years.

"The foundation of marriage is based on respect. The day

PETER BRYANT.
"... I'll listen for hours."

STEVE COCHRAN.
"... it stops being fun."

ROSSANO BRAZZI.
"... I was born married."

I ceased to respect my wife, the day she ceased to respect me, our marriage would end."

He prodded a poached egg reflectively. "Do women talk too much? No, I would rather talk to women than to men."

Taking a deep breath, I asked him what was the first thing he noticed about a woman.

He raised his eyebrows, implying that it was surely unnecessary even to ask. "But of course—the eyes. The eyes tell you everything."

Hastily I stared hard at my leg of lamb.

The most telling comment I have heard on the whole thing was made as I left Shepperton—"It's a pity you didn't have a chance to meet Mrs. Brazzi," somebody said. "Now, there's a clever woman."

Should 'Forty' Marry Miss 'Twenty-One'?

ANN TEMPLE'S
Human Casebook

My only son is in his early forties and proposes to become engaged to a girl of 21.

His mother and I are very concerned owing to the disparity in their ages. I have pointed out to him that when he retires at 60 she will still be in her thirties.

*We have never known or heard of a man of his age marrying one so young. There is nothing brilliant or striking about the girl. I feel he is making a great mistake, but our only concern is for his happiness. What are your views on this?—*FATHER.

THEY have been considerably jostled by my experience in this column. Like you, I used to think so wide a disparity must work out badly. But facts do not bear that out.

I really have been surprised by the numbers of letters I receive from couples of widely differing ages (in some cases the wife being the older partner) who assure me that their marriages have been most successful and proof against the risk of differing interests in the later years.

I still think twenty years' difference when the girl is only twenty-one rather risky. In such cases the young wife often suffers from loneliness, feeling herself cut off from friends of her own age. And I should certainly think it disastrous for a man of twenty-one to marry a woman much older than himself.

A very young man is given to liking the companionship of older women but also to making a violent *volte-face* in the thirties. I should not worry too much about this marriage if I were you.

After all it is your son's choice, and, goodness knows, he must be old and wise enough by now to know whether he and the girl have sufficient interests in common to give them an enduring companionship.

The extraordinary thing about this is that the smallest effort on your part in counteraction is effective. Not noticeably so at the time, but in that the next time it is easier to begin. The very first movement you make—sitting up, looking round, sending your mind *towards* a job—that is curative. In time you will be able to substitute patience, quietness, waiting, and hope for what is now melancholy.

COMMERCIAL ART

My daughter is very good at art, and has had a painting accepted at an art gallery.

*I feel that on leaving school she should try something in the commercial art line. Could you please tell me what training is required and what are the openings?—*P. O.

IN fairness to you I feel I must point out that many experts hold that the art schools of the country have been turning out more students with an art training behind them than there are salaried jobs or even free-lance openings.

Your daughter may find it very difficult to get established after her training. A commercial artist needs to have tremendous perseverance and "push" quite apart from her capabilities in her work.

The usual training is to take a three-year course at an art school which has a department for commercial art. After general training a pupil studies design and then applies it to the branch of work she is most interested in — advertisement lay-out, book and magazine illustration, fashion drawing, lettering, package design, posters, brochures, exhibition design, etc., industrial design, textiles, glassware, wallpaper, etc.

The mood before it reaches the stage of getting you down. Don't give it a chance to operate. Occupy yourself, preferably through the hands, immediately. The secret is *immediately.*

What's new in
VOGUE

1955

Equal Pay for Some Women

ABOVE: (L to R) *Edith Summerskill, Patricia Ford, Barbara Castle and Irene Ward with a petition demanding equal pay.*
BELOW: *Doris Day, pictured here in the film* Young at Heart, *epitomized the 'nice girl' image of the 1950s. Movies still had a strong influence on popular culture and promoted a series of female stereotypes from the girl-next-door to the blonde bombshell image of Marilyn Monroe, almost all of them helpless without a man.*

Despite the conclusion of the Royal Commission on equal pay in 1946 there were a number of areas in which successive governments had said that they approved the principle of equal pay. Women teachers had been promised equal pay during the war at the same time as the marriage bar was lifted, yet when salaries were reviewed in 1950 men teachers received £630 per annum and women £504, exactly 80 per cent of the male rate. Women in the Civil Service had long been promised equal pay. Even the 1946 Royal Commission had singled out the Civil Service as the one area where women should have equal pay.

The new postwar argument why women should not have equal pay was that the country could not afford it. Women teachers, Civil Servants and local government officers finally grew tired of the government backing off from its commitments and in 1951 organized a campaign to bring about equal pay. The campaign took four years to bear fruit: in 1955 women in the Civil Service, teaching profession and local government were awarded equal pay.

It was a victory of sorts for it showed what women could do if they organized and protested but it still left millions of women without equal pay. Even within the Civil Service and local government the awards were only granted to professional grades not manual grades, and many other women, such as nurses, in the public sector were also excluded, as were women in industry, financial institutions, agriculture and business.

1955 POSTSCRIPTS

July – Ruth Ellis was hanged in Holloway prison for the murder of her lover. She was the last woman to suffer the death penalty and her case again stirred debate on the issue.

October – After two years of speculation Princess Margaret announced that she would not marry the divorced Group-Captain Peter Townsend. Although public opinion looked favourably on the prospect of the couple's marriage the Establishment made it clear that it was not willing to accept the marriage of a member of the Royal Family to a divorced man.

IRIS ASHLEY

. . . introducing the other point of view
with 'LET'S BE FAIR TO THE MEN' Week

MOTHERHOOD IS TOUGH ON FATHER

THIS is Ashley's Let's Be Fair To MEN Week. It seems that, what with queries about he-manners, followed by a quiz on husband - value, the men are feeling low.

I've been getting buttonholed by males all around the town. "Look," they say, " how about *our* side of the question. What about us ? "

So LET'S BE FAIR about babies. Let's admit that the arrival of a new baby is tougher 'on Father than Mother.

TIRED FATHER

I MEAN, for instance, that if Mademoiselle Sophie or Monsieur Patrick Mirman has not turned up by the time you read this then Father Serge will be a very tired man. So will Benjamin the dog.

Modiste Simone Mirman, who designs Princess Margaret's hats, should have had her first baby on October 17, but didn't. Last seen 24 hours ago, she was calm, radiant, and prettier than ever.

Not so husband Serge, who was distinctly pale.

"In the middle of every night now," he explained, "Simone awake. She tell me 'Serge ! The baby is arriving !' . . . I get up. I get the car. Then I go to collect Simone.

"She is still in bed and has fallen fast asleep again. Me, I am too much awake to go back to sleep. So is Benjamin, my dog. He gets up when I do. He comes down to the car. We neither of us have had a good night for a long time. . . ."

Benjamin put his head on my knee and closed his weary Spaniel eyes. Undoubtedly there were dark circles beneath them.

Moved by all this, I called up

MRS. HEIDI SIMPSON

ERNEST MARPLES, M.P.

GOOGIE WITHERS

Mrs. John McCallum (Googie Withers). Her second child is due in five weeks

"How is John ? " I asked anxiously.

"Fine—but restless," said Googie. " I find I have to think up things to keep him amused. We're doing a new play after Christmas, but he's going *mad* doing nothing. I think he feels that I'm sort of busy," she explained.

There was, of course, the dissident voice.

"What! Think it's *worse* for men than for *us ?* " said Mrs. Nigel Campbell, outraged. " I certainly do *not* agree, darling. As far as *I'm* concerned Nigel can have the next one. . . ."

AND AT HOME

NOW, LET'S BE FAIR to Men in the Home. Let's stop admiring women with jobs who run homes as well. At any rate, let's see if we can't find one—just one man who can stand up to such a feat.

And I don't mean being willing to help wash up after she has dreamed up, bought, and cooked the dinner.

An American survey reports that U.S. men are doing " Home Work " and liking it.

It seems they cook, baby sit, help with the laundry, and turn all these tasks into *hobbies !*

What of the British male—the chap who flies to his club or the local at the sight of a broom, and hides behind his newspaper at the first rattle of china ?

I've made my own survey. And herewith report that our males have changed enormously in recent years.

Though far behind the American house-trained, home-is-my-hobby man, our men *will* lend a willing hand—when asked. Quite a lot of them can boil an egg now too.

Taking a leaf from across the ocean, where they nominate a Mrs. America every year, 1 wish to give the accolade of Mr. Home-maker to one particular Englishman, a treasure in husbands ; a man with weighty national affairs on his mind who takes to household chores as a joy and relaxation.

He is Ernest Marples. M.P. and former junior Minister.

"Cooking," he says " is the most complete and sensuous pleasure in the world. Far more fulfilling t h a n intellectual argument, because an argument is never really finished."

There is nothing, but nothing Mr. Marples doesn't know about the home. " Home-making is so restful to the mind." he says.

He shops : " Because you must get the right raw material to cook properly. Do *you* know how long a saddle of lamb should be hung to make it tender ? " asked Mr. M.

I blushed.

"Seventeen days," said Mr. Home-maker.

He cooks : " In my London dining-room I combine a charcoal grill with a spit, so I can cook on the spot."

He budgets : " I buy in large quantities for economy and plan menus a fortnight ahead."

He invents : " A special dining-table overlapping the seats."

He labour-saves : " With a special stuff so tables need polishing only once a year."

Finally : " You should do as little hard work as possible," says Mr. M. " And get as much fun out of it as you can. . . ."

WHAT I HEAR

THE best *diet gimmick yet*, Mrs. Heidi Simpson, w i f e of Dr. Leonard Simpson, high-fashion store owner as well as doctor, says : Just order the SAME MENU for lunch and dinner.

It's best if it can be based on plain proteins like steak. But if you can't resist rich dishes and ·you order the same thing twice a day it kills your appetite. You just can't face it. A brilliant idea and so simple.

A grimly lucid little hand-out which offers a healing and beautifying cream for "housewife's hands." It's good, though.

But the remarks that have given me a lot of fun around Town have been about my picture at the top of this column each Monday.

If it is smiling I meet a dear friend who says : " I prefer you serious."

If serious, a dear chum remarks : "You're *so* much nicer smiling."

But the darlingest of all are the ones who say : " Why don't they *ever* print a *good* picture of you in the *Daily Mail* ? "

◆◆◆◆◆◆◆The Newest Kind of Party◆◆◆◆◆◆◆

STARTED by a group in Colwyn Bay, N. Wales, it's called " A Circular Dinner." About 12 people with three cars dine in six houses ; each course is in a different place, and partners are exchanged en route. Apparently any woman will cheerfully undertake to provide a one-course meal, and I am assured the parties have gone well. A bit bouncy for me, I think.

✳   ✳   ✳

The most dubious Christmas Gift suggestion. A gift-token for one or a series of driving lessons. From husband to wife or vice versa, this could make for a bleak Christmas Day.

◆◆◆◆◆◆◆

1956

Marriage and Motherhood

ABOVE: *'Family at dinner – father carving.'*

BELOW: *'The fairytale princess herself . . . Grace Kelly'*

Marriage and motherhood were what every girl or woman in the 1950s aspired to, or at least was supposed to aspire to. There was a very real feeling after the war that family life needed to be rebuilt and re-established. Enforced separations of young children from parents by evacuation, and fathers, older sons and daughters being called up to the Forces or to do war work had all severely disrupted families.

The expectation on everyone's, including the government's, part was that women would reassume their role as homemaker, pull the family together and hold it together. Government policy was conceived with this in mind. The nurseries that had been opened for working mothers during the war closed, some even in the week the war ended. The financial structuring of the Welfare State assumed that wives and mothers would stay at home.

Women in the 1950s had fewer children than their mothers so that the period of their life spent pregnant or caring for young children was reduced from perhaps fifteen or twenty years to around five. Motherhood became much more of a career, a job to be done well. Research by the psychologist John Bowlby suggested that children separated from their mothers in the early years had problems later in life. A mother had to be there when her children came home from school. Even a part-time job suggested that a mother was not giving her full attention to her family. Growing juvenile delinquency was blamed on mothers not giving their children enough attention.

The image of marriage and motherhood was promoted everywhere from Hollywood films to the popular radio programmes like *The Archers*. Advertisers too used the image of the wife and mother caring for her family, desperately worried in case she was failing them by not buying the right brand of soap powder, polish or baked beans. The marriage of film star Grace Kelly, who announced that she was giving up her career to be a full-time wife to Prince Rainier of Monaco, was the social event of 1956.

The reality for many women was far from the fairytale marriage of the film star and the prince. Postwar housing programmes relocated and isolated many new mothers from family and friends. Clearly many women enjoyed the time they had with their children but as the children grew more independent they felt trapped and bored at home. Most women had had the benefit of a secondary education, had worked before they married and, increasingly, had remained at work until their first child was born. They knew they could do more than look after a home, husband and growing children.

1956 POSTSCRIPT

October – The Pope in an address to women urged them to subordinate all other activities open to them in order to fulfil their prime function. He said, 'Her sublime mission is maternity.'

NEW ATTACK

A fresh attack on the last of the 'men only' jobs is to be made by women.

An investigation is to be made by a committee of six of the National Federation of Business and Professional Women's Clubs into 'discrimination'.

Mrs Audrey Taylor, the organizing secretary, told me yesterday, 'The three chief remaining barriers are the Stock Exchange, the newspaper industry and taxi services.'

A woman can be a stockbroker but she cannot be elected to the Stock Exchange, cannot operate on the floor of the 'House'. Mrs Taylor described this as 'humiliating'.

But the Stock Exchange has a case, Mrs Taylor. One stockbroker told me: 'This business has its code but, make no mistake, it's ruthless.

'We are dealing in money – not furniture or books . . . and who wants to step on a woman?'

Daily Mail, 6 March 1956 – Extract from Tanfield's Diary

I T is my opinion t h a t women have gone too far, at any rate in England, with t h i s equality - with - men business.

A day I spent at Blenheim Palace with the Duchess of Marlborough confirmed it for me.

The duke was home, too. He was resting in his armchair, with an ITV programme blaring away, reading the paper with one hand and baby-minding with the other.

The duchess tottered in after an exhausting day in Oxford

Ladies, have you gone too far?

IN THIS BUSINESS OF EQUALITY . . .

doing a round of business meetings.

I sat awaiting her, surrounded by stately carpets only half-shampooed, and all the priceless Meissen china waiting to be washed up by the duchess in time for the palace to be opened to the public on April 1.

I changed my mind

MY business was to discuss with the duchess a festival of women which opens at Wembley in June, with the blessing of the Prime Minister, trade unions, and Treasury.

The duchess is president of the festival.

But what I saw when I followed the butler into the duke's sitting-room made me change my mind.

I stopped worrying about the festival . . . whether it would be a big success like the Festival of Britain, and all that.

Instead I started to worry about the awful change in men . . . and how we women were to blame for it all.

"The women of Britain," said the duchess, in her festival message, "are a power."

But look at the result.

Having pushed men into the kitchens and nurseries, where secretly they are quite enjoying themselves, are women going to budge?

Make no mistake, the situation is serious.

For example, Antonia, wife of Hugh Fraser, M.P., told me:

"My husband loves doing the cooking, breakfast, and so on."

Washes up in a dream

HER mother, Lady Pakenham, said: "My husband loves helping with the washing-up and carrying trays.

"He does all the drying himself, and he does it in a sort of dream."

You bet he does. Only men are able to dream nowadays.

Then Harold Macmillan, the Prime Minister. He is all for the festival of women.

Under his splendid portrait on the festival hand-out is a rousing speech by him. . . . "The festival is of particular interest to women, who do as much of the nation's shopping as they do of its work."

Jobs for the girls is clearly his motto.

I wonder why the men don't retire altogether soon. Now we even have to run our own festivals.

I doubt if the men will even turn up at the festival.

They'd rather stay home in the warm with baby and the washing-up.

But it was catching the Duke of Marlborough baby-sitting, with the help of the butler, footmen, and the staff of 21, in Blenheim Palace that really clinched it for me.

She was worn out

THERE was the duchess, still very pretty and very slender at 50 plus, but quite worn out, after a business meeting lasting all day at Wingfield Hospital . . . and now half-an-hour late for our business appointment.

"Horrible meetings," she muttered. She stood bravely against the jumbled but stately furniture.

Meanwhile the duke was having a lovely time.

He stretched his long legs in comfortable flannels and velvet slippers before the fire, puffed at his pipe, and kept one eye on TV and the other on his paper.

Said the duchess: "The duke says you can take his picture

THE DUCHESS . . . "HORRIBLE MEETINGS," SHE SAID.

By OLGA FRANKLIN

provided you don't expect him to get up out of his chair."

The duke sank deeper into it. "Those children," he said, waving his free hand at two fair - haired, angelic - looking grandchildren. Elizabeth, 5, and Michael Waterhouse, 7. "they have been so tiresome all day."

The children's mother is in America.

"Oh, do go away," he said to Elizabeth. She was wandering across his line of vision. Elizabeth sat down again, in front of the TV.

Never heard of it

THE butler came in, carrying a large fruit cake, followed by two handsome footmen wearing tails and a frilled touch of white at the throat.

I asked the duke for his views on the festival of women. "On the WHAT?" he said. I tried again.

"Never heard of it," said the duke.

I said: "The festival your wife is president of. In the summer."

"Views?" said the duke, "I haven't any views."

Said the duchess: "I think you're a bit early to ask about the festival.

"I can't say much because no one has told me yet what the programme is. I am in the hands of Miss Thirza West, the organiser.

"I expect we have to wait until we can get into Wembley after the football. Don't ask me when. I don't know. Really...."

Then the duchess had to rush off to yet another business meeting. She sits, when she does sit down, on a finance sub-committee, a general purposes committee, a county council planning and services committee, on Civil Defence, on the International Red Cross, and she has to open a fashion show this week and the stately home in a fortnight.

It is a hard life.

We must have been crazy

AS I walked back behind the butler through the hall, past its busts of all the Dukes of Marlborough with their round Churchillian faces, I stopped to look at a portrait of the beautiful red-head Sarah, wife of John, first Duke of Marlborough.

There she was, in low-cut gown, playing cards with her friend Lady Fitzhardinge.

And all around were the glinting breastplates of the men of the family who were out fighting some wars. . . .

Ah, that was the life. . . . We women must have been crazy to listen to that Mrs. Pankhurst.

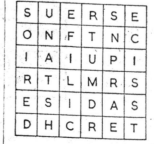

1957

The Perfect Figure

Ten years after the 'New Look' was created by Dior in 1947 it continued to dominate the female silhouette, even if the dresses narrowed to the sheath dress, which was popular alongside the classic 1950s' waisted, full-skirted and full-busted styles. Hollywood had reinforced and emphasized the hourglass figure by promoting women like Marilyn Monroe and Jane Russell.

Exercise and women's sport in general were not as popular as they had been in the 1930s. In fact vigorous exercise was rather frowned upon as unladylike. So for most ordinary women to obtain the perfect figure it required control over their diet either the hard way or the 'easy way' through the use of 'diet' or 'slimming' pills, the most effective of which later proved to be addictive. Corsets and padded bras helped trim the figure or supplement the bustline if it was lacking.

Make-up was used to draw attention to the eyes, particularly the eyebrows, and strong lip colours to emphasize the mouth, although towards the end of the 1950s pale pink lips as worn by Brigitte Bardot became fashionable. Bardot's backcombed and dishevelled hairstyle was also copied and marked a change from the neat cuts and waves for short hair and long hair smoothly held in a bun or roll.

Stiletto-heeled and pointed-toed shoes which flattered the legs of the wearer first made their appearance in the mid-1950s and became popular as skirts shortened.

1957 marked a watershed in the style of women's clothing as the 'sack dress' was the new shape to be shown that year and its unfitted line and shorter length was a distinct reaction to the postwar 'New Look' and presaged some of the ideas for women's dress in the 1960s.

ABOVE: Film Stars Mona Freeman (left) and Jane Russell in dresses which emphasize the bustline.

BELOW LEFT: An outfit from the late 1950s – accessories and hats were important.

BELOW RIGHT: The perfect figure as displayed by a Miss World contestant.

1957   POSTSCRIPTS

April – A survey by the National Council for Women showed that 3,570,000 married women worked outside the home. The great majority of them for economic reasons rather than because they were 'bored or lonely'. The survey also 'found that most husbands are accepting the fact that their wives should work, and were co-operating by helping with housework'.

May – The Church of England allowed remarried divorcees to take the sacrament if a bishop permitted it. They had been barred from communion before because they would be, strictly speaking, 'living in sin' with their new partner.

July – Prime Minister Harold Macmillan told the people of Britain that they had 'never had it so good' as the country enjoyed prosperity and a booming economy.

• Britain abstained from voting when UNESCO passed a resolution calling for full political rights and equal pay for women.

WOMEN – A right to be in the Upper House, says Lord Home

The government wants women to be admitted to the House of Lords, the Earl of Home, leader of the House said yesterday.

The peers, crowding their benches for a two-day debate on House of Lords reform, took the news manfully. There were even a few cheers . . .

'The admission of women,' he went on, 'is a recognition of the place which they have created for themselves as a right in modern society.'

Daily Mail, 31 October 1957

How to hide the HI-FI

WHERE IS IT? TRY THREE GUESSES...

HOW to hide the Hi-Fi is the home-planning problem of the moment, and nowhere has it been more ingeniously solved than by the Hon. Gerald and Mrs. Lascelles in that historic pine-panelled drawing-room in Fort Belvedere.

The whole works—amplifier, speaker, and turntable — are neatly housed in a mahogany Victorian bedroom commode picked up at a local auction for £12 by their neighbour Mrs. Peter Cadbury.

Fits in better

THE top section takes the amplifier, the centre drawer has had the earth works removed and now just takes the turntable. The speaker has been built into the back.

"We think it fits in better with our period furniture than any modern piece, and when we are not using the set it can be unplugged and the commode used as library steps," Mrs. Lascelles told us.

Now Peter Cadbury's customers in the Hi-Fi section of his famous radio and theatre ticket agency are seeking for similar conversions and Mrs. Cadbury is out searching the salerooms again.

"We've managed to find one or two commodes," says Mr. Cadbury, "but for customers who don't like them we've a nice line in converted grandfather clocks."

Another Mayfair firm is doing booming business making hand-made reproduction pieces for Hi-Fi and stereophonic equipment. You can buy a complete Hi-Fi outfit housed in what looks like a Regency chest of drawers for around £150.

Stereophonic equipment in Regency cabinets and with the second speaker undetectable in a small metal-fretted cupboard costs around £300.

We thought these pieces would look much better in the average home, with its mixture of period and new furniture, than any of the modern cabinets we have seen.

But we think it's one in the eye for our industrial designers that no one has yet produced a new piece which really is so attractive that we would *want* to have it in our homes.

THE LASCELLES ... and the Hi-Fi is out of sight

Peter Cadbury, Gerald Lascelles ... and here's the Hi-Fi

pan, stirring in the gelatine, and bring slowly to the boil.

Mix the custard powder and sugar with the remainder of the fresh milk until it is a creamy consistency. Strain hot milk and the gelatine mixture into this and then pour into a clean saucepan.

Cook for about four minutes. Beat the egg, add this to mixture and cook for a further minute. Don't let the mixture boil.

Allow to cool and then add the whipped evaporated milk or cream and pour into the ice tray. Leave until the mixture is hard at the edges, but still soft at the centre (for about 30-40 minutes).

Then tip the mixture into a bowl, whip thoroughly, and return to the ice compartment to chill until firm.

• • • • • • • •

Better than they were

NYLON SHEETS. The early ones were clammy. Newer versions were more porous. Better still, the latest, which are in a fleecy nylon. Prices £9 13s. 5d. for double set ; singles £7 15s. ; pillowcases 16s.

• • • • • • • •

Seen around

THERE have been plenty of good medicated and cover-up lotions for teenage girls with spots, but what about pimply boys who cannot go around daubed with cosmetic-type preparations ?

We've found the answer: an effective corrective lotion which is completely colourless and undetectable. It can make a marked improvement to spots and grease patches in a week.

The lady's not for shirking

GETTING DOWN TO THE ROOT ...

IN Mayfair hair salons experts have been studying the photograph on the right.

It is, in fact, the first-ever photograph of a human hair taken under an electronic microscope and magnified 1,500 times. And what it reveals means differences in hairdressing technique.

Says Mr. John Walters, technical manager of a leading hair preparations firm : "We never knew before that the surface of human hair was made up of a scaly formation

with a distinct rough and smooth grain. This put a lot

of my hairdressing methods out of date. I see that when I apply a hair tonic or oil and smooth it down the hair from root to tip, it is rather like water off a duck's back.

"There is little chance that any will be retained beneath the scaly layers. The same thing happens if I am applying a colour tint or rinse.

"It's obvious to do any good that both hairdressers and women doing their own hair at home should work in hair tonics and colours from tip to root."

• • • • • • • •

As they were

FROZEN VEGETABLES. The recognisable taste of the same old frozen peas, baby sprouts, and broad beans is becoming as monotonous now as the old canned foods. More variety, please.

• • • • • • • •

Ice custard

THE new orange, chocolate, and strawberry-flavoured custard powders are fine for home-made ice cream. Take 1½ teaspoons of custard powder, 3 oz. of castor sugar, half-pint milk, half-pint of cream or evaporated full-cream milk, one egg, a teaspoon of powdered gelatine, and a pinch of salt.

Turn refrigerator control to "lowest." Heat three-quarters of the fresh milk in a sauce-

★ ☆ ★ ☆ ★ ☆

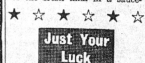
Just Your Luck

WHEN the children are off their hands some women take up dogs, good works, or baby-sitting. Lady Bullard, wife of Sir Edward Bullard, the famous Cambridge geophysicist, decided to try pottery and metalwork when Polly, the youngest of her four daughters, reached her teens.

But mother's part-time pottery grew into something bigger. Local shops discovered that hers was no folkcraft flair : the lady had high fashion style.

She soon had four workers employed in her garden workshop : the glossy fashion magazines hounded her out and she was swamped with orders.

Today she's opening a boutique in Belgravia to cope with the rush for her jewellery and pottery. Look at the exotic pieces in the picture and you'll understand why.

Made of hand-beaten copper and then dipped in a dull gilt Lady Bullard calls Roman Gold, the prices are 27s. 6d. each for snake bracelet and abstract pendant, £3 12s. for the necklace, which can also make a headband.

In lacquered copper the same pieces cost 5s. less.

1958

Women and the Church

Despite the fact that throughout the world women comprised the majority in the congregations they had no voice in the hierarchy of many of the Christian Churches of the world. While the Quakers and the Salvation Army had allowed women as preachers since their inception, most other groups, especially the older and established Churches, forbade any ecclesiastical positions to women.

Some of the more recently established Churches in the USA and Canada had allowed women as deacons and elders and a few of these Churches such as the American Methodist Church had even ordained them as ministers. Denmark had passed legislation in the 1940s to allow for the ordination of women as ministers in the State Lutheran Church.

None of the mainstream Churches in Britain had women in any similar capacities, although the Presbyterian United Free Church did have women ministers, and there were a number of women who had studied theology as lay members of the other Churches. The issue of women priests had been to the fore in Britain for some years, promoted by groups like the Society for the Equal Ministry of Men and Women in which the actress Sybil Thorndike was a prominent member.

ABOVE: Marie Stopes pictured early in the century at her work as a palaeobotanist.
BELOW: Hilda Harding at her desk.

1958 POSTSCRIPTS

April – The Church of England gave its unequivocal blessing to the use of artificial methods of birth control, accepting the idea of planning the number of children and frequency of their birth as a moral one.

July – Britain's first list of life peers included 14 women. Four baronesses were created including Baroness Wootton. Women who inherited a peerage were still not allowed to sit in the House of Lords.

October – Marie Stopes, pioneer of birth control in Britain, died.

November – Hilda Harding became the first woman bank manager in Britain when she took over the Hanover Street branch of Barclay's Bank which had been specially planned to attract women's accounts with 'a ladies' waiting room and a powder room, both in pastel shades and with deep carpets'.

December – Some early suggestions were made linking the anti-sickness drug for pregnant women, thalidomide, to a number of babies born with malformations.

WHY NOT A WOMAN ARCHBISHOP?

A group of distinguished churchmen have addressed an open letter to the bishops calling upon them to approve the admission of women to the priesthood.

The Church is the last bastion of male supremacy. Will it fall before their attack.

The Archbishop of Canterbury has said that the ordination of women is not a live issue . . .

Considering the shabby treatment given them it is not surprising that few women come forward for professional work in the Church.

Women who wish to serve God feel that they are more appreciated as teachers or welfare workers.

My guess is that the Lambeth Bishops will fob off this call for the ordination of women as they will many other demands for a bold decision. But I wish they would show real moral courage in this instance.

Daily Mail, 22 July 1958. Extracts from an article by the Reverend C. O. Rhodes, Editor of the *Church of England Newspaper*

How U
OR NON-U
is your home?

THE way you talk, the way you hold a knife can both fix your U or non-U rating. But the biggest giveaway of all, says a famous interior decorator, is the way in which you furnish your home. He is Mr. John Gillett, of Beauchamp-place, Knightsbridge, who for 20 years has been advising the top people how to decorate their stately homes. In a trade which today attracts more than its share of chi-chi, brides from Debrett still go to quiet Mr. Gillett for guidance (" Mummy always did ").

Years spent studying the best homes in Britain have given Mr. Gillett a fairly clear picture of what constitutes current U and non-U taste in furnishings.

" The best homes," he tells us, " are slightly shabby, a little untidy, in fact, an elegant hotchpotch of period-furniture. You come out thinking what a lovely home . . . without remembering details. If you go away with vivid memories of a handsome sideboard, it was most probably non-U and ostentatious."

Edited by
AMY LANDRETH

Mr. G's guide

Here is Mr. Gillett's guide to good taste:

It's non-U to have . . .

Three-piece suites, bedroom suites, carpets with a too-deep pile, linoleum (except for kitchens and bathrooms).

To have too much shine . . . shine in textiles, shellac shine on furniture is bad, so is new looking gilt.

Elaborate flower arrangements, like a florist's window. Potted plants in living rooms.

Plastic or paper lampshades, ding-dong door chimes, ashtrays on stands, harlequin glass or coffee sets.

Tinted glass walls, wallpapers with borders and panels. Folk weave fabrics. Blue rooms, red bedrooms.

Leaded windows, " baronial " chimney pieces and grates.

Ruchings and fringe pipings round cushions and chairs.

It's U to have . . .

Rooms without definite colour schemes with back-to-nature colours and flower - printed fabrics.

Odd chairs and sofas with non-matching covers. Covers with self piping and a simple fringe round the bottom. No ruchings.

Waxed floors and furniture.

Rare old carpets, or new ones in soft plain colours. Fitted plain carpets with Persian rugs on top.

Surprise!

Luscious furry rugs in your bedroom (but not living-rooms).

Regency stripes (surprise!), but they must be in traditional colours.

Lace table mats. Plenty of silver on the table.

On the subject of Contemporary, Mr. Gillett is undecided: " Of course, some of it is very nice, but none of my clients ever want it."

A WORLD FAMOUS PATTERN FOR YOU

THE wonderful handknits made by the homeknitters of the W.V.S. Women's Home Industries are world famous. The Duchess of Kent wears them ; so does the Duchess of Argyll, Elizabeth Taylor, and Rosalind Russell.

Now, for the first time, these beautiful patterns are available for you to copy. Exclusive to the Daily Mail, we present the first W.H.I. handknit. A holiday jacket in the casual Chanel mood of the moment. Send a stamped (3d.) self-addressed envelope for a free instructions leaflet to : " Jacket Knitting Pattern," Daily Mail, Gough-square, London, E.C.4 (Comp.).

THE WORLD OF DAVID PELHAM
● LIFE WITHOUT A WIFE GOES SLICKLY FOR THE
37-YEAR-OLD IMPRESARIO...

MR. P. relaxes . . . on his crimson-covered bed.

WHETHER after its first night tomorrow that controversial show The World of Paul Slickey booms or busts, the world of its 37-year-old impresario, David Pelham, will go on in its customary clever and efficient way.

He lives in a handsome bow-windowed flat in Montagu-square, London, W., and the Pelham Plan for life without a wife is a moral to all the girls who delude themselves that even gay bachelors around town must have a woman to run their homes.

Most of the week home is strictly for sleeping. Apart from a morning brew of instant coffee and croissants he seldom eats there or gets home before 1 a.m. or 2 a.m. He has no full-time domestic help, yet telephones are answered, flowers are fresh, suits pressed, and he can rustle up a surprise meal.

A valet

APART-TIME help does home cleaning and buys supplies from lists left by Mr. Pelham.

On Tuesdays Mrs. Pringle comes to do the flowers, and on Wednesdays a valet spends an hour or so checking up on the 12 lightweight suits, three overcoats, and ten pairs of shoes in the wardrobe.

" He sews on buttons and sees my shoes are kept repaired, so that once I have bought them I can forget my clothes completely. Since I began to make money the visiting valet has been my most economical luxury," says David Pelham.

Thursday brings the visiting masseur. " Apart from massage, I keep fit by walking to most town appointments."

He doesn't run a car but is on the special priority list a radio-cab firm keep for their best customers. You telephone your code number and you always get a taxi at once.

Another special service takes care of the telephone calls, and all incoming calls are intercepted direct by an answering service on the fourth ring.

On Sundays friends drop in, and, if the party grows, the doors between the fashionable " sludge - brown " living room and the bedroom are opened.

Guests sit on the large crimson-covered bed with a head made from the frame of a Victorian gilt mirror.

If they get hungry there are enough pork chops in the deep freeze to feed 20 people.

Yes, slickly goes the world of Mr. P.

Stacking craze

IN furniture the stack-away craze spreads . . . stacking beds go a stage farther and come in three decks. Price £10 12s. 3d., mattresses extra.

For only 10s. we've seen a really well-made stacking stool. In mahogany veneer, with black metal legs, tall enough to use at the table or to double as a coffee-table.

Out of town

THAT London institution the literary luncheon is moving out of town. A leading publishing group plans to give a series of luncheons for current best-selling authors in Manchester, Leeds, and Edinburgh. But they offer value for money in the North. The two-guinea ticket includes a signed copy of the book.

Old and new

IT'S time the greengrocers stopped cheating us about those so-called " new " potatoes. They cost about 8d. a pound, and when you get them home you find they won't scrape. Cooked, they taste little different from old potatoes. In fact, they are. Most come from Spain or the Canaries, and they are late varieties of maincrop potatoes which are lifted when still small. But greengrocers still label them " new."

If you want genuine new potatoes, the first Jerseys are in the shops now but at 2s. a pound.

ABOVE: *Launderettes were becoming popular for those who could not afford the initial outlay for a washing machine for their own home.*
BELOW: *A family-planning poster offering help and advice but only for married couples.*

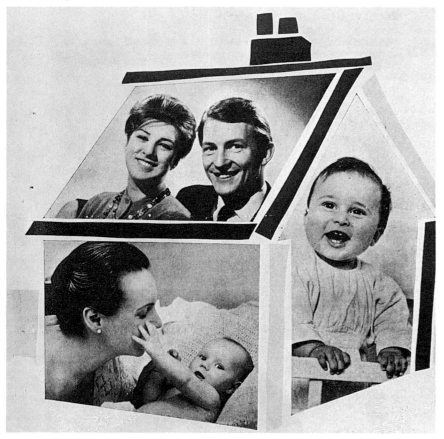

if YOU ARE GETTING MARRIED AND WANT FAMILY PLANNING ADVICE

if YOU ARE MARRIED AND WANT TO PLAN A FAMILY

if YOU WANT A FAMILY AND YOU CANNOT HAVE ONE

THE FAMILY PLANNING ASSOCIATION

will help you

1959

Women as Professionals

Throughout the 1950s newspapers were full of stories of women storming the last bastions of masculine preserves. Women gaining entry to the House of Lords in 1958 was one such story. But there were women who entered a wide range of, especially professional, jobs that had previously only been done by men.

Margaret Kidd in Scotland and Helena Normanton and Rose Heilbron in England had become King's, later Queen's, Counsels at the end of the 1940s. Hilda Harding had become the first woman bank manager in Britain in 1958 and John Lewis had appointed a woman managing director, Miss M. J. Ahern, in 1951.

Women were beginning to make careers for themselves outside the home. It was made easier for them by the fact that the marriage bar had disappeared from all spheres of work. But there were many obstacles in their way. Not least was the fact that for all the storming of male bastions in the 1950s there remained a number of areas where women were only permitted to a portion of the whole sphere of operations. Sometimes this was the result of rules barring them as with the Stock Exchange where they were not permitted 'on the floor'. But more often it was a lack of courage to appoint women to posts for which they were eminently suited. For example there were a number of women with the qualifications to be Ambassadors as early as 1952 but it was not until 1962 that Britain appointed its first woman Ambassador.

The chief obstacle in the way of any woman, especially a married woman, who wished to have a career was the social pressure; it was still maintained that a woman's place was in the home. It is interesting to note that many of the women who were successful at this period were either unmarried or did not have children.

1959 POSTSCRIPTS

February – A poll of the male electorate in Switzerland rejected the proposal to give women the vote.

• In India Prime Minister Nehru's daughter Indira Ghandi was elected as President of the ruling Congress Party.

October – The Conservatives were elected for the third time in succession and Margaret Thatcher won her first parliamentary seat.

DEBATORS OF OXFORD VOTE TO LET WOMEN JOIN

The Oxford Union Society last night decided by 383–294 votes that women undergraduates should be admitted to debating membership.

But the vote was not conclusive because the anti-feminists demanded a poll. If 150 members of the society support this demand in the next two days, all the 2,000 resident members of the society will be able to vote on the issue.

Since its foundation in 1823 the society has been exclusively for men.
Daily Mail, 27 November 1959

To the corseted, the girdled, the fashion-enslaved European woman, a startling report from uninhibited South America raises a query we may well ask . . .

What s-h-a-p-e is a woman?

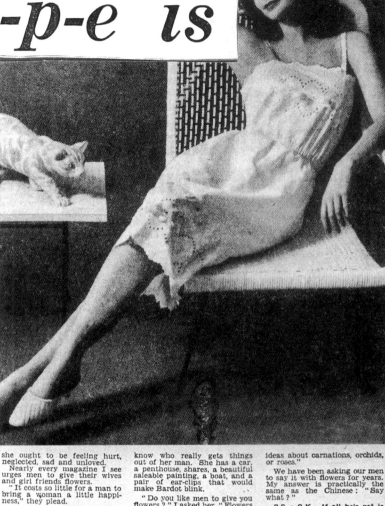

THEY can't sell corsets in the Caribbean, or girdles in Mexico, and women won't flatten hips and backs or build up busts in Buenos Aires. This shocking piece of news has been announced by **Mr. Fred Gann**, who is trying to sell American foundations to Latin-American women.

"It is all a matter of status," says Mr. Gann.

"Men treat their women much as European men did 50 years ago. Economically, the majority of women are completely dependent on their husbands or fathers.

"Consequently they must dress to please their men, whereas American and European women often dress to please themselves or one another.

"Latin-American men," he goes on to say, "like their women to show their curves and favour the hour-glass figure, with tiny waist, accentuated bustline, plump hips, and natural back."

New move

MR. GANN'S firm is so worried about the sales that they are attacking the problem with advertising.

"We are creating a psychological erosion," he states. "Through advertising women are being influenced to think in terms of chic rather than of comfort and of simply pleasing the men."

I do not envy salesman Gann his epic task.

But I am jealous of the uncivilised Latins who actually want to dress to please a man. Who are prepared to think in terms of a man being the boss and paying the bills. Who will even tolerate having hips and a waist and a natural back.

But I suspect I'm writing in the wrong country.

WITH A POSY

IN spring a young man's fancy is supposed to be getting violets and daffodils, roses and posies. If she isn't getting them she ought to be feeling hurt, neglected, sad and unloved.

Nearly every magazine I see urges men to give their wives and girl friends flowers.

"It costs so little for a man to bring a woman a little happiness," they plead.

Two sides

"**W**HAT a difference a small bunch of freesias makes," they argue.

"A rose a day will keep her sweet and loving far more than anything else," they suggest.

The young Americanised Chinese in *The Flower Drum Song* gives his girl friend orchids. "We say it with flowers over here," explains his aunt to the old Chinese sage.

"Say what?" he replies.

I talked to the one woman I know who really gets things out of her man. She has a car, a penthouse, shares, a beautiful saleable painting, a boat, and a pair of ear-clips that would make Bardot blink.

"Do you like men to give you flowers?" I asked her. "Flowers—certainly not," she replied.

"I don't mind another person choosing a car I don't particularly like, or a diamond that isn't exactly my taste, or even a painting that I wouldn't pay my own good money for.

"But the one thing I do want to do is to choose my own flowers. I hate other people's ideas about carnations, orchids, or roses."

We have been asking our men to say it with flowers for years. My answer is practically the same as the Chinese: "Say what?"

P.S.: O.K. If all he's got is 6d., a bunch of violets is better than nothing.

BUT, TELL ME...

HOT ITEM FROM MILWAUKEE, U.S.—People are buying drip-dry Waltz Gowns to take on their honeymoons. Will somebody please tell me just what is a Waltz Gown and just what you are supposed to do in it? Waltz?

THE FEMININE APPEAL OF HAIR OVER ONE EYE...

LISA DENIZ, the model above, has just had a new rinse, milk chocolate—a delicious pale browny blonde. Her hairstyle by Aldo, at Simon, is short at the back, long in the front. "So that it can fall over her eye," explained Aldo.

"I believe that there is nothing more feminine than hair that falls over one eye. It is so attractive to see a woman push it back with her hand." Aldo is, of course, an Italian.

Party-pale colours for every day make complete sense when they're in wonderful wash-and-wear Courtelle. Her shapely sweater, that keeps its shape, is by **DONBROS**, price about 39/11; the boy's hard-wearing sweater by **SABRE SPORTWEAR** costs about 47/6.

A new look for those expectant mothers

THERE'S A NEW look in maternity wear. The woman who makes the maternity clothes worn by **Princess Grace of Monaco** and **Baroness von Thyssen (Fiona Campbell Walter)** won't make those concealing cover-ups. She prefers to make use of that growing shape.

Mrs. Maisie Landon Silvers thinks that waiting mothers can even wear play clothes and swimsuits.

1960

An Education for Girls

Postwar education policy in England and Wales had been to offer a secondary education in grammar, secondary modern and technical schools for all, but in strictly segregated schools.

There was also overt and hidden segregation in the curriculum – boys' subjects and girls' subjects. Girls' schools were equipped for domestic science and needlework while boys' schools had woodwork and metal-work rooms. Even in girls' grammar schools it was rare to be offered a wide range of science subjects; most had just biology or general science on offer. Nearly all science teachers were male, reinforcing the idea that science was a boy's subject.

A number of government-commissioned reports in the 1960s, such as *Half Our Future,* sought to address the question of what should be included on the curriculum for boys and girls. In 1960 the Crowther Report was published. It said that it was a fact that in the last years at school, boys' first thoughts were most often about their careers and only secondly about marriage and the family, but the opposite was true for girls. The Report's solution to this situation was not to try to widen girls' horizons but, much to the protestation of the National Union of Women Teachers, to suggest that girls be 'specially directed to preparation for marriage and motherhood'.

Outside education circles the attitude that it was a waste of time to bother with much in the way of advanced education for girls was still prevalent. Girls who did well at school could still find their chances of sixth form or higher education sacrificed for the sake of a brother having the opportunity to continue his education.

Nevertheless most girls in the 1960s had an education which, while it might not have equalled the boys of their generation in terms of opportunity, was certainly superior to that of their mothers and probably their fathers.

ABOVE: A mother having her baby weighed at a child health clinic.
BELOW: Sirimawo Bandaranaike.

1960 POSTSCRIPTS

● Maureen Nicol who suggested the idea, helped set up the National House-wives' Register with the aim of putting women at home in touch with each other to offer support facilities to one another but also to talk, read, paint and discuss together.

July – Sirimawo Bandaranaike, widow of the assassinated Prime Minister, became the first elected female head of state in the world when she took office as Prime Minister of Ceylon.

November – D. H. Lawrence's novel *Lady Chatterley's Lover* was found not to be obscene following a colourful trial at which the Prosecution asked the jury, 'Is this a book you would wish your wife or your servant to read?'

SIGN FROM ST ALBANS
St Albans is run by women. Dominated by them.

It's useless for them to deny it (as in fact, they slyly do). Look at the facts. The mayor is a woman. The mayor's secretary is a woman. The town clerk is a woman.

Backing this triumvirate are women in charge of housing, welfare, the Post Office, a museum and an art school, and other strategic points of power and influence.

For weeks past the pundits have been predicting the course of the 1960s (we have done it ourselves.) Among them was MR GEORGE SANDERS who forecast in the *Daily Mail* this week that in the next decade women would throw off their pretended dependence on men and strike off on their own . . .

Now, it seems, they are ready to throw off all subterfuge and take over in earnest. And – vilest trickery of all – they are winning their positions of power through, of all things, sheer merit!

Daily Mail, 2 January 1960 – extract from Leader

The BIG sensation for this Wimbledon

At 20 guineas—a demi-wig

by PAT TAYLOR

FASHION at Wimbledon sometimes seems more important than the tennis.

Ever since the 1920's, when Suzanne Lenglen started the rage for bandeaux, we have come to expect a new sensation in feminine frivolities from the Centre Court. This year, I predict, will be no exception.

In recent years we've had Gorgeous Gussie Moran's original, famous lace-trimmed pants, plus her £80 pair of pleated chiffon bloomers, which launched tennis undies into the haute couture class. Later, with the dedicated aid of Mr. Teddy Tinling, we've craned for fascinating glimpses of anything from gold lamé to rows of baby lace.

Matching

BUT the accent switches this year to hair . . . false hair. Mrs. Ilse Davies (née Buding) is well on the way to game, set, and match in the Wimbledon glamour stakes with her notion of a bandeau of matching hair as a five-second beauty aid.

It takes just that long to slip on this Antoine-designed demi-wig, which comprises a fringe, side curls, and a touch of crown hair—and transforms a tousled sporting head into a slick, unruffled coiffure. The bandeau is made of real hair, stitched on to a fine elastic band, and dyed to match

IT IS THE FIVE-SECOND SWITCH

For Ilse—tennis and tousled look

. . . then instant grooming without a comb

exactly Ilse's own dark blonde hair. It costs 20 guineas.

The purists may sniff at such feminine distractions. The game's the thing. But for my part I'm all in favour of feminine charm and chic, whether it's facing a Wimbledon camera or the kitchen sink.

Practical note for non-sporting types :

Smaller hair accessories—say just a fringe bandeau — cost from around five guineas. As well as a fashion flash, they can be a handy aid to the woman getting a bit thin around the front hairline.

In Paris the top hairdressers are doing a big business in false hair pieces with summertime beauties who want to look well-coiffed at night after a day on the beach.

★ ★ ★

Mad dogs and...

WHILE half the world envies white skin, each summer the white races seek every opportunity to turn brown.

In Africa the biggest-selling cosmetic products are skin lighteners, whereas in the Western world a mahogany tan is rated high for reasons which vary from health and beauty to status.

Yet tanning, and the accompanying slight thickening of skin are only the body's way of endeavouring to absorb light and minimise the potential damaging effects of ultra-violet rays.

That reckless exposure to sunlight is highly dangerous is underlined by one medical report that 99 p.c. of skin cancer in Australia is due to chronic sunburn.

Admittedly in this country the dangers are very much less, but one skin expert gave me his opinion that "if we had many summers such as 1959 excessive exposure could lay the foundations of future trouble. Many people seem to go quite crazy faced with sunshine."

Tanning should never be rushed, but produced gradually, with pallid skins exposed in small doses. Where first exposure are too long, and bad blisters or burns follow, the way is paved for possible infection. In severe cases of sunburn the pigment cells may be destroyed or altered, with a consequent loss of capacity to tan for several years.

Baking

THERE are many good sunscreens on the market today. Use one, liberally and often, over the first few days of sunbathing, then less frequently when the tan is well on the way, BUT—even with adequate protection—note that it is considered that 20-30 minutes' "baking" is ample for the first day.

Even when it is a dullish, hazy day near the coast, go cannily . . . reflection from water or sky can result in an unpleasant burn.

There is a small group of people who, despite sensible precautions, find it hard to tolerate the sun. After even a small dose, their skin burns or blisters badly, and they may also develop rashes and bumps.

These unfortunates suffer from light sensitivity, either inherited allergy or acquired. One doctor, with a special interest in allergies, points out that the side effects of certain drugs are contributing towards a rise in light-sensitive subjects.

Suffering

FOR those who suffer in this way there is a medically approved colourless product (4s.) which contains a special pigment to deflect the sun's rays. Used properly it is a valuable aid. In the past I have had grateful reports back from light-sensitive readers to whom I suggested it, reporting that they had been able to cope with some sunshine without ill-effects for the first time in years.

Others who need special help are those who find that their lips swell, blister, and crack when exposed to strong sunlight and/or sea air.

There are two products for this form of allergy. One is a straight lip barrier cream (3s. 6d.) with a built-in light deflectant. The other (2s. 10d.) is an effective barrier cream, originally developed for medical purposes, which combines a natural screening agent with a conditioning ingredient.

Both are water repellent, odourless, tasteless, and colourless ; and ordinary lipstick can be applied on top.

BEAUTY BOX

HAVE WOMEN LOST THE ART OF COOKING?

Our under-40s are turning to the tin-opener and the ice chest for family meals

IS your marriage a marriage of convenience ? Don't get me wrong. What I mean to ask is whether your family is a "convenience food" family.

The Ministry of Agriculture, Fisheries and Food —which we will henceforth call "Ag and Fish" — calls "convenience" foods all "labour-saving, prepared or semi-prepared products."

In other words, sumptuous and colourful meals which just have to be unfrozen, boiled in a saucepan of water, poured out of a packet or shaken out of a tin.

Ag and Fish has just published a 142-page red-covered report, costing 8s. 6d., which contains some fascinating facts about "convenience foods," and other food trends.

It is a detailed account of what everyone ate in 1959, compared with previous years.

Quicker

IT shows quite plainly that housewives are grabbing the tin-opener, the packet, and the frozen pre-cooked package with increasing enthusiasm.

So much so that if things go on the way they have been going in the last few years the idea of preparing and cooking a meal from scratch will seem as ridiculous and unnecessary as, say, washing clothes by hand.

Women, in other words, are losing the art of cooking. At least, those under 40 are.

The facts are that four shillings out of every pound that was spent on grub in 1959 went towards "convenience foods." That is an increase of about a quarter on the 1955 figure.

Younger women spent more on these foods than the more conservative older ones. The tendency for housewives to carry on working has—as Ag and Fish cautiously puts it—"not been without influence in this respect."

There is, of course, one slight inconvenience attached to "convenience" foods. They cost more than, how shall we put it . . . the real thing.

Easier

THIS means that although we have all been spending more on food we have not necessarily been getting an equivalent extra amount back in what Ag and Fish calls "nutritional value." So that although we may never have had it so easy or palatable, we may certainly have had it as good.

As the report puts it : "When there is increased expenditure on the more desired foods such as meat, bacon, fruit, green vegetables and convenience foods"—and this is accompanied by decreased expenditure on bread, flour and potatoes, the intakes of many nutrients, especially of protein, calcium and riboflavin, will not necessarily be improved."

Families with four or more children seem to have got the worst bargain out of this trend towards spending more and getting less back than any other group.

Dearer

IT has been discovered that, first, their total spending on food has increased in recent years less than any other group's.

Not only that, but they have diverted more of their spending to foods like fish, poultry, eggs, canned vegetables, fresh fruit, chocolate biscuits, and breakfast cereals. These are all "more expensive sources of nutrients" than the humdrum old stuff, such as dried milk, potatoes,

by PEARSON PHILLIPS

carcass meat, sugar, bread, flour, and oatmeal.

The result is that in this age of affluence and plenty this group are not, on average, getting the required level of "nutrient adequacy" recommended by the British Medical Association.

As a parallel to this state of affairs the report points out that recent studies have shown that children in smaller families are, on average, taller and heavier than those in correspondingly larger families.

But we needn't get too gloomy about this. Ag and Fish says that our general diet in 1959 was "adequate." We are getting 5 p.c. more calories than we were in the years between 1934-39. But how our national eating habits have changed since then.

For one thing we are drinking 157 p.c. more coffee than we did. Our butter consumption has gone down by 25 p.c., but we are spending 67 p.c. more on margarine.

We are drinking more milk, but we still haven't reached a national pints per head, per day. (We drink just over five pints per head, per week.)

The roast beef of old England has dropped in favour, although, thanks to the broiler industry, we are eating double the amount of poultry. We are eating fewer oranges and lemons, but a lot more nuts.

We are drinking 3 p.c. more tea, but eating 15 p.c. less fish.

We should all feel healthier. In particular—thanks to the calcium from the extra milk—we should all be producing some splendid teeth.

The only thing which seems problematical to me is whether coming generations of housewives will be bothered to prepare anything worth biting.

WHAT THE AFFLUENT SOCIETY EATS compared with pre-war		
Dairy Products excluding Butter	UP	41%
Meat	UP	2%
Fish	DOWN	15%
Poultry, Game, Rabbits	UP	31%
Butter	DOWN	25%
Margarine	UP	67%
Tea	UP	3%
Coffee	UP	157%

Showing some percentage changes in estimated consumption for the year 1959 as against the period 1934-38

LINEN IS IN...

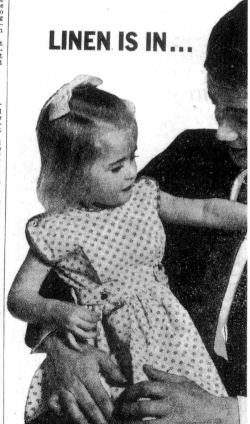

1961

The Pill

In January 1961 the oral contraceptive Conovoid was allowed to go on sale in Britain. By the end of 1961 it was possible to get the Pill, with a capital 'P', as it became known, on prescription through the National Health Service. Despite the fact that almost immediately doubts were raised over its safety, that it was virtually 100-per-cent effective meant it became a vital ingredient in a revolution in women's sexuality.

It is doubtful whether the 'Swinging Sixties' would have been quite so swinging without the Pill. Women could control their own fertility without having to mess about with caps or rely on the man to use a sheath. They could go to their GP or more likely a Family Planning Clinic where, if they were single, they would often pretend to be married, or at least not enlighten the clinic to the contrary. Once on the Pill all it required was that the woman remembered to take her pills at the right time.

The immense publicity for the Pill and the freedom from fear of unwanted pregnancy it gave women also meant increased knowledge about, and the freedom to enjoy, sex. But it also put pressure on some women to have sex with a man when they weren't ready or did not want to. Unwanted pregnancy was no longer an excuse and as the 'permissive society' grew it became distinctly old-fashioned not to have sex before marriage and increasingly it was regarded as a good thing for women to have as many sexual partners as possible. Pleasure and love were the aims and pursuits of the culture of the 1960s and sex was the route to both.

Controversy over the safety of the Pill has been constant since its introduction. It has been linked to thrombosis and other circulatory diseases and some forms of cancer. Subsequently some of these links have been proved, others remain speculation. There are also numerous more minor ailments or side effects, such as weight gain, headaches, dizziness and breast pains. Over the years on the grounds of safety more and more women have been excluded from using it, so that it has not fulfilled its early promise, or perhaps expectation is a better word.

For all the negative aspects of the Pill and the sexual revolution associated with it, it certainly gave women power over their fertility and the beginnings of power over their own sexuality, so that women began to think about their own bodies and responses to and enjoyment of sex. It also brought these issues into the open so that they were talked about in newspapers, magazines and the media generally and sex education began to find its way on to the curriculum in schools.

ABOVE: *A woman in Bolton cleans her back step.*
BELOW: *Women at work in a Lancashire textile factory.*

1961 POSTSCRIPTS

April – A government report revealed that 8,272,000 women were now working and earning money outside the home.

September – The first Mothercare shop was opened in Kingston-upon-Thames.

• The BBC announced that only men compères would appear in women's television programmes. Doris Stevens, head of BBC TV's Women's Programmes said, 'Men make better compères and women viewers accept a man much more uncritically than their own sex'.

WOMEN CRY THEMSELVES TO SLEEP IN NEW TOWN

Crawley, the bustling, booming new town with *all mod cons* for everyone, awoke yesterday to find itself branded a town of lonely women.

That was the conclusion in a survey by psychiatrist Dr Peter Sainsbury.

He found the rate of mental illness among women in Crawley (population 55,000) higher than elsewhere in the country.

Loneliness, boredom and separation from relatives were all linked with the problem, reported Dr Sainsbury . . .

Daily Mail, 12 January 1961

DINING ROOM CLUES TO YOUR PERSONALITY

SHIRLEY CONRAN

IT'S the greatest personality give-away since bookcases became showcases—seeing what people are like from the way they lay the table. This week I've seen tables planned by Dame Margot Fonteyn, Countess Jellicoe, David Hicks and internationally known sculptor Eduardo Paolozzi.

And I've come to my own conclusions about their personalities.

Around **DAME MARGOT'S** table stood fragile Italian chairs, ebonised with cane seats; the table was a thick circular slab of rosewood poised on a central, reverse - trumpet - shaped black pedestal.

Her bowl

Her centrepiece: a huge, low, midnight-blue glass bowl filled with green and black grapes, a few green apples, one orange and two magnificent sprays of real white orchids.

She used delicate white linen, candles and china, clear V-shaped wineglasses.

Cutlery was the most enviable I've ever seen, weighty Georgian silver with pistol-handled knives.

IT'S OBVIOUS: Dame Margot is elegant, graceful and sensitive and professional — her setting seemed effortlessly uncontrived, but obviously involved a lot of thought and work.

His day

PROPPED in front of the cornflakes bowl on **DAVID HICKS'S** breakfast table was a typed postcard from his secretary with a list of the day's nine appointments — which ranged from visiting the young Duchess of Rutland to checking his new silver designs.

"Get more razor blades. Cancel *The Times*," was scribbled on the pigskin-covered notepad which lay by his two boiled eggs supported in stiff-collared new eggcups.

Pale, shiny, bentwood chairs with woven cane seats stood round the circular table covered by dark grey and deep blue wide-striped cotton.

Round a central glass cylinder of cornflowers

PERSONALITY POINTERS (top to bottom) FONTEYN, HICKS, JELLICOE, PAOLOZZI.

Drawings by Nicholas Baker

stood sturdy white breakfast china with a bright blue smudge pattern, wooden bread platter, pepper and salt grinders.

IT'S OBVIOUS: Hicks is practical, well organised, sophisticated. The impact of the inexpensive objects used showed wit and imagination.

Black wooden rush-seated chairs, delicately painted with tiny flowers, stood round **COUNTESS JELLICOE'S** pink - black - and - gold oval dinnertable. Icing-pink linen cloth and matching napkins were teamed with matt jasper black china which had a tiny, raised black pattern (very subtle —black on black).

Glittering antique gold

YOU COULD CALL IT THE TABLE GAME

cutlery contrasted with the plain V-shaped stem wineglasses.

Flickering black candles were supported by tall, black Grecian figures on gold bases. Final splendid touch was old silver cigarette cases spilling over with gold-tipped black Russian Sobranie cigarettes. Only thing missing was James Bond.

IT'S OBVIOUS: Countess Jellicoe is serene and meticulous, cultured, rich. Trad splendour indicates stately-home background.

EDUARDO PAOLOZZI had scarlet Italian armchairs drawn up to a rectangular ash table.

Lying nonchalantly at ease in central place of honour, antique black sphinx gazed haughtily at a small brass pug dog and goat.

His idea

NAPKINS were thick, curly fringed white linen. White china service was gold banded. Soup was served in huge china teacups, cutlery was stainless steel, and huge teak platters held fruit and salad.

Table was guarded by Paolozzi brass crocodile, and behind it grey-and-white photo blow-ups of 19th - century engravings were drawing-pinned to the wall. Easy-to-copy idea: a selection from Paolozzi's old postcard

Picture by ALAN BOYD

collection — skyscrapers, birds and early aeroplanes —was glued to a charcoal card framed in white.

IT'S OBVIOUS: Paolozzi's superb simple shapes proved his visual sense. Chunky, solid, unusual and fascinating. Like him.

See the settings yourself at Rosenthal, Knightsbridge, where you can buy the china and glass.

WHERE DO COATS GO IN WINTER?

WHERE do the children fling their coats and satchels? Where do you keep visiting raincoats and umbrellas? In the hall? For narrow halls like mine that have no cloakroom, here's an easily made modern version of the invariably untidy Edwardian hatstand. My cloakroom—just a smart box really—is only 12in. deep x 6ft. high x 3ft. wide, but see for yourself what it takes.

Optional extra: Easily fixed, light Japanese wood blind slides silently across on overhead channel. 45s. Selfridges.

Write to me for instructions, enclosing stamped, self-addressed envelope to: "Hall Holdall," Daily Mail, Gough House Gough-square, E.C.4 (Comp.). Bowler-hatted beauty wears cream wool coat dress. £8 15s. Polly Peck. All outdoor accessories by Harrods.

Now that caravans lead a double life...

APART from the high cost of family holidays, children and hotels seem to be irreconcilable. Answer is a touring caravan which can be used as an extra garden guest room as well as a travelling holiday home.

So I've been asking designers what new tourer trends we can expect to see at the International Caravan Exhibition, which opens at Olympia on November 28 and continues to December 4.

Because there's a new crop of small, light cars and because you will soon be able to tour Britain at a dashing 40 miles an hour, tourers will be smaller,

lighter and easier to park, with independent suspension to give a better towing performance.

Through vision is the latest, most sensible idea. Wide, lower panoramic windows at both ends of the van enable the car driver to have an unimpeded view of the entire road behind him.

We can expect a better exterior standard of design and finish because manufacturers are jockeying for the start of the Common Market race and Continental buyers are far more demanding. Also, because now caravans are practically a status

symbol, everyone wants a tourer that's as smart as his car.

The three tourers which sound most exciting are all improved versions of tested models. They're all four-berthers with a fold-away double bed and separate interior lavatory.

SO SMART

THE Sprite Musketeer, 14ft. 4in. long, is ice-blue and white with flame curtains. It costs £320 and at 12½cwt. weighs 1cwt. lighter than the 1961 version.

Starred item: Fibre-

1962

The Housewives' Top Ten

The years of prosperity in the 1950s had seen a huge increase in the labour-saving devices in the average British home. Manufacturers and advertisers had pushed their wares telling housewives how much easier they would make their lives and insisting that 'every home should have one'. And indeed many homes did have and the rest aspired to having any one or all of a whole range of household items. In May 1962 the *Daily Mail* published the Housewives' Top Ten, presumably in acquisition order – vacuum cleaner; refrigerator; spin dryer; electric iron; sewing machine; washing machine; gramophone; electric toaster; television; electric floor polisher.

Also in 1962 Betty Friedan published her book *The Feminine Mystique*. In it she claimed, from her experience in the USA, where a larger percentage of women than in Britain went on to higher education, that the American manufacturers had manipulated women into spending a disproportionate amount of time, effort and money caring and buying for their home and family. Educated, and often highly educated, women at home were given goals to achieve to make the job of homemaker seem a more valuable one. Save up, buy the washing machine, then sort out all the various types of fabrics for the different washing cycles, and then experiment to find the best soap powder.

A similar thing was happening in Britain. Women at home were being called on to do more. While labour-saving devices freed them from much of the grind of housework they also created more work. Clothes were washed more frequently, houses cleaned more thoroughly, homes redecorated more often. Then in the free time left there was also the gardening, sewing, knitting or handicrafts to be done. Women with young children at home were also expected to provide a happy learning environment for them to grow up in. For some women this filled their time and fulfilled them but for most who had the benefits of education and had experienced the freedom and independence of paid work it was not enough and they found themselves bored and unfulfilled, their brains atrophying and their self-esteem wasting away.

ABOVE: Barbara Salt who became Britain's first woman Ambassador when she was appointed Ambassador to Israel in 1962.
BELOW: Sophia Loren with husband Carlo Ponti.

1962 POSTSCRIPTS

March – Mrs Thelma Casalet-Kier, one of two women among the nine governors of the BBC until she left in 1961, was quoted as saying that the BBC was unfair to women as only four of the top 150 jobs were held by women and there were only three female television department heads, in Planning, Women's Programmes and Wardrobe.

June – Sophia Loren and her husband Carlo Ponti were charged in Italy with bigamy as Italian law did not recognize Ponti's divorce from his first wife, indeed did not legally accept any divorce.

November – Lady Edith Summerskill, MP and a former Health Minister, urged a ban on the prescription of oral contraceptives until the results of a committee appointed to assess the reports that the Pill might 'predispose to thrombosis' were published. Lord Brain of the Family Planning Association dismissed the connection between the Pill and thrombosis.

Doctors Warn About THAT PILL

Britain's leading doctors came out today with their gravest warning about **that pill** and say it may be 20 years before they can give it safety clearance . . .

Only six years of evidence has so far been gathered by research doctors.

The *Lancet* says: 'We must accept for the present that this form of contraception could be dangerous, and we must try to balance this against its advantages.

'The balance struck will plainly be influenced by the circumstances of the individual or community for whom the contraception is proposed.'
Daily Mail, 1 June 1962

How to give a SWINGING party

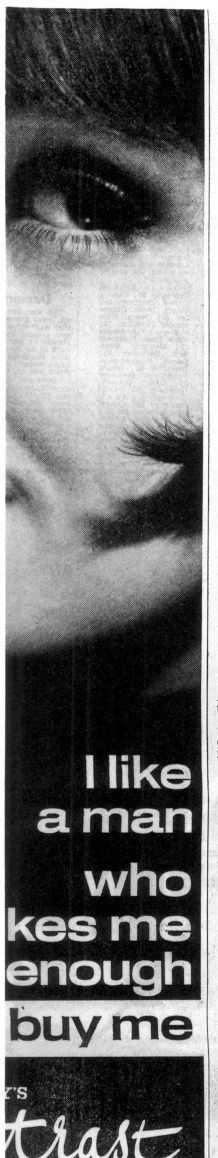

DRESS AS YOU LIKE we said . . . and how the men magnets reacted

by
JUDY
INNES

and

JOY
TAGNEY

Judy and Joy threw a party. It had to be relaxed, it had to be swinging, it had to be the sort of party YOU could throw this Christmas. The girls came in everything from velvet pants to long tweed skirts. They came prepared to twist and shake. It was a terrific party . . .

ANY girl off to a party knows the feeling of excitement at the thought of meeting lots of interesting new people.

She also knows the apprehension that she is underdressed or overdressed, the other guests will be too highbrow—or lowbrow—and worst of all, she won't know a soul and will be left to wilt in a corner all night.

She wants to be able to contribute something herself, either in appearance, ravishing, or conversation, witty, but preferably both.

She wants men to be whispering: "Who is that beautiful and clever girl?"

Basic party philosophy is fairly obvious; if you feel good, then you look good—and if you look good, the net result is usually a wonderful evening.

And this season party wear couldn't be easier. The Whips are off, the Party Line is relaxed.

You can wear what you please, how you please and this freedom extends right from the cocoa party through to the hard liquor party.

It means you can dress the way you feel happiest and most relaxed and not feel a social outcast who will never be asked again.

PARTY WEAR :

A sleeveless wool dress

THIS isn't just another version of that old bromide "anything goes." It's being the right anything for you that makes it go.

This we discovered when we gave our party. Guests were told : "You aren't expected to bring a bottle—but you are expected to twist, shake or something to a beat group."

We didn't specify dress, simply because we didn't think of it, but the couple of girls who did ask were told : "Well, we'll probably be wearing some kind of sleeveless wool dress with a lowish neckline."

The reaction was stunning. Our female guests turned up in everything from velvet pants to long tweed skirts. They all blended perfectly and the effect was tremen-

Pictures by Norman Eales

NOT ONE WAS LEFT TO WILT IN THE CORNER

IF you like a minimum of fuss . . . fling your clothes on and forget them . . . feel happier under-exposed . . . are lean and long - legged . . .

THEN try this polo neck tunic top in clinging black silk jersey and these leg - hugging trousers also in jersey. Top, 6½gns., trousers, 4½gns., at Peter Robinson's.

1963

Rising Hemlines

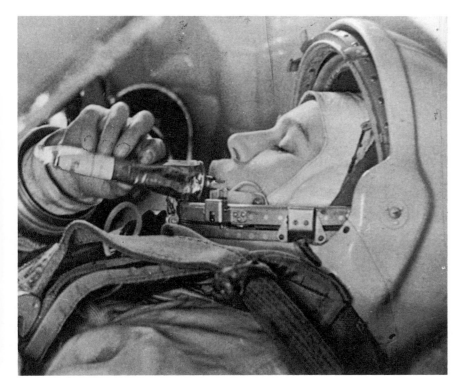

ABOVE: *Valentina Tereshkova pictured in training for her space mission.*
BELOW: *Woman wearing a mini dress.*

Mary Quant had opened her boutique 'Bazaar' in London's King's Road in the mid–1950s and by the early 1960s she had been joined by a number of other shops selling fashionable clothing to young people. Mary Quant and other young designers like her had a tremendous influence on the style of clothing that was to become emblematic of the 1960s.

The beach fashion of 1963 was for mid-thigh-length beach dresses and shirts worn over swimsuits and bikinis, reflecting a trend set by designers such as Mary Quant who had already been selling clothes with hemlines above the knee.

At the beginning of 1964 Mary Quant condemned Paris fashion as out of date; by the end of that year Paris too had raised its hemlines and the mini skirt was well on its way to becoming established. Throughout 1965 and 1966 skirts got shorter so that a skirt length of 18 inches (46 cm) was not remarkable even for some of the more staid clothing manufacturers. Dress styles were much simpler and freer, relying on pattern, detail and colour for interest rather than cut.

Hairstyles early in the 1960s were backcombed and piled up, a style which reached its peak in the beehive. By the mid-1960s Vidal Sassoon had begun to change hairdressing and simple stylish cutting became more important than shampooing, setting and backcombing. Mary Quant adopted a Vidal Sassoon cut and helped popularize the look.

Fashionable clothing was by now mass market, not just for the rich, although the styles were very much for the young reflecting the strength of youth culture. The mature, full-busted woman was no longer promoted as the ideal. Boyish adolescent figures like that epitomized by the model Twiggy became the accepted and sought-after shape. In many ways the shape of women in the 1960s mirrored that of women in the 1920s with a flat-chested, waistless and bottomless silhouette, although the 1960s one was altogether much thinner.

In all decades one style does not reflect the whole period of time and the 1960s was represented by more than just the mini. There were the unisex clothes such as trouser suits and the kaftans of the flower power period. There were also attempts which had some limited success to introduce mid-calf- and ankle-length dresses (the midi and the maxi), but the mini dress on a woman with a thin boyish youthful figure has become the stereotype image of the decade.

1963   POSTSCRIPTS

January – The BBC ended its ban on mentioning politics, royalty, religion and sex in its comedy shows. This paved the way for programmes like *That Was The Week That Was*.

June – Lieutenant Valentina Tereshkova, a Russian cosmonaut, became the first woman in space when she orbited the earth in a spaceship. In the USA, where thirteen women had passed astronaut tests but never been selected for a mission, it prompted Clare Boothe Luce, former ambassador to Italy, to say, 'Once again the Russians have shown us they know how to get ahead of us by letting women assume an equal share in society.

'We must stop trying to make paper dolls of women. They don't like it. They don't need it.'

• A Leader in the *Daily Mail* suggested that the time was long past for the eight million working women in Britain to have equal pay with men and not just the ten per cent who had achieved it by 1963. It also pointed out that husbands still legally owned any savings from the housekeeping money.

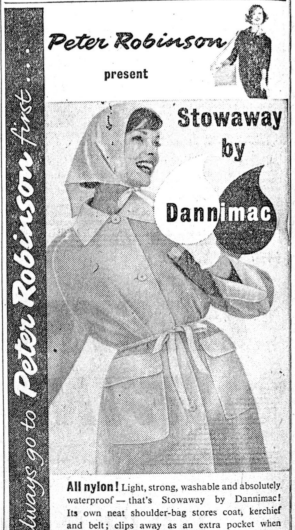
Monica Furlong

It's intolerable . . . but no one can save this child from her mother

THERE is one kind of problem which never seems to get enough publicity — the problem of foster-children.

It has many sides, all of them difficult to deal with, but some of the letters which sadden me most come from parents who have taken a child into their homes and looked after it with loving care with a view to adopting it, only to have it reclaimed by the mother much later.

Clearly, a mother who has to allow her child to be fostered needs to have her rights and feelings carefully considered. But the feelings of would-be adoptive parents need the utmost consideration too, and above all the child needs to have its emotional life jealously guarded.

Danger

The following letter suggests the kind of danger to which many children are exposed.

❛ For the past two years we have had a foster-child—a little girl now 4½ years old. She was voluntarily handed over to the county council when only nine months, since which time her mother has made no request to see her or made any inquiries about her welfare.

"H" came to us as a long-term foster-child, although we were not told at the time she had not been committed into care through the courts. Thus she is completely unprotected and we are powerless to prevent her mother claiming her at any time in her life up to the age of 15.

The mother is very unstable. The three other children of her first marriage are all in council homes. Sometime last year she became pregnant by the man she had been living with and remarried.

Later

The children's officer felt this would be an advantageous time to approach her regarding our adopting "H," and although at first she agreed to this, she changed her mind at a later date.

In August of this year she again became pregnant and was approached once more. She stated that she still did not wish to part with the child but will not commit herself to when she will take her back.

"H" came to us with all the usual behaviour problems associated with deprivation, but she is now a happy, healthy child, very advanced for her age.

Needless to say, we love her very dearly and the thought of parting with her is unbearable.

However, the child must have some permanence in life and under the present conditions that is impossible.

Putting our own feelings in the background we are wondering if it would be better for the child to return to her mother now, while there is still a chance of adapting herself to a completely different life. We feel that to uproot her when she is seven or eight years old would have a profound psychological effect on her. ❜

The unselfishness of the foster-parents stands out in moving contrast to the selfishness of the mother, who did not once bother to inquire about her little girl.

If, as seems likely, there is at the moment no legal way of solving this intolerable situation, then the only thing to do is to battle on as long as possible for the care of the child.

Future

I believe myself that no year, or week, or day of love is wasted effort—that whatever may lie ahead for this little girl, she is already receiving something infinitely precious which will help her to respond adequately to the future.

All the strain—and it must be agonising—falls on the foster-parents who cannot easily forget the shadow which lies over her happiness.

After all these years of neglect there seems an even chance that the mother may never wish to retain the child. Her refusal to agree to adoption, with all its implications for the child and the foster-parents, may merely stem from the fact that she lacks the maturity to make a decision. For all their sakes, one can only hope this.

FINDING THE WILL TO LIVE AGAIN . . .

WHEN I printed a letter last week from a mother who had lost her little boy in a road accident, I had no idea of the warm and sympathetic response it would evoke from readers. Nor of the depths of faith and of wisdom that must exist in innumerable families and innumerable homes.

Many mothers lived over again their private grief so that they could help my reader to believe that it is possible to go on living ; more important, they described the stages of coming out of depression, telling her what things helped and what didn't.

One letter suggested that the agony of mourning is a desperate attempt to escape the knowledge of what has happened, and that once it has been faced—"embraced" was the word she used—then it turns out to be less terrible and the pain begins to heal again. But no one suggested that the healing was — or should be—a quick process.

One remarkable letter came from a doctor who spends her life caring for incurable cancer patients and their relatives.

❛ I hope . . . you will encourage people to stand by those who are in this sort of desolation (i.e. bereavement). Those who know what it is like, who will listen and care, just be around and not try and hurry us, make it possible to live through the pain.

I do not think that we ever stop missing people we have loved, and I do not think we would want to, but finally it does not hurt so much.

I do not think that it helps to tell anyone of the rewards of the final peace, nor what it means to belong to the company who have been brought through depression, but I do know that we finally find our own reasons for gratitude. ❜

I'm still in the process of sorting the letters received, which amounted to several hundreds, and will be sending nearly all of them on to the mother concerned.

I hope readers will forgive me if I do not reply individually to every letter, but will accept this thank you for their concern.

1964

Married Women's Property

ABOVE: *Dorothy Crowfoot Hodgkin in her laboratory.*
BELOW: *Passers-by stare at a 'bare bosom dress' on display in the shop window. Although in 1964 they were seen as a 'bit of a giggle' and not expected to sell, topless and see-through styles enjoyed a limited fashion life later in the 1960s.*

Despite the fact that there were two million more women than men in the country in 1961 they owned only 40 per cent of the total wealth in the hands of individuals. But as with men the bulk of the wealth owned by women was in the hands of only a few individuals, the majority of women, especially married women, had very little.

Although most women now worked until they married or started a family it was expected that they would then give up work to be supported by their husband. Those women who worked usually did so part time and only because the family budget was desperate for the contribution of their wages. There was a growing number of women returning to work once their children were older teenagers but on the whole married women frequently had no money, apart from family allowances, they could call their own.

Property and possessions, too, usually belonged to the husband. It was rare for a coule buying their own home to put the property in their joint names. Any cars or household items would be regarded as owned by the husband unless a woman could prove they were bought with her earnings. Hire-purchase applications had to be signed by the husband so that even if the wife's money paid the premiums the item would legally belong to him. Nothing had changed since the Blackwell case in 1943, in that the husband still had a legal right to any savings from the housekeeping money. A wife could not secretly save money because her husband was required to declare the interest on his wife's savings on his tax return.

The Married Woman's Property Act of 1964 put into law the recommendation of the Royal Commission on Divorce that a wife should have a right to half of anything she might have saved from a housekeeping allowance. However the Act did nothing to change the position of women with regard to their right to live in the family home and in theory if a husband had sole ownership of the house he could have his wife evicted. A further law in 1967, the Matrimonial Homes Act, gave both men and women the right to occupy their home.

These two Acts removed some of the inequalities in marriage but the State's underlying assumption in terms of tax affairs, pensions and unemployment benefit was still that women were their husbands' dependants and as such did not need to be treated as individuals in their own right.

1964 POSTSCRIPTS

April – Geraldine Mock, a West German woman, became the first woman to fly solo round the world.

July – The first Brook Advisory Clinic opened giving birth-control advice to unmarried couples.

December – Briton Dorothy Crowfoot Hodgkin was awarded the Nobel Prize for Chemistry for her work in using X-rays to determine the structures of biochemical substances.

How's this for a really super kitchen?

- ● Island cooking area with electric and gas hobs.
- ● Burma teak units with built-in refrigerator.
- ● Spanish tiled walls.
- ● A wall wine rack which holds 168 bottles.

KITCHENS are becoming more imaginative day by day. There is a swing away from the laboratory - type kitchen towards something more personal, more intimate, more fun.

New kitchens are still planned as practical workshops but with a warm welcome built-in— schemes alive with colour and charm *plus* labour-saving finishes.

The swept-bare look is *out*. Rich patterns and bright colours are *in*. Smart British and American equipment is being given chic Continental surroundings with Spanish or Portuguese-style tiled walls, French or Flemish-style tiled floors, Italian rush - seated chairs and German or Dutch ceramic clocks.

Brightly

Or it is being teamed with country style British whitewash and timber and brightly painted furniture decorated with bold traditional bargee patterns.

Already on sale here are curvy bentwood chairs painted in strong primary colours and flaunting authentic fairground and barge motifs on the seats. They cost 5¼ gns. each.

Three enterprising young men called Binder, Edwards and Vaughan (whose father is a bargee) are behind the chair venture, and their distinctive chests of drawers in the same idiom are currently decorating the modern interior department of Woollands and

The super kitchen that Jack Frye built . . . masculine thoroughness with the glossy magazine look

PICTURE BY WALTER BROWN

several other big London stores.

Before Christmas, Michael Caddy hopes to produce kitchen dressers and cupboards with designs "based on bargee patterns but more sophisticated" on doors and drawer fronts; and, in the New Year, flowery - faced clocks.

Mullenger's Country Kitchenware is backing the pretty early American look described as Pennsylvanian Dutch.

Plain pine tables with edges and legs lacquered vivid orange and red (£17 5s. by Moag Designs) are being sold by Gear. They are also selling open-shelved units with backs enamelled in bright colours, plain or striped (5 gns.).

The most exciting new kitchens in London belong to Jack Frye, the chairman of Rotaflex, and Robert Carrier, the American-born gourmet and cook.

Carrier has *two* kitchens in his home in Gibson Square, Canonbury.

The large one in the basement he describes as his work kitchen. At garden level is his galley - style play kitchen, described by the man who planned them both, David Vicary, as "a very minimal space for someone very tuned-in who needs a cooking laboratory."

It is less than 9ft. wide by 14ft. long and revolves round a revolutionary American grill designed for open-air grilling or indoor barbecuing.

Fiery

In this Charco grill a bed of "coals," made from a space-age plastics material developed for missiles, is heated by high gas jets to a fiery glow which sears chops, steaks and joints in a flash.

Then the fats and juices flare up and char the grilled meat, giving it a distinctive charcoal flavour.

"Because of the terrific heat it gives out the grill was the governing thing in the room," says Vicary, who has

already planned more than 40 kitchens. "We had to make the area around it completely fireproof."

This meant tiles — a white tiled alcove bordered by decorative tiles and in front a white Italian mosaic-tiled counter top with four gas rings sunk flush.

There is only 3ft. left in the middle for circulation. The rest of the working space is taken up by storage units topped by an 8ft. long beech-wood chopping block.

Set in the wall are a re-frigerator and twin electric ovens for baking and roasting.

Utensils are washed up in the "work" kitchen downstairs.

Here the unit tops are in oiled, waterproofed teak. Walls are white with a border of 18th-century blue and white Delft tiles, or papered in a glowing damask pattern with 18th century still life over the sink.

Jack Frye and his Indian-born wife Lalita, who spent

18 months doing up their Chelsea home, moved in just seven weeks ago.

Her ideas went into some rooms, his into others. The living-room, dining-room and their bedroom they did together. But as he is the cook, Jack Frye designed the kitchen himself.

The result is the kind of super kitchen you see in glossy American magazines, planned with masculine thoroughness. The equipment is American — by Westinghouse — but the mood is Mediterranean.

Louvred shutters at the windows and cool walls and floor suggest a hot climate outside.

Curvy

Walls are whitewashed, or faced with exotic blue and white hand-painted tiles from Casa Pupo. The high ceiling is criss-crossed with curvy old beams and the floor laid with mellow, red tiles from an old house in Suffolk.

Over the island cooking area, which has a foldaway grill, plate-warmer and both gas and electric hobs, is a splendid copper hood made by a local blacksmith near the Fryes' country farmhouse in Buntingford, Hertfordshire.

It is fitted with concealed spotlights and an extractor fan.

There are more spotlights sunk in the ceiling. And over the old gateleg table hangs a Victorian brass oil lamp converted to electricity and fitted with a dimmer switch.

Twin Westinghouse wall ovens with doors in black-tinted glass are set in a rough brick wall linked to a line-up of storage units in rich Burma teak.

Built in are a massive refrigerator and deep freezer and a spacious store cupboard with doors lined with narrow shelves on both sides.

Six power points are spaced out above the work top. Near the double stainless steel sink is a chopping board and an array of kitchen knives slotted into a recessed rack.

There is also an impressive wine rack to take 168 bottles.

SITTING PRETTY

on TRAD ART

KITCHEN chairs with a difference— the seats are hand painted.

Left: The glossy, scarlet frame has brilliant red, yellow and blue Shazan pattern on seat.

Right: A red, blue and green Caterpillar-patterned seat on a curvy lime - green frame.

From 5¼ gns. each.

1965

Women With Careers

On 30 September 1965 Elizabeth Lane was sworn in as Britain's first woman High Court Judge. It was still rare to see a woman in such a position and many areas of life, such as financial institutions, in which power and authority were wielded still barred or restricted entry to women.

Few women pursued a career; it was expected that they would give up their job as soon as they had their children, if not when they married. Even women who had spent several years qualifying for a professional job would give it up with no intention of ever returning. The idea of taking a break to have a family and then returning to work was only just surfacing.

In 1963, there were 1,960 women practising as barristers. This was an almost fourfold increase on the numbers in 1953 but there were in both years many more women qualified as barristers who were not working but who felt their duty was to stay at home.

There were also 670,000 women in the Civil Service. As the Service did not offer part-time work at this time the female employee profile would have been much the same as in the legal or any other profession. A large proportion would be young women working until they married. A few would be returners and a few would be women pursuing a career.

Of these career women most would be single, some perhaps widowed or divorced, and if they were married it would be extremely rare for them to have children. Apart from the fact that it was not expected for a woman to have a career and children, absolutely no allowances were made for having children.

While most professional women such as doctors, lawyers, teachers, accountants and architects were paid equal salaries to men, a break in employment to have children would not be taken into account as a positive benefit when promotions were considered. Even in teaching where having your own children might be thought to be beneficial a woman returner resumed the position on the pay scale she had left on with no credit allowed for her years of motherhood.

Outside the professions there were often more effective bars to the career structures for women as when they were actively excluded from doing many jobs, especially in industry, which would lead them up the promotion ladder to satisfying and well-paid positions. A report entitled *Justice and Prejudice* published in 1965 by the National Federation of Business and Professional Women's Clubs found that women were still being treated as inferiors in most jobs and are seen as 'cheap labour in trade and commerce'.

ABOVE: Five of the 20,000 women shop stewards in Britain on a course to improve their skills as shop stewards. It was the first of these courses for women although men shop stewards had been catered for before.
BELOW: Judge Elizabeth Lane.

1965 POSTSCRIPTS

January – Yvonne Pope, a widow, was the first British woman to pilot a scheduled aircraft. A shortage of male pilots as air travel increased had given her the opportunity for the job.

November – The Customs and Excise Department changed the criteria for assessing what would be classed as children's clothing, and thus not taxable, from dress length to bust size so that mini-length women's clothing would not escape tax.

These are the earrings to wear with the hat that you wear with the shoes when you carry the bag that goes with this year's best fashions

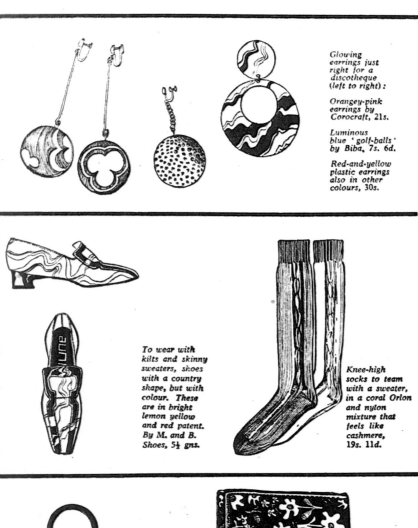

Glowing earrings just right for a discotheque (left to right):

Orangey-pink earrings by Corocraft, 21s.

Luminous blue 'golf-balls' by Biba, 7s. 6d.

Red-and-yellow plastic earrings also in other colours, 30s.

To wear with kilts and skinny sweaters, shoes with a country shape, but with colour. These are in bright lemon yellow and red patent. By M. and B. Shoes, 5½ gns.

Knee-high socks to team with a sweater, in a coral Orlon and nylon mixture that feels like cashmere, 19s. 11d.

Three separate PVC bags in beige, aubergine and mauve on a single plastic ring, 44s., by Sally Jess for Europa Handbags.

Daisy-printed PVC bag, that folds away flat. Open it's model-girl's tote-bag size, £4 9s. 11d.

Perspex ice-cube bracelet by Vendome, 4½ gns. Part of a range of Perspex jewellery which includes cube earrings, 35s.

Riding gloves, with pieces of crochet work on the fingers and palms. The leather is bright purple! Price 5 gns.

Drawings by NIKE WILLIAMS.

For information about stockists write to Daily Mail, Fashion Dept., Tudor Street, London, E.C.4, enclosing a stamped addressed envelope, or telephone FLEet Street, 6000, Ext. 495.

BY LIZ ATKINSON

IT ISN'T as though the "black-shoes-will-go-with-everything" school were still the safe, if dull, answer. It simply isn't true any more.

Black shoes might look right with some of this year's clothes — but with many of them they would be appalling.

Which leads us to the fashion truth that unless you are what used to be called a fashion intellectual of positively genius quality, the most harrowing moment still remains putting a rig together.

This autumn the complications are worse — largely because some fashions which have always had predictable accoutrements that you could go out with confidence and buy have been transformed. By the French, with the coloured mini-kilts; by us, in the case of what to wear in the evening.

With this in mind we have gone out to look for the accessories that are right with some of the best of this year's fashions.

Sporty

Those skinny sweaters and kilts, and the lean jersey dresses that are fast emerging as this winter's uniform, need low-heeled, sporty shoes, very country style down to the buckles and chains. But in non-country colours, like the yellow and red ones on the left.

Gloves are equally sporty, like the riding gloves on the left; but again, get them in some unlikely colour, like purple.

Best with the kilts are textured stockings or knee-socks with a cable stitch down the side. But the last thing you want with them are hearty earrings. Better some that glow in the dark like the papier-mâché golf-balls on the left, that come in a variety of colours. Or those orangy-pink globes with a stylised flower painted on them.

The bag to carry with the daytime uniform is no longer that quilted Chanel mini-bag which has been safe (like black shoes) for years. The tiny, square satchels in unbelievable blue and pink patents and PVCs are more interesting.

There's still more shine for the evening. To go with the silver stockings and shoes, there are a silver and gold leather watchstrap and some earrings painted with luminous paint to light up the discotheque twilight.

Buttercup-yellow wool ratine coat with a flared, tent-style back, a brass-button fastening and a neat rounded collar, by Wallis, 17 gns.; chocolate brown fur fabric beret with a buttercup-yellow zigzag on the crown, by Young Jaeger, 65s.; leather "driving gloves," 35s. 6d.; PVC satchel bag, 4 gns.
LEFT: the same fur beret showing a matching striped fur cravat, also from Young Jaeger, 55s.

Pictures by CRISPIAN WOODGATE.

1966

Women in the Universities

As Britain sought to keep up in a rapidly changing and developing world there was an expansion in the numbers of university places available and increasing numbers of women took up those places. Several new universities were established and polytechnics created to offer a wider range of degree courses. Women formed just under 30 per cent of the total university population. However at Oxford and Cambridge less than ten per cent of students were women in 1962, which was hardly any improvement on the percentage in 1922. All of those women were in all-women colleges.

In 1964 New College, Oxford voted to be the first men's college to admit women but the decision was reversed the following year after lobbying by the women's colleges who feared it would severely damage the standard of applications to their institutions. The women's colleges admitted 300 applicants each year while the men's colleges took in almost 2,500. It was not until 1972 that women were granted admission to any men's colleges.

Those women who did gain a university place often worked far harder than their male counterparts perhaps feeling they had to justify their presence in such establishments. A study by the University Grants Committee found that in 1965–6 almost 82 per cent of women passed their finals as against just over 76 per cent of men.

ABOVE: *Florence Nagle.*
BELOW: *Indira Gandhi being sworn in as Prime Minister of India.*

1966 POSTSCRIPTS

January – Following the death of Prime Minister Shastri, Indira Gandhi was elected and sworn in as Prime Minister of India by the members of the ruling Congress Party.

June – Barclay's Bank issued their Barclaycard credit card. In cases of joint accounts only the husbands were issued with cards, but most husbands returned them and asked that their wives be issued with one as well.

July – Florence Nagle won a long fight with the Jockey Club, eventually taking them to the High Court, over being allowed a trainer's licence. Mrs Nagle described herself as a 'ghost trainer' as she had trained racehorses for almost 30 years under a licence given to her head lad.

September – Margaret Sanger died. She was a pioneer of birth control in the USA and said in her 1938 autobiography that women needed 'first to free themselves from biological slavery'.

October – The Law Commission was charged to examine the practice by which the marriage prospects of a widow or single woman had to be taken into account when a court was assessing an award of damages. A women's conference had condemned the practice as degrading.

BRING ON THE BLUE STOCKINGS

Sir Denis Brogan, retiring Professor of Political Science, calls for more university education for women.

'Our greatest untapped source of ability', he said, 'is education for girls. If I had money to give away I would spend it on getting more women into the universities. That's where we are missing the bright ones. I don't think we are missing very many bright boys.

'The argument that it is a waste because they get married is bogus. We should make it easier for them to go back to their jobs ten years after they have their children . . . And anyway if a clever woman remains a wife and mother what is wrong with having clever wives and mothers?

Daily Mail, 4 March 1966

What a well-dressed wife can do

JUDY INNES

FOR A LABOUR MINISTER

Lady Kennet
. . . wife of the Joint Parliamentary Secretary for Housing and Local Government, a long empire line dress in orange chiffon

Mrs. Anthony Crosland
. . . wife of the Secretary of State for Education and Science, in a white silk suit with a long jacket and a high stand-up collar.

Pictures by
ROBERT LAMBERT

AS EVERY astute politician is well aware, there is no bigger asset than a pretty wife when it comes to getting votes at home or making friends and influencing people abroad.

Jackie Kennedy was the best ambassador America ever had. And even Kosygin (who hardly needs to worry about bringing in the votes at home) was sharp enough to include his photogenic daughter in the party when he came here.

But in the fuss over visiting dignitaries' wives and daughters, we tend to lose sight of the fact that we have a pretty formidable collection of talent at home in the wives of Government Ministers, from Mrs. Wilson down.

Mrs. Wilson hardly needs stressing. But as the Ministers' wives aren't as well known as they should be, I've picked five of the prettiest and best-dressed of an attractive bunch.

One of them, Mrs. Harold Lever, who inherited a £2 million fortune from her banker father, shops in Paris at Yves St. Laurent, Givenchy and Courreges. One of them, Lady Kennet, has raided her children's dressing-up box for some of her most successful outfits.

But they all have an eye for clothes and a flair for wearing them, which adds a bit of zizz to official functions and brings a sparkle to the jaded official eye.

Mrs. Lever, a 30-year-old who looks like Jeanne Moreau and has five children and a size 8 figure, is probably the most professional about her clothes.

She packs her clothes-buying into a couple of weeks in the year; she nips over to Paris, sees two or three shows, picks the outfits she likes and gets them made up.

She sometimes gets a reduction on very expensive beaded and jewelled dresses—being model size, she can wear the ones which have been shown in the collection. (It's nice to know couturiers aren't above making slashing reductions, too.)

She's rare among Labour wives in enjoying hats. Most of the five wear them only when they have to ; but as one of them said: " While Conservative politicians' wives wear hats to be respectable Labour MPs' wives either go hatless or wear a hat to cut a dash."

Mrs. Harold Lever
. . . wife of the Joint Parliamentary Under-Secretary of State at the Department of Economic Affairs, in a black-and-yellow Yves St. Laurent suit and a copy of a St. Laurent hat.

Trend setter

. . . IN FUN FURS

Lady Kennet is the most adventurous of the Ministers' wives. She loves clothes and gets her eye in to new fashions quickly ; she had a fun fur a year ahead of everyone else, loves jazzy stockings and finds that her skirts get shorter and shorter, " particularly when I'm wearing textured stockings or low heels."

No hat wearer, she has an Anthony Eden straw homburg covered in carnations, which is her standby ; a former standby "called the Gracious Pink Hat by the family " has been smartly relegated to the dressing-up box.

Some of the traffic goes the other way ; she recently realised that a black velvet cape lined with rabbit which had once belonged to her mother and was lurking in the dressing-up box was perfect for wearing over long evening dresses and promptly rescued it. " We all wear it now," she says. ("All" being her daughters and herself.)

1967

A New Abortion Law

With the growth of the 'permissive society' and much more open discussion about sex and contraception there was a growing public feeling that something had to be done about the existing abortion laws. The law dated back to 1861, despite a ruling in 1938 in the Bourne case which reinterpreted the expression 'unless the mother's life is in danger' to mean her physical or mental wellbeing. However, many doctors (and the agreement of two doctors was required to allow the abortion to go ahead) were not willing to risk their judgement on whether a women's health would be so disabled as to leave her a wreck, and in the majority of cases it was patently not the case. The only alternative was an illegal or 'backstreet' abortion.

Many plays and novels of the time, such as *Up the Junction,* dealt with or included the situation of a woman becoming pregnant and seeking an illegal abortion. They described graphically the often insanitary conditions and the pain, illness and sometimes death caused to the mother. It seems surprising that women would risk their lives in a backstreet abortion but during the 1960s, for all the talk of permissiveness and although there had been some softening of attitudes, the unmarried mother still faced rejection by society and often by her family.

In October 1967 the Medical Termination of Pregnancy Bill became law despite a campaign by anti-abortion groups such as the Society for the Protection of the Unborn Child formed in January of the same year. The new law effectively ended the practice of backstreet abortion by permitting abortion up to 28 weeks on the grounds that to continue with the pregnancy would cause injury to the mother's mental or physical health. Abortion was also permitted if the baby was at risk of being physically or mentally malformed.

The National Health Service was charged to make provision for abortion operations. However it was not always simple to obtain an abortion on the NHS as not all hospitals provided facilities, and some doctors, morally opposed to abortion, were unwilling either to refer women for, or to perform, the operation. Once in hospital a woman waiting for an abortion operation could find herself in an ante-natal ward alongside women anxiously trying to prevent the unborn child within them from spontaneous abortion.

The shortcomings of the NHS in relation to abortion lead to the establishment of bodies such as the British Pregnancy Advisory Service which offered contact with doctors willing to sanction and perform abortions and a more sympathetic treatment in private clinics.

The new law brought tremendous benefits to women: they no longer had to suffer for life the results of an unwanted pregnancy, or physical pain or terrible damage from an illegal abortion, although the law could not remove the mental and emotional suffering such an operation brings.

ABOVE: A group of Radio One disc jockeys. Radio One started broadcasting in September 1967 and all the DJs were male.
BELOW: A 'flower child' at Woburn Abbey.

1967 POSTSCRIPTS

February – A Bill was passed allowing local authorities to give contraceptive advice to married and unmarried men and women.

July – The Sexual Offences Act became law decriminalizing homosexual acts in private between consenting men over the age of twenty-one. Lesbianism had never been illegal as it was not acknowledged to exist by the law makers of earlier centuries.

Wanted: Angry young women

TO SAVE

2,500 LIVES A YEAR

IT should anger every woman in the land.

Pussyfooting and meanness by the Government and the mandarins of medicine are delaying the eradication of cancer of the cervix.

Each year cancer of the neck of the womb kills 2,500 women in Britain. The great majority of these deaths are preventable.

They go on happening for two reasons. The Ministry of Health will not spend enough on screening facilities for early detection of the disease.

And a row among medical men on the efficacy of screening looks likely to swamp the issue in years of sterile committee wrangling.

To take the second point first. A working group of medical experts, appointed by the Nuffield Provincial Hospitals Trust, has come down against cervical cancer tests because, they say, not enough is known about the disease, screening procedure and treatment.

Ignorance

And Lord Cohen of Birkenhead, president of the General Medical Council, seems to agree. He speaks of 'public ignorance' or imperfect understanding putting pressure on the Government to set up a service whose worth is not fully known.

Happily, his view is not shared by the Queen's gynæcologist, Sir John Peel, who is president-elect of the Women's National Cancer Control Campaign.

Sir John says: 'The cure rate for *pre*-cancer diagnosed by the smear test is nearly 100 p.c. Cancer of the cervix is therefore in theory a preventable disease.'

Even in clinically diagnosed and established cancer of the cervix the cure rate in Britain is 50 p.c.

He has a powerful ally in Professor H. G. McLaren, of Birmingham University, who found 300 cases of *pre*-cancer with the smear test. Not one developed cervical cancer.

Professor McLaren's message is that it is *fit* women who should take the test. The trouble is that 'a young mother of several children is always busy and thinks of herself and her health very rarely. She is, however, the key figure in any family or community.'

The test can be had in any National Health Service hospital. But not many fit young mothers have cause to go to hospital.

Closing

And Ministry of Health screening clinics throughout the country are closing, says Lady Donaldson, chairman of the Women's National Cancer Control Campaign.

The campaign has launched an appeal for £100,000 for mobile clinics which would tackle cervical cancer in factory yards and at country crossroads in much the same way that tuberculosis was tackled.

But what is more urgently needed is an evaluation of the impressive statistics given by Peel and McLaren, a massive publicity campaign, and *action*.

And no woman should let her anger abate until these things happen.

IF YOU THINK THIS IS GOING TOO FAR, JUST LOOK AT THE BACK PAGE

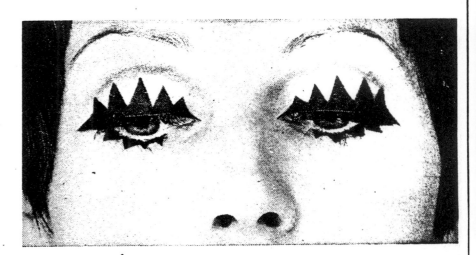

FEMAIL COMMENT ON MEAN MEN

MEAN MEN give you the housekeeping money two days late, borrow part of it back almost immediately and don't return it.

MEAN MEN say they hate Christmas because they like to give presents on the spur of the moment—only they never give presents at all.

MEAN MEN say they *like* margarine.

MEAN MEN don't pay housekeeping when you're on holiday.

MEAN MEN say 'Let's have scrambled eggs at your place' (not only mean men, of course).

MEAN MEN never order a taxi: they say 'We'll pick one up at the bus stop.'

MEAN MEN demand the family allowance money back and say that they pay for it in tax at the end of the year anyway.

MEAN MEN always buy the first round, because someone might come along later to swell the group.

MEAN MEN borrow your car and return it without any petrol.

MEAN MEN ask you to collect their dry cleaning.

MEAN MEN buy just one theatre programme.

MEAN MEN never give their wives pocket money.

MEAN MEN think it's a wife's duty to buy her husband's socks, ties and underpants.

MEAN MEN never have any stamps and their cars never have enough petrol.

1968

Birth Control Under Attack

Pope Paul published his Encyclical Letter entitled *Humanae Vitae (Of Human Life)* in 1968. The Vatican's deliberations on the subject of birth control had been awaited by Roman Catholics throughout the world with great expectation of a dramatic new approach. In the end most were severely disappointed for the Papal Encyclical stated that any form of artificial birth control was against divine will, although it did approve the 'rhythm method' of birth control where a couple had to avoid having sex at the woman's most fertile period. It was some small acknowledgement by the Church that sex was not solely for the procreation of children.

For many Catholic women this ruling put them in a very difficult moral position. Their Church ruled against artificial forms of birth control which were by far the most effective, and yet they felt that in terms of their own family's wellbeing and the world's population, to say nothing of the immense benefits to their own life and fulfilment, a strong moral case could be made for contraception.

If they chose to defy the Church's teachings, and many did, there was a growing range of possible alternative methods of contraception. There was of course the cap, the sheath and the Pill (although scares about the safety of the Pill had caused many women to stop taking it, sometimes only for a period until they could be reassured but often abandoning it altogether as a suitable method of contraception).

The Intra Uterine Device (IUD) became available a few years after the Pill and despite it not being as widely publicized it quickly became popular, especially among older women who had had their family and were at greater risk on the Pill. Wives, however, needed their husbands' consent before having the IUD fitted as once in place it made the woman temporarily sterile and only a doctor could reverse that sterility. By mid-1966 there was a year-long waiting list for the IUD, partly because of its popularity and partly because there were not enough doctors trained to fit it.

Sterilization was another, if drastic, method but a number of women chose that route although it was usually only offered to those with large families. Male sterilization or vasectomy was an alternative but usually only in cases where the wife was not considered fit enough to undergo a sterilization operation.

ABOVE: Sheila Thorns with her three surviving babies.
BELOW: Trying on fashionable military-style clothing at a Carnaby Street boutique.

1968 POSTSCRIPTS

● Epidural pain relief was first introduced for women during childbirth.

June – Women machinists at Ford called off a strike for better grading of their jobs after Barbara Castle, the Minister for Employment and Productivity, stepped in. She did not gain them better grades but the company ended the practice of setting separate rates of pay and the women were paid the same rate as men on the equivalent grade.

October – Sheila Ann Thorns gave birth to sextuplets after having been treated with a fertility drug.

MP SEEKS 'SEX BOARD'

Labour MP Mrs Joyce Butler yesterday moved the setting up of a 'Sex Discrimination Board' with powers similar to the Race Relations Board.

Mrs Butler (Wood Green) said in the Commons, 'There has been a failure by society to appreciate the full value of women.

'Fifty years ago they were granted the vote and ever since they have been struggling for something more tangible.

'Nine out of ten don't get equal pay,' she complained, and when pressure was put on the government, demands were met with 'constant procrastination'.

Her Bill, backed by other women MPs of all parties, was given an unopposed first reading.

Daily Mail, 8 May 1968

Baby's sitting pretty

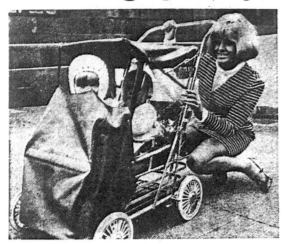

TOGETHER WE CHOSE A . . . Baby-Tandem, a weather-shielded partitioned pushchair with room for baby in the back, junior on a detachable seat at the front, and shopping in the tray underneath. In red vinyl with navy lining, £14.19s.6d. by Leeway.

MOTHERS with babies who want at all costs to be seen to be trendy, colourful and above all *different* when it comes to nursery accessories are going to have the time of their lives in 1970.

The only difficulty will be making a choice from among all the new-look ideas.

PRAMS, for example, are going into PRINT. On show at this week's Pram Fair in London is the Sandown baby carriage by Royale. With bodywork, hood and apron in Stylon (a new fabric of washable Bri-nylon and PVC), it's printed all over with a swirling William Morris design in red, blue or gold, and it costs about £30.

A strong colour contender in this year's pram stakes is a delicious new honey tan, a follow-up to last year's successful orange. 'Heavy-knit' vinyl for pram bodies looks like being another popular newcomer, while the traditional white pram interior is now very much an also-ran.

Practical

Today it's navy—smart, dark and much more practical—which looks like taking the prize here.

CANOPIES are going PSYCHEDELIC, in huge, printed abstracts or florals in mixtures of deep green, pale green and sugar pink. By Morlands of Glastonbury, they come in cotton or a new, shiny satin—as stunning as a jockey's

by ANGELA BROADBRIDGE

silks—and in 12 designs, from about 38s.

CARRY-COTS are getting BOLD—the latest, imported from Italy, are in shiny scarlet, brilliant yellow, green or white, £7 10s. at the new Bilba Boutique, Kensington.

Most hilarious idea around at the moment is the musical potty. In the shape of a pink or blue duck, it has a string trailing from the duck's mouth which the child can pull—and be rewarded by a cheerful little song.

Enough to give any child a musical hang-up for life, we'd think.

More practical is the Kiddirail, a telescopic handrail for fixing to a staircase at child-height. In silvery or ivory metal, it adjusts to any staircase up to 12ft. in length. By Bells of Southport, 59s. 6d.

Final colour note: a big plump rabbit in bright pink, to use as a table mat, with matching bib in towelling and a cotton wallet to store the bib 30s. the set, by Bassetti.

Dear FEMAIL

No love lost for David

DAVID, the architect who last week told Lynda Lee-Potter of his wife's successful career as an actress and how it was undermining his marriage, has stimulated a storm of protest from women readers.

'How many times,' ask several, 'has he been guilty of the crimes of which he now accuses his wife—not listening to her after a hard day at the office, not turning up at the children's school functions, being so immersed in his job he had only a superficial knowledge of world affairs, and thinking everything could be solved by sex ?'

'David obviously thinks marriage should be one glorious twosome—as long as both are sharing HIS interests,' writes Mrs Stevenson, of Wimborne, Dorset.

'The lady can't be such an unfeeling toad,' says another woman. 'She stuck it for seven years and only returned to her career when she could provide a presumably loving grandmother to look after her children.'

However, another woman says: 'What wouldn't I give for a husband like that. I didn't go out to work, but when my husband died I was forced to run my own business.

'This gives me an occupation and makes money, but give me my old life every time. I know exactly how a hardworking man feels at the end of the day and I am sorry for those unfortunate husbands who return to one of the moaning minnies.'

Mrs Salter, of Rochester, Kent, says she is sure all career women aren't like that, but adds: 'I have noticed that married women who work are either Bossy or Moaners or both. I think women are fools to try to attain equality with men.'

But a woman who decided not to work because her husband disapproved urges David's wife Carol to 'carry on working.' 'After 19 years of marriage,' she writes, 'my husband is bored with "the twaddle that comes out of my empty head." '

And most women correspondents agreed with her.

Lost

Another reader made the point that a woman who has no activity to fill her life will feel even more lost when the children grow up and leave.

But one working mother, Mrs Bowen, of Welshpool, who seems to have combined both careers successfully, writes happily :

'My work is geared to my home, not the other way round. I leave for work after everyone else and come home before the others. I'm at home if anyone is ill and during the school holidays. I wouldn't like a job without this understanding.

'My family are very happy with my job and the extra money we share.'

Those missing nice men . . .

Name and address supplied :
I WAS interested to read the frank and sincere letter from the woman who asked, 'Where have all the nice men gone ?'

After I lost my wife 18 months ago I had two or three lady companions. They were all in the late 50s, my age, but it wasn't long before I discovered they were seeking a marriage of convenience for security when all I wanted was a companion to talk to and for an occasional outing.

'I am optimistic that I will eventually find the person I want and hope your correspondent will find that "nice man." '

Name and address supplied :
. . . I would love a female companion to take out occasionally but I am reluctant to ask. Most females would think there was an ulterior motive and wouldn't believe I simply wanted a change from male company.

I lost my wife two years ago and her memory is still too dear to consider 'fun and games' or re-marriage, but how many women would believe that ? So it isn't as easy as you think for 'nice men' to ask women out.

1969

Divorce Reform

By 1969 anyone wishing to divorce their partner still had to rely on the 1937 Matrimonial Causes Act which required one partner to prove the other guilty of desertion, insanity, adultery or cruelty. Even if both partners wanted a divorce, because blame had to be attributed, the process was messy and unpleasant. In the light of all the changes in society and the relationships between men and women the Act seemed out of date.

During the 1960s legislation had been passed allowing a wife, and a husband in the rare cases where the woman owned the house, security of tenure in the family home. Further legislation had allowed her to keep any savings she had made from any money her husband might have given her. Laws like these which gave women a little more financial security, and a general feeling that they were not prepared to put up with unhappy marriages and situations their mothers might have accepted were part of what brought a growing pressure for a change in the divorce laws.

A Divorce Reform Bill was introduced into Parliament and passed in 1969, although it did not come into effect until January 1971. This new Act allowed for either partner to sue for divorce on the grounds that the marriage had 'irretrievably broken down'. After a couple had been apart for two years, if both agreed, a divorce could be granted; if one partner objected to the divorce a separation of five years was required.

The new Act did not always make divorce any less unpleasant but it did remove the necessity to apportion blame. However, it did not remove the need for partners to challenge one another over the major issues which follow from divorce. Couples still battled in the courts over custody of, and access to, any children of the marriage; maintenance payments and their upkeep; the division of the family home and property. The Divorce Reform Act made divorce easier to obtain and the dramatic 25 per cent increase in divorce petitions showed just how many unhappy marriages there were.

ABOVE: Golda Meir at a Socialist International Congress in Britain.
BELOW: The owner of a Carnaby Street boutique was arrested when he displayed women wearing only accessories in the window as a publicity stunt for the shop's opening.

1969 POSTSCRIPTS

February – Lloyds of London announced that it would admit women from the beginning of 1970.

• Scientists at Cambridge revealed that they had fertilized a human egg in a test tube but they said that there was a long way to go before this advance would have any practical use.

March – The Israeli Labour Party elected Golda Meir to be Prime Minister following the death in office of Prime Minister Cevi Eshkol.

Daughters of the new revolution

by PRISCILLA HODGSON

NOBODY jokes about women's liberation any more. Especially not men.

The U.S., home of the so-called matriarchal society and Doris Day, is gradually waking up to the realisation that apple pie like only Momma makes is all very well, but not if it means Momma is so frustrated and bored in her suburban ranch house making apple pie that she takes to the psychiatrist's couch twice a week.

On August 26 (50 years to the day after women in America got the vote) there's to be a national one-day strike by women in America to protest against discrimination.

Staggering

The majority will be protesting against job discrimination (which is probably only a little worse than it is here in Britain).

But this is only part of the picture. The staggering thing about the movement, which has hundreds of thousands of adherents and many more sympathisers, is that it stretches from the extreme Left to the far Right.

On one hand you have bra-burning militants who want test-tube births and the complete subordination of men.

On the other there are the working mothers who just want nursery facilities for their children.

In the centre there's the National Organisation of Women, which is unlike anything we have in this country. The fight against job discrimination is their main aim. And for this reason many groups on the Left split away because it was not radical enough.

They call themselves by a multitude of weird names, like Red Stocking, WITCH (Women's International Terrorist Conspiracy from Hell), WRAP (Women's Radical Action Protest), Bread and Roses and Keep on Truckin' Sisters.

Their collective nickname is Uppity Women, and they wear buttons to prove it.

You can't open a paper or a magazine without some reference to the movement.

The trouble with American womanhood in protest is that it is suffering from a terrible guilt complex. The women want to work. They want a certain independence. They want the stimulation of a world away from the deep freeze and the cocktail hour. Don't we all ?

Scornful

But they are feeling currently very guilty if they allow even one little anti-housework thought to pass through their minds.

Everyone I spoke to was eager to know about the situation in Britain, and when I said I couldn't see a comparative movement growing with the same strength here, they looked at me scornfully.

'Just wait,' said one girl.

I can see an interesting decade ahead.

'I want a child but it must be a girl...I hate men'

SARA DAVIDSON (above) combines marriage and a career as a freelance journalist. She's not freelance from choice. She finds it difficult getting a staff writer's job, although big magazines commission her to do important articles.

She recently undertook a major assignment for Life magazine on women's liberation. It ran to some 5,000 words and changed her life.

'I set out thinking they were probably a bunch of nuts. But I found myself getting very involved.

'Some of it I hated. But I started questioning everything in my career. The trouble I'd had getting established, how I was offered jobs as a cutting clerk or a mail girl.

'I also questioned aspects of my marriage. Why should I work all day and then cook and clean at night while my husband puts on the TV ?

'Now my husband does the dishes three nights a week. It's a start.'

DOLORES is slim, blonde and pale in an undernourished sort of way. Her tights are torn, and she's wearing a navy blouse and navy skirt which look like Wren surplus. She works in a library, is highly intelligent and articulate.

All her spare time is spent analysing the role of women. At 19 she went to a psychiatrist because she thought she should. She thought there was something wrong.

She was even more convinced when she left him.

Why is she fighting for the liberation of women ?

'Listen, my whole day makes me more and more convinced women are being exploited. I get up in the morning and I walk down the sidewalk and have to put up with wolf whistles.

'Then I pick up a newspaper at the corner stand and if I'm not looking happy the newsvendor says "Give a smile just for me."

'Then I get to work and I have to wear what my boss says. No trousers.

'I want a child, but it must be a female child. Soon it will be possible to know in advance. But I couldn't carry a male child in my body for nine months. I hate men '

BETTY FRIEDAN, the high priestess of Women's Liberation, started it all with her book 'The Feminine Mystique.'

She is founder of the National Organisation of Women, professional women working to end job discrimination, repeal the abortion laws and establish creches.

'Discrimination was crystallised in my mind when I went to Boston researching for my book. I had an hour to kill before my appointment, so I went into a large hotel for a drink. But the barman would not serve me because I was a woman alone. He said he would take me to where I could have a drink.

'He led me to the ladies' cloakroom.

'All I really did in my book was to put into words what millions of women have probably been thinking for years. That everything is against them.'

We enjoyed America. We'd like you to too ! So Femail has organised a special competition to start next week with a prize of five days in New York for two, all expenses paid

There's a direct BOAC flight, London-New York and back, accommodation at the 500-room luxury Berkshire Hotel in the heart of the smart Fifth Avenue shopping area, and sightseeing tours taking in Manhattan Island, the Empire State Building, Harlem and a visit to an ordinary American home. Plus pocket money. Plus a set of Revelation luggage to take with you and keep.

Full details of the prize and the competition next week.

Daily Mail Printed and Published by Associated Newspapers, Ltd., Carmelite House London, E.C.4. and Northcliffe House, Deansgate, Manchester, 3. Registered as a newspaper at the Post Office. Second-class postage paid at New York, N.Y., Tuesday, June 30, 1970.

1970

Women's Liberation Movement

ABOVE: *A demonstration at a Miss World Contest.*
BELOW: *Women beneath a protest banner which shows some of the Movement's targets for attack.*

After the Second World War Simone de Beauvoir, Vera Brittain and Betty Friedan had all published books drawing attention to the overt and subtle forms of oppression exercised over women. In 1970 Germaine Greer published a new work on the subject challenging the way in which men had stereotyped women and set out ways in which it was acceptable for them to behave, and the way in which society trained girls to be unassertive, undemanding and compliant to men. The *Female Eunuch* had a dramatic effect when it was first published, and a great deal of media attention, through which its message reached women who would never have dreamt of reading the book.

In 1970, responding to what they felt was a need, a number of women, including the feminist historian Sheila Rowbottom, organized the first national Women's Liberation Movement Conference. The conference, like Germaine Greer's book, was only part of a growing women's movement which questioned the role women were being forced to play in society. Very like the suffragettes before the First World War the Women's Liberation Movement held marches and demonstrations and lobbied Parliament and politicians on issues which affected women. And indeed they had success in terms of legislation. Several new laws were passed removing many of the inequalities women suffered in the legal system. The Movement was also international and brought changes in the legal position of women in countries such as France which was the first country to appoint a Minister for Women. It also brought changes in the social position and women's awareness of themselves and their value to society in countries with such vastly different cultural heritages as the USA and Japan.

The Women's Liberation Movement also drew attention to the way society and men in general perceived and treated women. Attacks on the exploitation of women and their bodies, with demonstrations at events like the Miss World Contest, had some impact. While at first the media dismissed such protests and did not treat them seriously the message was strong enough to change public consciousness. There is now no longer the same great media attention given to beauty contests and the winner of Miss World is often lucky to make it to the front page of even the tabloids.

There are critics who say the Women's Liberation Movement and the 'bra-burning, scrubbed-faced, dungaree-wearing women's libbers' went too far and denied their femininity in order to gain their freedom. Perhaps that is true but those women affected a whole generation of both men and women, and felt they had found a freedom for themselves while making freedom for other women a possibility.

1970 POSTSCRIPTS

February – The House of Commons gave an unopposed second reading to the Equal Pay Bill, introduced by Barbara Castle, the Minister for Employment and Productivity, which said that women and men doing the same job would have to be given the same rates of pay by January 1976.

May – The US Army appointed Ann Hays and Elizabeth Hoisington as its first women Generals.

June – The Methodist Church announced that women would soon be permitted to be ordained as ministers and be granted the same pay and status as men.

HIS AND HERS

. . . Female talent will continue to be under-used and under-paid as long as women are discouraged from training for the top jobs.

In Russia three quarters of the doctors are women, in Britain only five per cent. No wonder we are short of doctors.

All the same we believe that Mrs Castle's Bill will dent male prejudice as well as swelling female pay packets. Equal pay is the first step on the road to equal opportunity.

Extracts from a *Daily Mail* Leader, 10 February 1970

The love-life question

NOP
NATIONAL
OPINION POLLS

Day two of a fascinating Mail series on women and work

GIVEN the chance, two-in-five of Britain's housewives would take a job. And another 19 p.c. are thinking about doing so.

Their reasons, discovered by the National Opinion Polls survey, are that extra bit of money to do with as they please; the boredom of home life; and the companionship of people at work.

But of the 40 p.c. happy with their lot at home, a half said they wouldn't take a job—or go back to their old job—because they would have to do the housework at night.

As one young housewife with two children commented: 'Well, you don't have time for sex, which is the most important thing, because you're too tired. I think working wives *must* be irritable.'

Others said they would hate having to rush everything, and that the children would suffer. An accountant's wife in Devon commented: 'The house wouldn't be in the same condition that it's in, and my son would be annoyed if I was not there at 4 p.m.'

Among full-time mothers, 46 p.c. spend 41 hours or more a week on housework, including cooking, shopping and washing. At the other end of the scale, 11 p.c. of working housewives spend less than 15 hours on the same tasks.

Sixty p.c. of non-working women disagreed with the suggestion that married women can't find enough to occupy their minds just running a home.

But 79 p.c. agreed that it was important for a married woman to have

© *National Opinion Polls Ltd., 1971.*

HOW DOES A WOMAN SPEND HER SPARE TIME?

Watching TV	Crafts & Hobbies	Reading	Social Activities	Gardening	Going for walks	Doing nothing
80%	**71%**	**57%**	**46%**	**44%**	**37%**	**2%**

by Vincent Mulchrone

some money of her own, illustrating the frustration of those who would like to work but can't — usually because of the children.

More than half (53 p.c.) think working wives are less bored than themselves, and 45 p.c. think that women who work make more interesting companions for their husbands. (Only 34 p.c. disagreed with this.)

An inhibiting factor for those women who would like to work is the lack of nurseries and nursery schools —63 p.c. said their area needed more.

As to what effect all this has on a marriage, it is curious to find that, where the largest proportion of working wives think there are fewer rows in their home because they go out to work, exactly the same number of non-working women disagree.

Most full-time housewives consider their stopping work had not had any

effect on their marriage. But of those who did think it had made a difference, most thought it had made things better.

What full-time housewives most appreciate is their freedom—to spend time with their family, to visit friends, not having to rush. Some even mentioned the freedom to have a lie-in in the morning.

And what do they do with their spare time? In percentages, they mentioned: Watching TV, 80; crafts and hobbies, 71; reading, 57; social activities, 46; gardening, 44; going for walks, 37.

Two per cent share my hobby—doing nothing.

But many—those who would like to

get a job or go back to their old one—remain dissatisfied. They miss the money and the companionship. They are bored at home.

Like the middle-aged wife of a clerk in Lanarkshire, who said: 'Well, there's no interest apart from the home. I hate it. One becomes a cabbage.'

(Five p.c. of working wives actually used the word 'cabbage,' and their fear of becoming one, when explaining why they worked.)

A 40-year-old Surrey woman, wife of a commuter, and with three children at school, summed it up for many: 'It's a long day,' she said. 'And I feel frustrated.'

But, chiefly, it's the money. The

wife of a long-distance lorry driver said: 'I miss not having money for extras—or to give me a feeling of independence so that I can buy things like birthday and Christmas presents, and to help with holiday spending money.'

Money, friends at work—anything to escape the 'long day' between the same four walls.

These are the thoughts troubling the minds of most British housewives today.

Representative samples of 495 working wives, aged 16 to 60, and 490 full-time housewives in that age group were interviewed throughout Great Britain between June 18 and 22 this year.

Tomorrow: Whose side are the husbands on?

How does work affect a marriage?

FOUR WIVES GIVE THEIR VIEWS TO LYNDA LEE-POTTER

Mrs B: Sometimes I wake up, terrified

MARGARET B., who is 34, lives in Peterborough, is married with three children—and would love to go out to work.

But she has been unable to find a local job which fits in with her domestic schedule. And she says: 'You get the feeling of life passing you by very quickly.

'I can scarcely distinguish between the years. This time last month, this time last summer, my day was more or less the same.

'I wake up in the night sometimes, quite overcome with terror at the thought of my life just wasting away, with nothing to show for it.

'It's the silence, I think, that is so terrible. It's like being on another planet when John's gone to work and the children have got the school bus.

'There isn't a sound from any other human being from eight in the morning till four in the afternoon. I can hear the clock ticking away. I'm in such a state some days that I've just had to wrap it in a towel.

'The first thing people say is "And what do you do?", showing that this is how people evaluate you. When you say "I'm just a housewife," you see their interest just fading away.

'Put me in a room with 20 women and I could tell you without making one single mistake who went out to work and who didn't.

'There's a kind of gloss and confidence on the working wives, and a nervous boring hysteria about the stay at home ones.'

Mrs G: You do loiter with the milkman

BARBARA G., whose husband runs a car-hire firm, thought she knew what she wanted. . . .

. . . Four children, a cottage in the country, home-grown vegetables, domesticity and time to cook.

She is now looking for a good nanny for her only daughter as quick as she can find one—and says if she never tastes a home-grown sprout again, it will be too soon.

'Honestly,' she says, 'I nearly went out of my mind last winter after the baby was born. I've never lived in the country before and I never knew how things grew.

'I developed this terrible phobia about trees. I felt they were closing in on me and surrounding the house. I'd wake up in the night screaming and having terrible nightmares thinking they were strangling me.

'I know that makes me sound an absolute nut, but I've talked to a lot of other women and they've said they've had exactly the same feeling.

'I suppose it's part of this sensation of being buried alive when you're closeted in the house with a baby.

'All the hoary old jokes, you find, are coming true. You do talk to yourself, you do loiter with the milkman. On more than one occasion, may God forgive me, I've whined as Bill walked through the door: "I've never stopped all day."

'The awful thing is it's true, but out of all that labour you haven't achieved one constructive thing.

Mrs D: I couldn't bear an office . . .

JENNY D is married to an architect and they live in an old farmhouse with roses round the door, apple trees in the garden and home-made bread in the kitchen.

She rarely goes out but, at 34, with three children, she says: 'I'm blissfully happy.'

'He's not an ideal husband by most people's standards. He's rarely home before 11 and I know that two nights out of three it's because he's gone out with his friends for a drink.

'He can't knock a nail in straight and anything electrical is done by me, but just knowing that at the end of the day he's coming home to me is enough somehow.

'I love being at home. I'm sure that the only wives who are discontented at home are unhappy because there is something fundamentally wrong with their marriage.

'I went to collect Michael's car insurance the other day and looked round all the girls when I went into the typing pool.

'And I thought: "God, how can they stand it, day in day out, cooped up like chickens, battering their typewriters hour after hour."

'I'm not a bit cabbagy. I've got a bit of a brain between my ears, and it's being utilised now far more than it ever was when I was a secretary.

'I just don't know how anybody can say being a wife and mother is dreary. I feel quite drunk with power sometimes. I know I'm the pivot around which all their lives turn.'

Mrs W: Imagine—all day to yourself!

JENNY W. lived in the New Forest before she got married and says it was a rest cure compared with her life now.

She has four young children, and with the help of one local girl has painted her seven-bedroomed home inside and out.

She rides every day, deep-freezes her food in monthly batches, makes all the family jam and bread, and with the children has painted a huge mural on the drawing-room wall.

It nearly gave her husband a heart attack when it was being done, but it has turned out so successfully she's had two commissions.

'I drive my friends crazy because I keep saying what fun it is having the kids at home,' she says. 'But it's true.

'I can whip through the housework in about an hour and then we've got all day to go and have a picnic or paint or dig or play football.

'They're all in bed by about seven and David doesn't get home till 10, so I've got a lovely long time to fiddle with my face or make myself some more clothes.

'I'm not a bit of a selfless mum, devoting herself to her children. I'm a very self-indulgent lady, who is doing exactly what she always wanted.

'If it's your idea of hell to stay at home with the kids, why have children in the first place?

'I can't think of anything more cabbagy than trundling up to rotten old London on British Rail every day. I feel totally fulfilled at home.'

1971

Women Without A Vote

Women in Britain had been able to vote on equal terms with men for 43 years by 1971. Throughout the western world most women had been allowed the vote since before the Second World War and those who had an unequal franchise had remedied it soon after the war.

At the beginning of 1971 women in Switzerland, which would like to have described itself as one of the most civilized nations in the world, did not have the vote. Switzerland enacts much of its legislation on the results of referenda. Over the years there had been several referenda on the issue of giving women the vote. On every occasion the majority of the all-male electorate had vetoed the idea. However at the beginning of February 1971 a new referendum on the issue gave a majority in favour of women being enfranchised. This referendum only granted women the vote in national elections and half the cantons, which were a fairly powerful tier of local government, still barred women from the electorate.

At the end of February 1971 in a similar referendum the all-male electorate of the tiny state of Liechtenstein voted, unlike their Swiss counterparts, to continue to refuse to enfranchise women.

Women in Liechtenstein were not the only women in the world without a vote in national elections. Many Islamic countries where the religious authorities held sway, continued to refuse their women the vote. Despite affiliation to the United Nations and its Charter, Jordan, Kuwait, Saudi Arabia and Yemen had not enfranchised women, and in Portugal, San Marino and Syria women did not have the vote on the same terms as men.

ABOVE: A woman in 'hotpants' which became the fashion craze of the year.
BELOW: Despite the efforts of the Women's Movement it was becoming more common to see naked women used in advertisements. This one of model Vivien Neves caused a sensation when it appeared in The Times.

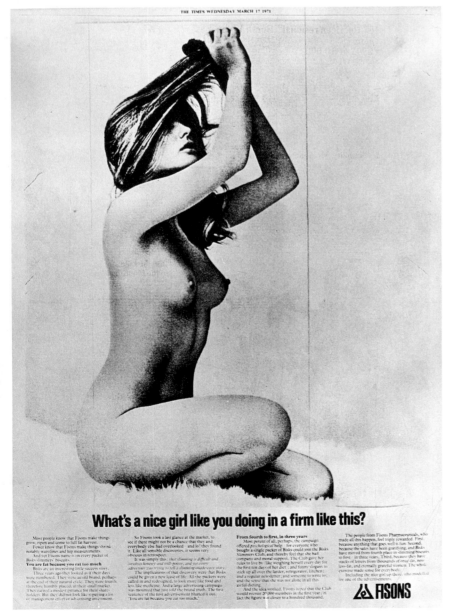

1971 POSTSCRIPTS

January – The first decree was granted under the new Divorce Act which allowed 'irretrievable breakdown' as grounds for divorce.

May – It was announced that 'ladies in hot pants' would only be allowed into the Royal Enclosure at Ascot if the general effect was satisfactory.

WOMEN'S BOREDOM LEADS TO BABIES

Father-of-four Lord Beaumont of Whitely was in trouble last night for saying that women often have babies because they can't think of anything better to do.

Lord Beaumont, former President of the Liberal Party, told peers debating the world's population problems:

'Towards the end of a period when women have two or three children, if there is not a chance of finding a worthwhile job, they find themselves lonely.

'And there is a great subconscious wish just to go on being a mother with more children.'

Daily Mail, 11 February 1971

FEMAIL: in a high spending mood

The woman who has everything

ASSUMING YOU HAVE £2,523 TO SPEND

IN TODAY'S consumer-conscious society, women are under ever-increasing pressure from the persuaders of industry to buy the labour savers and luxuries of modern life—to have everything, in fact.

Most women, as soon as they acquire one thing, begin thinking of the next item they would like to buy.

Femail wondered just how much it would cost to have everything.

VIVIEN HISLOP

Daily Mail Home Editor

has chosen what she thinks are the most sought-after essentials and luxuries—assuming you have central heating, furniture and the kitchen sink. The cost? £2,523·06. And that's allowing in the main for middle-of-the-range prices.

No list like this can ever be complete, of course. We are bound to have left out some items that some women consider absolutely necessary. Others will think that a few of our choices are frivolous.

See what you think. In all cases the prices given are those recommended by the manufacturer.

Drawings : KEN BAKER

SUPER 'Space Helmet' portable TV to hang up anywhere. Spherical case is glossy white and black with dark-tinted screen. Also in orange. Videosphere 3240 by Nivico. £75 at Harrods.

Picture : Jim Gray

IN THE KITCHEN

THE BILL £1,023.51

NO NEED to hold can or handle with the wall-fixed electric can opener by Philips. Stops automatically when can is opened. Price, £6·25.

☐ Streamlined, fully-automatic washing machine, white stove enamelled with stainless-steel trim. Front loading, it washes, rinses and spin-dries a 9lb. load. The Hotpoint 1600 costs £129·09.

VERSATILE food mixer with bowl, whisks and 12 attachments, including mincer, potato peeler and bean slicer. The Kenwood Chef, with extras, costs £91·45.

☐ Powerful waste disposer, with reversing facilities and safety cut-out. The Maxymatic de Luxe by Bell Home Appliances, £61·66.

ELECTRICALLY-heated air purifier cuts condensation, circulates clean, filtered air (warm in winter, cool in summer) even when windows are shut. The Skyport de Luxe, by Aircomfort Products, £43·40.

☐ The Creda Autoclean has a capacious oven that cleans itself silently and efficiently by electricity while you shop or sleep. With colour-coded controls, high-level grill, warming drawer, £129.

WHITE steam/dry iron that jets a fine spray just where you need it. The Shot-of-Steam iron, by Sunbeam, £9·60.

☐ Versatile stainless steel, wall-hung or table-top grill 15in. high, 21in. wide, will spit-roast poultry and joints, yet folds to 4½in. deep. The GEC/Cannon Foldaway Rotisserie has grill with kebab attachment, £48·51.

TRIM two-star refrigerator with automatic defrosting, 6·1 cu. ft. capacity, with white and dark-blue interior. By Kelvinator, £57·60.

MULTI - PURPOSE, push - button electric sharpener white/grey finish gives a razor-sharp edge to your knives and scissors, screwdrivers, etc. To adjust, twist head section to position indicated by appropriate symbol. By Philips. £5·65.

SMART, infra-red grill, in scarlet and black, for fast steak (90 seconds), toasted sandwiches (2 minutes), etc. By Rima, £12·99.

EFFICIENT, 32in. wide, stainless steel ducted cooker hood by Scholtes absorbs kitchen grease and smells when cooking. The 7080 costs £63·97.

☐ Smart, built-in dishwasher deals quietly and efficiently with the equivalent of eight place settings. The Colston Aristocrat £124·00.

CHOOSE the shade of toast you prefer on Hoovers' de luxe chrome/white toaster, £9·57.

☐ Ultra-safe electric kettle in chrome, boils three pints of water in two minutes, then automatically cuts out. By Russell Hobbs, £9·60.

☐ All-white, chest-model freezer, 13 cu. ft. capacity, with two storage baskets. By Tricity. £120.

COMPACT water softener, only 22in. by 6in., 200 gallons capacity, the Minisoft costs £88 installed.

☐ Power-driven carving knife, slices and shreds expertly with minimum effort. Ronson Electric Carving Knife costs £13·17.

AROUND THE HOUSE

THE BILL £731·34

☐ Chic, new, three-waveband transistor in smartly ribbed, moulded case 11½in. by 8in. Light grey or orange. The Fidelity RAD 22 costs £14.

RECHARGEABLE, automatic toothbrush, white with three detachable brushes in bright colours. By Ronson, price £9·64.

☐ Cylinder cleaner with powerful suction, automatic flex winder, whistle stop signal when dust bag is full. The Electrolux Automatic 310 costs £43·15.

VARY the light level in your living - room according to your mood with dimmer controls. Neat white Supaswitch SS300 fitting controls 300 watts, costs £6·81.

☐ Plug-in heated trolley takes complete dinner party dishes, plates, casseroles — for eight. The Ekco Hostess Royale has a four-heater compartment on top. Price £59·95.

NEAT 'memory bank' cassette tape recorder for taping mesages, recipes, shopping lists and memos to yourself or the family. By Philco Ford, price £23·28.

☐ Tea on tap first thing in the morning with an automatic teamaker which combines clock and bed side light, all controlled by a single switch. The Goblin Teasmade 835 costs £33·08.

☐ CINE camera, uses Super 8 film

stock. The new Bolex 233 Compact costs £63·59.

CINE projector with dual gate takes standard and Super 8 . . . geared to add sound to your reels. The Eumig S712D with zoom projection lens, two running speeds and automatic threading costs £115·51.

SLEEK, white, electric automatic sewing machine with smooth sculptured lines and simple controls (new back stitch, special stitch for stretch fabrics, embroidery stitches etc. all shown on a single knob). Necchi Lydia Mk 2. Cost £94.

SMOOTH hi - fi system — integrated stereo record deck/ amplifier/VHF radio in black and white moulded Perspex plus twin white 10-inch diameter glass fibre speakers. Compacta by Sykes and Hirsch. £228.

ELECTRIC floor polisher in sage green/ivory with three counter-rotating brushes for mobility and big coverage. The 322 by Electrolux costs £40·33.

SUPER LUXURIES

THE BILL £713·57

☐ Electric bath controls run your bath before you get up. Electrically operated valves (hot and cold) £7·50 each, by Damfoss; thermostatic hot and cold mixer valve (for 30 gallon bath at pre-selected temperature in six minutes) £50, by Walker Crosweller. Total, installed, £78.

COLOUR TV with 22in. tube in teak case faced with white. By GEC/Sobell. £271.

☐ Electronic door controls for peace of mind. Sentrymatic porter system offers two-way communication with callers and automatically opens door, £33·50.

ELECTRICALLY driven Powercord operates curtains by remote contol, while you laze in bed. Powercord by 505 Manufacturing Co. £31·07.

☐ Compact 3ft. square sauna, in scorched Finnish pine. The 'Minifinn' by Norpe Saunas of Finland costs £199 cash with order £225 (delivered).

BEAUTY

THE BILL, £54·64

☐ Pretty, pink - finish, salon-style hairdryer on adjustable, telescopic floor stand. By Moulinex, £9·75 complete.

ULTRA - VIOLET sun-lamp, with built-in timer which sets for up to eight minutes, so you can't overcook. The modern-styled, floor standing Baroness de Luxe, by Valor Ironcrete, has white finish with adjustable head. Price £18·99.

☐ Electric hair curlers that moisturise and condi-

tion your hair while it sets. The Carmen Conditioning Curl Set, £15·95.

FOR pampering your face, a facial sauna that bathes your skin in a fine mist and cleanses your pores. Lady Schick, by Carmen, £9·95.

And here, Vivien Hislop picks her top 12

EVERY woman has her own priorities, her own very personal reasons for what she wants and doesn't want, linked to her family's way of life . so her list may be longer, or shorter, than mine.

My top 12 would be cooker, refrigerator, washing machine, cleaner, transistor, colour TV, cine, stereo, food mixer, sewing machine, waste disposer, and cooker hood. But that's not to say I wouldn't like my bath run for me.

1972

Fair Shares

During the 1960s and early '70s legislation had given a wife more rights in terms of a share of the family's assets when a marriage broke up so that although divorce frequently brought financial hardship for both partners, especially where children were involved, the burden fell less on the wife with children than it had done in the past. However the same rules did not apply to common-law wives. A woman living with a man where he had ownership or tenancy of the property could be evicted by him and maintenance need only be given for any children of the relationship once paternity was proved.

By 1972 it was not an unusual occurrence for a couple to set up home together without getting married. In fact it had almost become a regular thing for couples to live together before making the commitment to marry. Sometimes couples decided to live together with no intention of ever getting married, others decided to live together until they had or decided to have children.

A case in 1972 reported in the *Daily Mail* illustrated clearly the position of a woman living with a man without the legal benefits of marriage. The woman, whom the judge described as 'a mistress' (her lover was described simply as a man), was granted a right to a share in the home they had built together. An initial court case decided that she was entitled to a twelfth share of the property and on appeal the percentage was increased to a third but not the half she had claimed and to which she would have had a right had they been married.

ABOVE: An all-woman production line.
BELOW: Nannies from the Princess Christian Training College wheeling their charges. The college which took in unwanted babies was closing as better contraception, easier abortion and a more tolerant climate for unmarried mothers had combined to reduce the numbers of unwanted children available.

1972 POSTSCRIPTS

March – The US Senate passed an Equal Rights Amendment to the Constitution making it against the law to discriminate against a person on the grounds of sex.

• The British government warned employers to make moves towards bringing women's pay into line with men's ready for equal pay in 1976 or they would bring in interim legislation to give women 90 per cent of men's pay by January 1974.

September – At the Munich Olympics Olga Korbut won three gold medals and one silver and captured the affection of the crowds in a Gymnastics competition where the USSR and East Germany and their 'perfectly formed' and trained gymnasts won every medal except one.

TOP PILL 'RISKS'

A table of women who should not use the Pill is given in a report published today for family doctors.

The young wife who has yet to start her family and the woman over 40 head the list as the type for whom the oral contraceptive is least advisable.

The report, the first of its kind to guide GPs on the groups of patients who could suffer unnecessary risk from the drug despite government reassurances on its relative safety, is prepared by Social Technology Associates of Manchester, and appears in the Journal of the Royal College of General Practitioners.

The report assesses the present death rate from blood clotting and unwanted pregnancy among women on the existing pill – a combination of the hormones oestrogen and progestogen – as 13 a year.

Daily Mail, 6 March 1972

'Now we're just chars and skivvies'

IT was a doctor, a visiting GP with more experience than tact, who first told the village midwife exactly how he saw her role today.

'You people,' he said, 'are the chars and skivvies of the Health Service. You are the cleaning women for the hospitals.'

He had not intended to be rude—just realistic.

And after a few moments thought, the midwife — a woman with more than ten years service as a district nurse in one of the more rural areas of Cheshire—decided that he had summed up her situation fairly accurately.

'That doctor,' she says, 'is basically right. We midwives are the losers all the way round. That's obvious.

'These days we do everything except the job we enjoy most—delivering babies.

'There was a time, a year or so

ONE OF BRITAIN'S MIDWIVES TALKS TO SHELLEY ROHDE

ago, when I felt very bad about it. But I've adjusted now.

'The trouble is that I can't see the young midwives, the students training now, wanting to come into the districts to take over when we older ones retire.

'They know they will miss out. They know that the chances of a home confinement are extremely slight.

'The last baby I delivered was in February, and some of my colleagues haven't had a delivery for over a year. It's very disappointing.

'And if it's disappointing for me, after all these years, how much more so will it be for the youngsters, who will never get the exhilaration and excitement of a home birth?'

The disappointment of Britain's midwives was mentioned fleetingly in the review of hospital services published the other day by the Department of Health—rather as if it were an irritating side-effect of increased efficiency.

Now, nearly nine out of every ten babies are born in hospital. Ten years ago one in three was born at home.

'Today,' says the Cheshire midwife, 'the big maternity wards are like sausage machines.

'The hospital midwives are coping with so many patients that there is simply no such thing as a bedside manner or personal attention.

Sad

'When I have to visit our nearest hospital I almost walk around with my eyes shut. I can't bear to see what things have come to.

'But then I have to remind myself that if all this means a baby saved and a healthy mother,

Midwife to base : Two-way radios were issued to some midwives a few years ago. Now, the call seldom comes . . .

6 These days we do everything except the job we enjoy most—delivering babies 9

then it is all worthwhile.

'Soon, it seems, they will have nine-to-five maternity wards, with inductions for breakfast, and birth before tea.

'I know that's called efficiency, but I personally find it awfully sad.

'But then I'm an old-fashioned midwife. I loved delivering babies. I never lost the thrill of helping a new life into the world.

'Now we are learning to compensate with thoughtful post- and ante-natal care. That's really our job now, and

it's almost as important as the delivery.

'Well, very important, anyway.

'So often, I'll go to see a young mother and she'll ask me something and say, "Sorry to bother you, but they didn't have time to tell me in hospital."

'I concentrate on building up a personal relationship with the mother, in giving what she needs most — sympathy, understanding, and personal care.

'And you can tell how

welcome we are by the way they greet us, almost literally with open arms.

'Today, we have to find our job satisfaction in that. We know we are not going to get the deliveries any more, so it's no good crying about it.

'We just have to tell ourselves that it's all for the best, and concentrate on doing what is left of the job to the very extent of our ability.

'You tell yourself that, even if you are the loser, it all results in healthier mothers and healthier babies . . . physically, of course.

'Their mental state is quite another matter. But then, you can't have everything.'

Beauty with a capital E

THE Vitamin E craze currently sweeping America shows signs of catching on here.

In the past year, sales of Vitamin E capsules have trebled in the United States, and health shops have been running out of supplies.

The latest health fad? Hardly, since beauty-conscious women aren't swallowing their capsules — they've been cutting them open to rub the oil into their skin.

Here's why Vitamin E is the latest beauty treatment.

A recent study was made of hundreds of people applying Alpha-Tocopherol (pure Vitamin E) on severe burns, wounds, and cuts.

Not only did their wounds heal rapidly, but there was only an

infinitesimal trace of scarring.

Equal enthusiasm came from women using pure Vitamin E to eliminate stretch marks, acne pits, vaccination marks and severe sunburn.

Last, though certainly not least, the oil helped to prevent lines and wrinkles if used regularly.

Pure Vitamin E, a thick oil, is now available at chemists and health food stores in Britain at £1·55 a half-ounce.

There is also a body lotion at 99p, skin cream at £1·65, and shampoo at 99p. All contain Vitamin E.

ALIX KIRSTA

1973

Entering the Establishment

Part of the work of the Women's Liberation Movement was challenging what the press continually referred to as 'the last bastions of male supremacy'. And there were many, some of them trivial, some of them in areas which wielded power and authority over society. Some bars such as El Vino's Wine Bar, a favourite haunt of Fleet Street journalists, banned entry to women. 'Gentlemen's clubs', which were meeting places for directors of businesses, financial institutions, high-ranking Civil Servants and politicians, denied membership to women, only allowing them to enter the club premises when accompanied by a male member. In these clubs men met and talked, and influenced direction and policy in many areas of British life.

One major financial institution which removed its final barriers to women in 1973 was the Stock Exchange. Since its foundation women had been excluded from trading on the 'floor' of the Stock Exchange building. Although there were a number of women working as stock brokers the governors of the Stock Exchange always maintained that the hectic pace and stress of work on the 'floor' would be too much for a woman, that they needed to be protected from such harsh and rough conditions. In February 1973 several women, amid much media attention, took to the floor of the Stock Exchange as traders.

While the Stock Exchange and men's clubs were very obvious places which excluded women from the Establishment which ran Britain there were other things which made it, and still make it, difficult for women to be part of it. Parliamentary hours, set to allow those in the legal profession to work by day and legislate in the evenings and nights, do not suit most women with a family. The selection process for candidates still frequently favours men as they appear to be a safer bet – no one in the electorate is likely to object to them simply because they are a man. The whole system of parliamentary 'debate', the shouting, abuse and insults MPs hurl at one another, is not something which appeals to many women. All these factors accounted for the abysmally low percentage of women MPs in the 1970s, and on into the '80s and '90s.

In business, too, women, especially those with children, were still expected to leave work to bring up children, and although most women who did so planned to return to work when their children were older there were no allowances given for taking time out to have a family. In 1973 no company or institution even paid lip service to the idea of a career break. Even in the Civil Service part-time workers could only work on the lowest grade.

![One of the three women allowed on to the Stock Exchange floor in March 1973.]

ABOVE: *One of the three women allowed on to the Stock Exchange floor in March 1973.*
BELOW: *Flexible working hours in offices was introduced in the early 1970s. Members of a City insurance company are pictured here clocking in.*

1973 POSTSCRIPTS

September – A report entitled *Equal Opportunities for Men and Women* proposed the setting up of an Equal Opportunities Commission which would have legal backing to ensure that neither sex could be discriminated against in employment, training or education.

• It was recommended in a government report that mothers bringing up children on their own should be given a weekly cash allowance which could also be given to fathers in the same position.

Femail

ADVERTISEMENTS like these are poignant reminders of the disruption a wife and mother often leaves behind her when she walks out. In such times of crisis most fathers succeed in bringing some order out of chaos. How do they do it ? *Femail* spoke to three men who suddenly found themselves in the role of father and mother....

What really happens after a mother says 'I quit'

BY
PATRICIA JACKSON

CHRIS is 43. A representative for a clothing firm, he spends part of the week away from home.

He and his teenage daughter and nine-year-old son were putting up the Christmas decorations a year ago when his wife announced she was leaving for good.

'We were absolutely stunned. She'd packed her belongings and gone within a couple of hours. I did know that she had had the odd affair, and never thought for a minute that this one was different from the rest.

'I believed she loved the kids too much to do it, but she told me they were old enough to manage without her any more.

'Talk about learning to cope the hard way. Oh, I could make a scratch meal — there was never any danger of us starving. It was the business of learning the routine job of running the home that almost swamped me.

Unfair

'My daughter took it well and I'm proud of the way she tries to take her mother's place. She gets up at six to do the washing and hang it out before going to school ; she irons and helps to keep the place tidy.

'I sometimes think it isn't fair to expect her to do so much—she should be out enjoying herself. If you can't be free from care at 15, when can you be ?'

His daughter says she doesn't mind the extra work : 'Quite honestly, although I love my mother things are better now she's gone. We seem more of a family than we have done for a long time.

'We don't have awful rows any more and really I don't do much because my Dad is very capable. He tries out all sorts of recipes and makes some super food. I like baking so we manage pretty well. Sometimes I worry because he looks so tired.'

Chris's major problem was the emotional blow to his son, James.

'For the first few weeks, he didn't seem to care what was going on. He'd speak when you spoke to him, yet all the time it was as if he were crying inside.

'He'd just sit, lost in his thoughts, and I knew he was wondering how his mother could have left him. It used to break me up to look at him.

'Thank goodness he's resilient. I had a straight talk to him. "Look," I said, "she's not dead, she still loves you and you can see her as often as you like. What we've got to do is manage without her and make some plans."

'Well, I don't know if it helped, but he's certainly doing well at school and we're great companions and do all sorts of things together we never seemed to have time for before.

'It's been a bit like being a mouse on a treadmill this past year. It's been a hell of a struggle but we're coming out of it pretty well.'

'Now we are very content'

HARRY is 30. A schoolteacher, he never had to face the problem of who would look after five-year-old Nicholas after. his wife left three years ago.

'My married sister was wonderful. She'd come and find the house in a mess and without saying a word, she would get going and sort it all out.

'If Nicholas or I were ill, she'd take over and I sometimes used to think she must be neglecting her own family to make sure we were all right.

'Anyway, about nine months ago I met Jean. She'd been married, but had no children. I'd always told myself I didn't want to get involved permanently with another woman, but, of course, I did.

'I was surprised she could feel the same about me—my ego took a great knock when my wife left me, but she does.

'When we got married last summer, everything seemed set for a happy ending. She and Nicholas have become fond of each other . . . my sister is delighted for us . . . we are very content.

'It's my ex-wife who plays me up over Nicholas. She keeps telling him he has to call the fellow she lives with "Daddy." The boy comes home very upset and once when I asked what was the matter, he burst into tears and said his Mummy had told him to call me "Uncle Harry."

'In a way, I pity her. How can she do that to her own son ?'

'I'd still have her back'

JOHN is 36. A partner in a reasonably successful firm of suburban architects, he was left to bring up two young daughters, now five and seven :

'When my wife left two years ago, I tried to muddle along on my own, working and running the home. I had a woman in to do the cleaning and the girls were shunted about between relatives and friends during the day.

'Everyone was kind, but it was an unrealistic state of affairs and I felt I was putting on people all the time.

'There were the times when Sarah and Jane had measles and I'd be at my wits end trying to divide myself between them and the office.

'The worst time was when they asked for their mother in the night. That's still a nightmare.

'Eventually, I talked things over with my parents who had just retired and bought a bungalow about 20 miles away from where we lived. They were marvellous, and insisted that the best thing was for me to sell up and move in.

'That took a lot of the strain away, but it meant extra work for my parents.

'They cooked meals for us, made beds, looked after the girls when I was away on business and somehow even seemed to anticipate what needed doing.

'They never complained, though, and I'm afraid I was the ratty one. We seemed to be living on top of one another.

'Anyway, we solved that by having a couple of extra rooms built on to the bungalow and things are easier now. My parents are getting old and deserve a little peace and quiet, but I'm afraid they don't get much because my girls are a lively pair and I'm very grateful for that because they have come out of it all so *normal*.

Misery

' "Look, lad," my Dad once said to me, "having them here has given your mother and I a lot more to think about than drawing our old age pension, so stop worrying."

'Six months ago my ex-wife started to ring me at the office. Now she rings almost every day. She keeps breaking down—I know she's miserable without the children.

'Once she said she regretted leaving us—"I wish I'd simply had an affair and got it out of my system," she said. The awful waste of it shocks me and I think, even now, I'd have her back and try again.'

A sauce that is above suspicion

A PURITANICAL streak arises in the average Briton when it comes to jazzing up food.

A cloaking of sauce, however subtle, arouses suspicion about the quality of the basic food underneath.

We even took the Latin-derived word 'sauce' and made it mean something impudent, frivolous and impertinent. The French despair of us, saying England has 360 religions and only one sauce : in France it is said to be the other way about.

Our most famed sauce is probably mint sauce . . . 'an occasion for humour,' says French chef and writer Raymond Oliver who owns the Grand Vefour restaurant in Paris.

Bitter

Mint sauce, so they say, came into being because Elizabeth I's ministers wanted sheep kept for their wool, not for feeding the queen's subjects.

An edict went out forbidding the eating of lamb or mutton except with a bitter

Herrings . . . traditionally served with a mustard sauce.   *Sketch: Liz Gill.*

herb sauce. Mint was found by Tudor gourmets to be the least bitter and still we add this cold vinegar concoction to our hot roast meat.

Although such decrees are unlikely even in the present austerity times high food prices mean we should make the most of our meats and use all the saucery we can to pep up cheaper cuts and stretch expensive joints.

Caper sauce for lamb or mutton is a simple variation on the parent English white sauce, that can be flavoured savoury or sweet as required.

The basic is a blend of 1oz. flour in 1oz. melted butter in a pan with about ½ pint water or milk (or a mixture of both), stirred in over a low heat till thick and smooth. Simmer for ten minutes, then add seasonings and flavourings.

Blend

For caper sauce, add one tablespoon capers to every ½ pint of sauce ; chop any that are large.

Adding wine to meat or game juices to create a sauce was as common among the British once as it is still with the French. For game, venison, or duck, Port Wine Sauce is easily made. Blend ¼ pint gravy from the meat ; 1 glass port, 1 teaspoon redcurrant jelly and ½ teaspoon lemon juice in a small pan and simmer for a few minutes.

Apple sauce is cold comfort with roast pork, instead try this old recipe for a hot spicy Currant Sauce. Gently simmer of pinch of mace, some black peppercorns, 1 or 2 chillies, and a small onion in ½ pint water for about 30 minutes. Strain and add 2oz. currants or sultanas to the hot liquid with enough crumbled slices of stale bread or breadcrumbs so that it boils up to a thick pulp. Add a glass of sweet white wine, a little nutmeg and about 1oz. butter. Bring to the boil again and serve hot.

Rind

With so many roasts in the national diet, it was inevitable sauces were discovered to go with cold meat.

Cumberland sauce is one which has survived widely. Boil two wine glasses red wine until reduced to half in volume. Add ½lb. redcurrant jelly, grated rind and juice of one orange and one lemon.

Stir over a low heat until the jelly has melted. Blend one rounded teaspoon cornflour with one tablespoon water till smooth ; stir into sauce. Bring to simmering point and cook gently for five minutes until slightly thickened. Sweeten to taste.

CAROL WRIGHT

1974

Free Family Planning for All

From the beginning of April 1974 family planning advice and contraceptives were free on the National Health Service. For several years the government had been campaigning actively to encourage the use of contraception, especially among young people of both sexes not ready to carry the responsibility of parenthood. Sex education in schools also included information and discussion about contraception. But until 1974 anyone requiring contraceptive advice had to go to a special family planning clinic, which could be funded by the local authority. After that date an ordinary GP could dispense contraceptive advice and any prescriptions were free of the standard prescription charges.

The move towards more freely available birth control was not without controversy. There was debate about whether it put pressure on young people, especially young girls, to start on sexual relationships before they were emotionally mature enough. There was also a great deal of argument as to whether doctors should be able to prescribe the Pill to girls under the legal age of consent.

However the biggest controversy over birth control in 1974 was caused by a speech by Sir Keith Joseph, the Shadow Home Secretary. His call for better birth control amongst the poor recalled the eugenicists of the pre-Second World War period. He said, 'The balance of our population, our human stock is threatened by the rising proportion of children born to mothers least fit to bring them up . . .' He was referring to a growth in the figures for births to young unmarried girls from the poorer sectors of society.

ABOVE: A militant women's liberation activist in Japan.
BELOW: The 'pregnant man' poster which caused great controversy when it was first introduced.

The Health Education Council

Would you be more careful if it was you that got pregnant?

Contraception is one of the facts of life.
Anyone married or single can get advice on contraception from the Family Planning Association.
Margaret Pyke House, 25-35 Mortimer Street, London W1 N 8BQ. Tel. 01-636 9135.

1974 POSTSCRIPTS

May – In the USA the Dalkon Shield contraceptive was taken off the market amid fears that it had caused infections, sterility and even death amongst its users. It remained in use in Britain although it was not a very popular form of contraception.

November – Helen Morgan, newly crowned Miss World, resigned when she feared that she would be named in a divorce case. The rules stated that only unmarried women were eligible as contestants and the implication was that they were virgins.

WOMEN GET THEIR CHARTER
Equal jobs for girls – and boys who want to work as midwives.

Women will be guaranteed equal treatment in almost every walk of life under plans announced by the Home Secretary, Mr Roy Jenkins, yesterday.

Anyone who refuses a woman a job or a mortgage or a pint of beer just because she is a woman will face legal action.

And so will anyone who refuses to employ a man as a secretary just because he is a man. . . .

The rules would break some old barriers. Men would be able to work as midwives and women prison officers could be recruited for men's jails.

But there would be some exceptions. The Army won't have to employ dolly girls in the front line and the Church won't have to ordain women priests.

Daily Mail, 7 September 1974

Daily Mail, Tuesday, June 10, 1975

Femail

Is this the price we have to pay for our liberation..?

Special report

by June Tarlin

WOMEN, according to many medical researchers, are beginning to pay the price of their liberation — increasing ill-health, stress and loss of sex drive and fertility.

They are smoking more, drinking more, attempting suicide more, taking more pills; and the incidence of heart disease, cancer and VD is rising.

Professor Ivor H. Mills, whose team of researchers at Addenbrooke New Hospital, Cambridge, has been studying the problem for eight years, says : 'My view is that women are gradually cracking up under social, sexual and business pressures. At present they seem biologically less able to withstand these pressures than men.'

Or, as Dr Max Glatt, who runs an alcohol and drugs dependence unit at St Bernard's Hospital, Southall, Middlesex, puts it : 'Give women enough rope and they'll hang themselves quicker than men.'

Boost

Professor Mills explained that the number of women over 16 going out to work has risen by 27 per cent. in the past ten years. And with increasing economic problems, the rate is rising—particularly among women who also have to look after a home and family.

'In many cases, women like this take a job for the money, then become compulsively interested in it, or the ego boost they get from it,' he added.

'Our researches have shown that women like this tend to subject themselves to more pressure than they need. They become compulsive nibblers between meals, and begin to worry about their weight. They find it difficult to sleep, so begin taking pills.

'All this means increased stress in the office and in the home, where there tends to be more irritability and conflict.'

Desperate

'If women push themselves too hard, their personalities — and even their hormone balance — changes. The result is a drop in sex drive and fertility.

'Fertility rates are dropping dramatically, and I am convinced this isn't due only to the pill.'

The birth rate dropped from 18·6 per thousand women in 1964, to 15·8 in 1971. But it went down to 14·4 in 1972, and was 12·7 last year.

'It is dropping so fast that our population is no longer replacing itself,' said Professor Mills. 'Yet our infertility clinics are swamped with desperate women.'

Professor Mills also points out that with the age of puberty having dropped to around 12, pressure is now put on girls at a much earlier age.

There's the sexual pressure of feeling that they are expected to give in to their boy friends, coupled with a decrease in parental control, guidance and communication.

The change in morals and codes of conduct have moved so fast that many parents can no longer control or even understand their children.

And with more marriages breaking up, vast numbers of children are being left to develop through the most crucial years of their lives in the disturbed and insecure environment of shifting social sands.

One of the most potentially dangerous problems the professor has encountered among teenage girls is slimming. Excessive dieting, he says, can lead to menstruation troubles and hormone imbalance that can cause serious problems later.

An interesting factor

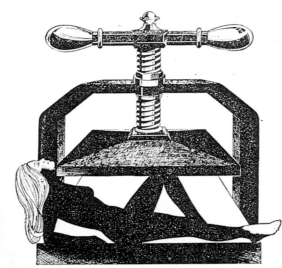

Illustration : DUNCAN MIL

emerged from the Cambridge hospital's studies of teenage slimming — the link between slimming and *studying*.

Professor Mills says: 'At first, we thought the obsession with slimming was because the girls were at a figure-conscious age. But our graphs show a definite link between girls studying for exams and starving themselves.'

Suicide

'The answer might lie in the fact that the brain is clearer after a few days without food and the girls subconsciously become aware of this.'

Also worrying are the increasing attempted suicide rates in women. Suicide attempts by girls under 20 have increased five fold in the past ten years. Attempts by those over 30 have gone up two or three times.

Sexual liberation is taking its toll in rising VD rates among women and, some doctors say, in cancer rates.

The female VD rate used to be half the men's rate. Now it's about two-thirds.

And it is now believed there is a link between cancer of the cervix and promiscuity.

Cancer of the cervix rates are rising, though this can partly be explained by earlier detection because of women taking cervical smears.

But Mr Stanley Way, surgeon at Queen Elizabeth Hospital, Gateshead, and a lecturer at Newcastle University, says : 'As a result of many years of research in my department I can categorically state that one of the causes of cancer of the cervix is sexual intercourse in a promiscuous fashion.

'The more promiscuous a woman is, the more likely she is to succumb to this disease.'

Smoking

Cancer of the lung among women also is increasing.

A spokesman for the Cancer Research Campaign told me : 'The latest figures we have—for 1971—show that male deaths outnumber female deaths by around 7-1. But there is evidence that the gap is narrowing by around 5 per cent. a year. This is clearly due to the increase in smoking by women.'

So, too, is the gap narrowing between men and women suffering fatal heart attacks in the forties and fifties.

A spokeswoman for the Chest and Heart Foundation says : 'It is generally accepted that the incidence of heart attacks in women has increased in the past ten years.'

The number of men aged between 45-49 who died from heart attacks rose by 12·11 per cent. during 1962-72 — while the figure for women increased by 15 per cent.

In 1962, deaths by women of

all ages from heart attacks totalled 52,000. In 1972 the figure was 64,204.

The increase in female drinking is another sign of the stress they are suffering.

Mr Derek Rutherford, Director of the National Council on Alcoholism, is particularly worried about the increase in hard drinking by teenage girls.

'Boys tend to be beer drinkers,' he points out. 'But girls start on spirits or wines at an early age and are more likely to become addicted to alcohol.'

Misuse

Dr Max Glatt feels that the reasons for increased female drinking is a combination of starting at an earlier age, drink easier to come by from supermarkets, a changed social climate in that the heavy female drinker isn't so much frowned upon, and the pressures of trying to do a job and run a home.

But he, along with other doctors to whom I spoke, agreed many women take to drink because they feel frustrated and unfulfilled by having to stay at home when other women are able to take up a career.

Doctor Glatt suggested that women tend to misuse drugs more than men. They are more ready to take pills for sleeping or for slimming, for example.

He says: 'Under stress, men have traditionally taken to drink, and women to pills. Now women are taking to both drink and pills.'

How is it all going to end?

Professor Mills sums up: 'Unless women ease up, there are going to be disastrous consequences for their health and the general stability of society.'

The cool eye for business

IT STARTED AS A HOBBY

ONE woman who has successfully turned a love of cooking and a large country kitchen into a £1,000 - a - month turnover business selling deep - frozen specialist dishes to food shops and restaurants, is Jenny Allday.

Mrs Allday, a 42-year-old widow with three children, started Country Cooks four years ago. Now she employs two girls full-time and a neighbour part-time, producing more than 40 dishes.

'I get a lot of women writing for advice on starting a similar business,' she said. 'There's no lack of part-time offers of help from widows and women whose husbands are away a lot. But I don't recommend it for a woman

Mrs Allday shops big at Smithfield

with a husband around. You may find yourself having to skin 40 hares the farmer has brought, just when you have planned a peaceful evening.'

The advantages are being your own boss, working from home and helping to pay for its upkeep and always being able to experiment with new dishes.

'You have to be prepared to work very hard — till 4 a.m.

if there's a rush order. It's also tiring, when starting the business, going from shop to shop trying to create an interest with your samples.

'The idea for the business grew out of the big cook-ups I used to do before the school holidays began. I loaded up the freezer so I could spend more time with the children. The business has now outgrown the family freezer.'

Discovering how to pack a deep freeze without wasting space was one of the most important things Jenny had to learn. Baskets are used throughout the chest-type freezers, and old onion nets segregate wrapped pheasants and different types of vegetable packs.

Square, shallow containers are the most space-saving. Sauces and soups are never frozen in more than 1 pint quantities, unmoulded, wrapped in polythene and stacked like bricks.

'I'm told by business experts I cannot make money from selling such a variety of dishes, but I change the list twice a year. People don't want desserts or grand food ; my most expensive dish is chicken breasts at 95p a portion.

'Most people seem to buy my products to cope with the emergencies of people dropping in unexpectedly, for weekend guests, or for when they return from a holiday.'

Carol Wright

1975

Flares, Hotpants and Punk

Flares, hotpants, punks, platform soles, midi skirts, trouser suits, Laura Ashley designs, jogging suits, military styles, work wear and of course denim jeans were just part of the multiplicity of styles in the 1970s. The '70s seemed to mark the beginnings of more rapidly changing clothes styles, as well as a wider range of styles being worn by any one individual. Advertisers created a market for fashion by promoting changes and crazes. This was part of a whole movement towards consumer goods of every description but the method was always the same: change or update the product and then persuade the consumer that they needed the latest version.

Unisex fashions, emphasized by men growing their hair longer, were a strong feature of the early 1970s. In fact men became increasingly concerned over how they dressed and how they looked and smelled, promoting a huge growth in the range of skin and body-care products for men. While men grew more aware of how they looked many women, bolstered by the feminist movement, refused to spend hours shopping, dressing and making up just to please a man.

Punk fashions which, for both men and women seemed deliberately to make the human form ugly but successfully challenged ideas of how people should look, was a fashion which was developed on the streets and by the promoters and performers of punk music. The fashion industry took up, copied and refined punk fashion.

During the seventies the first Page Three Girls began to appear in national newspapers. This exploitation of women was a strange paradox to the growing women's movement. Nudity, promoted by shows like *Hair* and *Oh, Calcutta!* was classed as a 'good thing'. But the most nude bodies anyone ever saw were those of young women in the tabloid press or selling some product. There were plenty of images of women around to make men and women believe that all women could look like these media images.

Nevertheless there were important spin-offs from a growing concern with body image in the late 1970s. While dieting came to rule some women's lives people became more aware of what was a healthy diet. Better, more wholesome nutrition and the fact that more and more women were taking up exercise would in the future have a beneficial effect on the general health of women. Women more than men embraced more wholeheartedly the advice and education about a healthy lifestyle.

ABOVE: The Sex Discrimination Act became law on 29 December and these women journalists, (L to R) Maggie Brittain, Sue Rose, Laura Kaufman and Francesca Hare tried to be served a drink at the bar of El Vino which clung to its men-only tradition and refused them.
BELOW: An outfit which combines many of the fashion ideas of the early 1970s – denim jeans, floral and geometric patterns, PVC fabric on the shirt collar and cuffs, hand jewellery and fancy belt.

1975 POSTSCRIPTS

● The year was designated International Women's Year by the United Nations with a view to promoting women's rights and position and campaigning on issues concerning women throughout the world.

● The Employment Protection Act was passed giving women the right to maternity leave with some pay and for their job to be held open for 29 weeks after the birth.

February – Margaret Thatcher, described as the wife of a wealthy businessman and mother of twins, was elected leader of the Conservative Party.

May – The internationally acclaimed sculptor Dame Barbara Hepworth died in a fire at her studio.

GOOD GOD, SIR! A Woman at the Carlton?

The Carlton Club, male bastion of the Tory Party, was last night faced with the greatest dilemma in its 140-year-old history.

For members of the exclusive club in St James's Street, London must now decide whether to break with tradition and allow Mrs Thatcher to join.

In the past every Conservative leader has been invited to join if he was not already a member. But to offer membership to a *woman* – the very prospect set some members shifting uncomfortably in their leather-studded armchairs, while other traditionalists sought comfort in large gulps from even larger brandies.

Women considered it a breakthrough when, in 1963, they were first allowed into the Carlton as guests of members.
Daily Mail, 12 February 1975

Femail

Getting round the law!

The advertisement that started like this

IT IS not so much what you say—it's the way that you say it.

Advertisers, in search of their elusive ideal requirement, are finding that a tongue-in-cheek approach can land the staff they want when they are not supposed to discriminate between the sexes.

Managing director Colin Hooton, for instance, got almost exactly what he wanted — an attractive mini-skirted receptionist. He advertised for one without actually breaking the Sex Discrimination Act.

His advertisement in an evening newspaper simply said what he could *not* do . . . : 'What we really wanted was a mini-skirted blue-eyed blonde but under the Sex Discrimination Act we cannot advertise for her. So we'll just say that we require a receptionist.'

The advertisement, quite within the bounds of the law, brought 60 replies. None of them were from men.

Mr Hooton, of Repete Publicity, Wellingborough, Northamptonshire, interviewed about 20 applicants and appointed 17-year-old Deborah Farden.

Absurdity

If there was any snag it was only that she isn't a blonde.

Mr Hooton said : 'People are having to word advertisements carefully to comply with the Act and, at the same time, get what they want. It's absurdity gone mad.

'In our case nobody took our advertisement frivolously and we made it clear what we wanted. We had serious applications from 17-year-olds t h r o u g h to middle-aged women. Significantly, no men applied.'

What does 17-year-old Debbie, t h e successful applicant, have to say ? :

'I think the new Act has advantages but it seems ridiculous when both sexes can apply for jobs which are obviously designed for a man or for a woman.'

Eton College were less fortunate. They popped an advert in the Slough and Windsor Express u n d e r 'Person Wanted' seeking a dining room assistant to 'share a room with another lady.' Most of the inquiries came from men.

The BBC's *That's Life* programme have had quite a collection sent in. This is among the better ones from the Romsey Advertiser :

'Experienced storekeeper, either sex, provided that they have at least five years' experience, are fluent in German and look like Marlene Dietrich in her early Twenties'

The Sidmouth Herald was a little more blunt. They published this one : 'Mechanic required, essentially fully qualified person. Responsible well-paid job, permanent. Sex immaterial provided they are prepared to share gent's toilet.'

Frivolous

And t h e Warminster Journal : 'Dental nurse-person required, either sex. Experience an advantage or suit recent school leaver with interest in people and sense of humour. Uniform comprising white coat, blouse and skirt.'

The sartorial theme is quite popular in the amusing adverts. The Weston Mercury c a r r i e d this appeal : 'Bar Staff required mornings and evenings—

...and ended up with a girl like this

From the Northampton Evening Telegraph

what we really wanted was a mini-skirted blue-eyed blonde ...
...but under the sex discrimination act we can't advertise for her so we'll just say we require a **receptionist!**
Repete
4. LONDON RD., WELLINGBOROUGH, Tel WELLINGBOROUGH 222350

ability to look good in women's clothing.'

The Northern Echo ran one for 'promotional team vacancies with the proviso: 'female costume will be worn.' .

And an advertisement in t h e Evening Gazette, Blackpool, offers as a perk for a sales consultant job: 'Grooming and hosiery allowance.'

How many men are going to have the nerve to apply for that one?

The Equal Opportunities Commission however, don't find them all that funny. An official said the 'more frivolous advertisements nearly all showed a blatant disregard for the spirit of the law '

Most of the complaints they receive, they say, are serious, and these are receiving attention. But, sooner or later, they could well get around to the funny ones—'and then they may not be quite so funny after all.'

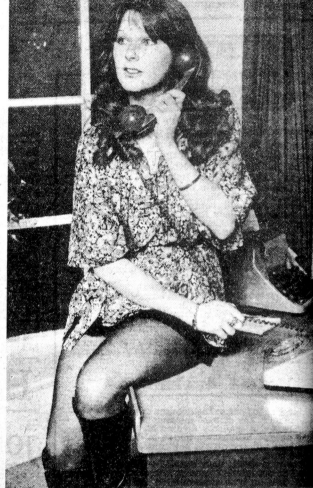

Deborah Farden, 17, at work yesterday.   Picture : BILL ORC

Have voice, will sell everything

BILL MITCHELL owes his success to an attack of mumps in early adolescence. At the age of 12, he suddenly found himself the possessor of an awe - inspiring deep voice.

'People thought I was an overgrown midget,' he complained, 'I came in for a lot of abuse.' Now, his is the growling, purring, basso profondo — with a pleasant North American slant—of a hundred commercials : Fabergé, Cadbury's, assorted airlines and Carlsberg.

A failed actor by his own admission, he drifted into doing voices for commercials because he was discouraged by t h e prowess of his acting friends.

He attributes his success to a sharp sense of timing. 'I know how to use space and silence' and an ability to 'get into the basement' with his voice, when there are so few bassos around.

As he talks, his voice curls lazily up and down the lower octaves and his

'who loves ya, baby' á la Kojak, makes your skin prickle.

H a r d l y an evening passes on Independent Television without the voice of Bill Mitchell doing a seductive turn on some product or other, yet neither his face nor his name are known.

He doesn't give a damn. He likes working and doesn't need the acclaim. He has reached that point in the profession where people devise their commercials to suit his style, not the other way round.

Tall, pale and always dressed in black and sun-glasses, his voice is s t r a n g e l y unfamiliar when you meet it larynx to larynx as it were. In fact, you have to bend quite close to him to hear what he's saying. It is almost as if his voice goes off duty when he's not working.

The ultimate accolade must come from Orson Welles, another remarkable voice. 'I did an ad imitating Welles's voice. Now I hear he's imitating mine.'

RENATE KOHLER

1976

Equal Opportunities

From the beginning of 1976 women were given equality with men. At least that was how the media interpreted the implementation of the Equal Pay and Sex Discrimination Acts. Indeed the year marked a change in the way women could be treated in a whole range of areas. In education girls had to be given the opportunity to do technical subjects such as woodwork and boys to take domestic science subjects. All training places offered in colleges and by employers had to be open to both men and women. Women could not be discriminated against by a system of quotas such as operated in medical schools which in effect controlled the number of female doctors.

In the supply of goods and services women were not to be discriminated against. In theory women would no longer suffer the indignity of being refused a mortgage simply because they were female and they could not be asked for a male guarantor to the deal. Job adverts could no longer request 'dolly birds' or 'pretty secretaries', or even say whether they wanted a man or a woman for the job. Employers interviewing women for a job could not ask her questions they would not have asked a man, such as whether she would be leaving to have a family.

There were, however, exceptions. Men and women were still not treated equally in retirement and pensions (women having to retire five years earlier than men), tax affairs and social security benefits. Some jobs in areas such as mining were still barred to women, and midwifery was barred to men. Some organizations and institutions such as private clubs, the Army and religious organizations were exempt from the law.

Apart from these exemptions there were employers and organizations who actively sought to get round, or use loopholes in the law to maintain the earlier status quo. And as with all laws of this nature the change in the law was really only a first step to changing society's attitudes and perceptions; no overnight successes could realistically be expected. By December 1978 a survey of 575 companies revealed that only 25 per cent had made any plans aimed at giving equal opportunities to women and only two per cent had actually taken steps to implement such plans.

ABOVE: *Mairead Corrigan (left) and Betty Williams surrounded by some of the 10,000 people who took part in the first demonstration for peace.*
BELOW: *Olga Korbut at the Montreal Olympics where her Romanian rival Nadia Comaneci scored the first-ever maximum of 10 points for her routine on the asymmetric bars.*

1976 POSTSCRIPTS

● Angela Rippon became the first woman ever to read the main evening news on BBC television.

August – Betty Williams and Mairead Corrigan began the Women's Peace Movement in Northern Ireland in an attempt to end the bloodshed. They were later awarded the Nobel Peace Prize for 1976 but did not receive the award until October 1977 as their nominations were submitted too late for the 1976 ceremony.

September – Dartmouth Naval College admitted its first women cadets.

A TOAST FROM...

Femail...

FROM
RODERICK
GILCHRIST

NEW YORK,
WEDNESDAY

'YOU'VE COME A LONG WAY BABY!'

Whirlwind way to wealth

BE A WOMAN...
BE GOOD AT SPORT

JUDY RANKIN, generally accepted as the best woman golfer in the world.

ROBYN SMITH, woman in the man's world of the Turf and fast horses.

DOROTHY HAMILL, poetry on ice, whose grace earns her a million-plus a year.

SPORTS QUEEN Chris Evert has a favourite T-shirt. It's black with white words across the front, and they say: 'I'd rather play tennis than stay home and cook.'

A look at her bank account would help you to understand that her affection for that T-shirt isn't purely an expression of her desire to promote female equality. Last year, at just 22, Chris, who defends her Wimbledon title next week, earned £857,142 for hitting a tennis ball.

That's £318,000 more than Henry Ford was paid for guiding the destiny of the world's most famous motor company and only £60,000 less than the salary received by the highest-paid U.S. executive, which in itself was a record pay-out.

Female athletes, even the best of whom 10 years ago often struggled to make the kind of money a well-paid Manhattan secretary received, are really striking it rich in America today.

This year an estimated £20 million will be put up in purses for them to win, with three times that amount available in sponsorship from commercial companies, which reap high profits from identifying with women winners.

At least 30 female sports stars in the States earned in excess of £57,000, last year, and among them were Britons like Virginia Wade, whose pay-day was by no means confined to her activities on court.

She received a healthy salary for advice she gave a sports complex attached to a luxury New York apartment block. The directors thought it would look good having her name on a plaque outside the gym.

LAST YEAR
Chris Evert
earned
£857,000
YES...
£318,000
more than
Henry Ford

from her endeavours sponsoring commercial goods.

Amazingly, she could probably earn £1·5 million a year if she added more endorsements to the tennis rackets, shoes, clothes and blue cheese commercials she is already committed to.

'If you're Number One, the opportunities come knocking at your door,' she says. 'I spend as little time promoting products as possible in order to devote as much time as I can to my game.

'The agents I have talked to want to squeeze everything out of me. They want me to work every day.'

Chris puts all her money into a family corporation, Evert Enterprises. 'But I just don't have time to enjoy it,'

When people think of money and women's sports, they think of Chris, or maybe Billie-Jean King, who earned £57,000 last year solely from playing doubles matches.

But the highest earner of all is Dorothy Hamill, the Olympic ice-skating champion. Last year, before tax, she earned nearly £1·2 million.

Her money came from a contract with a touring ice show, TV specials and, most lucrative of all, a hair conditioner which resulted in a much-

Splash

Unlike many male sports stars who suddenly come into the big money and splash out on Rolls-Royces and general pursuit of the good life, ending up broke when arthritis creeps into their ageing limbs, most of the women bank their cash and adopt a modest life style.

But Chris Evert, the epitome of the clean-as-surf young Californian woman, could well afford the £800 she put down for a single black chiffon gown when she went to dinner at the White House.

When you're earning £2,348 per day or, put another way, £97 per hour, every hour, it's small change.

True, more than two-thirds of that comes, not from her ability to swing a racket, but

CHRIS EVERT : £97 an hour, every hour, because she can play shots like this.

copied trend throughout America.

Czech tennis star Martina Navratilova, who defected from the Communist ideology in 1975, has embraced the American dream with a full-bodied hug.

Envy

In three years, she has bought a £50,000 house in Dallas with its own swimming pool, a luxury apartment in California, a Mercedes-Benz and a full wardrobe of Gucci clothes. Off court she lives a pampered life that Raquel Welch might envy.

Of course, tennis and ice-skating have traditionally drawn big crowds. Women's golf and downhill skiing have not.

But the financial backing of companies like Colgate—who have budgeted £8 million for sport in 1977—last year kept Marion Post, the 21-year-old American downhill champion, in the £70,000-a-year life style to which she has become accustomed.

American golfer Judy Rankin earned £150,000 from her

ability to pitch and putt last year and is accepted as the best female golfer in the world.

But, intriguingly, it was not she but the girl who actually finished as far down as 19th in the ranking who picked up the most money—£130,000.

That was perky, blonde, Californian Laura Baugh, who became an instant celebrity in places as diverse as Japan and Hawaii, not simply because of her skill with a four-iron, but because she looked cute on the green.

Every night you see her on

American TV advertising toothpaste. Sadly, however, she now confesses she has spent so much time in front of the cameras her game has suffered.

'It was Billie-Jean King, the first woman to earn a million dollars a year from sport, who led the way, and she says it wasn't just money that made her fight for recognition that women on the playing field can show a degree of expertise as attractive to crowds as that of Jimmy Connors or an Arnold Palmer. Her motive was the desire to propagate sexual equality as well.

She has made her point. Last year at Wimbledon, Chris Evert received only £2,500 less than the men's winner, Bjorn Borg.

Winners

But, ironically, it isn't the girls who are the really big winners, but companies like Colgate and Virginia Slims, the cigarette manufacturers, who sponsor women's sports, gain a distinct product identity—the object of every manufacturer—and have really found women's sports a bankable investment.

In their first year of investment in 1967, Virginia Slims spent £100,000 backing women's tennis. Since then, they have put close to £6 million behind it, but the success of that investment is reflected in their corporate profits.

Sadly, the chase to win sport's big-money prizes takes its psychological as well as physical toll.

The majority of the girls involved in women's sports are still single, and when they are down they are more emotionally depressed than men in a similar position.

Inevitably, the competitive element, especially when so much money is involved, leads to gamesmanship and broken friendships. Chris Evert recounts how she sat down with her friend Martina Navratilova and they decided not to spend time with each other any more. Says Chris :

'We said we both wanted to be Number One and that it was very hard emotionally to play your friend. We both know how she and being Number One means to us and there are no bitter feelings at all.'

It's tough when you decide you can't afford to take tea with your best pal. But Chris does have the comfort of a million in the bank, and I'm sure that, when Ms Navratilova drives her Mercedes or takes a dip in her pool, she feels they compensate just a little.

1977

Battered Wives

In 1970 Erin Pizzey opened her first refuge for women seeking shelter and protection from violent partners. Throughout the 1970s the issue of violence within marriage was brought into the open and the term 'battered wife' was coined. Of course the violence was not always against wives. Often the women in question were not married to the men who battered them but felt just as helpless and fearful, trapped by children and financial dependence, just like wives who would have to go through the courts to gain a legal separation. A woman living with a man could, if she had the emotional strength and a willing police force, have a violent partner charged for an attack. Wives had no such recourse to law. In 1976 pressure from women's groups brought about the Domestic Violence Act which gave wives more protection from violent husbands and the police powers to arrest husbands who breached injunctions.

Before the issue of domestic violence was brought out of the confines of the family home many people simply ignored or were ignorant of its existence. There was also an underlying inheritance, especially among the victims and the perpetrators that it was somehow acceptable for a husband to beat his wife, and indeed in the days when a wife quite literally belonged to her husband society accepted that she was his to do as he liked with. In marrying she gave away her rights.

This last issue of what a woman was giving up when she married was the crux of a ruling which said a husband could not rape his wife. A judge had ruled in the eighteenth century that when a woman gives her marriage vows she gives away all rights to refuse to have sex with her husband for the rest of the marriage. A case in December 1975 had reaffirmed this to be the legal position in Britain with regard to rape in marriage. However some states in the USA had changed their laws to allow for a man to be prosecuted for raping his wife. And in 1978, in what was believed to be the first case of its kind, a man in Oregon was prosecuted for raping his wife while they were still living together. He was found not guilty after claiming that his wife consented voluntarily to sex, because the jury felt there was insufficient proof of guilt.

ABOVE: *Rosalyn Yalow.*
BELOW: *The Marie Stopes Well Woman Clinic began offering female sterilization on an outpatient basis.*

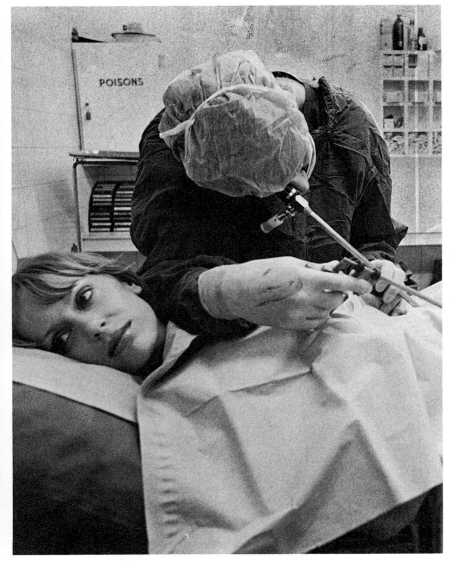

1977   POSTSCRIPTS

● New adoption laws gave adopted children the right to seek out their natural parents. But the law did not and still does not give natural parents the right either to refuse disclosure of their name and address to the child or the right to trace a child they have given up for adoption.

December – Rosalyn Yalow was awarded the Nobel Prize for Medicine for her discoveries relating to hormones.

● Florence Nagle, the first woman ever to hold a racehorse trainer's licence, was one of three women admitted to membership of the previously all-male Jockey Club.

JOCKEY CLUB CHAUVINISTS MAY DROP BAN ON WOMEN

The Jockey Club, one of the last great bastions of male chauvinism, is poised to accept women members for the first time in its 226-year-old history.

The club, which controls racing in Britain, has been an exclusively male preserve since its foundation in 1751.

Even a Royal Charter granted in 1970 and the patronage of the Queen and the Queen Mother failed to breach the dedicated masculinity of the self-electing body.

Daily Mail, 12 December 1977

Femail

SUDDENLY, everybody's doing it. Some from necessity. Some from choice. Not all are married, and some are still looked at askance. They are the women for whom work begins at 40.

There are now 66 per cent. of all women between 35 and 54 who have jobs. Most of them are working office hours . . . plus. They leave their 9 to 5 jobs simply to start their domestic chores.

For many, work is a burden. But there are some women for whom it is a relief — a release from the boredom that sets in when children grow up, and they suddenly realise they are no longer needed in the only job they have trained themselves for.

A daunting future? It doesn't have to be. If they are happy with the dusting and baby-sitting for their grandchildren, good luck to them. One of the more damaging aspects liberation is that it makes otherwise perfectly contented wives feel inadequate.

But if they are unhappy at home, they can get out of the rut. I have been talking to four women who solved their problems with more than usual style, and have turned incipient frustration into demonstrable success.

NOW THAT...
Work begins at 40
BERYL DOWNING

MEETS THE WOMEN WHO

ARE DOING IT IN STYLE

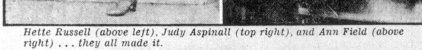

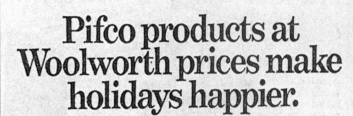

Hette Russell (above left), Judy Aspinall (top right), and Ann Field (above right) . . . they all made it.

HETTE RUSSELL, owner of three Young Motherhood shops, is the first to acknowledge the debt she owes her husband.

She was bored when her children grew up, but had no experience of a job before marriage. So she leased the basement of a friend's shop, 'just to see if I liked working.'

She says. 'I had always loved clothes, and 16 years ago maternity wear was so dull and miserable. I just wanted to do something to make it young and pretty.

Excited

'But I did tend to overbuy at first because of my lack of experience. When my husband saw all the stock left at the end of the first season, he put his foot down and

'Bluff your way into a job'

wouldn't let me spend any more until I had sold it. I soon learned.'

Her eye was so good that in no time she had opened branches in three of London's busiest shopping areas, was advising manufacturers on design, and had Princess Margaret and, later, Princess Alexandra and the Duchess of Kent among her customers.

A six-day-a-week job keeps her slim and elegant, and still leaves her with enough energy for her two grandchildren, aged 11 and 13.

Her success recipe? 'Enthusiasm. You've got to be excited by what you're doing. Once I started I wondered how I could have stayed at home all that time.'

So, pick a basic idea—an agency, a shop, a business—and give it an individual twist. Or you could, like **Judy Aspinall**, take a different route to personal freedom. At 43 she is in her second year of a degree course in economics at University

College, London.

'I married at 20, and had three children very young, as one did in the mid 50s. But the marriage broke up, and as the youngest was just three I could only work two afternoons a week and had to cope with the nightmare of holidays.

Natural

'I became a picture researcher because the work was flexible, and I kept the job when I re-married because I felt the children were my responsibility, and I should provide for them.

'But I had always wanted to go to university — my father died when I was young, and we couldn't afford it. So when my son started working and my elder daughter got a university place, I applied too. We were both accepted the same year.

'I didn't find the academic work difficult—I'm just a natural student, I suppose. But I did feel a

bit left out at first because I couldn't join in student events and societies, as I had to be home in the evenings.

'And, of course, it's difficult to adjust to preconceived ideas about looking after your home and family. But something had to give, and now I hardly ever do any housework.

'The result is we all benefit. It's much better to stay sane and have a reasonably relaxed family than a spotless house. My husband and children enjoy me so much more because I'm happy.'

Ann Field, joint head of TIPS secretarial agency, has an office in Regent Street, linked directly to the Hilton Hotel, where she provides temporary secretaries for visiting tycoons.

When she started, 19 years ago, in a £6-a-week room behind a barber's in Whitehall she and her co-directors never expected their idea to be such a runaway success.

'My children were in their teens, and I was bored, she says. 'We had all been secretaries before we married, so we started temping to get our hand in.

Answered

'We wanted to build up a round-the-clock secretarial service for people visiting London—tycoons, film stars, business people doing deals outside normal office hours.

'My friend and I did the day-time jobs, and my sister Laura did the evening and weekend calls. We didn't take any money for ourselves, but put it all into the business to build up a little capital so that we could employ staff.

'When we had enough we advertised for "temp. secs., days, weeks, evenings, odd hours." But somehow it was printed "temp. sex," and the phone never stopped ringing.

'But among the women who answered the ad out of sheer curiosity, some turned out to be a really good shorthand typists, and were in business. Now all the people we employ are in the £4,000 a year class.'

Eve Shepherd at her shop in Cobham.

EXPORTER Eve Shepherd began her business career in a rather unusual way. She and her husband were thrown out of Egypt at the time of Suez . . . their property confiscated, all their savings gone.

'I had never been allowed to work. I married at 19, had three children, and never even made myself a cup of coffee. This was my opportunity to prove to myself that I was as good as the next person.

'I bluffed my way into a fashion manager's job and went straight in at the deep end without any training. I hated every minute of it, but I stuck it for 12 years because it taught me so much about business.

'But my real love was antiques, and

in my lunch hours I used to go to auctions and buy an odd piece—just to be in a sale room.'

The experience paid off, for when her husband was posted to Australia, she took one look at the Outback, sized up the antique market there, and opened her own import company. It did so well that she now has an export company here, and an antique gallery in Cobham.

Didn't she have any problems? Well, of course. It is always difficult to go to a new country. You don't know the way they think. They don't trust you until you have proved yourself. Everything you do is a risk.

'But as long as you are doing something you enjoy, you will do well.

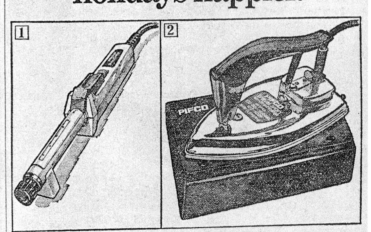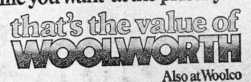

1978

Babies from a Test Tube

Nine years after scientists at Cambridge first announced that they had succeeded in fertilizing a human embryo outside the womb, the world's first test-tube baby was born. Louise Brown was born on 26 July 1978 amid huge publicity. Her birth brought hope to thousands of infertile couples, although the treatment was originally only available privately at specialist clinics like the one run by Dr Patrick Steptoe who treated Louise's parents.

In the 1960s several infertility treatments were developed, including artificial insemination and the use of fertility drugs. Many of these treatments were a result of research into contraception which demanded a better understanding of both male and female fertility. Infertility became another of the issues which were far more openly talked about in the 1970s. The fact that there was more help available meant couples no longer had to suffer in shame and silence over what were now often curable conditions.

Test-tube fertilization might have captured the public imagination but it and science generally could not provide the cure to every form of infertility. In America, there was a growing practice of surrogacy, where one woman, usually paid for the service, was impregnated with the sperm from a man whose partner was infertile. The woman carried the child and when it was born handed it over to the father and his partner. Agencies were set up to introduce infertile couples and surrogate mothers and arrange the payment of fees.

The huge advances medical research and practice had yielded in the 1960s and '70s in the field of human, and especially female, fertility gave women much greater freedom and choice. They could choose when and how many children they wished to have and if they found getting pregnant was more difficult than they expected there were medical treatments available to help. But there were disadvantages. Multiple pregnancies with all the attendant dangers to both mother and babies often resulted from the use of fertility drugs, especially in the early days, and this problem was transferred to pregnancies resulting from in-vitro fertilization. As fertility, contraception and birth itself became more scientific and hi-tech, doctors, and especially male doctors, took much more control over all these processes. It was a balance which women themselves began to address in the 1980s with calls for less medical intervention in pregnancy and childbirth.

ABOVE: Baby Louise Brown with her mother Lesley.
BELOW: Anna Ford prepares herself for her newsreading début as ITN's first woman newscaster on the major evening news slot.

1978 POSTSCRIPTS

February – A Life Assurance Company reported it would cost £6,000, that was one and a half times the average male salary of the period, to replace the services of a woman looking after a home and children.

June – Naomi James arrived in Britain after sailing her yacht around the world in two days less than Francis Chichester's record time.

• The Inland Revenue announced that in future correspondence about wives' tax affairs and any rebates owed to them would be sent to them and not their husbands.

September – France appointed Monique Pelletier as Minister for Women. With government commitment and funding the Ministry made some strides on women's issues particularly that of abortion but after the first few years the funding and commitment faded and women's issues became more marginalized.

OLD LAW ENDS LIFE OF SHAME

Ann McLean kept a secret for 28 years from her son and her neighbours.

The shame of the ex-nurse was that she was not married to the man she lived with. But yesterday, 20 months after her 'husband' died, a judge in Edinburgh decided that under an old Scottish law she had been married by 'habit and repute'.

Miss McLean, of Kirkintilloch, near Glasgow – now officially Mrs Frederick Roberts, 66, was granted a marriage decree.

She told the court that when in 1953 she returned to the village of Lattermorar in Kintyre, she and her husband had a son. She did not dare admit that she was not married.
Daily Mail, 8 June 1978

Femail

by ANGELA LAMBERT

The Perfect Wife —for 'yesterday's' husband!

KENNETH HARDE is 36, a successful self-made man, with his own house and decorating business. He married his Indian wife, Veronica, 28, six weeks ago.

'It is,' says Kenneth, 'what you'd call an arranged marriage.'

Indians have long accepted the custom of arranged marriages, and point out with pride that — whatever the Western ideals of romantic love — arranged marriages tend to be more stable, more lasting and at least as happy as those based on the unpredictable, if glorious excitement of two people in love.

But Kenneth Harde is no Indian. He lives in an Oxfordshire village and is as English as his name suggests, although many people would regard him as an Englishman of the late 'fifties', rather than an Englishman of today.

Attitude

His happiness with married life is unmistakable as he explains what made him contemplate an arranged marriage with an Indian girl, who arrived here from Delhi only three months ago and whom he met only half a dozen times in the month before their wedding.

'I've had lots of English girlfriends, but none that I would have married,' he said. 'I've come to the conclusion that white English girls have lost the art of marriage.

'The modern woman's attitude makes a man feel he's not really needed.

'Asian girls are *brought up* to make good wives—that's the difference. And if you treat them well, you'll have a wonderful marriage.

'In fact, most of them make superb wives : they're beautiful girls, very clean, good cooks and absolutely faithful.

'They give you a sense of satisfaction in your own achievements that today's career-chasing English girls who don't forget, are often financially independent, just don't provide.

'What more,' asked Kenneth, 'could any man want from a wife ?

'In return, I give my wife 100 per cent. — in my work, my home and my love — and, well, you're speaking to a very contented man.'

And what about Veronica ? Was she equally contented ? Had being 'brought up to be a good wife' included the acceptance of being little more than a beautiful, obedient, domesticated, faithful, functional . . . object ?

'You can't speak to her,' said Kenneth quickly. 'She's very shy. She wouldn't speak to you without my permission. No, I'm afraid I can't allow that.'

Kenneth met Veronica through the Suman Marriage Bureau in Southall, Middlesex, which was set up by Mrs Suman Bhargava in 1972, mainly to cater for young Asians.

Nowadays, there is an ever-increasing number of inquiries from Englishmen. It has over a thousand clients, and of these just over 100 are non Asian, wanting to marry Asian girls.

They range from a wealthy film producer with estates in three countries to clerks, shop assistants and young professional men.

What, I asked the bureau's proprietors, Mr and Mrs Bhargava, are these men hoping to find ?

'Many of them have had problems in their relationships with English girls,' said Mrs Bhargava. 'They're slightly old-fashioned perhaps ; they can't cope with Women's Lib and the notion of equality in marriage.

Faithful

'They want a docile, faithful wife ; preferably a girl who doesn't want to go out to work; who won't drink, and is prepared to devote her life to looking after her husband and children. Many have lived in India or have Asian friends, and like what they've seen of Indian family life.'

Why should an Asian girl want an English husband ? 'It works well both ways,' explained Mrs Bhargava. 'Englishmen are more helpful in the house than most Asian husbands ; their parents don't put the same kind of pressures and demands on a wife that Indian

Marriages are made like this : Mr and Mrs Bhargavas matching like with like . . .

parents-in-law often do; there's no question of expecting the girl to bring a dowry (though even among Asians this is dying out, too)—so the girl gets a good deal as well.'

The Bhargavas introduced me to a young professional Indian girl who had said she was willing to marry an Englishman. Charming, university educated and highly intelligent, it was as hard to imagine her as any other career woman in the role of the obedient, stay-at-home wife. Nor was it one she was prepared to adopt.

Pressures

Perhaps that was why she said, of one of the two Englishmen she'd met through the bureau, 'I felt I was beyond his comprehension.' Yet her attitudes were not entirely English.

'Of course I would like to fall in love. But for me, that's not the first essential. I think most people fool themselves about love anyway. In 98 per cent. of cases it means no more than that two people find each other suitable—compatible—and their personalities interact. An arranged marriage can be a very good way of *making sure* that happens.'

Once a client is on the books (registration fee £35 plus VAT; a further £50 on marriage) the Suman Bureau will arrange as many introductions as necessary. Many people marry the second or third person they meet ; others take two or three years and up to 40 introductions before pairing off.

But what are the problems ? Do the families on both sides approve of 'mixed' marriages ?

Kenneth Harde told me, 'People are having to wake up to the fact that prejudice

'What more could any man want?'

against mixed marriages is a thing of the past. Veronica's parents were quite happy to accept me ; my family came to our wedding — every one of them. We've had no problems on that score, and I don't expect any when we start our family — yes, we both want children very much.'

But another Englishman seeking an Asian wife with the help of the Suman Bureau, 33-year-old James Harden an accountant from Windsor, was less sure.

'There *are* still certain pressures from other people,' he said, 'although more are becoming more tolerant.

'I've never actually told my parents that I'm looking for an Asian wife, and I'm not sure what their reaction would be— or their neighbours'—if I married an Indian girl. But it's my life and my decision. I hope they'd recognise that.'

In the seven years since they established the bureau, Mr and Mrs Bhargava (whose own marriage was arranged and is very happy) have been responsible for several thousand weddings. Of those, about 75 were 'mixed' marriages which, they say, have proved highly successful.

'We keep in touch with lots of our clients; we have a reunion here every year and we can see for ourselves that people are really happy,' said Mr Bhagava.

'Asian women *do* seem to be more flexible — more able to adapt to their husbands' wishes. Once they're convinced that his decision is right, they'll accept that and not be stubborn. In the end, the man is in charge.'

And that, it seems, is what the Englishmen who marry Indian girls are looking for. But I still wish I could have asked Veronica what *she* thought . . .

ILLUSTRATION : BOB WILLIAMS

Femail

LETTER

'Personal Chemistry' (Femail last week) was evident in the office where I worked with five other audio typists —ALL blonde, ALL 5ft. 5in.-5ft. 8in. tall ALL 36-26-36 and ALL with husbands frequently working away from home. Immediately I realised my boss's 'personal chemistry' I left !

Daphne Hudson (Mrs), Solihull, West Midlands.

1979

Women and Islam

The Shah of Iran left his country in January 1979 following demonstrations against his rule. In February the spiritual leader and opposition figure Ayatollah Khomeini returned from exile to take power. Almost immediately the Ayatollah and his government set about making Iran, which was, under the Shah, fairly westernized, an Islamic State. Just as quickly Iranian women began to protest and voice their fears over how their position would be affected by this new Islamic Revolution. Many women had been at the forefront of opposition to the Shah but now dreaded the alternative they had helped to promote.

A major issue for women in Iran became the wearing of the *chador*. This traditional Islamic dress cloaks the female form in voluminous black material from head to foot, demanding that no man apart from a husband or close family see any of the woman's body or face. Despite the women's protests within a relatively short space of time Islamic rules on female dress were imposed and soon no woman would be seen on the streets of Iran not wearing the *chador*.

The treatment of women in Islam varies widely from country to country depending upon the extent to which the religious authorities hold power. The followers of Islam, like those of many other religions, will often take what they want from it and leave the bits they find unpalatable. For example, the teachings of the Roman Catholic Church with regard to birth control are quite patently not observed by many people who consider themselves 'good Catholics'. So with Islam in countries where there is more freedom the religion can exist without women feeling overly oppressed. Indeed, in countries like Egypt, some women choose to wear Islamic dress as a statement of their cultural identity. They have a choice. But where, as in Iran, the State is controlled or run by religious figures and it follows the fundamental teachings of Islam, women are not just affected by the question of dress. Their whole position is similar in many instances to that of women in the West at the beginning of the century. Unequal divorce laws, the barring of women from several jobs and activities (even western women are not allowed to drive a car in Saudia Arabia), their lack of voting rights, of the right to hold political office and of rights to custody over their children are all still evident to a greater or lesser extent in some Islamic States.

ABOVE: Mother Theresa.
BELOW: Margaret Thatcher with Israeli Prime Minister Menachem Begin on the doorstep of 10 Downing Street soon after her election as British Prime Minister.

1979 POSTSCRIPTS

March – Lee Marvin's long-time girlfriend, who took his surname, sued him for 'palimony' after their relationship broke up. She claimed that she had given up her own career to be with him and so deserved half of the £3.6m he made during the six years they were together.

May – Margaret Thatcher became the first woman Prime Minister of Britain when the Conservatives won the general election.

July – Portugal's first woman Prime Minister, Maria Pintassilgo, took office.

October – Athlete Greta Weitz won the New York Women's Marathon in 2 hrs 27 mins 32.6 secs and beat the 2½-hour barrier for women runners over the distance.

November – The Swedish Parliament voted 165 to 21 with 147 abstentions to grant the right of succession to the Swedish throne to the monarch's first-born child. This meant that two-year-old Princess Victoria would take precedence over her six-month-old brother, Carl.

● An Employment Tribunal ruled that an employer who sacked a woman from her job because she was pregnant was not guilty of sex discrimination. The tribunal said that because there was no male equivalent to pregnancy the woman should sue for redress through the Employment Protection Act not the Sex Discrimination Act.

December – Mother Theresa, the Albanian nun who had worked for years with the poor, the sick and the dying in Calcutta, was awarded the Nobel Peace Prize.

Femail

ON THE DAY SOME DISQUIETING STATISTICS ARE DISCLOSED...

Do Britain's babies lose out?

STATISTICS released today will be viewed by many as nothing less than an indictment of the National Health Service : at least 5,000 babies dying—unnecessarily—at or near birth every year and a further 5,000 handicapped for life.

The call, from the Parliamentary Social Services Committee following a two-year investigation, is for MORE midwives, MORE paediatricians and ROUND-THE-CLOCK cover for maternity hospitals by

experts in resuscitation—the absence of which is one of the main causes of these deaths. On figures alone, comparisons in this area are disquieting to say the least : more than double the number of babies die in Britain than in Scandinavia, and far more than in the Netherlands or Japan. Is the ante-natal care in these countries significantly better ... how does having a baby in Britain compare ... what, if any, are the lessons to be learned ? FEMAIL reports ...

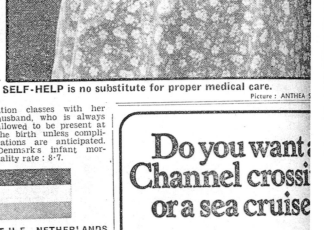

A cartoon . . . with a very serious message. One of the posters from the current campaign to persuade expectant mothers that delay can be dangerous for them AND their baby.

FINLAND is rapidly becoming one of the most health - conscious countries in the world, not least because of the very high — and as yet not fully explained—incidence of heart attacks there.

By contrast, its infant mortality rate is one of the *lowest* in the world, decreasing steadily from 18 per thousand in 1951 to only five per thousand in 1977 (the last available figures).

An effective inducement to persuade women to attend ante-natal mother-and-baby centres is the Finnish maternity benefit, which is witheld if a mother-to-be has not registered with the clinic before she is four months' pregnant.

They are given the choice of a lump sum maternity benefit (about £40) or a pack of baby clothes and nursery equipment. Most choose the pack because the contents are worth double the £40.

ITALIAN law insists that any gynaecologist or doctor delivering a baby *must be assisted by a fully qualified obstetrician.*

Mothers have the choice of going to a state hospital for pregnancy confirmation and examination or to one of the numerous private medical clinics in almost every city.

At private maternity clinics a pregnancy check costs £10, instruction courses for expectant mothers £10 a session, delivery anything from £150 to £250.

Mrs Angela Gugielmi, a secondary school teacher who had her second baby a few days ago, said : 'When I learned there would be complications I applied

for, and was granted, nine months' release from work.

'Despite the ante-natal advice available, many women still leave it all to the last minute.'

NORWAY'S campaign to encourage women to have babies in hospital has been so successful that only 0·3 per cent. of babies are now born at home.

Most hospitals have specially-trained resuscitation teams and there are only a handful of maternity homes still operating which deliver fewer than 5 per cent. of the country's babies.

The infant mortality rate is 9·2 per thousand births.

JAPAN has little difficulty in persuading its mothers-to-be to visit their doctors regularly. Hypochondria is said by some to be a national disease—and has

become a national joke !

With home confinements strongly discouraged in recent years the number of midwives has decreased significantly. But in remote districts the equivalent of a British health visitor makes regular calls on expectant mothers.

Medical treatment, including maternity care, has to be paid for by the patient. But as a company 'perk' many husbands are able to claim a 100 per cent. refund from their employers of the cost of their wives having babies.

The latest infant mortality rate : 8·9 per thousand, almost half that of Britain.

DENMARK is one of the few countries where checks for abnormalities like mongolism are made on *all* women during pregnancy instead of being restricted only to those most at risk (usually over the age of 35).

In addition a health visitor calls on the mother and her baby nine times during its first year.

During pregnancy the mother can attend relax-

ation classes with her husband, who is always allowed to be present at the birth unless complications are anticipated. Denmark's infant mortality rate : 8·7.

THE NETHERLANDS have more babies born at home (more than 60 per cent. !) than in hospital, yet the infant mortality rate has dropped dramatically from 23·1 per thousand in 1965 to 12·5 per thousand two years ago.

Expectant mothers have a team of three to help them through a home confinement : their local doctor, community nurse and midwife. Obstetricians can also be called from the nearest hospital.

FRANCE is so determined that every mother has proper ante- and postnatal care that they 'fine' those who do not attend clinics.

Women are entitled to grants of about £250 before each birth, £300 after the birth of the first two and £750 for subsequent offspring—but only if they register their pregnancy with the local health service by the third month and attend three compulsory clinics before and after the birth.

Too many too late

BRITAIN'S doctors—and the Department of Health—are worried that many pregnant women delay going to ante-natal clinics, especially those expecting their second or third baby.

Early and regular attendance at these clinics greatly increases the chance of detecting possible abnormalities and either treating them or offering the mother an early abortion.

The Health Education Council is currently running a poster and TV commercial campaign urging mothers to help themselves and their babies by attending clinics as early as possible.

In 1971 the Department of Health recommended a two-tier system of care for babies in hospital : 'special care,' where one nurse looks after only three babies, and 'intensive care,' where three nurses care for one baby, with specialist doctors and sophisticated feeding and breathing aids to fall back on.

So far there are only 42 intensive care units with 176 cots, in large general hospitals, and another 208 special care units with 224 beds.

SELF-HELP is no substitute for proper medical care.

Picture : ANTHEA S

1980

Work and Marriage

In 1951 only 20 per cent of married women worked outside the home but by 1980 official statistics showed that the figure had risen to 50 per cent. In most other European countries the percentages were lower – 35 per cent in Germany, 22 per cent in the Netherlands and 25 per cent in Italy. A study suggested that the main reason for this high percentage of married women in paid work was the relatively low wages paid to men in Britain. The study's conclusion was that economic necessity had driven women to find work and not equal pay opportunities. Throughout the 1980s the number of married women doing some kind of paid work steadily increased so that now at least two out of every three have a job outside the home.

By 1980 it was extremely rare for a married woman with no children not to be working full time and most women who had children felt they would almost certainly be back in the job market in some capacity before their children had left school. Changes to employment laws to allow women to take maternity leave meant many more mothers were able to pursue a career and remain in full-time work. However large numbers of women felt that working full time, bringing up a young family and assuming most of the responsibilities for household chores was simply too demanding. They wanted time to spend with their family but also wanted to have a career.

Part-time work had, since the war, been popular with married women, especially those with children, as it has advantages in terms of hours worked outside the home. For despite a growing willingness of men throughout the postwar years to help with child rearing and domestic duties, the burden of responsibilities fell and still falls on the woman. Working part-time allows more time for household duties and more energy to deal with the emotional demands of a growing family.

However part-time work had many disadvantages. Pay rates and employment protection levels were, and still are, generally lower than in full-time work. And part-time workers were rarely considered for promotion which meant that a large number of women found themselves struck in boring and often menial jobs far below their capabilities simply because they had chosen to spend more time with their families. This has changed to a small degree in the last few years as job-share schemes and more flexibility on the part of employers about their women workers' hours make it a little easier for mothers to work part time while taking on more stimulating and interesting posts and maintaining some foothold on the career ladder if they so wish.

ABOVE: *At the beginning of the 1980s office work was beginning to change as word processors and computers began to make their appearance. The remainder of the decade would see rapid change and require a change in office skills to deal with the new equipment.*

BELOW: *A trained, uniformed nanny takes her charges for a walk. As more women worked outside the home childcare became an important issue in the 1980s. Nannies were for the well-off, middle-class and professional couples. Most working women relied on nurseries, child minders or relations to look after their children.*

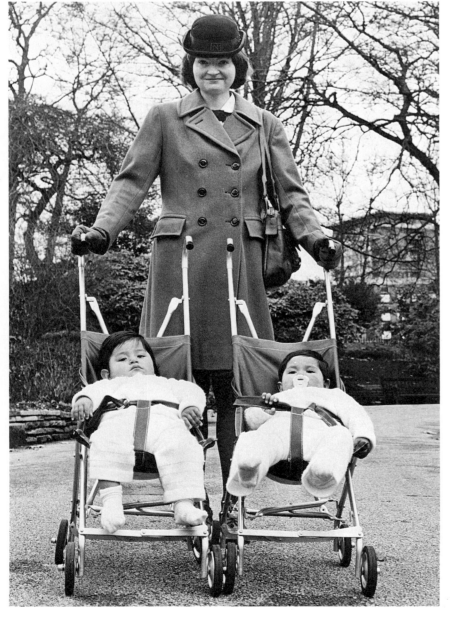

1980   POSTSCRIPTS

● A working Paper on Sexual offences published by the Criminal Law Revision Committee recommended that husbands who forced their wives to have intercourse should be liable to prosecution for rape.

January – The government announced that Child Benefit (Family Allowance) would be paid monthly and not weekly as had traditionally been the case. Existing recipients could elect to continue to collect the benefit weekly.

● The US Surgeon General warned that lung cancer was the leading killer cancer in women.

June – Vigdis Finnbogadottir became Iceland's first woman President. The Icelanders claimed her as the first freely elected female Head of State as she was voted into office by the people and not because she was leader of a political party.

WOMEN FLOCK TO TAKE SAFER PILL

Thousands of British women are going back on the Pill following the introduction of a new low-risk oral contraceptive, it was revealed yesterday . . .

The new pill contains the same two hormones, oestrogen and progestogen, as those in most current pills, but in proportions that are more in line with the latest medical findings on safety.

Another change is that it follows the pattern of the natural cycle more closely, using tablets of three different formulations at different times of the cycle.

This has considerably reduced the total hormone intake, while 100 per cent effectiveness is claimed.

Daily Mail, 5 July 1980

Femail

by CONNIE FRANCIS

Chart-topper of the fifties, whose career came to a tragic end

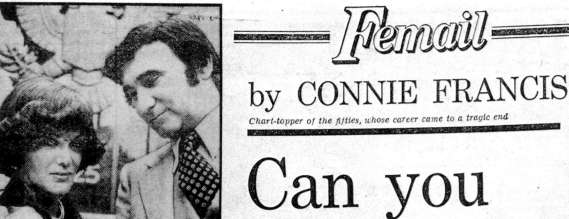

Can you ever get over rape?

THEN: At the time of the trial . . . Connie Francis with her husband, Joe, who was supportive at the time

NOW: Connie Francis today . . . putting her life back together but never able to forget the night she was raped

I HAVEN'T AND I DON'T KNOW ANYONE WHO HAS

SHE sang of teen dreams and puppy love to the innocent Fifties and spun gold records from tunes like Lipstick on Your Collar. Yet for singer Connie Francis a night of terror six years ago damaged her life for ever. While she slept in a motel room after a concert appearance in Westbury, Long Island, an intruder jemmied a lock on her door and raped her at knifepoint. He was never caught.

The ordeal contributed to the break-up of her marriage and virtually finished her performing career. Connie, 42, now shares a suburban New Jersey home with her parents and adopted son, Joey, six. Today she tells about the impact that rape had on her life.

AFTER I had been raped I was afraid to be with people, couldn't pick up a newspaper or listen to the news. I would lie in bed for a month at a time and wouldn't want to get up.

To this day I never go anywhere alone and never do anything by myself. I have never been in a motel since. Performing scares me to death.

But when you have had a knife at your throat and your life has been hanging in the balance for over two hours, you realise you're lucky to be alive. And you have to build on that.

Relive

How a woman survives an ordeal like rape depends on what kind of husband and family you have. If you have someone who sticks by you until you return to normal, you are lucky. My husband, Joe, was marvellous at the time.

I decided to sue the motel owners, Howard Johnson, but not for the money. My attorney, who is also a good friend and my son's godfather, said I had an obligation to come forward and encourage other women who experience the same thing to do so as well. And to force hotels and motels to give their guests better protection.

Nevertheless, the trial was disastrous for me, my husband and my family. I had to retell and relive everything that happened that night . . . details which I hadn't discussed with anyone before.

There I was on the witness stand, opening up my whole life, testifying for about three months after the incident I was not sexually responsive. For me and my husband—a proud man and very Italian—that was a violation of our privacy.

Afterwards we split up. He went back to live alone in New York. I do not believe we would be apart today had it not

THE FIGURES

● Rape is on the increase in Britain.

● The London-based Rape Crisis Centre, set up to help victims, claims that for every woman who reports a rape at least another six keep quiet.

● In 1969 the number of rapes reported in England and Wales was 869. Ten years later in 1979 — the latest figures available —there were 1,170.

been for the attack and the trial.

Yet the trial did have a positive effect on many women. A lot of them wrote to me and said they had been afraid to report being molested or raped because they couldn't face the ordeal of a trial, or because they were afraid to tell their husbands.

I answered every letter myself and advised them to be brave and report any incidents.

Other women wrote telling me that it had happened to them in exactly the same circumstance—in a motel. Most women said they had still not fully recovered. Not one said she had conquered it.

Unfortunately, some people don't think of rape as the horrendous crime it is. Everyone is sleeping around so much, so what's the difference they say. They don't realise how much of an ordeal it is.

I had a very traditional upbringing and a mother and father who loved me. I was a very disciplined performer. I didn't drink. I didn't go to clubs or after-the-show parties.

Pity

Instead, I'd go back to my room with my aunt or my mother and play Scrabble. I was never abused. My manager was very protective.

I never saw agents directly. I never knew the old show business story about having to deal with

the producer's couch. I was never asked for money by disc jockeys. I was never asked for sexual favours.

So of course that rape totally changed me. I began to live my life like a Greek tragedy. Eventually, after wallowing in self-pity, I decided I had to get out and do something.

I read everything I could about rape and its implications. Now I have been elected chairman of the National Association for Crime Victims' Rights, based in Portland, Oregon, and I hope to do some public appearances for them.

Joys

Last year I appeared before Senator Kennedy's committee which was looking into the way the law protects the criminal and puts the victim through hell.

Slowly I got my life back on the tracks.

One of my greatest joys is my son, Joey. He has made a tremendous difference, and if I had to experience some of these things without him I don't know what I would have done.

I will never be the same again, but maybe that's an advantage. I think I have put this attack in the right perspective, because I am enjoying life again. You have to work at being happy. It's not a right; it's a privilege.

Connie Francis was talking to Richard Rein. ©
People Magazine.

1981

The Changing Family

Society in 1981 was based on the assumption, and to a large extent is still run on the assumption, that most people lived in a family with a mother married to a father living together and bringing up their own children. In this family father went out to work and mother stayed at home. A startling report in 1981 showed that this was the case in only fifteen per cent of families. The report also found that one child in every eight was living in a single-parent family, that in only a third of families were both parents living with their own children, and that one in four marriages ended in divorce.

There were also growing numbers of children being born outside marriage – by 1986 the figure was 20 per cent. Many of these children were born into stable relationships but there were still a large number of women left with a baby and no partner to help financially, physically or emotionally. Unmarried mothers were no longer shunned to the extent they had been in the 1960s and earlier. The State did provide money and housing, but for a young mother bringing up a child or children alone and relying on State provision it was not a particularly easy life. Statistics show that they were, and still are, among the poorest in society.

Children born to unmarried parents in a stable relationship were usually better off emotionally and financially. But if that relationship broke up the mother still was not entitled to the same rights as a wife. Her partner could evict her from the family home if he was the sole owner or tenant and she would have to sue for maintenance for herself and any children of the relationship and be required to prove paternity if the case was contested.

Some women with children found that a lesbian relationship provided a more fulfilling life for themselves and a stable home for their children. There were also a number of lesbian couples willing to have a baby by artificial insemination or to foster chldren. The fact that local authorities accepted lesbians as foster parents demonstrated just how much perceptions of the family unit were being challenged, although it was not without a great deal of controversy.

ABOVE: *Baroness Young.*
BELOW: *Oxford cox Susan Brown.*

1981 POSTSCRIPTS

● The House of Lords had its first woman leader when Baroness Young was appointed.

February – Gro Harlem Bruntland took office as Norway's first woman Prime Minister.

April – Oxford were steered to victory in the Boat Race by Susan Brown, the first woman cox in the history of the event.

July – Following a campaign promise by Ronald Reagan, Judge Sandra O'Conner was appointed to the US Supreme Court. Her pro-abortion and women's rights stance ran counter to the moral majority campaigners who had a great deal of influence over the administration.

November – The Church of England Synod voted overwhelmingly in favour of admitting women to Holy Orders as deacons, enabling them to conduct weddings, funerals and baptisms but not to give Holy Communion.

Femail

No 4 in a new series: The secretaries who made it to the top

Sally's never the celebrity ...but always a star

SIPPING from a cup of coffee Sally Anne Egan says suddenly : 'Often I think I'd like to do a job that was a little less taxing.

'Then I get back at my desk and say : "Come on Sally Anne, if Mark can do it, so can you".'

Of course it's not easy following in the footsteps of a man like Mark McCormack, the 24-hour-a-day workaholic who runs the giant International Management Group, guiding the careers of celebrities like Angela Rippon, Michael Parkinson and Bjorn Borg.

But Sally Anne Egan is not easily daunted — and she knows that the way to get on if you work for a man like McCormack, as she does, is to emulate his tough, no-nonsense disciplined style.

It is her ability to do this that won her the highly paid position of Vice-President at IMG, the only woman to attain this goal throughout McCormack's offices in Europe.

'Mark is the most efficient and well organised person I've ever met,' she says. 'And he expects the people he employs to have the same attitudes.

Headaches

'So on bad days I just remind myself that he is not asking me to do anything he couldn't do—and it spurs me on.'

With all the headaches of success come the benefits too —a salary in excess of £20,000 and a smart blue Volkswagen Jetta company car.

Her job is two-fold. She handles the leasing of entertainment marquees at big sports events like Wimbledon and, more importantly, acts as a kind of literary agent, negotiating with publishers on behalf of IMG clients who want to get their autobiographies published—people like Chris Evert-Lloyd or Billie Jean King.

She is the devoted helper, giving constant support working to ensure that other people enjoy their time in the limelight. And at this she is a star.

Yet she joined the company ten years ago as a secretary ... to Mark McCormack.

Interview: TERESA SKELLY

And her ascent was hardly meteoric.

As a girl, she admits she was only interested in having a good time—'I didn't really begin to get ambitious until I was 30.'

Coincidentally, that was her age when she joined IMG in London. Suddenly, she found herself taking dictation at 6 am in the back of limousines speeding from Heathrow airport and *still* toiling away at the office until 8 or 9 pm.

Soon she found she enjoyed it and after five years, her uncomplaining dedication paid off.

An executive handling the leasing of entertainment marquees left and Sally Anne was offered the job.

'I was terrified,' she says. 'After all, when you are a secretary the responsibility always lies with somebody else but once you take on a job like that the buck stops at one person — and that's you.'

She accepted, partly in a spirit of adventure and partly because a strong streak of stubborn Irish pride made the very notion of saying 'No' out of the question.

From then on there was no stopping this attractive, bright-eyed woman from Dublin, who looks younger than her 41 years.

Soon, she was travelling Europe and the States, leasing out marquees at events like the prestigious Italian Open Golf Tournament.

'I found the transition from being a secretary to becoming an executive a relatively easy one,' she says, 'although it did mean a lot of damned hard work.'

The name behind the big names ... Sally Anne Egan.

PICTURE: MARTIN LAWRENCE

'I found that the key to success in business is efficiency. It was ideal for this job because it entailed a lot of attention to detail, dealing with big companies, caterers, wine suppliers and so on and I believe women are better at details than men.

'I also realised that it didn't matter not having a degree or diploma in business because all I really needed was a lot of common sense.'

There's no doubting that Sally Anne has her feet planted firmly on the ground.

Yet even her outward calm was shaken when she was offered the job of literary agent and vice-president.

'Again I agonised over whether I could do it, because I knew little about books and nothing about negotiating.

'But again I decided that if Mark didn't think I could do it he wouldn't have offered me the job, so I accepted.

'It can be tough but usually we are dealing with such big names it's not too hard to persuade publishers to take an interest in a client's book.'

In a typical day she gets up at 6.30 a.m. and leaves her elegant three-bedroomed flat in Barnes by car to be in her office at 9 a.m.

She then spends a couple of hours going through her mail with her secretary, then it's on to the hard work of the day — making umpteen telephone calls to ensure there are no last minute hitches on negotiations on the latest book by, say, Arnold Palmer.

When possible she reserves her lunchbreak to go shopping—and whether it's clothes or food she'll probably find her way to the nearest Marks & Spencer.

If it's a business lunch and she's paying she'll choose a small, friendly Italian restaurant. 'They may not be patronised by the rich and famous but they are always good value for money.' Then it's back to work until around 6 p.m.

She says her biggest success was negotiating extra money for Virginia Wade, whose autobiography was published in 1977—the year she became Women's Singles Champion.

Sally Anne secured an almost unprecedented amount for a tennis star in advances —£40,000. 'We all did quite well out of that but it was more by luck than judgment,' she says, clearly rather self-satisfied.

So it comes as a surprise to hear Sally Anne say emphatically : 'Anyone who doesn't see that there is more to life than work is a fool.'

Bemused

'I've known people, mainly men, who are so committed to their jobs that they start getting ulcers and their marriages break up.

'So, while I am involved with my job and work hard, I would never let it rule my life.'

It is a telling statement from a woman who is plainly bemused by her success.

'I don't regret not marrying. I've had offers but something always held me back.

'In fact I'm glad because when I was young I was far too immature and selfish to have made a marriage last. Now I feel I would like the kind of relationship marriage can be and I am more giving. Only now do I feel ready to make the kind of commitment I believe you need.

'But I'm not making any plans. I never have — there are enough things to worry about today without worrying about what might happen when I'm 50.'

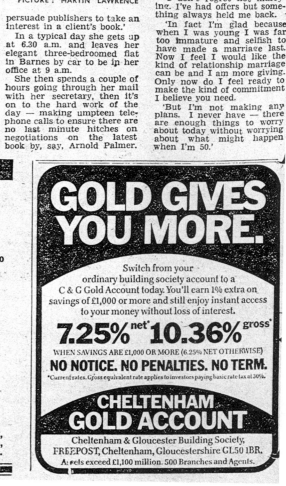
LETTER TO FEMAIL

The price of saying 'No'

SARA BARRETT is absolutely right to warn us never to underestimate the purpose of the office party (How Are Your Party Politics ? Femail, December 21).

I remember when returning to the office in the New Year, I discovered that three annual salary increase envelopes, which should have been posted with more than 20 others before the Christmas break, were still lying on the personnel manager's desk.

When I asked his assistant why, he said, 'Who do you think said "No" at the office Christmas party ?'

What he didn't realise was that I was one of them and one of those envelopes was addressed to me. The next day I handed in my resignation.

ANNE DERE,
Cathays,
Cardiff.

1982

Rape

Until 1958 a man who forced a woman to have sexual intercourse against her will would be charged with 'indecent assault' and not rape. The penalties if found guilty of a serious indecent assault were severe but frequently women did not report such an assault. Even after the law was changed, and in the supposedly more permissive and open 1960s, rape victims frequently remained silent. Exposure of the crime often led to more censure and victimization of the woman than of the guilty man by both the police handling the case and society at large. Many women and their families, especially if the victim was unmarried, did not want to admit that anything had happened. The woman might be regarded as 'damaged goods', perhaps severely affecting her marriage prospects. There was no anonymity for rape victims until the mid-1970s so that newspapers were allowed to publish their names.

The judge at any trial involving a sexual offence had to warn the jury then, as now, not to convict on the basis of the victim's evidence alone. This is not required in any other type of trial and places the victim of such an offence in a weaker position than any other witness, as their testimony cannot be believed without corroboration, which is usually supplied by forensic evidence.

In 1982 there was a great deal of discussion about a rape case which reflected the long-held attitude that somehow the victim of rape had to bear some of the guilt for the crime. In January Lord Hailsham rebuked a judge who said that a woman who was raped was guilty of 'contributory negligence' by hitch-hiking. The man in the case admitted his guilt and was fined £2,000 and not jailed. There was a public outcry against the judge's comments and the leniency of the sentence. But it was not the last such case to be reported in the 1980s where judges have deemed that in some instances women have 'led a man on' or where men have been rewarded by ludicrously lenient sentences because they pleaded guilty and gallantly saved the woman from testifying.

Despite these much-publicized cases, or perhaps because of the very fact that they brought the issue into the public eye, reports of rapes have increased dramatically. Rape victims are far more sympathetically treated by both society and the police. Following the broadcasting of a documentary on the Thames Valley Police in 1984 which included an interview with an alleged victim of rape where the woman was treated most insensitively the police have done much to change the way they deal with such cases.

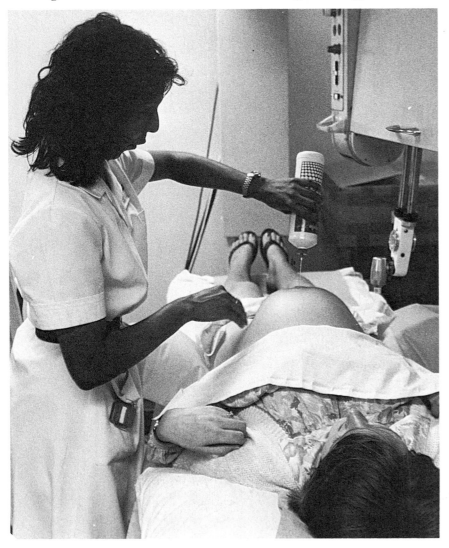

ABOVE: *The Prince and Princess of Wales with their son William whose birth scotched the debate about the question of succession if the heir to the throne's eldest child was a girl.*
BELOW: *A pregnant woman having an ultrasound scan which was rapidly becoming routine as childbirth became more reliant on high technology.*

1982 POSTSCRIPT

June – NALGO, National Association of Local Government Officers, decided to amend its rule book to acknowledge the existence of 50 per cent of its membership. Reference would now be made to 'he/she' and 'him/her' instead of just he and him. NALGO also reported that two thirds of women were in clerical grades while half of their men members were in professional grades and that half of the men earned over £8,000 while only 4 per cent of women did.

HOW WOMEN ARE CHEATED OUT OF PENSIONS

Mary Taylor is a senior consultant at a major London hospital. She is 46, has four children and is the chief breadwinner in her family.

She earns the same salary as her male colleagues and pays the same amount of money into an identical pension scheme. She has to – it's a condition of the job.

But there the similarity ends. When a male consultant dies his wife and children automatically receive a lump sum and a pension.

But if Dr Taylor dies her husband and children receive nothing . . .

Mary Taylor has decided it is time for her to make provision for her family so she is about to take out an insurance policy which gives them a lump sum worth three times her salary when she dies.

'My insurance broker tells me it's the only way of providing for them,' she says. 'It means I have to pay into two schemes to get the same benefit as a man doing my job.'

Daily Mail, 6 January 1982

You could be haunted by the child denied birth...

That's the view of Femail readers to a woman who sought their help

NO issue has touched such a responsive chord in Femail readers as the letter we published recently from a professional woman asking: 'Should I have an abortion?' Hundreds of letters poured in daily, and, after reading them she has finally made her decision. She says: 'I am grateful to everyone who wrote, particularly those who bravely told of their experiences and gave their names and addresses, even though what they were writing about was often a total secret from their own families.'

A GOOD man may be hard to find and it is not easy to be a single parent.

But life is too precious a gift to destroy and anyone who decides to have an abortion is likely to saddle themselves with lifelong feelings of haunting regret.

That was your overwhelming verdict.

One reader, who signed herself simply 'Mary', has an illegitimate son of nearly 20 ('His father was not free to marry me and 20 years ago any scandal would have cost him his job, house, pension, everything') and had an abortion when she found herself expecting a second child.

She writes: 'I still count each year how old my second child would have been and wonder all the time what he or she would have looked like.

'Show the world how brave you are and cry only when you are alone —because that is what you must do whichever of the two paths you choose to take.'

'I am 28, an adopted child like you and experienced an abortion and its emotional consequences nearly 10 years ago,' wrote a Dover woman. 'It seemed the right thing to do at a time when society was not as broadminded as it is now. But I still mourn the child whose life I terminated.'

A year ago, a Cheltenham reader found herself pregnant by the married man, father of two children, with whom she was deeply in love.

Yearn

She, too, was married with two children. She and the father of her unborn child decided they would leave their respective families and set up home together. But the only way they could afford it was if she had an abortion.

'Afterwards he changed his mind and said he couldn't leave his family,' she writes. 'I feel no resentment. Instead of a new life together, we carry on as before.

'But I yearn desperately to become pregnant again, to bring up the child of a man I love very deeply but whom I can never be with in the normal way.'

Ray Spencer of Ealing offered a man's point of view: 'As a man I should—like your boyfriend—feel an initial desire to reject the prospect of becoming a father unexpectedly. It takes time to recover from the shock.

'But talk to your boyfriend, explain how you feel, about your present pregnancy and your previous abortion and still birth. If he truly loves you he will accept the situation and encourage you to go ahead with the pregnancy.'

The joy and fulfilment to be found in motherhood were a recurrent theme, particularly in letters from happily-married women who had resisted medical advice in favour of abortion.

Wrote one reader from a Lancashire village: 'Before my marriage I was given an injection against German measles which, as an infant teacher, I thought I might catch from my pupils.

'I was not warned not to become pregnant for three months. When I soon started the family I wanted, my doctor told me my baby had a 30 per cent chance of being deformed — blind, or deaf, or mentally retarded, or suffering from a hole in the heart.

'The doctor strongly advised me to have an abortion, but my religious beliefs held firm. Besides, how could I abort my baby, my flesh and blood, my husband's flesh and blood?

'The baby hardly anyone wanted, except for me, my husband and — to be fair — the consultant at the maternity hospital, was born a lovely, healthy, normal girl.'

Mrs J. R. Harris, of Congleton in Cheshire, pleaded: 'Please do not have an abortion. Life is so precious, easily taken away but impossible to give back.

'I was advised 12 years ago to have an abortion on medical grounds because it was feared my baby would be abnormal. But I gave my baby the gift of life. Today he is a healthy and mischievous lad of 11 who makes me laugh, cry and worry over him.'

Fear

Nobody minimised the problems which a woman faces when she has to bring up a child on her own—choosing a surname . . . having to explain why there is no Daddy about the house . . .

'I dreaded being faced with having to tell the truth when my son grew older,' wrote one reader. 'But at a certain age you must tell the truth, even if you fear hurting him and hope only that he will not think too badly of you.'

'You are used to the freedom your lifestyle at present allows,' wrote Mrs R. O. Carmichael, a State Registered Nurse from Pewsey in Wiltshire. 'That would be curtailed by a baby and cause resentment.'

Joan M. Orange of Leeds took the view: 'Your correspondent knows herself how it feels to be an "unwanted" child. Her lover doesn't want her to have the baby and she is desperately undecided. I should think an abortion is the only possible answer to her dilemma.'

Nearly everyone wished our worried correspondent good luck in making a difficult choice which, in the end, would have to be hers alone.

A LONELY CHOICE . . . and you're not the only one who stands to be hurt.

And this was her decision

THOUGH overwhelmingly you advised me not to have an abortion, I have decided to do so.

I know only too well what it will do to me mentally but to do otherwise is to mess up too many people's lives.

A lot of you thought if it was a question of the man or the baby I should choose the baby—with which I agree—but in the end, as things have transpired, I shall have neither.

Nanny

My relationship with my boyfriend has inevitably deteriorated dramatically over the past few weeks to the point of no return. Suffice to say he has been totally unsupportive.

I am a self-employed lawyer and would rapidly become unemployed once it was known I was pregnant.

If going back to work with the aid of a nanny were at all viable, then that is the choice I would probably have made. But to have no career is, I am afraid, something I could not consider.

Despite what might have seemed an odd choice of 'going to the country like a Prime Minister' as one reader put it, some of your letters were tremendously helpful.

By the end of this month I hope life will have returned once again to what it was before I met my now ex-boyfriend. I do not choose to delude myself that the path I have chosen is an easy one, but as the alternative is no job and no man I feel it is the only sensible one.

Thanks again to you all. I am sorry I can't possibly reply to you personally. You have reinforced my opinion that the majority of people in this country are kind, feeling people.

1983

Peace Women

In the early 1980s, before the advent of President Gorbachev and *perestroika* and *glasnost,* the Soviet Union was continuing to put much of its energy into its armed forces and military hardware. With President Reagan in the White House the US response was to increase its military spending and to plan to deploy nuclear weapons in Britain and Continental Europe. Despite talks and treaties aimed at reducing arms on both sides, the military and particularly the nuclear capability on each side had escalated to such a degree that many people considered it madness.

In such a climate movements such as the Campaign for Nuclear Disarmament, which had been popular in the 1960s, re-emerged to express great public disquiet and to press for peace. A change from the 1960s CND movement was that in the early '80s the movement for peace became very much associated with women. In the peace movement many women, like Joan Ruddock, found their political voice. Great stress was placed on women's history as givers, nurturers and sustainers of life against men's history of death, destruction and the creation of killing machines.

The focus of attention and a symbol for the whole peace movement in Britain became the American Military Base at Greenham Common. In 1982 it was announced that Britain would allow the USA to deploy Cruise, its newest nuclear missiles, at Greenham from where the weapons could strike at the heart of the Soviet Union. From September 1982 a group of women established a protest camp outside the base's perimeter fence. The makeshift camp became the scene of a permanent vigil for several years and Greenham Common saw many demonstrations and protests throughout 1982 and 1983. In December 1982 over 20,000 women joined hands to encircle the airbase in protest and in April 1983 a fourteen-mile human chain linked Greenham to two other defence establishments at Aldermaston and Burghfield.

All the protests failed to stop the deployment of Cruise missiles but the point had been made to politicians, not just in Britain but throughout Europe and the rest of the world, that people were seriously worried by the escalation in the nuclear arms race. Subsequent moves to call a halt to this and the removal of many missiles have been claimed as a success for both the policies of the doves of the peace movement and the hawks like Margaret Thatcher and Ronald Reagan who insisted on outfacing the Soviet Union.

ABOVE: Peace women outside the main gates of Greenham Airbase.
BELOW: Victoria Gillick feeding some of her ten children.

1983 POSTSCRIPTS

April – Jenny Pitman became the first woman trainer to win the Grand National when her horse Corbière was first past the post.

May – Mary Donaldson was the first woman Lord Mayor of London since the office was created in 1192.

July – A judge ruled in a case brought by Victoria Gillick that doctors who prescribed the Pill to girls under sixteen were not guilty of aiding and abetting a crime by encouraging an underage girl to have sex but were medically encouraging contraception to limit the results of such a crime. The judge also ruled that it was not a crime for a doctor not to inform the parents that a girl under sixteen was on the Pill as there was no law requiring this.

December – Barbara McLintock of the USA was awarded the Nobel Prize for Medicine.

NOT A PENNY FOR THE LOVER OF 20 YEARS

A woman who kept home for her lover for 20 years and bore him two sons was not entitled to a share in their home when they split up, three Appeal Court judges ruled yesterday.

'I think she can justifiably say that fate has not been kind to her,' said Lord Justice May of 40-year-old Valerie Burns. But together with Lord Justices Waller and Fox he could offer her only sympathy because the law did not give her the same rights as a wife.

She 'has no rights against him,' said Lord Justice Fox. 'But the unfairness of that is not a matter which the courts can control. It is a matter for Parliament.'

Daily Mail, 27 July 1983

Femail

21 years ago the tranquilliser revolution swept Britain—but what was the cost...

Valium—Mother's helper or Mother's ruin?

THE lynx wasn't spitting any longer. The wild cat was acting more like a kitten. The scientists who had come to the San Diego zoo were astonished. They had never seen anything like it.

It had been achieved by the injection of a new drug called Librium. They were surprised because the animal was wide awake despite the drug and reacting normally. Yet it was tame. A new type of tranquilliser had been born. That was in 1957 and it signalled the start of a revolution that was to sweep the world. The man behind it was Austrian-born chemist, Leo Sternbach. Two years later he made another drug that was even more remarkable—Valium. As a muscle relaxant it was found to be ten times more effective than Librium.

It was capable of removing the sharp edges of emotional anguish while enabling people to carry on normal lives. That was the way the company behind it, the Swiss-based giant, Hoffman La Roche, sold it. It meant you could suffer acute anxiety and still go to work. It was, they said, a drug of its time—a means of combating the ever increasing stress of the 20th century.

It is now 21 years since the drug came to Britain. An estimated seven million people take Valium and other so called 'minor' tranquillisers each year.

It has been far too freely issued because it is easier for a doctor to scribble a prescription than to listen to a complex problem when his waiting room is full of patients. The fact that it is cheap compared with other NHS drugs also makes it popular.

A course of 100 tablets (5mg) costs only £1·65 and can provide five weeks' treatment. The average cost of an NHS prescription is about £4·50. However, the drug once hailed as 'the housewife's choice' and immortalised by the Rolling Stones as Mother's Little Helper is now subject to a barrage of criticism.

Far from softening the cruelties of 20th-century life, it is claimed, tranquillisers can hook people—especially women.

BY BARBARA GRIGGS

'I CAN'T explain the fear ... your head's ringing ... when you go outside, the trees are swimming.

'I always had the same hazy, swimming head: I haven't enjoyed a summer in seven years. You're in a world of your own—a world of fear. It's as though something else is living your life for you. It's taken over your life and its not a nice person . . .'

Sophia is middle-aged, smartly turned out, her hair beautifully coiffured. But her features are drawn, there are big circles under her eyes, her whole face is expressive of deep and desperate fatigue.

She started on Valium seven years ago ...

Bitter

'I can't say it ever really worked. I couldn't even concentrate any more. My life changed—I turned into a bitter, selfish, weepy woman.

'When I think what a rotten snivelling bitch I was, I think my family deserve a medal for putting up with me. I didn't know it was the Valium—until I realised I had to take more—and more — or I got a bad turn. Then I was frightened, and I tried to come off without any help.

'It's been the most terrifying, horrible experience of my life . . .

'I've been off Valium for seven months now, and I have variable days, that's all I can say.

'I took my last tablet on July 1, last year and I just hope there's light at the end of this rotten dark tunnel.'

Is Sophia one of untold thousands suffering from a frightening modern drug dependency problem, or is she a rare sufferer from a syndrome that afflicts only a tiny percentage of tranquilliser users? It depends to whom you talk.

When I first started to research the problem of withdrawal from Valium, I telephoned Roche, its makers. Their friendly, helpful PR Jean Kilshaw sent me round a huge stack of literature, including articles reprinted from prestigious medical publications.

I found that dependency or withdrawal problems received little attention. One authoritative two-part study, part-funded by a U.S. Public Health Service grant, and published last summer in the New England Journal of Medicine, concluded such problems were largely the creation of irresponsible journalists.

Dr John Marks, in his study, The Benzodiazepines : Use, Overuse, Misuse, Abuse, said of the dependence risk, that 'the incidence of total recorded cases appears to be in the range of one case per five million patient months . . .'

So how does it happen that when a London radio station ran a two-week phone-in project on the use of drugs in families, tranquillisers emerged as by far the commonest problem—more than 61 per cent. of callers worried about taking them.

And how is it that when a tiny item appeared in a popular newspaper about the work of the drug-help agency Release, their switchboard was jammed with desperate calls from people with tranquilliser problems for two weeks?

And how is it that there are now about 70 self-help groups for tranquilliser addicts in Britain?

Meanwhile, the Wolfson Unit of Clinical Pharmacology at the Royal Victoria Infirmary in Newcastle, published a special statement last year on the subject of Benzodiazepine Dependence and Withdrawal, in which they estimate that about a quarter of patients taking benzodiazepines for four months become dependent, while some patients show withdrawal symptoms after only a few weeks.

They list a horrifying catalogue of symptoms they have found to be common, including insomnia, anxiety, depression, panic attacks — as well as physical symptoms such as nausea, blurred vision and muscle pain. Furthermore, these symptoms 'may last for many months.'

Dr Anthony Thorley, consultant psychiatrist to Oakwood House, Regional Drug and Alcoholic Unit, told me: 'It's beginning to emerge that coming off heroin is easier than coming off Valium.'

There's a growing recognition that the cure may be worse than the disease. Release reports 'The degree of distress which many people experience on withdrawal is often far more extreme than when the person went to the doctor for the original problem.'

One explanation for the yawning gap between such assessments and the verdict of the scientific literature, is the difficulty most victims experience in convincing doctors that they have a problem of either withdrawal or dependence.

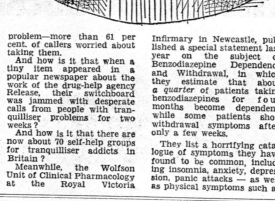

Man who started it all...

EXPERTS estimate that 100,000 people in Britain would have severe withdrawal problems if they stopped taking minor tranquillisers like Valium.

But Dr Leo Sternbach, above, the 75-year-old chemist who invented the drug, has no regrets about having done so.

He told me: 'I am proud to have been associated with both Librium and Valium. The development of these drugs represent the high point of my working life.'

And he hit out at claims that patients are being prescribed the drug for too long.

'I don't think this happens any more. There has been so much propaganda about this that doctors now tend to under prescribe.

Furthermore, although the problems of addiction have now been well publicised, the agonies of withdrawal have received less attention.

Newcastle nurse, Shirley Trickett, runs a tranquilliser withdrawal support group called Come Off It and has held the hand—quite literally —of nearly 200 people suffering withdrawal.

Unique

'The benzodiazepine withdrawal syndrome seems unique,' she told me. 'It's quite different from other dependencies such as heroin or alcohol, not only because it is not self-poisoning, but also because physical and not psychological dependence is the major problem. The duration is also different. Some people are not symptom-free for 18 months to two years.'

'I'm not saying—Ban the Benzodiazepines' — emphasises Shirley. 'They can be lifesaving for some people. There's nothing to replace them, and many people—probably most—have no problems coming off when they want to. But there must be much more careful prescribing, and there must be recognition of the true nature of the illness caused by the therapeutic use of the drugs, and reactions to their withdrawal.'

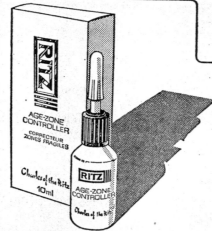

Of Equal Value

The Equal Pay Act which was passed in 1970 and finally implemented in 1976 said that where a man and a woman were doing the same job they should be paid the same wage. However there were many areas of work which despite the Sex Discrimination Act had remained through tradition and practice all male or all female. Where jobs had no male pay structure because there were no male employees before 1976 the pay structures remained the same. If a man was not doing the job it was likely to be low paid. So many women doing what had by tradition become women's jobs were unaffected by the Act.

It became evident in the years following the implementation of the Act that in many cases women were doing work of 'equal value' to a man in a different job within the same company or institution. Following a ruling in the European Courts the British Government were forced to amend the Equal Pay Act in 1984 to allow women to be given equal pay for work of equal value. This of course was a less clear-cut law to implement and required a court ruling in some instances to define 'equal value'. In 1988 a cook won equal pay with joiners, painters and insulation engineers in the same company when an industrial tribunal ruled in her favour. And in 1989 Lloyds Bank had to increase the pay of 5,500 secretaries and typists to match that of senior messengers. A tribunal said that the difference had originated because of the traditional assumptions that 'the messenger was a family man and needed to be paid a family wage'.

The Equal Pay Amendment has still to prove its worth to women in areas of work such as some factory production lines which are exclusively female where there is no man's job to compare the value of their work with but where the tradition of women workers, with their past willingness to work for lower wages and their lack of trade-union organization, has established rates of pay which male workers and unions would not have accepted.

ABOVE: *Brenda Dean.*
BELOW: *Graham and Janet Walton pictured with their six baby daughters born in November 1983 after Janet Walton had been treated with a fertility drug.*

1984 POSTSCRIPTS

March – The 250,000 members of SOGAT 82 elected Brenda Dean to head the union. She was the first woman to lead a major trade union.

• British Airways announced that all cabin staff would in future be placed on five-year contracts and the maximum starting age would be 26 so that no one would be over 31. Before the Sex Discrimination Act came into effect in 1976, the maximum age for women was 35 and 55 for men, after the Act the maximum age for both sexes was 55.

July – In the USA Democrat Walter Mondale named Geraldine Ferraro as his running mate. Women had become powerful within the Democratic Party and the selection of the first woman to such a position reflected this.

August – The first Women's Olympic Marathon was run at the Los Angeles Games.

Femail

You're one in a million!

The facts and figures that go to prove why the British woman is anything but average

LOVE

THE average woman makes love once every 3·8 days—96 times a year—and will burn up about 200 calories doing so.

First choice of location for lovemaking for 96 per cent. of women is the bedroom. As an alternative, 78 per cent. chose the living room, 46 per cent. elsewhere in the house and 41 per cent. in the car.

Most women receive a formal proposal, over dinner, and generally are engaged for 19 months. Today, 52 per cent. of all weddings are in a register office. The average single woman marries when she is 22·3 years old, single men 24·5. Second-time around women are 33·4 years of age, men 35·8.

Once married, she'll stay that way for 44·5 years—longer than at any time in history.

Church weddings are less popular than register office now.

The average UK adult is not a toucher. In a restaurant survey over one hour, a British couple did not touch at all, an American couple touched eight times, a Puerto Rican couple 20, a French couple 110.

CHILDREN

WOMEN are pregnant for an average of 266 days from conception. She stays in hospital for five days when having her baby which weighs 7lb 5oz.

To be average, the parents will name a daughter Charlotte or Sarah and a son, James. In fact, James has been the most popular boy's name for 21 years. And if it's James Smith, well . . .

The average cost of raising a child to the age of 16 is about £70,000 (including wife's loss of earnings) but each additional child will cost only an extra £1,000 a year.

Girls spend most time on homework—38 minutes, compared to 18 minutes for boys. Nearly one-third of girls and half the boys say they do no homework at all.

The average teenager is not going out with anybody of the opposite sex. Fewer than 40 per cent. have a steady boy or girl friend.

HOW many times does the average woman make love in a year? What's the size of the average woman's bust? How much sleep does she need on average? And who do most women want to look like? The answers to these questions and many more statistics that shape the mind and body of the average woman in Britain have now been compiled* and provide fascinating insights into the female sex.

THE ideal woman as seen by women, is 35-25-36 and weighs 8st. 12lb.—a full 13lb. lighter than reality. The most sought after figure is one like Felicity Kendal's who is rated above Victoria Principal, Bo Derek, Raquel Welch and the Princess of Wales.

But in reality, busts are bursting out—the average is now 36in. Only a decade or so ago the most popular bra size was 34in., in a modest B cup. The average hip measurement is now 39in.

BODY-TALK

WOMEN generally start dieting when they are 20, though one in four start at 15. Most weigh themselves once a week, but 25 per cent step on the scales daily. Most women think they're overweight and 20 per cent think they are very overweight. Five per cent think they're just right and diet to stay that way.

Women take a bath four times a week, men only three. Both spend about the same time in the bath — women 24 minutes and men 26.

A woman will sleep for eight hours and 20 minutes and doesn't snore : a man sleeps for eight hours and does snore. Both sexes dream, with an average span of 1¼ hours in five separate periods. Whatever the interpretation of dreams, they're slimming stuff — women and men lose about 1lb while asleep.

Most women will live until they are 75·6 years old, men to 69. British children born now will do better than their parents. Girls will live until they are well over 80, men to 77.

HOME

The average home is a house—beating flats into second place by four to one. One-third are terraced, one-third semi-detached and the remainder are split equally between detached, bungalows and 'others'.

The average fuel bill in the average home is between £450 and £500 a year.

Most women do NOT have a tumble dryer (in only 27 per cent. of households) ; video recorder (33 per cent.) ; home computer (25 per cent.) ; microwave oven (8 per cent.) ; blender/liquidiser (47 per cent.) ; pressure cooker (44 per cent.) ; deep-fat fryer (25 per cent.) · toasted sandwich maker (44 per cent.) ; slow cooker (14 per cent.).

Every day we put 50,000 tons of rubbish into our waste bins. In a year the average dustbin contains enough paper to save six trees, enough waste to keep a garden in compost and half a ton of glass, metal and plastic.

When it comes to accidents in the home, it's women and children first. Children under five are involved in 27 per cent. of all household mishaps. Every day 300 women fall out of bed and more than 200 crash into doors—many of which are made of glass.

WORK

Today, 60 per cent. of women work—against only 20 per cent. in 1954—and women make up 40 per cent. of the total UK work force.

Fifteen years after the Equal Pay Act and nine years after the Sex Discrimination Act, women earn only two-thirds as much as men.

Most people work 40 hours a week which breaks down into 37.2 hours a week for women and 41·4 hours for men.

The average working man and working woman puts their earnings into a joint account from which both partners can draw. One in five men puts his money into a personal account ; one in three working wives do too. One in three men give their wives all or most of their earnings. Four in ten give wives a housekeeping allowance.

The average time a woman with a job must spend working to pay for household goods is :

1 pint milk, 4 mins ; 125gm tea, 7 mins ; Large white sliced loaf, 8 mins : 1 pint beer, 12 mins : 1 dozen medium eggs, 13 mins ; 500gm butter, 19 mins ; 20 cigarettes, 20 mins ; 100gm instant coffee, 22 mins ; Cinema admission, 34 mins ; 1 gallon petrol (4*), 35 mins ; Weekly telephone bill, 40 mins ; 1lb rump steak, 58 mins ; Weekly gas bill, 1hr. 7 mins ; Weekly electricity bill, 1hr. 14 mins ; 1cwt coal, 1hr. 31 mins ; Long playing record. 1hr. 41 mins ; 1 bottle whisky, 2hrs. 20 mins ; Colour TV licence. 14hrs. 40 mins : Car tax. 27hrs. 10 mins ;

one member out of work. In the high-income group (households where the woman and the man both have jobs) the weekly spend is £200. Throughout the country, food takes the highest percentage of our weekly income.

* The Mackeson Book of Averages is published by Andre Deutsch, price £4·95.

Women spend £25·73 on household food a week

MONEY

Women shopping for the household spend £25·73 on food every week and a complete family shop, including food, costs £38·58.

Two in ten men have no idea how much of the family income goes on food, even though four out of ten men actually help with the weekly shop. Most don't mind doing it and 17 per cent. positively enjoy it.

Every week households in the middle income group spend about £150, broken down to £56 per person. That's about double the figures for the low-income family with

LEISURE

Our most popular national sporting activity is hardly a sport at all—it's walking. Eight million of us—slightly fewer women than men—regularly walk more than two miles at any one time. For the most part we want to walk in rural surroundings like a park, by the canal or along leafy roads.

Next in popularity is swimming—both indoor and outdoor. Five million people, equally divided between women and men, swim regularly. Most is done in indoor pools. If we swim outside, we prefer the sea, or rivers and ponds, to outdoor pools.

Swimming is by far the most dangerous sport. It is more dangerous than soccer, rugby, sailing and horseriding put together.

love is...

... discovering he's a good cook.

© 1985 Los Angeles Times Syndicate

2842

1985

A Growing Divorce Rate

Since the new Divorce Act had come into force in 1971 there had been almost a threefold increase in divorces. In 1985, one in every four marriages ended in divorce, affecting large numbers of women, men and children. Wives and children were in theory reasonably well provided for when a marriage broke up but of course finding enough money to keep two households going generally made everyone less well off. Problems occurred if the husband remarried and had a second family to support. Statistically a husband was two and a half times more likely to remarry than his ex-wife who most usually had custody of any children. Keeping maintenance payments regular and at a reasonable level was, and remains, a perennial problem for divorced women.

In 1984 a further divorce law was brought into effect which allowed for divorce after only one year of marriage. The Matrimonial and Family Proceedings Act concentrated on providing maintenance for any children of the marriage. Where no children were involved and both partners were self-sufficient they could make a 'clean break', divide up their property and have no more financial ties to one another. Where there were children maintenance was allocated to them and then the wife, where it was deemed necessary for her to look after them. When the children left home or the woman remarried, her maintenance from her ex-husband would cease and she would have to provide for herself.

There are obvious benefits to more easily obtained divorce. Women no longer have to remain tied to a relationship that is unhappy, violent or simply emotionally dead. But there are disadvantages. Many people now no longer regard marriage as a lifelong commitment which means it is no longer the secure and stable institution it once was; although of course in Queen Victoria's reign as many marriages were ended within sixteen years by the early death of one or other of the partners as are ended by divorce today.

It is the mother who more often has to cope alone, for even if the father is granted access it is common for fathers to no longer have contact with their children only a few years on from the divorce. Bringing up a child or children alone and coping with all the demands they make emotionally, physically and intellectually is not easy. Without a partner for support single-parent status leaves women at a severe disadvantage in terms of career prospects as it is difficult to take a demanding well-paid job and childcare costs make lower-paid jobs uneconomic.

ABOVE: *Pop singer Madonna performs as a sex symbol but with herself very much in control of the image she projects, unlike many of the girl singers, such as the young Tina Turner, of earlier generations whose image had been controlled by men.*

BELOW: *Anita Roddick had become a business success when The Body Shop was quoted on the Stock Exchange. Her philosophy of selling body-care products based on natural ingredients in simple bottles without fancy labels or extravagant claims to make the user more beautiful, captured the imagination of millions of consumers.*

1985 POSTSCRIPTS

January – Surrogate mother Kim Cotton gave birth to a child whom she gave up to the father. Her case brought the issue of surrogacy which had been practised for some years in the USA to the attention of the British public and a law was passed banning commercial surrogacy.

February – In the face of a threatened Aids epidemic the Dail in Dublin passed a Bill legalizing the shop sale of condoms to people over 18.

October – The Law Lords reversed a ruling made by a lower court in February which banned doctors from prescribing the Pill to girls under sixteen. The ban had been won following campaigning by Victoria Gillick.

Femail

For love of Catherine...

She starved to 'aid' her family. Now her tragedy may save others

TO AN outsider, the Dunbar family seem to have it all. But it is not the elegant house on a Surrey hillside, the three cars in the drive and John's business successes that one should envy. It's the dedicated closeness of the family—so close, it's almost tangible.

Yet wife Maureen, a colonel's daughter, admits: 'Once we came close to splitting up. Our family was in deep crisis. But nothing could part us now . . .'

Family portraits are all over the house. There is Simon, recently qualified as a doctor, Richard, Anna blonde and clever. But there is a fourth child. A dark-haired waif with large eyes. Catherine, unnaturally thin and haunted, looks out from these photos. She is the source of the family's heartbreak. And its strength.

For Catherine is dead at 22. She and her parents fought for seven years against her self-starvation . . . and lost.

Maureen said: 'It started when the family was under great financial stress. At one point, I left home for a short time. It ended with us all trying to understand, to help to save Catherine.'

John explained: 'We discovered her illness right from the beginning. We could afford to go to the top medical people and try every treatment available — and we did. We weren't ashamed to admit our problem: we kept nothing hidden.

'We did everything we possibly could to break the dreadful pattern. We sent Catherine to boarding school when she wanted to go. We brought her home again when she wanted to be with us. We sent her to school in France because she fell in love with the idea. We offered her bribes. We made threats. We tried everything anyone could try. And we still lost.'

It is only now after they have written a book* about Catherine that mother and father are beginning to find reasons for what went so terribly wrong.

Maureen castigates insensitive medical treat-

by DIANA HUTCHINSON

ment based on a childish punishment and reward system—unsuitable when dealing with the enhanced cunning of a highly intelligent young woman.

BUT for John, a dominating, driven figure raised in a council house in Liverpool, looking over his relationship with Catherine and Maureen has meant coming to terms with the awful idea that his business crash in 1973, and his response to it, may have supplied the trigger which started his daughter's illness.

John explains: 'At 18 I'd started work in a factory in Liverpool, and within a year I'd moved south and begun building up a business. We had a

large Victorian house we all loved. I ran an investment trust for a European company. I was happily married to someone who took pleasure in being a wife and mother.

'My sons were at boarding school and my daughters were at private schools, too. We decided to look for another house and found one with a swimming pool and tennis court nearer to Catherine's Convent school.'

But a few months after the Dunbars bought their dream house, the world economy crashed, the European investment group sold off their business, John found he could not sell his former home and he was saddled with an immense bridging loan.

Maureen's response was to suggest the children

went to State schools and that they sold their big new house.

But John's attitude was there could be no going back. 'It was my sense of achievement and my ambition. When I was a lad I worried that I would never achieve anything. To take the children out of their schools would be a personal failure and intolerable.

'I became very anxious and depressed. I had two survival mechanisms. One was to go to bed for the whole weekend. The other was consciously to sit down and get drunk. I have never gone out drinking. I used to do it at home.

EVERYONE can get nasty when they drink. Obviously Catherine would see outbursts of stress. I am an emotional person and if I feel something and want to shout, I shout. Catherine used to shout back. She was very outspoken.

Her mother says : 'Catherine took it upon herself to try to keep the family together at this difficult time. And she couldn't do it. She was just a little girl really.

'Stopping eating was a

Wasting away : Catherine with her mother, and (above) with the family at their idyllic home

way of deliberately making herself ill. It was her form of protest. But she didn't foresee the tragic consequences.

'She'd always been finicky with food. Giving up eating was the easiest way to rebel. She was trying to control her life. She was trying to get the family stable again.'

There were good times. Catherine got first-class results at O-levels and landed a job at Reuters. John Dunbar started to become more successful. A house was sold to pay back the bank loan. Maureen, who had left home for three months, realised she could never leave John finally. Nor Catherine.

But anorexia, once triggered, is relentless. 'Catherine grew to detest her illness but she couldn't live without it. She had no hope of leading a

normal life and in the end she just wanted to die,' her mother says.

JOHN remembers how she asked him to take her to the hillside cemetery at their local church. 'She said she loved it there and hoped we had reserved a plot for her. I used to say "No Catherine. I can not accept that you are going to die. And to the very end I will try to fight to change your mind".' On January 2nd 1984, he lost that fight.

Says Maureen : 'Nothing can bring Catherine back but we are setting up a trust fund to help other children like her. I can only hope that by speaking out we can get a debate opened on the medical treatment of anorexics, because so much is being done so badly.'

* Catherine, by Maureen Dunbar, published by Viking, £7·95.

What you can do if your child stops eating

BOYS as well as girls are at risk of becoming anorexic. Dr Bryan Lask, head of a group of specialists at Great Ormond Street Hospital for Children, says that at least 25 per cent. of new cases are male.

Dr Lask says: 'Parents tie themselves in knots trying to find the reason why their child gets it. The truth is, there are many complex factors. One common strain is the issue of staying in control. Children who do not like what is going on in the family, find very quickly that by stopping eating they become the centre of attention and occupy a strong controlling position in the family.

'It is very addictive. It is often the bright conscientious child who does this. And once started it is very hard to stop. Any parent should keep a close

watch on their child's weight. If they lose half a stone they are in trouble and need professional help. And families will need therapy to try to find out the underlying difficulties.'

At Atkinson Morley Hospital, Professor Arthur Crisp runs a regime where anorexics are put on a calorie controlled diet of 3,000 calories a day. A spokesman said: They are kept in bed and they have to agree to give over their willpower to us. If they do not make that agreement then we don't take them on. Those who stay have a good prognosis.

'We treat the whole family in pyschotherapy sessions. Often the parents will have to change their ways with dealing with problems or look very hard at their marriage.'

1986

Feeling Fit and Looking Good

ABOVE: *An aerobics class.*
BELOW: *Weightlifting for women also became popular.*

Jane Fonda's *Workout Book* sold 160,000 copies almost overnight when it went on sale in Britain in 1982. Capitalizing on the fashion for jogging and a healthy lifestyle that emerged in the late 1970s Jane Fonda became something of a high priestess of fitness. Her message was to 'go for the burn', and that if it wasn't hurting it wasn't doing any good. Aerobics became the fitness craze of the early 1980s and following Jane Fonda's there were many similar books, and women on television exercising the nation in the early mornings. As in the 1970s it was mainly women who took the fitness message to heart and aerobics became almost exclusively a female pastime.

The fashion for fitness and health has remained and developed to include dance and less vigorous forms of exercise, such as walking, appealing to and enabling a wider range of women to participate. There has also been a massive increase in the whole fitness and leisure business with more sport and leisure centres opening, more courses on offer, more books and magazines dispensing advice about what to eat and how to keep the body in perfect shape.

The search for the perfect shape and the desire to remain youthful looking has led to a boom in cosmetic surgery, particularly in the USA, although it is being promoted more and more in Britain. Even girls as young as sixteen are having the shape of their noses or their breasts changed to make them more attractive.

In many ways women in the 1980s became freer to dress as they pleased. There was a wider range of styles, from the power dressing of the woman at work to floaty, flowery Laura Ashley designs or comfortable leisure and jogging suits. Older women were no longer required to wear either young fashions or be left with frumpy styles. On the other hand, there was continued pressure in the media promoting images of how a woman should look, from the Princess of Wales who became an icon – the glamorous working wife and mother – to the continued use of women to advertise products, to Page Three Girls, to Joan Collins and other television and film stars who remained young looking at 50.

Eating disorders among women became more talked about with cases of bulimia being reported as well as anorexia nervosa which surfaced in the 1970s. The tip of an iceberg had been revealed and some dieticians say that the iceberg is growing with younger and younger people, mainly girls, being afflicted by eating disorders. To attribute the cause of the increase to the images of women portrayed in the media is too easy a solution but it is in part to do with body and self-image and the way girls are conditioned to feel about themselves.

1986 POSTSCRIPTS

June – Sixty-three per cent of voters in a referendum in Eire rejected a government proposal to amend the constitution to allow divorce.

November – Following 278 deaths and 548 cases of Aids in Britain so far the government launched the largest ever health campaign to try to combat the spread of the disease.

December – The Institute of Directors reported that there were only nine women on the boards of Britain's largest companies and that whereas in 1975 women held ten per cent of the 'top jobs' in business in 1985 that figure had dropped to just over six per cent.

Femail

The 'sun care' sell that burns me up

Our only real protection is to stay indoors

It takes more than just a blob of suntan oil to protect your skin and your children's from the sun's damaging effects.

by ANTHEA GERRIE

THE SUN does your skin no good. No one any longer has any excuse for not facing the saddest and truest beauty fact we have had to come to grips with this century.

Dr. Albert Kligman of the University of Pennsylvania, world's leading skin care guru, says brusquely that if you want your skin to look younger for longer, you need to keep it out of the sun.

Even our own Royal College of Physicians have this year taken the unprecedented step of warning us against the damage sun can wreak on your skin. To early wrinkling, add scaling, pigmentary irregularities and skin cancer.

Business

The news is bad for sunworshippers, but the weight of medical evidence is solid. So it's a surprise to see the companies that have built their fortunes and reputations on a serious approach to skin care getting deeper into the suntan products business — rather than making a stand by getting out completely.

Clarins, the French beauty house of almost 40 years standing which has made a sizeable impact in Britain with its pure ingredient claims and clinical packaging, has a huge sun care range of no fewer than 12 products. And new this year comes not a more powerful sunblock but a Deep Tanning Gel, SPF only 2 — what the trade terms 'minimal protection'.

Clinique, which owns a quarter of the top-end cosmetics business, his built an unparalleled worldwide marketing success on the concept of no-nonsense skin care. Yet along with an impressive range of sunblocks, they promote the minimal protection Suntan Encourager — hardly a name to put you off the sun.

Cancer

And they have not been able to resist capitalising on the new technology pioneered last year by their parent company Estee Lauder, by introducing a Pre-Tan Enhancer guaranteed to accelerate your tan.

RoC, also born in France of pharmaceutical origins, have had sun care in their line since 1960. They too have chosen to get into minimal protection products this year — and, almost laughably, they are banding a free sample of their After Sun Repair Cream to every pack!

RoC scientists know full well that sun does skin no good: their own Sun and Skin hand-out points out that 'premature ageing of the skin is a long term effect of sun exposure' and that excessive sun can result in skin cancer.

But, they continue cosily 'although the sun is in many ways harmful to the skin, it nevertheless has a positive psychological benefit, a generally enjoyable and a suntan remains socially desirable.'

There you have it. The sun products market was worth £51 million last year — and it's growing by an annual 16 per cent. Cosmetics research specialists Syndicated Data Consultants predict that the invention of the pre-tan accelerator could actually set the market growing even faster —

meaning big profits for all who participate.

'Cost of goods is very low on these products — ingredients may amount to only 50p, but the product can be sold for 10 times that amount,' says SDC director Imogen Matthews.

'People do not mind spending good money on suntan products when they have already laid out £400 on a holiday. The manufacturers have picked up on this, and product prices have shot through the roof.'

Do the skin care companies who tout themselves as authorities on protecting the epidermis not think it stretches their credibility just a little when they fly in the face of medical opinion?

Yveline Duchesnes, Clarins' Paris-based director of international training, says: 'We tell fair women to start out with a total sunscreen and dark women to start with SPF6.

'We tell them to stick to this regime for 10 days' minimum before switching to a lower protection factor. But of course human beings are free, so we can never refuse to sell a product.'

At RoC, the consultant is not always around to babysit the customer, who is notoriously bad at serving herself with product information leaflets. Most RoC sales are made through independent chemists, and 15 per cent are sold in Boots, straight off the shelf, self-service.

'We do put our leaflets out, but Boots will not let us put up a sun-typing chart,' says UK marketing executive Mary Wray. 'Our research shows there is a place for SPF2 products — they are defined as being for skin that rarely

burns, tans profusely, looks dark brown and is insensitive.'

In truth, few of us in Britain can honestly lay claim to that sort of skin. We are English roses blessed with a humid climate that gives us the best skin in the world, and if we had any sense we would make a point of trying to keep it that way.

The good news is that sunblock products too are on the increase, and they've never been easier to apply. Clinique's Lip Block (£4.75) and Eye-Zone Sun Block (£7.50) are portable little crayons you can carry with you always, and new this year is a Face-Zone Sun Block (£8) that offers serious protection while staying truly matte and transparent on the face.

Really innovative new ways of applying sunblock come from La Prairie of Switzerland in the form of a mousse for the body and a sunblock compact for the face, both SPF15. But these are for the real jetsetters — they cost £19 apiece.

COOK OF THE YEAR: HEAT THREE

Strawberry surprise

Maureen Mulley

PAMELA Nelson wants to be a best selling romantic novelist. She spends six hours a day studying the works of Jeffrey Archer and Jackie Collins in an attempt to meld the two.

But the Daily Mail Cook of the Year competition was an altogether more inspiring story. Her designer menu for the Duke and Duchess of York and Blake and Alexis Carrington was high on glamour and colour. Particularly her saffron stuffed shoulder of lamb and a marbled gooseberry fool which survived the journey from Nottingham to our Birmingham final.

'Fergie watches her weight, Andrew ought to. I'm sure Blake has false teeth so no seed in the dessert. And Alexis must look good and glowing

. . . that's how I planned my menu,' said Pamela.

Ann Jenkins was worried her rose pink Champagne Spoon, a delicate water ice, would disappear in the heat. So the judge tasted it first.

The easy winner was Maureen Mulley from Banbury,

who was entered by her appreciative mother-in-law. Her meringue basket cake with strawberries got full marks from specialist Jane Asher and the lamb en croute was delightfully pink in the middle.

The next final is in Maidstone next week.

Prizes include a luxury kitchen from Alno and the sensational Creda circulaire combination microwave oven with magnetic induction hob, cooker hood and de luxe dishwasher. Value of this kitchen is £7,250. There will also be Royal Doulton fine china and glassware and hampers of top quality food from Dairy Crest including English cheeses.

DIANA HUTCHINSON

1987

Women as Priests

By 1987 women in the Church of England had already been able for four years to conduct weddings, baptisms and funerals in their role as deaconesses. But they were still barred from being ordained as priests and so were not able to give Communion and minister fully to their congregation. Most other Protestant Churches in Britain had moved in the 1960s and '70s to ordain women as ministers and the liberal Jewish faith had ordained women rabbis. Outside Britain the Anglican Church, particularly in the USA, had ordained several women.

The Church of England had hesitated for several years over the ordination of women on two grounds. First, it had long hoped that it could form closer and more binding ties with the Roman Catholic Church and as the Vatican was totally opposed to the idea of women priests it was thought that a move to ordain women in the Church of England would remove any hope of a joining of the two faiths. The second reason was fear of a schism within the Church itself. Indeed when in February 1987 the General Synod of the Church of England voted overwhelmingly in favour of the ordination of women the Bishop of London and lay members like MP and government minister John Selwyn Gummer said they would leave the Church.

The Archbishop of Canterbury, Robert Runcie, an advocate of women priests, tried to calm the divisions by stressing that no legislation would be enacted before 1991 and that it would be at least 1993 before any women were ordained. But the crucial decision had been taken and it was reinforced in 1988 when the Lambeth Conference of Bishops voted to allow women to become bishops.

ABOVE: Women who wished to be ordained as priests hold a service to draw attention to their cause outside Southwark Cathedral while an ordination service is being held inside.
BELOW: Deaconess Antonia Lynn.

1987 POSTSCRIPTS

● Legal and General took Rosalind Hines as a typical example of a woman at home looking after children and estimated that she worked on average 92 hours per week and that the cost of replacing her labour would be £19,253 per year.

● A survey showed that quarter of all small businesses were run by women.

June – In the general election in which Mrs Thatcher was the first prime minister this century to win a third successive term in office a record 41 women were also elected to Parliament – this was still however only six per cent of the total membership of the House of Commons.

YOUR BABY MUST DIE

A father-to-be yesterday finally lost his dramatic battle to save the life of his unborn baby.

Three Law Lords ended his hope of stopping his former girlfriend having an abortion. The operation, scheduled for tomorrow, can now go ahead . . .

Yesterday's decision came after a whirlwind of courtroom activity, and effectively confirms that a father has no rights over his unborn child.

Daily Mail, 25 February 1987

Femail

A recipe for disaster

"The average globe artichoke,"

said Mark, "has a water content of 36%. The average human being has a water content of 66%.

"Which throws a new light on its relative value and ours," he continued, looking gloomily at the tanned, healthy bodies around the swimming pool.

Jane poured herself a glass of Volvic mineral water from the blue plastic bottle.

"Artichokes don't drink Volvic," she said. "It is naturally filtered through alternate layers of fine porous rocks and the hardest volcanic stone. Andesite, for example, and Basalt. Which makes it unusually pure, even for mineral water, and remarkably low in mineral content. Conventially pure."

"That only means," said Mark, unwilling to be comforted, "that they have more substance but we are a better class of water."

by HELEN FIELDING

BEST-SELLING novelist Shirley Conran coined the phrase: 'Life is too short to stuff a mushroom.' Now, it seems life is too short to bake a cake.

The British housewife is slowly being replaced by a 'Flash Harriet' figure with a liking for fancy foreign food, a tendency to fudge the truth about what she serves up and about her total inability to cook.

A soon-to-be-released survey suggests the British person (woman if we're honest rather than ideologically sound) is losing the inclination and, therefore, the ability to prepare home-made food.

The survey, by Taylor Nelson Research, studies the consumption of home-made food in British households and concludes: 'One of the greatest changes in our eating habits this century has been the shift away from home-made food toward branded replacements.'

From 1980 to 1987, the number of meals made in the home has fallen by 30 per cent. In the last year alone, 17 million fewer home-made hot pies were eaten than in the previous year, 27 million less helpings of home-made savoury dishes, and a cataclysmic 51 million less home-made cakes, tarts and pastries.

There are good sociological reasons for this. Far more people live alone today than ever before — they leave their parents' home earlier, marry later and divorce more. More importantly, 50 per cent of British women now work. There's less incentive to cook if you're on your own or short of time. But there's also less incentive if there are substitutes which are as good as home-cooking.

Fresh

Five years ago, Marks & Spencer introduced us to the chilled meal: a dish you could buy in a container, ready-cooked and — most importantly — fresh. Its Chicken Kiev started the revolution.

The trend toward convenience food was already established. You could buy dried soup, cake mix, curry, tins of beans or steamed sponge, and just about anything in frozen form. But nothing so fresh that people might actually believe you'd cooked it yourself.

Now that's changed, and the mental wrestling in the supermarket is less about ingredients than which ready-made meals to purchase. Surrounded by Trout Meunière, Roast Chicken Dinner for Two and Lobster Thermidore, we are seduced by convenience: 'No one need know... It would be a hassle to buy the ingredients...'

Holidays abroad first made people want to eat spaghetti and taramasalata, but having spotted the desire to experiment, supermarkets have done more for the British palate than trips to Malaga or Rimini.

The constant pressure to find the

SANDWICH CAKE FAILURES: From left, Emma Thompson, Jilly Cooper and Edwina Currie

Could you rise to the cake challenge?

THE Victoria Sandwich Cake was a standard part of the family diet 20 years ago. Any woman worth her salt would have had the recipe off pat. But not any more, as these hapless victims of our telephone spot-check demonstrate.

Actress Emma Thompson gave double the correct amount of flour, half the sugar, missed out an egg and mixed it up all wrong. Emma's Victoria recipe would produce a cake with the consistency of a leaden stageweight.

Novelist and journalist Jilly Cooper was close on the ingredients but her oven temperature would have reduced the mixture to a smouldering pancake.

Edwina Currie, Mrs Thatcher's Junior Health Minister, had no idea how to make one. She said she wouldn't dream of making anything so unhealthy as a cake anyway!

So how *do* you make a Victoria sponge? According to Pru Leith's School of Food & Wine, use 6 ozs butter; 6 ozs sugar; 3 large eggs; 6 ozs self-raising flour. **Method:** Cream butter with sugar. Beat in eggs, adding one tablespoon of sieved flour with each. Beat well. Fold in remaining flour. Divide mixture between two greased tins and bake for 20-25 minutes at 370F/Gas Mark 5. Cool, then sandwich sponges together with jam.

Convenience meals may kill the art of home-cooking

next Chicken Madras or Beef Stroganoff demands a permanent M&S staff of 50 selectors and four master chefs searching for new ideas.

Sainsbury's has long shared the thirst for innovation. It tentatively introduced eight ready-cooked dishes two years ago: now it sells a range of 60 which is increasing all the time. Its tagliatelle with mushrooms and ham has doubled its sales in just two years.

The chilled food area is undoubtably the biggest new growth market. Sainsbury's, Tesco, Safeway and Asda all have their own rapidly expanding chilled food sections. A recent survey by Mintel pinpoints chilled food as the major growth sector in British food retailing — a trend which seems set to continue.

Which brings up fudging the truth about who really made the supper. The question of whether it's seriously bad form to serve up bought food as your own, is one of the great new moral dilemmas.

I used to pretend. You know, tart it up with some fresh veg, hide the wrappers, mess the kitchen up a bit. But things have a tendency to bounce back at you. Tragically, the question is no longer 'Will this ready-cooked meal taste as good as my own?', but 'Will anyone believe I could cook this?'

Dreams

Human beings evolve. But if you lose your fins, you've got to be sure you're not going to need to go back into the water. And, if you lose the ability to cook, you've got to be sure you're always going to be within easy reach of a convenience store.

These days, if the hunk of your dreams asks for a steak and kidney pudding like his mother used to make (and you're not the sort who tells him to make it himself and stop being such a sexist creep), with a lot of concentration and recipe-book studying, you could have a sporting dash at it.

But think about our daughters. Presumably their hunks will ask for seafood tagliatelle like mother used to buy.

1988

Tax Free

When government first began levying taxes, wives were regarded as the property of their husbands, anything they brought to the marriage then belonged to the husband and he paid tax on it accordingly. In 1870 married women were granted limited rights over their own property or earnings and throughout the remainder of that century and into the twentieth those rights were extended so that by 1988 wives had a right to their own earnings and savings, and a right to a share in the family property and possessions. What a wife did not have a right to was to be taxed independently of her husband. A husband and wife could elect to be taxed separately but then they did not receive the married couple's allowance.

The system was archaic and patently unfair to women. The Inland Revenue had by 1988 ceased to send to husbands correspondence about, and any tax rebates due on, wives' income but that was about the only concession to women. There was a catalogue of discrimination.

A woman whose husband earned below his threshold for tax could not, if she earned more than him, be given the married allowance so long as her husband was in employment. If her husband was in full-time education she could have both her personal tax allowance and the married allowance. For a husband with a wife in full-time education, or at home with children, her tax allowance was not transferable to him. Women whose husbands fell into the higher-rate tax bracket paid his highest rate of tax on anything they earned over their allowance. The interest on any savings a woman made out of her own income and banked in her own name had to be declared on her husband's income tax return and he was held legally responsible for any tax that might be due.

The Budget of 1988 swept aside all of these anomalies and made way for a complete and long overdue change in the taxation of husbands and wives. From April 1990 wives were to be responsible for their own tax affairs and their incomes were to be taxed independently of their husbands'.

ABOVE: Male secretaries were still a rarity.
BELOW: Benazir Bhutto.

1988   POSTSCRIPTS

March – A survey revealed that nine out of ten women were dissatisfied with the facilities for screening for cervical cancer – a completely curable cancer if treatment is administered early enough, and the incidence of which is growing.

April – A Bill introduced by MP Clare Short to ban the publication of sexually provocative pictures of women in newspapers was given support by a large majority of MPs who had been told by women that they found such pictures degrading. The Bill however did not become law as it ran out of time.

May – Liberal MP David Alton's Abortion Bill which sought to reduce the time limit for abortion from 28 to 18 weeks' gestation failed when it was 'talked out'.

November – Benazir Bhutto of Pakistan was the first woman ever elected to lead an Islamic country.

NEW CHARTER FOR WIVES

After years of debating the way husbands and wives are jointly taxed, and bemoaning the fact that couples who live in sin get all the tax breaks the government has confirmed its commitment to marriage in a major reform of family taxation to come into effect in 1990.

At the same time the Chancellor's shake-up of the system will remove some of the sex inequalities which married women have been complaining about for years.

In future women will be treated as tax payers in their own right instead of merely appendages to their husbands – a relic of the Victorian era when women as well as children knew their place.
Daily Mail, 16 March 1988

Femail

The real-life Shirley Valentines

Escaping the drudgery for a new start in the sun

by PAUL PALMER

THE middle-aged housewife (two kids, a husband and a mid-life crisis) could hardly believe what was happening to her. It was sunset. The wine was chilled. The Greek island of Mykonos lay serene and enchanting before her.

It was many miles from the drudgery of life at home, a small semi in Liverpool. Sipping her retsina as waves lapped the shore, she was alone, but she knew she had found paradise. 'I have,' she declared to the seagulls, 'fallen in love with life.'

Pauline Collins' portrayal of a born-again woman in the marvellous new film Shirley Valentine touches the most basic human emotions of hope, escape, happiness and regret.

Made by the same team responsible for Educating Rita, Shirley Valentine is about a rebellious teenager turned automatic housewife. Her children neglect her. Her husband, played by Bernard Hill, uses her. Life in general just doesn't have the kick — or the promise — it once held.

In desperation, Shirley takes a holiday in Greece with a woman friend, and discovers she can't, just CAN'T, return home. Throwing caution and her airline ticket to the wind, she sends her bags home to hubby while she stays in Greece.

There are times when we have all felt like Shirley. As the end of our annual holiday approaches we think to ourselves: 'If only life could be like this all the time. If only I didn't have to go back.'

AND the remarkable thing is that there are very many real-life Shirley Valentines who have done just that, women in the midst of a personal crisis who have decided that the body clock is ticking too fast and it is now or never to make the break.

Pat Kilby holidayed in Cyrpus nearly three years ago, and has stayed ever since. In the process she, like Shirley, found happiness, and a sybaritic new life in the sun.

'I wanted to live a different life abroad,' said Pat, 36. 'My marriage was on the rocks. We had separated, and I just needed to be away from home for some time.'

Like the film character, Pat had married young, had a boring, mundane life, and found herself living in suburban stupor in St Albans. Now, like Shirley, she is running a restaurant on the island.

She said: 'Looking back, I found that I had started to feel unhappy with my life in England, particularly after the separation. Fortunately we had no children and this made things easier. My decision to live abroad was an escape from that boring life.'

Joan Conroy: A love affair with Italy   PICTURE: JIM DUXBURY

In the little town of Kyrenia she has discovered her independence, and mutual affection with the local people. 'I didn't have the slightest doubt about making my life here. For two-and-a-half years I have lived a pleasant and happy life. That's why I am not contemplating a return home, at least for the time being.'

Shirley Valentine's life had been spent caring for her husband and being a constant slave for her children. In real life, facing up to the fact that the birds have flown the nest and that few people will miss you once you're gone is the catalyst for some women to go it alone.

Trish Litton has successfully raised three children: Guy, 29, Karia, 27, and Jason, 25. She divorced early, and raising the children single-handed meant constant money and emotional pressures. After a holiday in

Spain with a girlfriend last year, she decided to give England the push and escape to a plush apartment in Javea, near Alicante.

'I am a completely different person in Spain,' she says. 'I could hardly believe how much better I felt. I tasted a different life, and wanted more. In England a woman on her own is rarely included in dinner parties our outings. But in Spain everyone includes you, however young or old you are.

SHE has returned to Britain briefly to sell her flat and make final arrangements for her permanent move to the Costa Blanca. She will return to a new love affair with Belgian jazz

musician Emile Caron. 'With all these things happening to me,' she says, 'I feel years younger.'

It was ten years ago that Joan Conroy, a Glaswegian, first set eyes on the Italian resort of Rimini — and said to herself: 'This is it.'

Joan, now 35, had what she describes as 'a boring, normal job' in an office. 'And the way I was living in Scotland — let's just say it wasn't great,' she says with a laugh.

Italy was the stuff of her dreams and she is still clearly enraptured by the place. 'It's the classic things that make it so special, the weather, the way everybody is relaxed, the sorts of lives that the Italians lead. It's the stuff of love affairs.'

In the film, the Shirley Valentine character has an affair with a smooth-talking Greek named Costas,

played with po-faced style by Tom Conti. Then, predictably, she discovers that Costas' line of patter is wheeled out to every female tourist.

But having caught Costas chatting up a leggy blonde, Shirley realises it isn't him she's staying for at all it's her. 'I've found myself,' she says elatedly.

The same is true of those real women who have followed Shirley Valentine's path. Love was a factor but facing up to themselves was a much larger consideration in dumping their old lives. It is a journey into their own hopes and emotions.

Joan Conroy is now living with a 39-year-old Italian cinema owner but she had been in Rimini for a number of years before the love affair started 'I came to get away from Scotland, and because of my love for this place and all it stands for.'

BUT are there no regrets? What of those they leave behind? 'I don't even know where my husband lives or what he does now,' says Pat Kilby. 'And I had no problem in adapting myself to life in Kyrenia. This is a lovely town, the people are very friendly. I really do not feel homesick.

'I can think of nothing that I miss. I find everything here — bacon, sausages and even smoked salmon. It's just like living in England, but with warmer weather. There is a lot of entertainment too, lots of discos, but I am not that young any more.

'I'm surrounded by good people, both British and Turkish Cypriots. My parents come here quite often. My two sisters and their children also came recently, so I am not alone. As for my friends in England, I have new ones here now.'

Joan Conroy, hundreds of miles away in Italy, echoes the same theme: 'I won't leave here. It's my life — my new life.'

Island Ideal: Pat Kilby has found happiness running a restaurant on Cyprus. Role model: Pauline Collins in the film Shirley Valentine
PICTURE: DENIS BEAVAN

And now for aerobics of the mind

by MIRANDA INGRAM

IT'S the latest craze in America. First you do your workout, then a spot of psychocalisthenics — or psychocals for short.

Now that their bodies are in tip-top condition, Americans are into *mind* aerobics — exercises that firm up the grey matter as well as the flesh.

Superstar Shirley MacLaine has already brought out her Inner Workout video — 'a total workout for mind, body and soul'. Basically, it's a westernised version of relaxation techniques practised for centuries in Asia and the Orient to untap the power within.

And now there's psychocalisthenics, the

latest innovation from alternative guru Oscar Ichazo of the Arica Institute in New York. It takes precisely 16 minutes to complete your daily psychocalisthenics routine, and if you do it regularly you'll expand your lung capacity and experience a sense of profound calm; you'll feel emotionally stable, healthy, energetic and alert. At least that's what Oscar claims.

In case you're wondering, psychocalisthenics is a series of simple exercises and deep breathing, but

trust the Americans to give it a flashy name. You needn't be particularly fit or young to cope, says to Oscar — though to be honest, some of the floor work needs fairly strong stomach muscles.

Each routine is followed by the *integration breath*, for which you clasp your hands in front of you and raise them up and over your head to a count of six, inhaling until your hands reach the back of your neck. Then exhale. Between integration breaths, each appropriately

named exercise — picking grapes, axe, camel and windmill — sends oxygen to parts of the body it doesn't usually reach.

To do the Camel, for example, you stick your neck and chin out like a camel, and draw it down and in so that your chin meets on your neck, inhaling on the way out and exhaling as you draw it in. This flashes oxygen and vital stimulation to the brain which, with any luck, will leave you feeling doubly alert.

Like any self-respecting American obsession, psychocalisthenics and Shirley's Inner Workout are due in Britain — soon.

1989

Equal Pay?

Figures in 1988 showed that women's average pay was still only 74 per cent of the average man's pay. Thirteen years on from the Equal Pay and the Sex Discrimination Acts women still were not anywhere near the equal pay the law had seemed to promise.

In 1989 there were almost 10 million women out at work, four and a half million working part time, the rest full time. A study by the Equal Opportunities Commission showed that in Britain women workers in non-manual jobs earned only 61 per cent of the pay of men working in equivalent jobs. Part-time workers fared even worse earning below 50 per cent pro rata of their full-time male equivalents.

Domestic ties have been the major and abiding reason why women's pay has remained so far behind men's. Most women, especially if they are wives and mothers, still bear the responsibility for the bulk of the housework whether or not they work outside the home. A government report called *Social Trends,* published in 1989, bore out this fact and confirmed the EOC report that women were being paid less than men. With responsibilities for children and housework, most women look for jobs which give them flexibility of hours and an employer who will not make too much fuss if they have to have time off to look after a sick child. Very often they are willing to forgo higher pay and some of the job perks they might find elsewhere to have the conditions which most suit them. The trouble is that most employers imply that women working hours to fit round a family is of great detriment to the company or institution while ignoring all the beneficial advantages of having a mature, well-trained, experienced and committed worker.

In 1989, before the economy went once again into recession, there was much talk about the future need for many more women in the workplace and of how employers would have to change their attitudes and work practices to allow women to return to work in large numbers. There would need to be provision of crèches or payment of childcare vouchers, more flexible working hours and job-share schemes. Once these were accepted as normal working conditions and women were really needed the theory was that equal pay would come. In 1989 the future looked fairly bright for women at work and indeed the need to entice more women into jobs remains, for in the next century women returners will make up a large proportion of the workforce.

ABOVE: The all-woman crew of the yacht Maiden *preparing in the Solent before the start of the Whitbread Round-the-World Race. They came home fourth in May 1990.*
BELOW: There was much speculation in the media that the Chancellor would cease to tax workplace nurseries as a 'perk' but that measure was introduced the following year after pressure and campaigns by both employers and employees.

1989 POSTSCRIPTS

September – A majority of magicians in the Magic Circle voted to admit women members but the majority was short of the 75 per cent required to carry the motion so women continued to be excluded. There were six women members of the Magic Circle in 1905 but after they left a rule banning women was introduced in 1909.

October – Following a pilot scheme in 1988, Midland Bank, which has a 56 per cent female workforce and already offered a five-year career break, opened its first crèches for employees' children.

Femail

Why 90s women now say no to careers

by ANNE BARROWCLOUGH

> ‘I don’t want my job to be my life’

SHE'S thrown away the shoulder pads and picked up the carry-cot, swapped the expense account for the Sainsbury's bill and the boardroom for the nursery. She's the New Feminist, and she will be the woman we aspire to in the 1990s.

The Eighties was the decade of the Feminist Fatale. She fought her way to the top, crushing skulls under her Charles Jourdan power heels.

The family suffered, of course, but then families do, don't they, when you're an ambitious career woman? She joked in the office that the children were calling the nanny 'Mummy'. She was even proud of the fact that dinner with her own husband happened only once a week and had to be pre-booked via the Filofax.

This was success. This was achievement. This was a pain in the neck.

Missing

'In about 50 years' time,' says journalist Jane Poole, 'they'll look back at us women of the Eighties and they'll say, "That was the time women went mad. They knew what they fought for it, they gave up everything for it — and when they'd achieved it they found they hated it."'

The woman who is emerging from the Eighties is no born-again housewife. She hasn't suddenly decided that baking cakes beats sealing million-pound deals. She has simply taken another look at her life — and decided that there's something missing.

You might call it quality of life, you might call it happiness. But it's not there waiting for her when she gets home after working all hours God sends. After all, as one top businesswoman said: 'What does a roomful of accolades mean if you never have the time to go on a picnic with your husband?'

Women who have made it to the top are now saying: 'Who

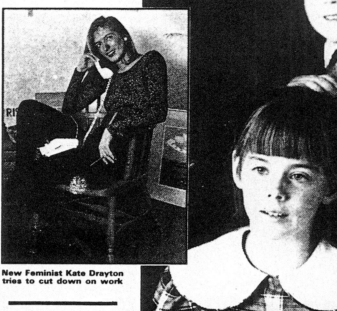

New Feminist Kate Drayton tries to cut down on work

> ‘The 80s was the time that women went mad...’

needs it?' They might not mean they're giving up work totally, but they're putting their careers in second place. In the Eighties, families came last. In the Nineties, they'll come first.

But there is a tiny little catch. No-one seems to believe them...

TV researcher Kate Drayton spent the Eighties turning her barrister boyfriend into a New Man, ready to accept she had ambitions too. But then a year ago, Kate took time off from work and everything changed.

'I suddenly had time to think, time to read, time to learn the clarinet,' she says. And although she returned to a job she adores, it's not what it used to be.

Crucial

'I do not want it to be my life. But it seems that if you want to do this kind of job, then it has to be. If the programme is at a crucial stage, we work all weekend. I get well paid and I love the people I work with. But where is my life?

'I don't want a relationship run on co-ordinating diaries and unenthusiasm fuelled by exhaustion. These are *my* years. I want to spend them seeing my family, making my flat into a home.'

Cutting back on work in favour of a better quality of life isn't easy. Now that we're used to good salaries and equally good lifestyles, the idea of managing on just one salary is anathema to many, impossible for some.

And we didn't do ourselves a lot of good when we turned up our noses at housewives as we battled to be taken seriously,

either. It's a double-edged sword, this. After fighting for years for our right to get out of the home, now we're facing just as big a fight to get back into it — even if it is only for a few days a week.

Jane Poole, a highly successful journalist, decided she'd rather give up work and become a full-time mother when she was on maternity leave last year. Now she's decided that she must return to work — partly because she can't afford not to.

'I went back to work five weeks after my first daughter

NO REGRETS: Christine McCarthy gave up work more than two years ago, mid-way through her second pregnancy
Picture: Sandra Lousada

was born, and I felt I'd really missed out. I'd watch the nanny taking her off to parties and wonder. "Why aren't I there?"

'So when my son was born, I wanted to be with him, to share his infancy. Yet there's tremendous pressure everywhere to work. People start saying "Something is wrong with her — why hasn't she come back to work yet?" My own children don't have any friends whose mothers don't work. You actually hear them talking about what their Mummy does.'

It was made a lot easier for Christine McCarthy because she not only had the moral support of her husband, but they could afford to keep up their lifestyle on one salary.

Stress

Christine, who ran her own fashion PR company, gave up work mid-way through her second pregnancy. She had had problems with her first pregnancy, partly brought on by the stress of her work, and had to stay in bed for a month early in her second pregnancy.

'It was a terribly difficult decision. And for the first year after Max (now two) was born, I really did miss the stimulation of work. But I certainly haven't regretted my decision.

'When I had my daughter, there was a feeling that I had to prove myself and so I went back to work five days after she was born. Now I feel very differently. I don't want to find the children don't have a gym kit on Monday mornings. I don't want them growing up and saying, "We never saw you".'

But even with a husband who supports her, Christine has found society hasn't been so encouraging. 'You're made to feel worthless. At drinks parties, when people ask what you do and you say "Nothing", they can't accept it.'

These women say they are not copping out. They have simply re-evaluated their lives and realised that life is more fun on the other side of the boardroom door.

‘A quick shampoo and snack, madam?’

Good enough to eat. Daniel Field tests his hair products

HAIRDRESSER Daniel Field has a rather peculiar habit. He colours, conditions and shampoos like any other hairdresser. But what doesn't end up on a client's head usually disappears into his mouth. This man *eats* his treatments.

He also makes all his products, so there is a method in his madness. Daniel Field is the first organic and mineral hairdresser. All his concoctions use only the purest of ingredients that never damage the hair — or apparently the stomach.

Proof

'I have to eat the damn stuff,' he says chewing thoughtfully, 'because of the opposition from other hairdressers.'

The world of highlights and curlers is not a friendly one. And as 50 per cent of women have bleached, permed or coloured hair, there are a lot of

by NEWBY HANDS

STYLE AND BEAUTY EDITOR

iel has been laughed at and put down by other crimpers.

'When I eat my hair restructuring treatment, it proves how natural it is. This new attitude to healthy hairdressing will eventually help all the other hairdressers.'

Daniel offers the first real alternative to bleaching, colouring and perming that does not damage hair. One top Harley Street trichologist recently pronounced the hair was in better condition *after* Daniel's organic highlights.

Go to any other hairdresser who uses the infamous bleach, peroxide, ammonia mixture and you leave baby blonde but with a bleak future of split ends and other such delights.

ruffled follicles out there.

Field's highlights are achieved by a mixture of seaweed ash, 'percolated like coffee then evaporated in iron pots', volcanic spring water and other secret natural ingredients. Avocado is a favourite, used to remoisturise hair

Raw

The colours are the only ingredient that have not passed Daniel's lips. He insists he can do any hair colouring or perming technique with his specially formularised products without ruining the hair. 'I can bleach hair to pure white if you want it — without using one drop of bleach.'

Daniel's obsession with hair began at 14 when he took a job in a salon. After three Saturdays his hands were raw and bleeding from the harsh shampoo.

So armed with a bottle of salon shampoo and a library

book on herbs he made his first shampoo. The salon bought it up as a scalp treatment.

He now runs four salons and sells his products in more than 400 branches of Boots. For the salons tel. 01-439 5223.

love is

1990

Women and Aids

In July of 1990 a World Health Organization report said that Aids was now the most common cause of death for women between the ages of 20 and 40. Ten years before no one had ever heard of Aids. Suspicion of the existence of the disease was first revealed in 1981 and the Aids, or HIV virus, was identified in 1984.

The principal ways of contracting Aids are through having sex, both male homosexual and heterosexual sex, with an infected person or by injecting drugs with a contaminated needle. A number of haemophiliacs and other patients who received contaminated blood products in the early and mid 1980s also contracted the disease but blood is now screened to stop that route of infection.

There is as yet no cure for Aids – only precautions to be followed. Intravenous drug users can be given free sterile needles. The dramatic reduction in the infection rate among the homosexual community has shown how effective the use of condoms can be in limiting the spread of the disease. But for women, using condoms also means that they cannot become pregnant so the issue of safe sex for them is also caught up with the question of fertility. Although surveys among young people have suggested that many are beginning to avoid having sex with men after only a brief acquaintance, figures released in 1991 following anonymous screening in 1990 revealed that in inner London 1 in 500 pregnant women (1 in 200 at St Thomas's Hospital) were HIV positive.

Most of the women who have contracted Aids or the Aids virus have done so through sex. Many of the women that make up the WHO figures come from Africa where the disease, 'slim' as it is known there, is a disease affecting principally heterosexuals. In some areas it has reached epidemic proportions – 1 in 4 of the adult population in some cities in Central and East Africa is HIV positive. Many of these infected women have passed the virus onto their children during pregnancy and the future is bleak for those children not infected but who are left parentless. The WHO estimates that before the end of the century there will be 10 million children worldwide orphaned because their parents have died from Aids.

In Africa, illiteracy, limited methods of mass communication, and the isolation of areas make it difficult to distribute information, education and condoms to prevent the further spread of the disease. Further, a lack of willingness on the part of men to practise safe sex and the importance to women of bearing a child means a great deal has to be done to change attitudes and sexual practices.

1990 POSTSCRIPTS

April – King Baudouin of Belgium, an opposer of abortion, stepped down for 24 hours to allow the passage of a bill legalizing abortion.

July – Martina Navratilova beat Zena Garrison in the Wimbledon Ladies Final to win a record ninth Wimbledon Singles titles.

November – Mary Robinson, pro contraception, women's rights campaigner and an advocate of divorce and abortion in a State whose constitution denies both, was elected as the first woman President of Eire.

• Margaret Thatcher was ousted as leader of the Conservative Party and Prime Minister. She was succeeded by John Major who announced a cabinet devoid of women although women are promoted to many advisory roles.

DOCTOR MOTHERS SHARE A TOP JOB

Two women doctors have won a victory for working mothers by securing a top consultant's job for two and a half days a week each. Cilla Macguire-Samson, 41, and Dorcas Kingham, 42, convinced health authority employers that they could share the job and do it as well as any single candidate. They believe their success will open the way for other women trainees who make up 50 per cent of newcomers to the profession.

Mrs Kingham did not want a full-time post because she wanted to spend more time with her sons, aged 5 and 9. She found the perfect partner in Mrs Macguire-Samson who has two daughters aged 5 and 3 and who said, 'Women are fed up having to take lesser part-time jobs'.
Daily Mail, 28 November 1990

ABOVE: Martina Navratilova.
BELOW: Condom advertisements became much more overt and for the first time targeted women as well as men.

"THEY'RE AWFULLY FIDDLY TO PUT ON.
ISN'T THAT HALF THE FUN?"

...er, you are gay or straight, promiscuous or ... condoms are a must these days. Few people ... ue with that. ... makes Mates condoms such a good idea is that ... they're just as reliable and sensitive as other brands, yet they cost less. ... What's more, every last penny made by Mates Healthcare Ltd. goes to help fight AIDS. ... The range includes Natural Mates, Ribbed Mates and Coloured Mates. Every one of which carries the official BSI Kite-mark. ... So they'll greatly reduce the risk of AIDS, cervical ...

FEMAIL Forum

■ TEN days ago Kathy Gyngell wrote in Femail about the despair she feels for stay-at-home mothers who regard themselves as second-class citizens. She described how she herself had given up her job as editor of TV-am's After Nine programme following the birth of her son Adam, and how she is now involved in setting up a movement to raise the status of the full-time mother. Many of you wrote in to describe your own experiences of motherhood and society's attitudes . . .

How having a baby changed your lives

THE DREAD I felt at returning to work was not laziness, I just couldn't bear the thought of leaving my baby, Lottie.

I had no assistance with childcare and my husband and I ended up having to work opposite shifts so one of us would always be at home. We realised this wouldn't work and employed a live-in nanny. She takes a third of my salary, but we can get by.

This week I've worked six days. I've spent one hour in the morning with my baby and three hours at night. I don't see my husband at all. I come home and ask my nanny: 'Has she eaten all right?', 'How much did she sleep?'. I shouldn't be asking someone else these questions. I should know, I should be there.

Why am I doing this? My husband says: 'So we can live here, a perfect place to bring up a child.' But what good is a perfect place without a mother?

There is only one way to get out of this — to sell or rent our lovely house and move into one provided by our occupation. Reading your article, I realised what I had known but wasn't brave enough to face. I *have* to give up work. I *have* to give Lottie a mother. There is no choice.

**Rosie Lane,
Albury, Ware, Hertfordshire**

BEING a full-time mother is something I feel very strongly about, and it is exactly the phrase I use when people ask me what I do.

I am six months' pregnant and have two daughters aged eight and five. I have a BA in languages and my job before my first baby was as account executive/director of an advertising agency.

My husband has a high public

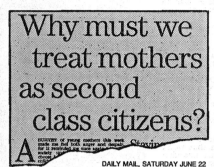

Why must we treat mothers as second class citizens?

A SURVEY of young mothers this week made me feel both anger and despair for it reminded me once again how society treats mothers as [...]

DAILY MAIL, SATURDAY JUNE 22

profile in Scotland, and when we attend events together it is inevitably him whom people want to talk to. When they ask me what I do and I say 'full-time mother', they usually make some kind of patronising remark like 'well, yes, it is a full-time job' then turn away.

One friend who went back to work shortly after her baby was born said to me: 'I want to be able to buy her the things she wants and give her all she needs'. To me it's an achingly painful statement. It's so obvious the child could want nothing more than her mother's time.

Linda Donnelly, Glasgow.

I AM the headmistress of a girls' preparatory school and feel passionately on this topic.

For a few years, especially when the child is of pre-school age, its care and upbringing should be the mother's chief concern. It does a child no good to feel she is less important than her mother's job.

It is just not possible to 'have it all'. The people who tell us otherwise are those working mothers with access to the media who feel the need to justify themselves to assuage their guilty feelings. Surely no one else is good enough to bring up one's own child. Sometimes I wonder who will look after

Is a mother any less loving towards her baby because she goes out to work?

these working mothers in their old age!

**Lady Smith-Gordon,
London SW10.**

I HAVE chosen to be a working mother but I feel no animosity over any woman's decision to stay at home to care for her children. Why then, should she feel the right to throw scorn at my decision to combine a career with motherhood?

On many occasions I have been verbally abused by stay-at-home mothers — asked why I bothered to have children only to 'farm them out' to another woman.

Yes, my life is divided between the demands of my family and the

demands of my career but that is exactly the way I like it and my children are certainly not third class citizens — they have as much love, security, time and attention as any child of a stay-at-home mother.

**Reilly Carver,
Central TV, Birmingham.**

THREE years ago I gave up work as a senior programme researcher at Yorkshire TV. My daughter Sophie was 4½ and I was expecting another baby. I wanted to stay home and care for her from the moment she was born, but whenever I broached the subject with family or friends, I was greeted with cries of derision.

When my daughter was two, I

was working every hour God sent and the misery of never being with my little girl seemed endless. All the articles I read about working mothers harp on about quality time spent with the kids. All I remember is coming home to rush around organising the following day's responsibilities.

**Elizabeth Harris,
Pool-in-Wharfedale,
West Yorkshire.**

MY SONS are no longer babies but I stay at home where I consider I have a full-time job. People assume that as children get older, it's easier to leave them. I don't think so.

When people ask: 'Do you work?', I always mean to say: 'Yes, very hard.' Instead, I feel guilty because I stay at home, and say something flippant like 'I'm a lady of leisure'. Why do I feel like this? Is it because I'm not paid for all the various jobs I do that I feel like a second-class citizen, or is it because of the way society views stay-at-home mums?

**Caroline Watson,
Great Barton,
Bury St Edmunds.**

AS A man, I have often felt uncomfortable explaining how my wife and I decided that she stay at home rather than return to work (we have children aged seven, six and two).

People seem to look upon it as a very chauvinistic attitude, as though I want my wife to be at home just so she'll have my meal on the table when I get in.

**Stuart Roberts,
Southport, Merseyside.**

MY DECISION was made 20 years ago, leaving a well-paid civil service post. It isn't that easy watching acquaintances gathering material wealth and having to do without yourself.

The rewards are greatest when your eldest son, 21, puts his arm round you and says: 'You were always there, Mum' and your 18-year-old daughter, having a traumatic time, comes to you and says: 'You're my best friend, Mum'.

No amount of salary or pension can compensate for those words.

Eileen Salmon, Blackburn.

Jaci Stephen

THE LAST WORD

A SIDELONG LOOK AT SEX . . . AND THE SEXES

IT'S THAT time of year when people are turning to thoughts of holiday romance. British women in particular, bemoaning the quality of British male lovers, set out for the Continent, where they have been led to believe more loving, enthusiastic breeds await them.

The French are allegedly romantic, the Germans pleasantly aggressive, the Dutch open minded, the Spanish flamboyant and the Italians passionate, even if it is in a 'nice legs, shame about the olive oil' kind of way.

British women believe Continental men make better lovers largely because they live in countries which have better weather. A warm climate, they say, is an incentive to strip off, and we know what happens when people do that. Continentals therefore become more practised at sexual technique and therefore, goes the argument, better at it.

■ ■ ■

BUT is it really as simple as that? Regional sex is as varied as regional cooking, and it seems unfair to lump all British men together in the pie and chips and brown sauce

category. Indeed, being of French nationality is no guarantee of sexual competence, and I suspect that in many cases, the men reflect nouvelle cuisine: it looks appetising, but in reality promises more than it delivers, and you're rarely satisfied afterwards.

There are certainly broad conclusions which can be drawn from a general observation of English, Scots, Irish and Welshmen.

The Welsh, for example, don't know how to make a decent pass unless there's an oval ball in their hands, and on the evidence of their rugby team's performance in recent years, not even then. Unlike Welsh women, whom surveys reveal to be the most highly sexed in the country, Welshmen are happier spending the night in a pub talking about The Match. It's only possible to get them into bed at all by telling them there's a barrel of Felinfoel ale in the wardrobe.

Irishmen are keen enough to get there. The problem is sobering them up sufficiently to make the journey without their breaking a leg en route. They also almost always love themselves more than the person they're with, so if an Irishman wants to make love under a mirrored ceiling, be assured it's only

because he can't bear the thought of not seeing himself for the time the act takes.

National characteristics traditionally associated with a race invariably find their way into the bedroom, so a Scotsman will probably ask his lover to bring her own pillow. However, this meanness is more than made up for by a generosity of spirit in the sexual act. Scotsmen lose their brusqueness behind closed doors and tend to show more consideration for their partners than men from the other three countries. But then I suppose there's precious little else to do in a place like Dumfries.

■ ■ ■

ENGLISHMEN are so repressed, their idea of foreplay is locking themselves in the bathroom. If and when they finally get to the bedroom, they're so embarrassed about the whole thing, they insist on wearing a paper bag on their heads. And afterwards, they don't light up a cigarette, they set fire to the bedroom in order to destroy the evidence.

I am willing to admit that within each

country there are regional variations which reflect more wide-ranging levels of sexual skills, but there are things which can and should be done to bring the sexual skills of all British men up to the standard of their Continental equivalents.

For this reason, I am currently engaged in devising the ESU, a programme of European Sexual Unity, which will ensure that in 1992 a woman will be able to travel anywhere in Europe and find the same degree of sexual competency among all the men she encounters. So far, the programme reads:

1. The time men spend talking about themselves before, during and after the sexual act, to be cut from six to 4½ hours.

2. The British national average of 6.2 minutes per act of sexual intercourse to be extended to 90.3 minutes.

3. No stopping during the sexual act to read The Spectator.

4. Men to wash their bedding at least biannually.

5. The phrase 'I'll call you' to be followed up by a phone call.

6. No biting, scratching or similar activity to take place before the pudding course.

7. Men to ask women whether they have taken precautions before, rather than after the sexual act has taken place.

Until the ESU becomes common currency, the most important point for women to remember is that an Englishman is a man who says Yes when he always means No.

1991

Abortion

Medical advances have made the life of a 26-week-old foetus viable. In April of 1990 the 1967 Abortion Act was amended to take account of this fact and the limit for terminations reduced from 28 to 24 weeks. However, abortions as late as 28 weeks were by then extremely rare.

In 1991 a survey revealed that it was almost impossible to have an abortion on the National Health Service after 10 weeks gestation. The survey also revealed that only a quarter of all abortions were carried out on the NHS and that less than half of Health Service areas provided abortion facilities.

Most abortions in Britain are carried out in private clinics, often run by non-profit making organisations such as the British Pregnancy Advisory Service. This means that for most women abortion is not free, it costs £200 or more.

Nevertheless abortion remains a legal operation in Britain, unlike the Republic of Ireland, and there is no serious threat at present to change the law. In recent years in the USA some states have brought in legislation which severely curbs the ability of women to gain abortions. For example in 1989 the US Supreme Court upheld a Missouri State law which stated that life begins at conception, that the foetus had rights from 20 weeks and forbade the public funding of abortion or abortion counselling.

The law in Britain has so far been inclined to interpret the rights of the pregnant woman seeking an abortion as more important than those of the foetus or the father. A judgement in 1987 stated that a man could not prevent his girlfriend from terminating a pregnancy in which she was carrying his child. And in 1991 a judge said that the interests of a 12-year-old girl, seeking an abortion against her mother's wishes, were 'paramount' and ruled in favour of a termination of her pregnancy.

ABOVE: *Kate Adie, whose reporting in the Gulf War was one of several assignments in the past few years from scenes of conflict or strife. She reported from Libya following the USA airstrike on Tripoli, from Romania as the Ceausescus fell and from Tiananmen Square.*
BELOW: *Helen Sharman became the first British person in space when she spent two weeks on the Russian Mir Space Station.*

1991 POSTSCRIPTS

January – The beginning of the Gulf War brought to public attention the issue of women soldiers, especially those who are mothers, and question of whether they should be deployed in combatant roles as American women troops had been in the eighties in military actions such as the invasion of Grenada. British women military personnel are still kept from combat even though they may be armed and serve close to the front line.

March – A husband was found guilty of raping his wife and the judge, Lord Lane, said, 'The time has now arrived when the law should declare that a rapist remains a rapist subject to the criminal law, irrespective of his relationship with his victim.'

• Great controversy was stirred when it was revealed that a woman who had never had sexual intercourse was receiving fertility treatment with a view to being artificially inseminated in order to conceive a baby.

April – 'The Condom Crisis' in Ireland broke when the Irish Prime Minister reduced the age at which condoms could be bought from 18 to 16, which was the legal age for marriage, without consulting the Catholic Church. Condoms were only supposed to be sold as a means of preventing the spread of Aids and not as a contraceptive device.

• The 'abortion pill' which had been used extensively was withdrawn in France from use after a number of women had died after taking it. British trials of a similar method of abortion remained.

• In the Swiss canton of Apensfal women voted for the first time in local elections.

May – Women workers forced to retire from their jobs at the age of 60 under British law were granted the right to compensation for the loss of earnings up to the age of 65 by the European Court, as Britain had agreed to equal employment laws but had not brought them onto the statute book.